Anglican Eucharistic Liturgies 1985–2010

Edited by

Colin Buchanan

CANTERBURY
PRESS
Norwich

© Colin Buchanan 2011

First published in 2011 by the Canterbury Press Norwich
Editorial office
13–17 Long Lane,
London, EC1A 9PN, UK

Canterbury Press is an imprint of Hymns Ancient and Modern Ltd
(a registered charity)
13A Hellesdon Park Road, Norwich,
Norfolk, NR6 5DR, UK

www.scm-canterburypress.co.uk

British Library Cataloguing in Publication data

A catalogue record for this book is available
from the British Library

978 1 84825 087 1

Typeset by Regent Typesetting, London
Printed and bound in Great Britain by
CPI Antony Rowe, Chippenham, Wiltshire

Contents

Acknowledgements of copyright sources

Permission for publication has been obtained from the copyright holders shown below. The texts concerned are shown by the code used in this volume, and the code is explained on pages vi–ix below.

The Archbishops' Council of the Church of England (**EngCW1A, EngCW1B, EngCW2A, EngCW2B**); The General Synod of the Scottish Episcopal Church (**Scot2A**); Church in Wales Publications and the Representative Body of the Church in Wales (**Wal2, Wal3, Wal4**); The Bishop of the Lusitanian Church (**Port3**); The Representative Church Body of the Church of Ireland (**Ire3**); The General Synod of the Anglican Church in Canada (**Can5**); Church Publishing Inc, New York (**Amer4**); The Provincial Secretary, The Church in the Province of the West Indies (**WInd2**); The Church of Nigeria (Anglican Communion) (**Nig1**); Uzima Press, Nairobi (**Ken**); The Publishing Committee of Provincial Trustees of the Anglican Church of Southern Africa (**SAfr3, SAfr4, SAfr5**); The Church of North India (**CNI1, CNI2**); The Church of South India (**CSI1, CSI2**); The Prime Bishop of the Episcopal Church in the Philippines (**Philp**); Broughton Books of Australia (**Aus6, Aus7**); The Archbishop of Papua New Guinea (**PNGR**); The General Secretary of the Anglican Church of Aotearoa, New Zealand and Polynesia (**NZ1A, NZ2A, NZ2B, NZ3A, NZ4, NZ5, NZ6**); The Liturgy, Worship and Doctrine Commission of the Anglican Church of Melanesia (**Mel2**).

Other Acknowledgements

I also wish to acknowledge the help given by the following friends, colleagues and acquaintances, without whose valuable assistance this volume could not have been compiled:

The Most Revs: Ian Ernest, Archbishop of the Indian Ocean; Paul Kwong, Archbishop of Hong Kong; Anis Mouneer, President-bishop of Jerusalem and the Middle East; Carlos Touche Porter, Primate of Mexico

The Rt Revs: Solomon Amusan, Christopher Boyle, Terry Brown, Ezekiel Kondo, Harold Miller, Robert Paterson, Humphrey Peters, Henry Scriven, Fernando Soares

The Rev Canons: Cynthia Botha, Roger Bowen, Ian Lam, David Kennedy, Tomas Maddela, Brian Mayne, Ruth Meyers, Ian Paton, Charles Sherlock, Ian Tarrant, Gianfranco Tellini, Francis Zanger

The Rev Drs: Ian Darby, Paul Mooney, Clayton Morris, Eileen Scully, Phillip Tovey

The Revs: John Bennett, Anthony Eiwuley, Shintaro Ichihara, Samitiana Jhonson, Joseph Nak-Hyon Joo, Joyce Karuri, Dominic Moghal, Terrie Robinson, Dushantha Rodrigo

Dr Narmasena Wickremesinghe

Mr Dan Bavington, Ms Karen Evans, Mr Michael Hughes, Mrs Awais Moghal and Mr Zabir Moghal, Ms Angela Robinson, Ms Mary Rollin, Mr Andrew Symonds, Ms Susan Woodcock

Abbreviations and typographical rules

Liturgical texts are represented throughout this book by a code in bold type as shown in the list below. The texts are each to be found in the volume shown opposite it in the right-hand column by a volume-code (each except the first edited by me): **LiE** (Bernard Wigan (ed.), *The Liturgy in English*, Oxford University Press, 1962, 1964), **MAL** (*Modern Anglican Liturgies 1958–1968*, Oxford University Press, 1968), **FAL** (*Further Anglican Liturgies 1968–1975*, Grove Books, 1975), **LAL** (*Latest Anglican Liturgies 1976–1984*, Alcuin/SPCK, 1985), and this present volume, **AEL** (*Anglican Eucharistic Liturgies 1985–2010*, SCM-Canterbury, 2011). Four texts from the Iberian peninsular were published in a separate monograph, *Liturgies of the Spanish and Portuguese Reformed Episcopal Churches* (Grove Liturgical Study 43, 1985), and this is coded as **LS43**. Where a text is only shown by description or by *apparatus* to another text, an asterisk is added to the volume-code in the right-hand column. The Church of England texts of 1549, 1552, 1662 and 1928 (the proposed revision) are denoted simply by their dates and no other code. They were shown in **LiE**.

Afr	The South African Liturgy (1929)	LiE
Amer	The American Liturgy (1928)	LiE
AmerR	The American Experimental Liturgy (1967)	MAL
Amer1	The American Experimental Liturgy (1970/3) 'The First Service'	FAL
Amer1-1	Rite One from the American Book of Common Prayer (1979)	LAL
Amer2	The American Experimental Liturgy (1970/3) 'The Second Service'	FAL
Amer2-2	Rite Two from the American Book of Common Prayer (1979)	LAL
Amer3	The American Experimental Liturgy (1970/3) 'The Order of Celebration'	FAL
Amer3-3	'The Order of Celebration' from the American Book of Common Prayer (1979)	LAL
Amer1-3	Liturgical Material common to **Amer1, Amer2, Amer3**, appended to them all (1970/3)	FAL
Amer4	Supplemental Material from *Enriching Our Worship* (1998)	AEL
Aus1	The Australian 1662 recension (1966)	MAL
Aus1A	The Australian 1662 recension modernized (1972)	FAL
Aus1B	The 1662 recension in *An Australian Prayer Book* (1978)	LAL
Aus1C	The 1662 recension in *A Prayer Book for Australia* (1995)	AEL
Aus2	The Australian 'A Modern Liturgy' (1966)	MAL
Aus3	The Australian Experimental Liturgy (1969)	FAL
Aus4	The Australian Experimental Liturgy (1973)	FAL
Aus5	The Second Order in *An Australian Prayer Book* (1978)	LAL
Aus6	The Second Order in *A Prayer Book for Australia* (1995)	AEL
Aus7	The Third Order in *A Prayer Book for Australia* (1995)	AEL
Bangla	The Church of Bangladesh Liturgy (1989, 1997)	AEL
Bom	The Bombay Liturgy (1923)	*LiE
BomR	The Revised Form of the Bombay Liturgy (1948)	LiE

Braz	The Brazil Experimental Liturgy (1967)	MAL
BrazR	The Brazil Experimental Liturgy (1972)	FAL
Braz1	'Rito 1' from the Province of Brazil *Libro de Oração Comun* (1988)	AEL
Braz2	'Rito 11' from the Province of Brazil *Libro de Oração Comun* (1988)	AEL
Braz3	'Orações Eucarísticas Alternativas' from the Brazil *Libro de Oração Comun* (1988)	AEL
Burm	The Liturgy of the Province of Myanmar (Burma) (1999)	AEL
Can	The Canadian 1662 recension (1919)	*LiE
CanR	The Canadian Liturgy (1959)	LiE
Can1	The Canadian Alternative Liturgy (1974)	FAL
Can1A	The Traditional Language Rite in the Canadian *Book of Alternative Services* (1985)	LAL
Can2	⟦Number left unused, but would have been a better numbering of **Can1** above⟧	----
Can3	The 'Third Canadian Order' (1981)	*LAL
Can4	The Modern Language Rite in the Canadian *Book of Alternative Services* (1985)	LAL
Can5	Supplementary Eucharistic Prayers (2001) for the Canadian *Book of Alternative Services*	AEL
Cey	The Ceylon Liturgy (1938)	LiE
Cey1	The Liturgy of 1988 of the dioceses of Ceylon	*AEL
Cey2	The Liturgy of 2009 of the Anglican Church of Ceylon	AEL
Chil	The (South) Chilean Experimental Liturgy (1967)	MAL
ChilR	The Chilean Liturgy (1972)	FAL
CNI	The Church of North India Liturgy (1973/4)	FAL
CNIR	The Church of North India Liturgy (5th edition, 1983)	LAL
CNI1	The Lord's Supper from the Church of North India's *Book of Worship* (1995)	AEL
CNI2	'An Alternative Order for . . . the Lord's Supper' from CNI's *Book of Worship* (1995)	AEL
Cong	Holy Communion in the Anglican Church of Congo Book of Common Prayer (1998)	AEL
CSI	The Church of South India Liturgy (2nd edition, 1954)	LiE
	(*also* Proper Prefaces, 3rd edition, 1963)	MAL
CSIR	The Church of South India Modern English Liturgy (1972)	FAL
CSI1	The Order for the Lord's Supper from the CSI *Book of Common Worship* (2006)	AEL
CSI2	The 'Short Order' from the CSI *Book of Common Worship* (2006)	AEL
EAUL	The East African Union Liturgy (1966)	MAL
Eng1	The Church of England *Series 1* Liturgy (1966)	MAL
Eng1-2A	The Church of England *Series 1 and Series 2 Revised* draft Liturgy (1975)	FAL
Eng1-2B	The Church of England *Series 1 and Series 2 Revised* Liturgy (1976)	*LAL
Eng2	The Church of England *Series 2* Liturgy (1967)	MAL
Eng3	The Church of England *Series 3* Liturgy (1973)	FAL
EngA	The Church of England Rite A Liturgy (1980)	LAL
EngB	The Church of England Rite B Liturgy (1980)	LAL
EngCW1A	The Church of England Common Worship Order One Liturgy (2000)	AEL
EngCW1B	The Church of England Common Worship Order One (Traditional) Liturgy (2000)	AEL
EngCW2B	The Church of England Common Worship Order Two Liturgy (2000)	AEL
EngCW2A	The Church of England Common Worship Order Two (Contemporary) Liturgy (2000)	AEL
EngAgape	The Agape outline in *Lent – Holy Week – Easter* (1986)	AEL
HK1	The Hong Kong and Macao Liturgy (1957)	MAL

HK2	The Hong Kong and Macao Experimental Bilingual Liturgy (1965)	MAL
HK3	The Holy Eucharist Rite Two of the Province of Hong Kong (2000)	AEL
ICL	The Indian Concordat Liturgy of CNI, CSI and the Mar Thoma Church (2006)	AEL
Ind[1]	The Church of India Pakistan Burma and Ceylon 1662 Recension (1960)	*LiE
IndR	The Church of India Pakistan Burma and Ceylon Liturgy (1960)	LiE
IndS	The Church of India Pakistan Burma and Ceylon Eucharistic Propers (1960)	MAL
Iran	The Iran Experimental Liturgy (1967)	MAL
IranR	The Iran Experimental Liturgy (1971)	FAL
Ire	The Church of Ireland Liturgy (1926)	*LiE
IreR	The Church of Ireland Experimental Liturgy (1967)	MAL
Ire1	The Church of Ireland Experimental Liturgy (1972)	FAL
Ire2	The Church of Ireland *Alternative Prayer Book* Liturgy (1984)	LAL
Ire3	Order Two from the Church of Ireland Book of Common Prayer (2004)	AEL
Jap	The Japan Liturgy (1959)	LiE
Jap1	The Holy Eucharist of the modern Prayer Book of Japan (1990)	AEL
Ken	Holy Communion from the Anglican Church of Kenya's *Our Modern Services* (2002)	AEL
Kor	The Korean Liturgy (1939)	LiE
Kor1	The Korean Experimental Liturgy (1973)	FAL
Kor1A	The Korean Experimental Liturgy Revised (1980)	*LAL
Kor2	Rite 1 from the Anglican Church in Korea Prayer Book (2004)	AEL
Kor3	Rite 2 from the Anglican Church in Korea Prayer Book (2004)	AEL
Kuch	The Kuching Experimental Liturgy (1973)	FAL
LfA	*A Liturgy for Africa* (1964)	MAL
Mad	The Madagascar Liturgy (1945)	MAL
Mel	The Melanesian Liturgy (1972)	FAL
MelR	The Melanesian 'Second Form' (1984)	LAL
Mel2	The Second Order rite of the Anglican Church in Melanesia (2003)	AEL
MLT	The modernization of **Eng2** in *Modern Liturgical Texts* (1968)	------
NG	The Papua New Guinea Liturgy (1970)	FAL
Nig	The Nigerian Liturgy (1983)	LAL
Nig1	The Eucharist in the Church of Nigeria Book of Common Prayer (1996)	AEL
NUL	The 'Nigerian United Liturgy' (1965)	MAL
Nyas[2]	The Nyasaland Liturgy (?1929)	LiE
NZ	The New Zealand Experimental Liturgy (1966)	MAL
NZR	The New Zealand Liturgy (1970)	FAL
NZ1	The New Zealand Alternative Liturgy (1984)	LAL
NZ1A	NZ1 as in *A New Zealand Prayer Book: He Karakia Mihinare o Aotearoa* (1989)	AEL
NZ2	The New Zealand Alternative Liturgy for Special Occasions (1984)	LAL
NZ2A	NZ2 as in *A New Zealand Prayer Book: He Karakia Mihinare o Aotearoa* (1989)	AEL
NZ3	The New Zealand 'Order of Celebration' (1984)	LAL
NZ3A	NZ3 as in *A New Zealand Prayer Book: He Karakia Mihinare o Aotearoa* (1989)	AEL
NZ4	'Service' in *A New Zealand Prayer Book: He Karakia Mihinare o Aotearoa* (1989)	AEL
NZ5	Aotearoa: An Alternative Form for Ordering the Eucharist (2006)	AEL
NZ6	Aotearoa: Eight eucharistic prayers authorized by Synod (2010)	AEL
Pak	The rite of the Church of Pakistan (1985)	AEL

---

1 The Code 'IndE' was used in the writing of **MAL**, inconsistently with the coding set out in this section in both **LiE** and **MAL**.

2 The titles 'Nyas' and 'Rhod' are retained for the sake of conformity with **LiE**, in which the texts appear, and for no other reason. The countries and dioceses concerned changed their names with decolonization in the 1960s, and both texts lapsed from use from around the same time. The dates of origin shown arise from bare inference: no dates were given in **LiE**.

Philp	The Eucharist from the Episcopal Church in the Philippines (1999)	AEL
PNG	The Papua New Guinea Liturgy (revised from **NG**) (1978)	*LAL
PNGR	The First Order in the Papua New Guinea *Anglican Prayer Book* (1991)	AEL
Port1	The Liturgy from the Prayer Book of the Lusitanian Church (1882)	LS43
Port2	The modern Rite of the Lusitanian Church (1969)	LS43
Port3	The modern Eucharistic Rite of the Lusitanian Church (1991)	AEL
Rhod³	The Northern Rhodesia Liturgy (?1925)	LiE
SAfr1	The South African Experimental Liturgy (1969)	FAL
SAfr2	The South African *Liturgy 1975* (1975)	FAL
SAfr3	The Rite in Southern Africa's *An Anglican Prayer Book* (1989)	AEL
SAfr4	'Alternative Order for Celebrating the Eucharist' in *An Anglican Prayer Book* (1989)	AEL
SAfr5	Supplementary Eucharistic Prayers, published in *Worship Resource Manual* (2009)	AEL
Scot	The Scottish Liturgy (1929)	LiE
ScotE	The Scottish 1662 Recension (1929)	*LiE
ScotR	The Scottish Experimental Liturgy (1966)	MAL
ScotRR	The 1970 form of **ScotR** (1970)	*FAL
ScotS	Propers authorized to supplement those in **Scot** and **ScotE** (1966)	MAL
Scot1	The Scottish Episcopal Church Experimental Liturgy (1977)	LAL
Scot2	The Scottish Episcopal Church 'Scottish Liturgy 1982' (1982)	LAL
Scot2A	The new eucharistic prayers and other supplements to **Scot2** (1996)	AEL
SouCon	The Eucharist of the Province of the Southern Cone of South America (1993)	AEL
Span1	The Liturgy from the Spanish Reformed Episcopal Church Prayer Book (1889)	LS43
Span2	The Experimental 'Rito 1' of the Spanish Reformed Episcopal Church (1984)	LS43
Tan	The Tanzanian Liturgy (1973/4)	FAL
TanR	The Tanzanian Liturgy Revised (1977)	*LAL
Tan1	The Liturgy in the Province of Tanzania Book of Common Prayer (1995)	AEL
WAfr	The West African Experimental Liturgy (1980)	LAL
Wal	The Church in Wales Experimental Liturgy (1966)	MAL
WalR	The Church in Wales Modern English 'Study' Liturgy (1972)	FAL
Wal1	The Liturgy in the Church in Wales Book of Common Prayer (1984)	LAL
Wal2	The Church in Wales Modern English Liturgy (1984)	LAL
Wal3	The Alternative Order for the Holy Eucharist of the Church in Wales (1994)	*AEL
Wal4	The Liturgy in the Church in Wales Book of Common Prayer (2004)	AEL
Wal5	The Outline Order in the Church in Wales Book of Common Prayer (2004)	AEL
WInd	The West Indies Liturgy (1959)	LiE
WInd1	The Liturgy in the West Indies *Revised Services* (1980)	LAL
WInd2	The Liturgy in *The Book of Common Prayer* (1995) of the West Indies	AEL
Zan	The Swahili Mass (Zanzibar Diocese) (1919)	LiE

At various points in the volume references to eucharistic prayers are done by citing the rite and giving the number or letter, such as '**NZ7** – EP/F'. 'BCP' means 'Book of Common Prayer' in every context in which it occurs, and as this denotes a modern and/or current worship book in many provinces, readers in England are warned not quickly to imagine it means '1662'. Wherever in introductory paragraphs 'Book' is written with a capital, it refers to whatever worship book has been described or named as the use of that province.

---

3 See note 2 above.

The liturgical texts have been laid out with an eye to their original presentation, but subject to the constraint of sustaining some uniformity of appearance throughout the volume, and under a greater necessity than with the previous volumes to describe some of the material rather than reproduce it all *verbatim*. This is in part an inevitable outcome of the passage of 25 years since the previous volume (in contrast to the intervals between the prior volumes being six, seven and ten years respectively), but is also due to the creation of initial provincial rites in parts of the Communion which either used more traditional rites until after 1985, or have only come into existence as provinces in the years since then; and furthermore texts are now authorized with a far greater range of alternatives than was the practice in the past. The basic principle of selection of material has been that the 'liturgy of the sacrament' in each rite from the peace onwards, and particularly the eucharistic prayers, should be presented in as full a way as possible, while the prior sections of the rites have been more open to summary description, and/or to the use of smaller typeface. Many rites have their individual items numbered, and for convenience an editorial numbering has been imposed on those that had not originally had it. In one case, Wales, the original numbering has been simply from 1 to 7, to indicate large sections of the rites, and in that one case it has not been practical to number specific items.

In Appendix B there are set out two categories of 'Common Forms', first the 'ELLC' ones (from the interdenominational English Language Liturgical Consultation), and second the notably Anglican 'CF' ones. Throughout the texts these forms are cited by reference only, with variants from them shown within the beginnings and endings shown, or by *apparatus* beneath.

Throughout the texts, *italic* is used for rubrics, notes or other directions, roman type is used for the words of the officiant (and rubrics stating *'The president says'* are regularly omitted in the interests of economy); and **bold** type for congregational or responsive spoken text. These conventions are regularly observed in the original texts from which this collection is drawn, the main exception being from the Episcopal Church in the USA, which, as in its 1979 BCP, so in its recent texts reproduced here, does not usually distinguish typefaces. Capitalization (save in cross-headings) and punctuation have been generally reproduced as in the original text, with occasional corrections of what appears to be an original misprint. Editorial elucidation (whether in the text or in footnotes) is included within double brackets ⟦ . . . ⟧, or by small capitals in an *apparatus*, thus guaranteeing that all material not so bracketed is original. Within bracketed editorial descriptions of liturgical material the use of an asterisk * indicates that that section is optional. The practice of 'lining' printed text, which began (see earlier volumes) as an aid to congregational recitation by indicating where breath should be drawn, has spread almost universally to presidential texts, and most obviously in the eucharistic prayers. In the interests of saving space, eucharistic prayers are therefore regularly presented below in two columns, but with care taken, in the interest of ease of reading, to avoid turnovers in them. With each text there is a note as to whether the lining is original or has been imposed editorially. The double-column presentation so uses space as to entail the elision of the marginal rubrics such as *'President'* or *'All'* or even *'All say together'*. I apologize for the editorial heavy hand at such points, but it is only rubrics which are strictly otiose (because they indicate simply what the typeface of text indicates anyway) which are elided.

Preface

This volume stands fifth in a line of Anglican liturgical reference works. The first of these, Bernard J. Wigan (ed.), *The Liturgy in English* (Oxford University Press, 1962 and 1964), provided almost all the Anglican eucharistic texts from 1549 until 1960, including a whole series of different provincial recensions of 1662. I have myself edited the four subsequent volumes to supplement the Wigan collection, each volume in turn adding from round the world all the new eucharistic texts authorized within its stated period. The titles concerned are: *Modern Anglican Liturgies 1958–1968* (Oxford University Press, 1968), *Further Anglican Liturgies 1968–1975* (Grove Books, Bramcote, 1975), *Latest Anglican Liturgies 1976–1984* (Alcuin/SPCK, 1985), and now *Anglican Eucharistic Liturgies 1985–2010* (SCM-Canterbury, 2011). The volumes differ in their publishers, and differ somewhat in size, as the third of these four, the Alcuin Club Collection (**LAL**), was limited by the Club's finances and thus had no room for the general introductory chapters and the essays introducing each province's rites which I had been able to provide for the first two volumes. I am glad to be able to provide fuller introductory material again here. They also differ in that this fourth volume is the first to have been composed by word-processing, a great relief to the editor. But the particular change of content is that there is far more material for the editor to process than in the previous volumes, and this results not only from the 25-year time-gap since **LAL** was published, but also from the growth of independent provinces of the Communion, the growing importance to each province that it should have its own rite, and the multiplication of options and alternatives within each province's actual provision. I have judged therefore that the first priority in presentation was to get the structure of each rite clear and to provide the sacramental part of the liturgy in full; though even then the seasonal and other propers have so increased as to make the folding charts of such material which I compiled for previous volumes unimaginable for this one.

The 25-year time-gap has been marked in my own life by my being removed in 1985 from teaching liturgy in a residential context, and also in early 1986 by my being removed after 21 years from the Church of England Liturgical Commission. I have, however, had every incentive to continue the gazetteering task of collecting Anglican rites from round the world into a single volume (indeed I made an exploratory start twelve years ago, but my lap-top was stolen and life was too busy then to restart). Furthermore, the International Anglican Liturgical Consultations (IALC) began just before **LAL** was published in 1985, and I have been at every Consultation and interim Conference since, always meeting in tandem with the biennial Congresses of *Societas Liturgica*, which I have also attended. I was for six years (1995–2001) on the Steering Committee of IALC, and was also a participant in the two African consultations on liturgy convened by the Council of Anglican Provinces in Africa (CAPA) in 1993 and 1996. I was privileged to be secretary to the group considering liturgy at the Lambeth Conference of 1988 and, as a member of the Chaplaincy Group at Lambeth 1998, held responsibility there for gathering and editing the texts from the different provinces to be incorporated into the worship handbook of the Conference, *Lambeth Prayer: Daily Worship for the Conference 1998* (SPCK, London, but not on general distribution). I have further had opportunity in this time to visit 17 of the provinces and Churches of the Anglican Communion, and within the Church of England itself I sustained until 2003 my monthly journal of liturgy, *News of Liturgy*, and took a full part in the handling of liturgy in both the General Synod and the House of Bishops.

Throughout this period I have been privileged to keep alive to academic studies, as I have chaired the Joint Editorial Board for the Alcuin/GROW Joint Liturgical Studies (published by Grove Books from 1987 to 2004, and by SCM-Canterbury since 2005), and this series has contributed strongly to Anglican liturgical studies generally and to this collection in particular, not least through the publishing it has afforded to IALC Statements and allied documents. One further major work from IALC-5, which addressed eucharistic issues, was David Holeton (ed.), *Our Thanks and Praise* (Anglican Book Centre, Toronto, 1998). There have also been two marvellous volumes published in recent years from wholly outside of the official structures of the Communion: first was Charles Hefling and Cynthia Shattuck (eds), *The Oxford Guide to the Book of Common Prayer* (Oxford University Press, New York, 2006), a large part of which comprises a survey of the whole contemporary Anglican liturgical scene worldwide; the other is David J. Kennedy, *Eucharistic Sacramentality in an Ecumenical Context: The Anglican Epiclesis* (Ashgate, Aldershot, 2008), which is a study in depth of one of the most significant and sensitive parts of the eucharistic prayer as it is manifested in the rites of the whole Communion.

I need to issue a warning, as I have in the past. Putting rites into print in a comparative way is a great leveller. Quite apart from the issue of how texts are used in practice (which I have discussed briefly as a cultural issue below), there is no evenness of use. A trial rite used for a short time in a few congregations will appear here alongside a text used by millions over many years. An alternative service may be rarely used, as the previously existing rite is still much-loved, is available in the congregations and continues current. Printed texts will illuminate (it has been a thrill to me to work with so many from round the world), but unless their use can be penetrated and understood, they can also mislead.

I must add that I have been hugely assisted by friends, pen-friends and e-friends throughout the world, and I have endeavoured to list them elsewhere (see page v). In short, it is friends and colleagues, the coming of e-mail (and to a lesser extent of websites) undreamt of in 1985, and the lessening of daily pressures during retirement, which have all made this volume possible.

Colin Buchanan
Epiphany 2011

A. Introduction – The Worldwide Scene

1. The Eucharist in the Anglican Communion 1985–2010

The Anglican Communion

The Anglican Communion has grown in organization, if not in numbers, since 1985. Then there were 26 autonomous provinces or Churches[4], and since then eight new provinces have been formed – some by separation from an existing Church (such as Mexico and Central America) and others by the reshaping and grouping of extra-provincial dioceses to become new provinces (such as South-East Asia and Hong Kong). In addition the united Churches of the Indian sub-continent – those of Pakistan, North India, South India and Bangladesh – have become full members of the Communion, and the two dioceses of Ceylon (Sri Lanka), without becoming a Province, have become a separate and constitutionally united Church. At the same time, there have in very recent years been pressures within the Communion leading to ruptures in some provinces, and the recording here of eucharistic revision in those provinces, which almost entirely antedates such rupturing, is not intended to convey any judgement about the rightness or otherwise of the rupturing, or the standing in the Communion of any of the resultant bodies.

The various provinces have during these 25 years been addressing the compilation of their own provincial eucharistic liturgies, sometimes as part of the way of asserting their provincial identity or coming of age. The following chapters contain details of the new rites of 28 provinces, in some cases with two or more stages of compilation revealed – as, for instance, in Wales, where the 1994 eucharist was succeeded by the definitive 2004 one, or in Ceylon, where the 1988 rite has been revised to become the 2009 one. A survey has to identify some general trends, the task of this chapter, as well as looking in more depth at specific features of liturgical and sacramental theology which the texts exhibit, the task of Chapter 2.

---

4 Hereafter called 'provinces', though with the recognition both that in England, Ireland, Canada, the USA, Nigeria and Australia there are more than one ecclesiastical 'province' within the Church, and that there has been a widespread tendency for provinces to rename themselves as, for example, The Anglican Church in Southern Africa.

Monitoring and Reporting

In a diverse Communion with few central resources and less central control, it is unclear whose task it is to monitor and report liturgical developments, and it is equally unclear to whom such reports should go. In 1973 Ronald Jasper wrote a report for the second meeting of the Anglican Consultative Council, and his report contained the 1968 Pan-Anglican Document on 'The Structure and Contents of the Eucharistic Liturgy and the Daily Office'. He included with the Document a somewhat uneven set of vignettes of liturgical revision in 20 provinces or regions of the Communion. His report was published within the ACC-2 report, *Partners in Mission* (the Structure Document is also in **FAL**). In 1984 I was asked to do a report in succession to his for the 1984 ACC in Nigeria, ACC-6. This was circulated to the delegates in duplicated form, along with a paper from a sub-group of the Primates' meeting in October 1983 which I had been asked to keep in view as I wrote my report. Neither of these documents was published in the report of ACC-6, *Bonds of Affection*, so I added them as an appendix to the Grove Liturgical Study I was compiling, number 41, *Anglican Eucharistic Liturgy 1975–1985* (Grove Books, 1985). This Study is relevant as it was written to serve as an Introduction to **LAL**, and thus, read in conjunction with **LAL**, it brings the overall picture of the development of the rites around the Communion to the beginning of the quarter century covered by this present volume. My report on liturgy appended to it broke somewhat new ground, as, unlike Ronald Jasper's province-by-province report in 1973, it endeavoured to chart general trends. This provided a background to the survey of the eucharistic rites I was making in the Study, and the survey itself, introducing the rites in **LAL**, followed the introductory pattern I had been able to use within the actual volumes in **MAL** and **FAL**.

International Anglican Liturgical Consultations (IALC)

A turning point came in 1985. At the very point that **LAL** was being printed, there was convening for the first time the International Anglican Liturgical Consultation (IALC). As this new gathering bid fair to have a continuing life, there was for the first time the prospect of a place of reporting, advice and accountability that would be formed of liturgists from the Communion, thus replacing for these purposes both meetings of bishops and non-directive communication to and from the Anglican Communion Office.[5] IALC has had few resources, though the years when Paul Gibson was seconded from the Anglican Church of Canada to be the Liturgy Co-ordinator for the Anglican Communion (a role he continued in retirement until 2007) facilitated the organizing and networking of the Consultations.

The 1988 Lambeth Conference

The first two Consultations (1985 and 1987), when IALC was still getting on its feet, did not touch on eucharistic rites. Before IALC-3 could convene, there came the Lambeth

---

5 The exact status of IALCs, and negotiations over that status, need not detain the account here. It is largely set out in David R. Holeton and Colin Buchanan, *A History of the International Anglican Liturgical Consultations 1983–2007* (Alcuin/GROW Joint Liturgical Study 63, SCM-Canterbury, 2007). IALC outlived slightly threatening proposals for an international official Liturgical Commission from ACC-7 in 1987, and for an international 'policing' doctrinal watchdog from the Lambeth Conference of 1988.

Conference of 1988. Its 'Mission and Ministry' section included a long statement on liturgy. Most of this concerned general principles, as some extracts demonstrate:

§182: 'Thus we commend and encourage authentic local inculturation of the liturgy, and fear lest in some parts of the Anglican Communion we have been all too hesitant about it.'

§184: 'If we do not dwell on its [1662's] *strengths* today it is because we judge its era is slipping irretrievably into the past.'

§185: 'The presuppositions of the 1662 Book itself were of a static "Christendom" England, so that little awareness of mission touches its pages; its requirements of the laity were of largely passive participation; and, for all its ancient beauties, its liturgical structuring has been called into question in Province after Province . . . '

§186: 'Provinces should be ready to have basic authorized forms for the central parts of certain rites such as the Eucharist, and for those forms to give an appropriate part to the congregation. But they should also provide outline structure into which a choice of materials, already existent or written for the occasion, can be fitted.'

§187: 'A modern liturgical English is emerging. For somewhat more than twenty years worshippers have used texts which have abandoned "thou" and address God as "you" . . . We welcome the coming of "inclusive" language.'

There were however two paragraphs directly concerning the eucharist:

'EUCHARIST: MEETING AND MISSION

203. We do not attempt here to discuss textual technicalities of the eucharistic rites. Instead we note that in the eucharist the Church unites in the praises of God, receives God's holy word, expresses her life in the Spirit, sustains the mutual fellowship of her members, recommits herself to Almighty God, and, from this holy feast, returns to the world to fulfil God's mission. The eucharist is a locus for mutual sharing and ministry for the "building up" of the Church (1 Cor. 14). The eucharist may include: various teaching methods to minister the word, drama, dance, extemporary prayer, groups for study or intercession, healing ministries, weddings, and other public activities of the local Christian community. Christian mission itself is vitiated if the Church's eucharistic practice does not in fact build up the people of God.

THE AGAPE

204. We note signs of the re-emergence of the *agape* or love feast. It appears in two forms; eucharistic, in the sense of having the sacrament of the Lord's Supper at its heart, or non-eucharistic, though still with elements of Christian worship within it. It is interesting to note that, in its non-eucharistic form, it is often used by local groups of Christians in the absence of a duly ordained minister.'[6]

Along with the report, there were two unopposed resolutions of the Conference, similar to each other and bearing upon liturgy: Resolution 22 ('Christ and Culture')

---

6 The 1988 Lambeth Conference, *The Truth Shall Make You Free* (ACC, 1988), §§182–204 of 'Mission and Ministry', pp. 67–73.

and Resolution 47 ('Liturgical Freedom'), the latter being the sole resolution submitted by the group working on liturgy. They read:

'22. This Conference (a) recognizes that culture is the context in which people find their identity; (b) affirms that God's love extends to people of every culture and that the Gospel judges every culture according to the Gospel's own criteria of truth, challenging some aspects of culture while endorsing and transforming others for the benefit of the Church and society; (c) urges the Church everywhere to work at expressing the unchanging Gospel of Christ in words, actions, names, customs, liturgies, which communicate relevantly in each contemporary society.'[7]

'47 This Conference resolves that each Province should be free, subject to essential universal Anglican norms of worship, and to a valuing of traditional liturgical materials, to seek that expression of worship which is appropriate to its Christian people in their cultural context.'[8]

These resolutions provided the peg upon which IALC-3 the following year could hang its 'York Statement' on inculturating worship, 'Down to Earth Worship: Liturgical Inculturation and the Anglican Communion'. The Statement is over 2,000 words in length, and wide-ranging in its application. It was not intended to be specifically related to the eucharist, though illustrative mention of language, music, architecture, and ceremonial in §7 paragraphs (a)-(d) has a broad and obvious eucharistic relevance. More specifically §7 goes on to include two pointed eucharistic questions:

'(e) Sacramental elements: here there are special problems, needing more work. Should wafer bread be as dominant as it seems to be – even to the point of being imported? Should local staple food and drink supervene? How far can variations be allowed?

(h) Agapes: Christians have gathered for meals from the start. The growing revival of agapes in our Communion we welcome, not only for the breaking down of the walls between the 'sacred' and the 'secular', nor simply for their fellowship aspect, but also because both these factors enable people wherever they are to be themselves with their own customs, and to be free to bring those ways into the heart of church life.'[9]

Both these questions have hung at the edge of eucharistic liturgy, but neither has greatly affected the textual revision and creation with which this volume is largely concerned.[10]

---

7 Ibid. p. 219.

8 Ibid. p. 232.

9 The York Statement is available in a pamphlet, *Findings of the Third International Anglican Liturgical Consultation* (Grove Books, Bramcote, 1989) or in the front of the essays on the Statement, David R. Holeton (ed.), *Liturgical Inculturation in the Anglican Communion: Including the York Statement 'Down to Earth Worship'* (Alcuin/GROW Joint Liturgical Study 15, Grove Books, Bramcote, 1990).

10 While the matter of eucharistic elements recurs below (see pages 12–14), Agapes, spotlighted by both the Lambeth Statement and the York Statement, remain almost invisible. In the USA Amer3-3 in 1979 had concluded the informal 'Order for Celebrating' with the rubric '*When a common meal or Agapé is part of the celebration, it follows here*', but that appears to treat the agape as by definition separate from the eucharist. A more integrated pattern was aired by the Church of England's Liturgical Commission in the (non-statutory) 'commended' services in *Lent – Holy Week –Easter* (SPCK, 1986), pp. 97–8, and this is reproduced in part

IALC and Eucharist

In 1991 the next IALC, meeting in Toronto, was due to consider Christian initiation. The Boston Consultation in 1985 had already called for baptism to be the sole requisite qualification for admission to communion, and the Toronto Statement took that much further. The Statement was going with the flow of rethinking Christian initiation in the Communion, and undoubtedly itself reinforced that flow. If Toronto did not spell out implications for eucharistic texts, yet it was perhaps adding some weight to the incipient desire for eucharistic prayers to be used with children, a provision which has come a short way above the horizon in 2011.[11]

But IALC was moving on towards a full treatment of the eucharist. In 1993 an 'interim conference' was held in Untermarchtal in South Germany to do preparatory work towards a full Consultation in 1995. The conference is especially remembered for the keynote and far-reaching paper given by Thomas Talley of the USA, 'Eucharistic Prayers, past, present and future'. Its thrust, carefully grounded in a favouring of the Greek Fathers, was to move revision of rites towards lifting all consecratory weight from the narrative of institution, thus diminishing existing conflicts in relation to the anamnesis, and overtly asking in the subsequent epiclesis for the Spirit's role to be fulfilled.[12] There was one further main address, but otherwise the Untermarchtal papers, typically in chapters of two-page briefings, air the kinds of questions the next IALC would have to address. Thus the chapter titles include: 'Eucharistic Consecration, the Role of the Institution Narrative in the Eucharistic Prayer, and Supplementary Consecration', 'Ceremonial, Ritual Gesture, and the Eucharist', 'The Epiclesis and the Role of the Holy Spirit in the Eucharistic Prayer', and 'Offering and Sacrifice'.[13] The issues were coming to the crunch.

Kanamai

1993 also saw the first ever pan-African Anglican consultation on liturgy. This was held under the auspices of the Council of Anglican Provinces in Africa (CAPA), and was convened by David Gitari at Kanamai on the Kenyan coast just prior to the Untermarchtal Conference. Its theme was 'African Culture and Anglican Liturgy', and the participants compiled a major 'Kanamai Statement' under this title, and the published papers include an Introduction by David Gitari in which he clearly hopes that the Kanamai Statement will feed into the forthcoming IALC in ways parallel to

on page 56 below, and was written up in a helpful coaching manual, Trevor Lloyd, *Celebrating the Agape* (Grove Worship Booklet 97, 1986).

11 In some quarters the very fact that Rome had had such prayers from the early 1970s was of itself sufficient reason why Anglican rites should have them. Rome, however, had never had any compunction about using eucharistic prayers which prayed (as surely all eucharistic prayers do?) for fruitful reception of communion at rites where, at the starkest, no one but the priest would in fact receive. Except in places where Rome was idealized, Anglicans have wanted a surer relationship between the prayer and the reception, so with a strong tradition of admission to communion coming at confirmation when candidates have been almost invariably ten or more years of age, Anglicans have been slower to look for prayers specifically written for young-age children (see page 23 below).

12 Talley's address is the vital component of the Untermarchtal papers, which were published as David R. Holeton (ed.), *Revising the Eucharist: Groundwork for the Anglican Communion* (Alcuin/GROW Joint Liturgical Study 27, Grove Books, 1994). It is well summarized in David Kennedy, *Eucharistic Sacramentality*, pp. 221–5.

13 See Joint Liturgical Study 27 cited in footnote 12 above, *passim*.

the way the Untermarchtal conference was expected to.[14] The Kanamai Statement itself had six sections, the first of general principles of celebration and inculturation, and the next five considering specific categories of liturgy. Of these five, number 2 addresses the eucharist.

2. EUCHARIST AND CULTURE

2.1. INTRODUCTION

We take 'culture' to mean 'cultural trends' since Africa does not have a unified culture. Changes in eucharistic liturgy need now to be thorough, not cosmetic. A serious challenge must be faced. The process recognized as Indigenization—Adaptation—Inculturation (Atta-Bafoe and Tovey) has reached the second phase in Africa, generally, and, where this is so, it is ready to move to the third. Up to this point liturgical renewal has been more a matter of adapting previously given forms. Moving on to the third phase is a lengthy process.

In drawing up eucharistic liturgies, each province should carefully examine the relevant cultural practices of its nation or region as they might affect eucharistic worship or reflect upon it. In the process of drafting eucharistic rites, provinces should judge whether the cultural practices it has defined can be affirmed in the liturgy.

In drafting, provinces need to allow for local variations within their area of responsibility by providing for flexibility. Provinces should recognize that suggestions made in this report are not recommendations for implementation but are intended to raise questions and issues of importance.

2.2 THE SPIRIT OF AFRICAN WORSHIP

Africans do not only spectate, they participate. The liturgy needs to be open to opportunities for the expression of joy and suffering, of death and hope, affirming people's deepest affections.

One of the problems we face is the mentality which existing buildings have created, changing attitudes and restricting freedom of expression. Architectural features, such as pulpits, can be a problem in certain contexts. Some thought needs to be given to the shape and atmosphere of our buildings, providing spaces for the expression of the Church as the body of Christ, and at no time is this more important than at the eucharist. Alongside this needs to be an appreciation of the nature of holiness associated with places and buildings, and an awareness of the negative fears that need to be combated. There is a real need for African art, sculpture, woodcarving etc. in our churches. It would appear that the wealth of artistic talent (as well as the artistic offerings of children) could be used to greater extent.

2.3 MUSIC

We encourage the use of local words and music to make worship more joyful and authentically African. Attention needs to be given to creative writing and composition. Music should not appear to decorate the liturgy but should be regarded as integral.

2.4 ATTIRE

There is a longstanding tradition that liturgical leaders, particularly those who preside, should wear distinctive clothing which symbolizes their role on behalf of the community and the community's identity in and with them. While such vestments should follow a similar, and therefore recognizable, pattern in a given area, in both style and material they may be drawn from local patterns of ceremonial dress.

---

14 David Gitari (ed.), *Anglican Liturgical Inculturation in Africa: The Kanamai Statement 'African Culture and Anglican Liturgy' with Introduction, Papers read at Kanamai, and a first Response* (Alcuin/GROW Joint Liturgical Study 28, Grove Books, 1994).

2.5 DETAIL

For the purposes of this paper, the eucharist may be divided into seven elements. Before proceeding to outline these elements, it needs to be stressed that provinces should discern the shape of the liturgy before proceeding to detail.

1. *The greeting*

Lively worship may be encouraged before (and after) the liturgy itself. It is a common practice in many African cultures to greet the gathering before the business begins. The eucharist might begin with greetings as a way of encouraging one-ness at the outset. These greetings should be real, rather than a formality.

The call for Peace (and the greeting of peace) is very important and the best place for it in each rite needs to be found. Wherever it is placed (even if in place of a greeting) it is important to recognize that the 'peace' is much more than a greeting.

2. *Penitence*

There are a number of possible positions for this penitential element in a eucharistic liturgy. At present it would appear that we use too many words in confession of sin. We recommend the use of silence, singing, gestures, appropriate symbolic acts and any other means to lead worshippers away from sin into a deeper relationship with the Lord. There are African ways of expressing penitence and the church in each setting needs to explore them.

3. *Proclamation of the word*

The divine authority of the word needs to be stressed with the use of local customs. For instance, in some cultural groups, when a person gives an important message in a gathering, that person uses a staff which symbolizes authority in the community. This kind of custom might be brought into the proclamation of the word, and each area needs to discern its own local practice.

Sometimes the provision of lectionary readings themselves may be too long for the people to concentrate on them. The readings might be shortened, dramatized, danced, memorized, drummed, etc.

4. *Intercession*

When we have heard and responded to the word, we bring the world before God. Nothing is beyond the scope of prayer. Posture and gestures in prayer vary from one cultural tradition to another and the natural form needs to be discerned. Liturgical provision may need to reflect this diversity. How do Africans – or a people of a certain area – normally express themselves in prayer? Some close their eyes, some kneel, some raise their hands. Again we note that our texts for intercession are sometimes too wordy. We should consider a wider range of styles, including chanting, music, and led extempore prayer. This will involve further education of worship-leaders and people.

5. *Eucharist*

No attempt should be made to follow a set pattern, though provinces should be familiar with the basic elements of eucharistic prayer in the wider church. It may be right to lay more stress on the doctrine of creation and to express the close affinity which Africans feel for the whole created order.

We wish to encourage local people to produce the eucharistic bread and ask the provinces to consider whether they should permit the use of local staple foods and drinks for the eucharistic elements, also carefully considering this alongside the biblical tradition.

6. *Sacramental eating and drinking*

As much as we respect our cultures, it is necessary to stress the importance of the unity of the family of God and, therefore, to encourage men and women to come together to the Lord's Table. Occasionally, a common-meal might be celebrated and provision for this (guided by biblical principles) might be made if provinces so decide. It would not be inappropriate for the consecrated bread and wine to be passed around the people on some occasions, rather than being served by the ministers.

7. *Dismissal*
It would seem to be vital that the two elements of continuing in the Church's fellowship and sharing in God's mission should both be expressed in the dismissal.

2.6   CONCLUSION
In all of the above, it will be necessary to combine new thinking and practice with a clear and careful process of education throughout each province.

⟦This section then lists six 'Issues Arising' which include (a) consideration of celebrating the eucharist at a larger meal, and (d) the issue of using 'local foods and drinks' in place of 'wafers and wine'. The other 'Issues' do not impact sacramental practice.⟧[15]

While Kanamai had a great sense of having enthused its participants, its actual impact has been more limited. Of the African provinces which have produced new eucharistic materials since 1985, the highly creative Kenyan eucharist of 1987 and 1989 (**Ken**) and the more traditional Southern African rites in *An Anglican Prayer Book 1989* (**SAfr4**) were produced before Kanamai. The Nigerians had been unable to come to Kanamai, and their 1996 book (containing **Nig2**) shows little sign of an awareness of it. In Tanzania, where sustaining the sensitive balance of churchmanships was a major factor in the creation of **Tan2** in 1995, Kanamai came rather late in their process to have much impact – they, like the Kenyans, were feeding into the Consultation more than they were drawing from it.[16] However, the province of Congo, having shortly before embarked on an initial drafting of an indigenous liturgy, was able to take full advantage of a Consultation which came at the right formative point in their own process of writing a eucharistic liturgy (**Cong**, 1998).[17]

A second CAPA consultation on liturgy in Africa was convened in Johannesburg in November 1996. It suffered in organization and energy through the absence of David Gitari, the prime mover of Kanamai.[18] There is nothing to record from it.

IALC-5, Dublin 1995

IALC-5 duly met in Dublin in August 1995 to consider the eucharist, and a fuller representation of the whole Communion than at any previous Consultation attended. The participants worked in five sections, and the substantial Dublin Statement which emerged was composed largely of the five sections' drafts. However, the whole Consultation accepted nine fundamental 'Principles and Recommendations' as follows:

---

15 David Gitari (ed.), *Anglican Liturgical Inculturation in Africa*, pp. 39–42.

16 See Ian Tarrant, *Anglican Swahili Prayer Books* (Alcuin/GROW Joint Liturgical Study 62, SCM-Canterbury, 2006) p. 16.

17 See Ian Tarrant, *Anglican Swahili Prayer Books*, p. 18.

18 By one of those oddities of history, he had to be in Kenya that week in order that an election of an Archbishop (which required 100% attendance of the House of Bishops) could proceed – and he was then himself elected.

Principles and Recommendations
(adopted by the whole Consultation)

1. In the celebration of the eucharist, all the baptized are called to participate in the great sign of our common identity as the people of God, the body of Christ, and the community of the Holy Spirit. No baptized person should be excluded from participating in the eucharistic assembly on such grounds as age, race, gender, economic circumstance or mental capacity.

2. In the future, Anglican unity will find its liturgical expression not so much in uniform texts as in a common approach to eucharistic celebration and a structure which will ensure a balance of word, prayer, and sacrament, and which bears witness to the catholic calling of the Anglican Communion.

3. The eucharistic action models the way in which God as redeemer comes into the world in the Word made flesh, to which the people of God respond by offering themselves – broken individuals – to be made one body in Christ's risen life. This continual process of transformation is enacted in each celebration.

4. The sacrificial character of all Christian life and worship must be articulated in a way that does not blur the unique atoning work of Christ. Vivid language, symbol, and metaphor engage human memory and assist the eucharistic action in forming the life of the community.

5. In the eucharist, we encounter the mystery of the triune God in the proclamation of the word and the celebration of the sacrament. The fundamental character of the eucharistic prayer is thanksgiving, and the whole eucharistic prayer should be seen as consecratory. The elements of memorial and invocation are caught up within the movement of thanksgiving.

6. In, through, and with Christ, the assembly is the celebrant of the eucharist. Among other tasks it is appropriate for lay persons to play their part in proclaiming the word, leading the prayers of the people, and distributing communion. The liturgical functions of the ordained arise out of pastoral responsibility. Separating liturgical function and pastoral oversight tends to reduce liturgical presidency to an isolated ritual function.

7. The embodied character of Christian worship must be honoured in proclamation, music, symbol, and ritual. If inculturation is to be taken seriously, local culture and custom which are not in conflict with the Gospel must be reflected in the liturgy, interacting with the accumulated inculturation of the tradition.

8. The church needs leaders who are themselves open to renewal and are able to facilitate and enable it in community. This should affect the liturgical formation of laity and clergy, especially bishops as leaders of the local community. Such continuing formation is a priority and adequate resources for it should be provided in every Province.

9. Celebrating the eucharist involves both reaffirming the baptismal commitment to die to self and be raised to newness of life, and embodying that vision of the kingdom in searching for justice, reconciliation and peace in the community. The Spirit who calls us into one body in Christ equips and sends us out to live this divine life.[19]

It is perhaps fair to conclude that these principles are largely general, unspecific and uncontroversial, and offer little practical help to provinces engaged in revising their rites. However, the section reports contained more detailed help. Section III on 'The Structure of the Eucharist' included the following:

---

19 The Dublin Statement was published on its own as David Holeton (ed.), *Renewing the Anglican Eucharist* (Grove Worship Booklet 135, Grove Books, 1996), and was published with a series of accompanying essays in David Holeton (ed.), *Our Thanks and Praise* (Anglican Book Centre, Toronto, 1998). It was also published as an appendix to the report of ACC-10, held at Panama City, *Being Anglican in the Third Millennium* (Morehouse, Harrisburg, for the ACC, 1997).

'We therefore recommend recognition of the following basic structure for the Sunday assembly:

1. *Gathering of God's people*. The people of God gather as an assembly to draw near to God and to celebrate new life in Jesus Christ.
2. *Proclaiming and Receiving the Word of God*. The Scriptures are read and the word of God is celebrated in song and silence, reflection, preaching, and response.
3. *Prayers of the People*. The people of God, as a royal priesthood, intercede for the world, the church, the local community, and all in need.
4. *Celebrating at the Lord's Table*. The assembly offers praise and thanksgiving over the bread and wine, and partakes in the body and blood of Christ.
5. *Going out as God's People*. The assembly disperses for a life of faith and service in the world.'

The next paragraphs expanded on this structure, and the treatment of paragraph 4 included a careful analysis of the structure of the eucharistic prayer. The section exhibited three such structures, each similar to the other two, and they are perhaps made most accessible by being tabulated.

'A common arrangement ... is ...'	'Other developed forms might include' ... 1	'Other developed forms might include' ... 2
Dialogue	Dialogue	Dialogue
Thanksgiving	Thanksgiving for Creation	Thanksgiving for Creation
Creation	Sanctus	Sanctus
Redemption (as recorded	Thanksgiving for	Thanksgiving for
by both the Old and New	Redemption	Redemption
Testaments)	Institution Narrative	Institution Narrative
The work of the Spirit	Anamnesis	Anamnesis
Sanctus	Thanksgiving for the work	Supplication
Narrative/anamnesis	of the Spirit	Epiclesis
Epiclesis	Epiclesis	The work of the Spirit
Doxology and Amen	Supplication for the	in the Assembly and
	Assembly and the	the Mission of the
	Mission of the Church	Church
	Doxology and Amen	Doxology and Amen

The section urged that this kind of view of the overall nature of a eucharistic prayer evaded the use of the traditional word 'preface' and, without drawing attention to it, also evaded the use of 'consecration', save to warn that the narrative, if it 'is part of the supplication, . . . risks being understood as a formula for consecration' – part of the tendency (displayed in the outlines above) to play down a western shape of the prayer. More explicitly, Section I (on 'Eucharistic Theology') amplified and reinforced Tom Talley's promotion of an eastern, Trinitarian, shape to the eucharistic prayer, and clearly adopted the concept of 'consecration by thanksgiving'. On the other hand, it did not attempt to define or describe what consecration effects, and its discussion of 'The Presence of Christ in the Eucharist' avoided all questions of localization and objectivization and, in line with Cranmer and the Thirty-Nine Articles, concentrated on the separable, more dynamic, question of the inward part of what the communicant receives.

While the Dublin IALC was a landmark in inter-Anglican networking in relation to liturgy, it is not clear that its findings have been widely influential. The province which has most overtly engaged with it is the Church of Ireland, where the 2004 BCP expressly mentions IALCs in its modern Preface. The Anglican Church in Aotearoa, New Zealand and Polynesia also makes specific reference to it in its 'alternative order' (NZ4).

After Dublin

IALC passed on in the next decade and a half to address ordination, liturgical formation, Anglican identity, and funeral and marriage liturgies. With one exception, arising below, there was no recurrence to the eucharist. However, the Dublin Consultation was to bear further fruit in the publication of David R. Holeton (ed.), *Our Thanks and Praise: The Eucharist in Anglicanism Today – Papers from the Fifth International Anglican Liturgical Consultation* (Anglican Book Centre, Toronto, 1998). This volume seriously addressed the nature of the eucharist in Anglicanism. Along with the Dublin Statement (and a Study Guide to it, devised by Ruth Meyers) it presented substantial essays, partly expounding, partly expanding, the work done in Untermarchtal and Dublin. In these William Crockett further buttressed the Talley thesis that the 'Trinitarian' shape most fully satisfied the purpose of the eucharistic prayer, and David Holeton himself confirmed this by setting out a structure for the Great Thanksgiving which is both simpler and clearer than the sketches reproduced above from the Group at Dublin:

Introductory dialogue
Proclamation
   Thanksgiving
   Sanctus/Benedictus
   Institution
   Anamnesis/Oblation
   Supplication
     Epiclesis
   Doxology
   Amen

Another weighty essay was by Charles Sherlock from Australia, on 'Eucharist, Sacrifice, and Atonement', with a subtitle, 'The "*Clarifications*" of ARCIC', exploring the significance of sacrificial and propitiatory language in statements about the eucharist. He had himself been a signatory of *Clarifications*, in which ARCIC-2 had addressed itself solely to papal disquiet about ARCIC-1's Statements on the Eucharist, and had apparently gained the desired papal acceptance of their work by thus 'clarifying' the text to meet the points of disquietude.[20] The general Anglican reaction had been (and

---

20 ARCIC-2, *Clarifications on Eucharist and Ministry* (Church House Publishing and Catholic Truth Society, London, 1994). While this present record does not divert to address *Clarifications* further, it is worth noting that one major flaw in the original ARCIC-1 Statements on the eucharist (which were overall a genuine breakthrough in ecumenical agreement) was that neither Communion's eucharistic rites were brought into consideration at any point, and there was even a possibility that parts of the Statement would not sit easily with the actual texts. *Clarifications*, however, somewhat extraordinarily cited 1662 itself, and used

has been since) to deplore both the process of 'clarifying' to one Church only, and also the actual exposition of the eucharist used by ARCIC-2 to meet the papal hesitations. The 1998 Lambeth Conference, while welcoming all the 'Statements' of ARCIC-1 and ARCIC-2, deliberately left *Clarifications* out of account (perhaps relying on the technical ground that it was not a 'Statement'), and its signatories have been embarrassed by it. But not so Charles Sherlock, whose robust, even eager, defence of *Clarifications* gives both visibility and, from his angle, thorough defensibility to the document others on the Anglican side have wanted to bury.

While the Dublin Statement was published in the report of ACC-10, and was therefore in the hands of the Lambeth Conference members in 1998, no follow-on Statement from it appeared in the Lambeth report.[21] In Section 3 of the Conference a group prepared a Statement which both expressed confidence in IALCs and commended the Principles and Recommendations of the Dublin report. Their draft was blocked by Section 4, so never came to the plenary sessions, and hence no Statement on liturgy came from the Conference; but the blocked draft has been published in *A History of International Anglican Liturgical Consultations 1983–2007*. The Conference did pass a resolution of confidence in the IALCs, and did experience eucharistic worship from many provinces around the world. But one portion of the final section of the draft Statement under the heading of 'Inculturation' addressed a need strongly articulated by African participants:

> 'One particular instance of the tension described earlier between the liturgical expression of the culture and the worldwide unity of the Church has emerged strongly at this Lambeth. It concerns the sensitive issue of the sacramental elements at holy communion. On the one hand there is an almost unbroken universal practice of nearly two thousand years of celebrating communion with wheat-bread and grape-wine; on the other we have heard compelling pleas (including the findings of the pan-African Kanamai Consultation and IALC-5 in Dublin) that in some parts of the world these forms of food and drink may well be culturally alien or prohibitively expense or both, and that the traditional practice is therefore to be severely questioned . . . '

The twenty-first century

Lambeth 1998 was silent on liturgical renewal. IALCs, with the substantial treatment of Untermarchtal and Dublin behind them, thereafter moved on in their agenda to tackle other liturgical issues. So the Communion was unlikely to enjoy from that source any helpful overview of textual revision of the eucharist on the one hand, nor benefit from advice about such revision from the Consultations on the other. There was, however, an ongoing topic, well adumbrated above, which the IALCs did not let rest. At IALC-6 in Berkeley, California, a paper entitled 'Eucharistic Food – may we substitute?' asked what breadth of interpretation might be allowed in the provision of sacramental food

---

it as a basis for arguing for votive masses and reservation of consecrated elements and paying reverence to them. Lovers of 1662 may find this surprising – but the purpose in hand was simply to convince the Vatican, not lovers of the rite, and it apparently did that.

21 ACC-10, held in Panama City in October 1996, had one of its four sections address 'Looking to the Future in Worship', and the section produced a Report under this title. The section's own five sub-groups handled five different topics, none of which was specifically eucharistic, and the section report therefore only touched on eucharistic issues in most general or passing terms. It made no reference to Kanamai or Dublin.

and drink. The IALC asked the Standing Committee of the ACC to conduct a survey 'to determine practice in relation to the elements of holy communion throughout the Communion'.[22] However, before the Standing Committee could meet, in December 2001 the new Inter-Anglican Standing Commission on Ecumenical Relations (IASCER), which included an IALC member, William Crockett, considered the Berkeley request – and produced a Statement which was 'cautious to the point of immovability on this issue, citing "the Church's constant tradition"'.[23] The Joint Standing Committee of the ACC and primates met just before ACC-12 in Hong Kong in September 2002, and 'It was agreed that a survey be undertaken of practices in relation to the elements of Holy Communion'.[24] Then at the actual ACC meeting a few days later, Paul Gibson presented the Joint Standing Committee's recommendations about a survey, and added that he had already conducted a preliminary survey, to which half the provinces had replied, and of them half had said that variations from the traditional composition of the sacramental elements were known and even allowed.[25] The ACC itself then resolved:

Resolution 16. Inter Anglican Liturgical Consultation
This Anglican Consultative Council:
1. awaits a survey by the Inter Anglican Liturgical Consultation of practice in relation to the elements of Holy Communion, and of the reasons given for any departure from dominical command; and
2. requests that the results of such a survey be presented to the Joint Standing Committee upon completion.[26]

The Steering Committee of IALCs acted on this, and set up a task force to conduct the survey and report on it. The three members conducted the survey, and presented a full report to IALC-7 at Prague in 2005. This 'revealed a wider spread of variations than IASCER was likely on previous form to approve'.[27] The IALC itself 'was minded to affirm a norm and yet be wholly tolerant of variants'[28] – and sent the report on to the Joint Standing Committee in line with the ACC resolution above. The Joint Standing Committee had referred the report back to IASCER, which, along with polite thanks for the report, 'reminded all provinces of the third article of the Lambeth Quadrilateral' (which refers to the 'unfailing use of Christ's words of institution and of the elements ordained by him'), and 'viewed with concern evidence indicating that elements other than bread and wine are used in some provinces'.[29] The Joint Standing Committee had also endorsed IASCER's findings. The IALC-8 itself, meeting in 2007, learned that each element in this process was now out of embargo, and requested the Secretary-General of the ACC to post the documents together on the Anglican Communion website.

---

22 *A History of the International Anglican Liturgical Consultations 1983–2007*, p. 49.

23 *A History of the International Anglican Liturgical Consultations 1983–2007*, p. 49.

24 *For the Life of the World: The Official Report of the 12th meeting of the Anglican Consultative Council, Hong Kong 2002* (Morehouse Publishing for the ACC, 2003), p. 63. The text of the recommendations is on p. 395.

25 *For the Life of the World*, pp. 395–6.

26 *For the Life of the World*, pp. 466. The incorrect title 'Inter Anglican' appears to be due to a misprint or possibly sheer ignorance.

27 *A History of the International Anglican Liturgical Consultations 1983–2007*, p. 52.

28 *A History of the International Anglican Liturgical Consultations 1983–2007*, p. 52.

29 Both these quotations are from the minutes of IALC-8 at Palermo in 2007, at which William Crockett reported from IASCER.

Other sources

This highlighting of the very narrow, and strictly non-textual, issue of the limits of what constitutes 'bread' and 'wine' illustrates by contrast in recent Anglican history the sheer lack of any other guidance on eucharistic revision by any central bodies of the Communion. There have of course been long-standing relationships of communion with the Old Catholics, the Philippine Independent Church and the Mar Thoma Syrian Church of Malabar; and there have been new agreements and concordats with other Churches (as, for example, with Lutherans in both the Porvoo Declaration in Europe, and the concordats in the USA and Canada, and with non-episcopal Churches in Southern Africa). These have sometimes led to the use of each others' rites, but not to making ecumenical statements to the whole Communion, nor to entrenching texts which Anglicans have 'owned'. An exception duly included here is the new text agreed for shared eucharistic worship between the Churches of North and South India and the Mar Thoma Syrian Church. This is contained within the Church of South India *Book of Common Worship* (2004), and it is presented here at the end of the South India chapter.

The major Communion-wide ecumenical accord which might have borne upon the eucharist in the last decade is *The Church of the Triune God: The Cyprus Agreed Statement of the International Commission for Anglican-Orthodox Theological Dialogue 2006* (Anglican Communion Office, 2006). It does, as such dialogue always does, discount the *Filioque* clause in the Nicene Creed; and it does not have any section devoted to the eucharist; but it does, in the context of a discussion of the priesthood of Christ and the nature of ordination, describe what the participants believe the eucharist to be:

> 'In taking bread and wine, giving thanks, breaking and giving, the priest is configured to Christ at the Last Supper. The president draws together the life and prayer of the baptized, and offers them to the Father with the bread and wine. In the eucharistic prayer, the offering of praise and thanksgiving for the mighty deeds of God, culminating in the sacrifice of the paschal mystery, is offered for all creation. Received by the Father, the gifts of bread and wine are returned in the Holy Spirit as Christ's risen life, his body and blood, the bread of heaven and the cup of salvation. In the eucharistic action, the Church is renewed in its prayer and self-offering as the priestly people of God.'[30]

The difficulties with this description are both that it does not look typical of Anglicanism, and that at its heart there are ambiguities as to what it means that the president 'offers them to the Father with the bread and the wine', and what is 'culminating in the sacrifice of the eucharistic mystery'. It is also curious because, although all kinds of recognition-marks of Eastern Orthodoxy appear in the passage, there is one which does not. Anglicans round the world have been wrestling with the role and character of the epiclesis, as the next chapter here shows; the Eastern Churches have in the past insisted that the integrity of the eucharist stemmed from the key role played by the epiclesis; yet here, where the actual role of the Spirit in the eucharist is being invoked, the Agreed Statement coyly avoids any explicit reference to the epiclesis. The Agreed Statement is not, of course, at this stage actually agreed by the two world Communions – it is simply

---

30 *The Cyprus Agreed Statement*, Section VI, §19, p. 72.

agreed by the participants. And the participants would no doubt insist that they were not really addressing the eucharist – the chapter concerns the ordained ministry.

The Lambeth Conference in 2008 made no Statements and passed no Resolutions. But it did give rise to 'Reflections' by a chosen band of bishops, who 'heard' the outcomes of the 'Indabas', or discussion groups, into which the participants were distributed. The Reflections hardly bore upon worship issues at all (when they did, they did so in the hope that environmental issues would figure more strongly on worship agendas). And, more specifically, they did not at any point address the character of eucharistic rites.

Other eucharistic concerns

While the most recent decade has seen the textual issues which are of concern here little addressed by central bodies, the Communion at large has been more regularly engrossed in questions of the terms of communion between churches, the possibility of lay presidency, the use of reserved eucharistic elements for distribution at a satellite liturgy later or elsewhere, the admission of the unconfirmed (and in some places the unbaptized) to communion, and the status of the eucharist as a main Sunday worship event. The mind of nearly all the provinces to create or revise their own eucharistic rites has, in an electronic era, led to considerable borrowing, interchange and cross-fertilization between these various provinces. But as IALC-5 at Dublin in 1995 has faded from corporate memories, so the initiative and energy for such creativity has sprung, often unguided, from the individual provinces themselves. Common principles may be arising from the rites of the Communion, and may be discerned by inspection in those published here – but it is less clear that such common principles have underlain the work of each province's liturgical work.

2. Provincial Eucharistic Texts

Structure

It will be clear from the previous chapter, as well as from the individual rites in the succeeding chapters, that the structure of the eucharist has been accorded a widespread priority in the 25 years under review. Furthermore, the structure has become almost entirely agreed. We may set it out as follows:

1. A gathering (sometimes including penitence, usually including Gloria in Excelsis, most frequently concluding with the collect).
2. The Ministry of the Word, with two or three readings, culminating in the Gospel, optionally interspersed with psalmody or hymnody, and followed by first the sermon and then the Creed.
3. Intercessions or Prayers of the People.
4. The Ministry of the Sacrament, usually starting with two preliminaries, and then with the eucharistic action:
     Peace
     Preparation of the Table

     Taking of the Bread and Cup
     The Eucharistic Prayer (followed by the Lord's Prayer)
     The Breaking of the Bread
     The Distribution of the Bread and Wine.
5. Post-communion, including thanksgiving and dismissal.

This structure determines the major part of this chapter. However, there are some general trends which need recording before the specific matters are addressed.

Alternative services and the English Language

Earlier volumes saw the transition from 'traditional' liturgical language (i.e. that of 1662) to 'modern' English (i.e. that which addresses God as 'you'). In various provinces 1662 itself, or a local variant of it, has run on as the foundational liturgical standard of the province, even if the vast majority of actual celebrations of the eucharist have used a modern alternative. This is the case in Canada, Southern Africa, Australia, Aotearoa, Scotland, and England itself, where 'alternative services' have been widely used without impairing the canonical authority of the foundation texts. In others, as in the USA and in Ireland, the traditional services have been incorporated in a modern Book in such a way as to mean that that Book has become *the* BCP, and not an alternative book of services. The Church of England has managed to have it both ways – adapting 1662 and **EngB** from 1980 to be 'alternative services', even while 1662 also still remains (unadapted) as the foundational liturgical text of the Church.

However, the process since 1966, when the first modern-English rites appeared in Australia and New Zealand, has not been that of a single change, the crossing of just one linguistic watershed. Writing in 'traditional' English certainly passed away quickly.[31] But within ten years the issue of 'inclusive' language was overtaking texts only recently authorized. This change was not simply that the coming of women ministers meant that rubrics could no longer refer to ministers as '*he*'; the case was much more forcefully being made that the terms 'man' and 'men' no longer smoothly included 'woman' and 'women', but that they had developed an exclusive ring, such that Jesus did not become incarnate 'for us men and for our salvation', women were not required 'to love and serve all men' (at least not in an exclusive sense!), and 'mankind' was a perilous way of indicating the whole human race. Thus the American BCP of 1976 (proposed) and 1979 (definitive) had taken this step in time. However, the Church of England *Alternative Service Book 1980* and the Church of Ireland *Alternative Prayer Book* (1984) were published in fairly authoritative hardback form only a year or two before their own compilers would have wished to have gone 'inclusive' – but by then it was too late.

The change is well illustrated in the move from the Common Forms of 1970, 1971 and 1974 of ICET (the International Consultation on English Texts), provided as an appendix in **FAL** and **LAL**, to the re-touched forms from ELLC (the English Language Liturgical Consultation), which are part of Appendix B in this volume.[32] It parallels changes in secular use, and is not easily discerned as a feature of new liturgical writing – it is when it outcrops in the altered form of well-known texts (whether Bible, liturgy or hymnody) that it is most noticeable and is often then least agreeable to the traditionalist. It is particularly a feature of the English language, though other languages have other pitfalls and similarly have to surmount them for contemporary worship.

The obvious element in inclusive language is the transcending of masculine nouns, pronouns and possessive adjectives, in the interests of unprejudiced communication. However, within this broad change a question inevitably arises about language concerning God. There is little sign in this volume of texts which seek to remove all hints of maleness from references to the Son of God (we can still say 'he came down from heaven'), and there is little evidence of excluding references to God as Father ('Our parent in heaven' does not have much official credence). But ELLC has tactfully eliminated, or greatly reduced, general references to God as 'he', so that the second line of the Gloria in Excelsis now has 'God's people' where ICET had 'his people', and the opening dialogue of the eucharistic prayer ends with, 'It is right to give *our* thanks and praise'.[33] There is a scrupulous tendency among some English-speakers towards using the 'reign' of God in place of the 'kingdom', because of the male overtones in the word 'king' – but ELLC did not go that far. And a finely poised text is earlier in the Nicene

---

31 There is hardly any new liturgical writing subsequent to 1968 which uses 'traditional' language. There have been a few cases (as in **EngCW1B**) of translating the modern into the traditional, in order to enrich the latter or give a symmetry of content between two styles. And there was the amazing case of Wales, which produced a complete range of new bilingual rites in 1984, in which the English version displayed a marginally adapted traditional text (see **Wal1** in **LAL**).

32 It is mirrored in the change from the New International Version of the Bible (the NIV) to the New Revised Standard Version (the NRSV).

33 However, a third candidate is the Church of England's variant from ELLC: '**It is right to give thanks and praise**', and that form has also been adopted elsewhere.

Creed, where ICET had 'and was made man', and ELLC has 'and became truly human' – and not every province has been ready to adopt the ELLC text.

A different way of softening the apparent male-gendering of God is to use feminine-type imagery alongside the terminology of kingship, fatherhood and lord. Thus (with a background in the prayer devised – not for authorized use – by the Roman Catholic International Commission on English in the Liturgy (ICEL) in the 1980s) in **EngCW1A** prayer G says God cares for us 'as a mother tenderly gathers her children', and further echoes from the same source are found in **Amer4** EP 2 and in **CSI1** EP C.

The Lord's Prayer has had the hardest task in winning its way into modern-language use, though (apart from the very issue of 'Our Father') it has not precipitated inclusive language issues. In the Indian sub-continent, 'holy be your name' runs on from the earliest ICET texts of 1970 and 1971. But the chief stumbling-block with the ELLC text is the ninth line and 'Save us from the time of trial', and in England, Ireland, Nigeria, Papua New Guinea and elsewhere the main text still has 'Lead us not into temptation'. It has possibly been preserved in that form by the weight of the traditionalists in those churches who do not desire a modern text in any case.

Enormous Variety and Cultural Adaptation

The Anglican liturgical tradition began with imposed uniformity, a straitjacket which allowed virtually no scope for choice between alternatives within the rite and equally no scope for importing extraneous materials into it.[34] It is a matter of simple observation that this constricted provision has now burgeoned into a skeletal framework (the structure) upon which any manner of material may be placed at the president's or other people's discretion. While in **LAL** it was still possible to edit forms for intercession which were at least printed within the original rites or as appendices, the discretion now given stretches to the horizon. It is similar with the introduction to confession, the introduction to the Peace, and the post-communion prayers. In part there is a vastly increased seasonal provision, but in larger part the liturgy has burst the boundaries of set texts, and allows home-produced forms or extemporary utterances to characterize any particular celebration. And, while the eucharistic prayer may sometimes look like the one immutable form, yet provinces may have a choice between eight or ten eucharistic prayers, with further variety provided by 40 or 50 proper prefaces, and sometimes by other discretionary options built into the prayer at other points. There was precedent for the 'matrix' concept in **Amer3-3** and **NZ3**, and it is found again here in **Amer4** and **NZ3A**, and it is taken further here in **CNI2** (which is little more than a directory) and in **CSI2**.

While much of the desire for variety (or permissiveness) in Anglican rites arose from the emergence of anglo-catholicism in the 19th century, some of it sheerly doctrinal, some of it more obviously seasonal, the modern opening of almost all the boundaries owes more to pastoral considerations. The texts are in practice allied with a vast range of musical styles, and an equally vast range of hymnody, anthems and songs which the music accompanies; and as practically no hint of any of the contents of these items appears in the authorized text, the texts can be read with little sense of the

---

34 1662 offers choices between two prayers for the monarch, a variety of offertory sentences, and two post-communion prayers, and no other.

actual three-dimensional celebration which they precipitate on, say, a Sunday morning. The freedoms which exist mean that Anglican eucharists around the world may vary culturally from the severely poker-faced Victorian England formality to the wholly indigenous, 'incarnational', adaptation to local cultures in language, architecture, art, music, vesture, ceremonial, dance, and use of multi-media communication. This great range of styles may be found within one province, where the officially authorized text gives little hint of what local conventions or creativity may overlay the given minimum that the structure provides – and to that extent also, a reading of the texts here provided will yield few hints about the characteristic features of local culture which are, whether frequently or occasionally, embodied within the actual celebrations to which the texts give rise. If the provinces are taking seriously the recommendations of both Lambeth 1988 and the IALC 1989 Statement 'Down to Earth Worship' to inculturate their liturgies, it is, it seems, not greatly within the authorized texts that this is to be found.[35]

A parallel trend in liturgical expression should perhaps be set alongside this freedom. Throughout the liturgy – and particularly within the eucharistic prayer – the vogue for congregational responses has found increasing expression. The bold type in every rite is evidence of this. But such participation requires some rigour in the composing and authorizing of texts and some discipline in worshipping with them. Presidential parts can be adapted almost at the drop of a hat, but congregational ones are relatively immutable.

Well-loved and Once-off Liturgies

The lack of central control or guidance has clearly encouraged mutual borrowing. Furthermore, international travel has multiplied vastly over the last quarter of a century, and it has been more than matched by the astonishing immediate access from anywhere on earth to information anywhere else on earth, such as the electronic revolution has provided. Thus provincial commissions writing or revising liturgies have usually had a great range of materials before them. Some of the evidence of the use they have made of this range can be found in the recourse to the Common Forms (in which the Anglican ones, labelled 'CF', mostly stem from England). Thus, to take one instance, David Frost's 'second post-communion prayer' (CF 11(b) – 'Father of all'), is now to be found in **EngCW1A**, **Ire3**, **Nig1**, **CSI1**, **Aus6**, **NZ1A** and **Mel2**.

However, it is in the eucharistic prayers that the most fascinating patterns of borrowing and cross-fertilizing are to be found. 1662 remains somewhere in the parentage of some rites; the original **CSI** has had impact (partly through Lambeth 1958 and *A Liturgy for Africa* (**LfA**, 1964)); a devotion to Hippolytus is found in nakedly Hippolytan prayers, in prayers filtered through the adaptations of the Roman Catholic Prayer II and, in a more remote way, in the stages that Prayer A in **EngCW1A** has undergone through **Eng2**, **MLT**, **Eng3**, and **EngA**. In some cases specific lines have travelled (as in the **Mel** and **Mel1** use of the Qu'Appelle rendering 'Do this in memory of me and *know that I am with you*' (italics mine)[36]). In others, ideas – such as concluding the prayer

---

35 Exceptional instances are: the recommendation in **Nig1** re the peace, 'a sign of peace; African fraternal or traditional embrace or traditional handshake or double handclasp'; in **Ken** the sweep of the worshippers' arms as they approach the blessing; in **CSI1** 'a hymn or bhajan'

36 This instance is illustrated in earlier volumes – see the footnote on p. 306. But see also the prayers from **NZ6** on pages 304–5.

with the sanctus – have crossed borders. In others again, the substance of a prayer has been marginally altered in the place of its adoption (as with the 'star-trek' prayer from **Amer2-2** as found here in **Braz2**, or with Prayer H from **EngCW1A**, adapted to become Prayer 3 in **Ire2** and, rather differently, to become a Prayer for Eastertide in **SAfr5**). And in some cases prayers from elsewhere have been adopted entire, such that **EngA** from 1980 is now to be found here in Portugal and Nigeria, whereas it has been somewhat changed in the Church of England itself, as can be seen in **EngCW1A**. Further instances of this are: the use in Ireland, in both **Ire1** and **Ire2**, of Prayer 4 from **Aus3** (not now featuring in this form in **Aus6**); the adoption in Wales, as Prayer 5 in **Wal4**, of the original eucharistic prayer from **Scot2**; texts from **Amer2-2** in **HK3**; and from **Can4** in **SAfr3**.

However, in with the products of borrowing and cross-fertilizing, there have also been serious creative ventures of 'thinking outside the box'. An interesting pioneering in this area came in 1984 in **NZ2** and **NZ3**, and there are continued examples in the further Aotearoa New Zealand rites. Prayers for specific use with children (discussed for their content three pages further on) are another category of new thinking; but for newly innovatory compilation go to **EngCW1A** Prayer D, **Scot2** Prayer V, **Can5** Supp Pr 1, **Cong** Prayer 3, or **CSI1** Prayers B and C.

Within the Structure

There is little reason to go closely over the whole structuring, as it has settled down to such a standard order. The 'Gathering' sometimes includes penitence, sometimes not, and sometimes includes Kyries and/or Gloria in Excelsis and sometimes not. In a few cases the collect is attributed to the 'Ministry of the Word' rather than to the conclusion of the Gathering.[37] The Ministry of the Word always provides for three readings, with an option of two, but the absolute requirement of the Gospel as the climax of the readings. The Creed (with a growing readiness to allow the Apostles' Creed as an alternative) follows the sermon and rounds up the section. The 'Prayers' (or similar title) almost invariably come next, and their general character is outlined above. They have become a subject for specialized study in their own right, not necessarily connected tightly to the eucharist. In one or two rites the Lord's Prayer can, optionally, conclude the prayers. And in one or two rites the Peace is grouped under the heading of the Prayers, perhaps a formal recognition that Tertullian says that the Peace is 'the seal of prayer'.[38]

The Peace is more regularly viewed as the beginning of the liturgy of the sacrament, which mirrors its role in Justin, where the newly baptized are joined with the faithful as they come to the eucharist. This was fairly clearly the rationale followed by the Church of South India as it reintroduced the ancient sharing of Peace from 1950 onwards. It has been almost uniformly followed by Anglicans throughout the world as they

---

37 **EngA** must take some responsibility for this, as the two-year 'thematic' eucharistic lectionary which was integral to it led to thematic collects to lead into the readings. But further back, the whole 1662 grouping of 'Collect, Epistle and Gospel' had perhaps lodged a supposed mutual relationship quite deep in the corporate psyche – even in a rite where none of the three items connected with each other save at high seasons. The widespread currency of the three-year Sunday lectionary, providing for semi-continuous readings in three strands, has rendered void any idea of a common 'theme' to be introduced by the collect.

38 Tertullian, *De Oratione* 18. For a discussion of this, see L. Edward Phillips, *The Ritual Kiss in Early Christian Worship* (Alcuin/GROW Joint Liturgical Study 36, Grove Books, Cambridge, 1996), pp. 19–20.

have created modern eucharistic rites. Even placing the Peace formally to conclude the Prayers still gives it the same place in the sequence of the order! Nor has the fascination of Roman Catholic ways, to which some Anglicans are subject, led any Province into an official following of the Roman Catholic location for the Peace, after the consecration.[39] However, there are a few paradoxical exceptions to this uniformity. One is in **Mel2**, which locates the Peace as the conclusion of penitence in the Gathering, but a footnote there shows how the Melanesians have not taken to this. Another exception is, wholly unexpectedly, the Church of South India itself, the very Church that pioneered Justin's position! In **CSI1** a position similar to that in **Mel2** is adopted, linking the Peace with penitence and forgiveness, a principle also adopted in the Indian Concordat Liturgy (ICL), where two penitential sections occur, the second specifically concerned with any lack of peace with each other, and therefore appropriately concluded after absolution with the sharing of the Peace – but in ICL's case this use of the Peace does lead straight into the sacramental section of the rite.

The preparation of the Table is an ambiguous event. Cranmer in 1552 had an 'offertory' which was solely money (and occurred even when there was no communion), and no rubric about preparing the table. In 1662 Cranmer's offertory remained, and bread and wine were placed on the table when the offertory was concluded.[40] This clear distinction between two different functions has been retained in some rites, but often Anglicans have been muddled through the Roman Catholic labelling of the preparation of the bread and wine as the 'offertory', and through the juxtaposition of the two functions in 1662 (with the added readiness of Anglicans incorrectly to expound 'offertory' in 1662 to relate to the bread and wine). The situation was further prejudiced by Gregory Dix's insisting that the first of the dominical actions was the 'taking' of the bread and wine, which was *tout simple* the 'offertory' – and the 'offering' theme in the word 'offertory' meshed beautifully with his exposition that the elements were a token or means of the offering of our lives. Any patristic basis for his thesis (let alone any biblical one) is threadbare to the point of invisibility, but the processing with the elements and the according them value as symbolic offerings to God has burgeoned and flourished, and appears (all mixed up with the money) in many rites – whether or not the word 'offertory' is used. It is helpful when the word is *not* used.

This understanding of 'offertory' is further expressed and reinforced in a recourse to the Roman Catholic 'offertory prayers'. These have been sufficiently widely adopted in the rites to warrant inclusion here in the Common Forms (see CF 5(a) and (b)). The standard translation of these is that we have bread/wine 'to offer'; that is how the texts are found in **Wal4**, **Nig1**, **SAfr3**, **PNGR** and **Mel2**, and the use of these prayers simply reinforces the Dix interpretation of the rite. There are variants around – in **EngCW1A** (see §46 in its appendix), we have the bread/wine 'to set before you', a nuancing of the meaning which some thought at the point of drafting would gather more support.[41] In

---

39 The exception is an option in **Braz1**. Nor, it should be added, has there been much evidence of a borrowing of the (surely unsatisfactory?) Roman text, 'look not on our sins but on the faith of your church'. The introductions to the Peace displayed in this volume are almost entirely concerned with mutual belongingness and sharing among the people of God.

40 For a full treatment of this – including the meaning of 'accept our alms and oblations' – see Colin Buchanan, *The End of the Offertory* (Grove Liturgical Study 14, Grove Books, Bramcote, 1978).

41 For a fuller account of the handling of this in the Church of England Synod, see Colin Buchanan, *Taking the Long View: Three and Half Decades of General Synod* (Church House Publishing, 2006), pp. 81–84.

Cey2 the wording has been turned round splendidly to say 'Blessed are you . . . you are the giver of this bread/wine'; and in **Aus4** 'we have this bread to share'. However, quite apart from whether the wording goes beyond anything warranted in scripture, there is also an open question as to whether the form of the thanksgiving in these prayers does not anticipate the eucharistic prayer itself, and, so to speak, do its work for it in advance. In England much reflection on the Commission in the 1970s led to the conclusion that preparing or laying the table is a functional preliminary to the sacramental action (perhaps comparable to the disciples getting the Upper Room ready in the scriptural account), and is of little or no symbolic significance. The first of the dominical actions – the 'taking' – is to be carefully distinguished from this preparation, and whether the ceremony is modest or ebullient, it demarcates the two elements over which the thanks are now to be given, and starts the sacramental action moving towards its climax in reception. Other provinces vary in the way they interpret Jesus' taking of the bread and cup, and vary accordingly in how they then execute their interpretation. There is, however, as we shall see, a very widespread move away from ordering a ceremony of 'taking' within the narrative of institution.

The Eucharistic Prayer

At this point in the structure, the central feature of this volume comes under scrutiny. As it is the locus of most of the eucharistic doctrine in each rite, it clearly requires both an examination of some general trends, and then a close look at the component parts of the prayer's own structure. Some of the family relationships within the prayers have been glimpsed on pages 19–20 above, and there is reference there too to a slightly random set of innovatory prayers found in different provinces.

(i) Identifiable themes

The handling of specific themes in eucharistic prayers has traditionally been done by the provision of proper prefaces. 1662 had a very limited set of these, and all revision since has tended to expand the supply.[42] Some new rites, and some EPs within the rites, have a fixed preface, and no variation during the year. But other rites have not only traditional prefaces, but also 'extended' ones which mark a season with a lengthy narrative of God's deeds. And along with the 'matrix' concept, there has been a growing unconcern about whether prefaces to be inserted in the rite need all be fully synodically approved; alternatively they may be provided ad hoc, as occasion suggests.

But a larger way of handling specific themes has dawned with EPs written wholly to highlight and celebrate a particular theme. This goes beyond the idea of a 'votive' rite (in which the EP was but little affected) – it is the writing of a whole prayer anew. Much writing of EPs in the last 50 years has in fact had a thematic thrust, for the

---

An irenic, but not wholly sympathetic, discussion is to be found in Paul Bradshaw (ed.), *Companion to Common Worship 1* (Alcuin/SPCK, 2001), p. 122.

42 In LiE, Bernard Wigan had an appendix with 71 proper prefaces. In **MAL**, the growth of rites and the widening of provision meant there were 99. In **FAL** seven further years of rites yielded around 175 (now contained in a folding table). In **LAL** the next ten years had provided over 200 (again in a folding table). No attempt at charting their further multiplication has been part of the preparation of this volume. They have become a specialized subject in their own right.

unique concentration of 1662 upon the cross of Christ and his all-sufficient sacrifice has led to other EPs which emphasized other features of God's mighty acts, and sometimes included a *sotto voce* advice that Cranmer was still good for passiontide, but a variation of emphasis was needed at other times of year. None of this, however, ever led to a labelling of EPs for particular seasons. The first signs of such labelling were in NZ1, NZ2 and NZ3 in 1984 (and found in LAL, though also found entire in chapter 32 here). There were EPs entitled 'Thanksgiving and Praise' and 'Creation and Redemption' and 'For Special Occasions', this last being an outline matrix. There are now similarly labelled prayers in Scot2A ('Anticipation', 'Returning to God' and 'New Life, the Lord, the Spirit'), though these themes give away their being written for specific seasons. SAfr5 has, *inter alia*, two for 'Creation', one for 'Eastertide' and one for 'Lent and Good Friday'. And Mel2 has a third alternative EP labelled 'Melanesian Environmental Theme'. One suspects that this tendency will grow.

However, there is a wholly different category of 'thematic' EPs arising more or less simultaneously in the last decade. This is the specific case of EPs 'for use with children'. The Roman Catholic Church provided such prayers in the early 1970s, and the genre has therefore since then been in the offing, posing a question, or even an opportunity, to Anglicans. However, Roman Catholic masses, although including in the canon prayer for fruitful reception, have been generally viewed as having a value and an efficacy which was not closely connected to reception of the elements. Anglicans have been more doubtful, and have regularly concluded that, even if non-communicant children were present (as happens, for instance, at eucharists in church schools), there is a fundamental oddity in writing EPs specifically to be user-friendly for non-communicants. However, a slow theological and canonical shift in Anglicanism over the last 40 years has led to a widespread admission of young children to communion on the basis of their baptism, and that in turn has slowly changed the climate for EPs written for ease of understanding and participation by children. Thus around the world such prayers have been written and authorized, and are to be found here in: Wal4 EP6 and EP7 (2004); SAfr5 'EP with children' (2008); NZ6 EP 'for use with children A' and 'for use with children B' (2010); and Mel2 'Alternative Great Thanksgiving suitable when there are many children present' (2003). The Church of England, where General Synod first asked for such prayers in 1991, is in the process of addressing drafts as this volume goes to press. Interestingly, within the Church of England's existing services a child may already have a role in one of the prayers at the preparation of the table (see EngCW1A §46). The modes of making the texts child-friendly have varied enormously, and while there is a general thrust towards brevity, simplicity of language and congregational participation, some of the standard 'adult' prayers may well rival the actual examples here in one or more of these features. Asking and answering questions within the rite (cf. Exod. 12.26–27) is more innovatory. But overall there is a field for research and further experiment opening before the Churches.

(ii) The biblical sweep

1662 was held to exhibit but one biblical feature of the acts of God – the crucifixion. In the first half of the 20th century, as Cranmer's language was adapted for rites with a 'long prayer', so the coming of an anamnesis provided mention of Jesus' death, resurrection and ascension – but the link from the sanctus to the narrative retained the exclusive 'by his one oblation of himself once offered . . . ' and so on. In **Afr** (originally drafted in 1924) this was extended to 'thou of thy tender mercy didst give thine only Son Jesus Christ *to take our nature upon him*, and to suffer death . . . ' (italics mine). The focus was slowly widening. The issue was not raised at Lambeth 1958, but new rites in the 1960s (see **MAL**) tended to slip in reference to creation, and sometimes also to the fall. The kind of standard preface of **Eng2** in 1967, drawing upon Hippolytus, included creation and fall, but also went on to the gift of the Holy Spirit and the forming of the church, the people of God. The widening of themes continued in the 1970s and 1980s without much placarding of the process – the issue was more usually the more pressing question as to how the distinctive role of Christ's unique sacrifice on the cross could be protected, and not simply be lost in a great sequence of events of smoothly equal status.

However, the texts in this volume display a vast breaking of the bounds in standard texts of EPs, and not simply in proper prefaces. There is wide reference to the Old Testament, to the patriarchs, the Exodus, the Law, the Exile, the prophets;[43] and the Gospels are laid under contribution to depict Christ's earthly ministry. Thus we find the ministry of John the Baptist, Jesus' interview with the woman at the Samaritan well, his touching of lepers, his being anointed in Bethany. After his resurrection, we find mention of Mary Magdalene and of the two on the road to Emmaus. And his reign in heaven and his promise to return also figure strongly. These references tend to go beyond mere recitation of reported events – they are usually linked (as in homiletics) to some way in which the Son of God deals with us today in the light of his relationships with men and women when on earth.

(iii) Consecration

Anglicans tend to say in sophisticated contexts that consecration is done by thanksgiving, that an EP is a single thanksgiving, and therefore that the whole prayer 'consecrates'. That is, however, sophisticated; and popular devotion and the accoutrements of elevation, genuflection and the ringing of bells may well distort worshippers' understanding of the rite. The issue is deeply affected by the use, in rites which are still western at this point, of a 'preliminary epiclesis', so that it has been natural to view as in logical sequence and connection a prayer for consecration, followed by an action which effects consecration. It is this sort of sequence, from 1549 to 1662, which gave credibility to the assertion that 1662 was 'more Roman than Rome'.[44] It is, of course, not easy to sustain when there is no preliminary epiclesis and the substantial one, after the anamnesis, appears to pray for consecration to be effected after the manipulation of the elements and the

---

43 Perhaps the prize for the mention of the most obscure prophet – actually a prophetess (which may account for her inclusion) – should go to Huldah (2 Kings 22.14–20), who is honoured in the preface to S1 in **Can5** on page 92 below.

44 Rome has, by a long-standing tradition, fully backed by the kinds of ceremonial mentioned above, allocated the consecratory role to the key words 'Hoc est enim corpus meum' and 'Hic est enim calix sanguinis mei'. However, this traditional attribution, though the basis of disputes with the Eastern Churches at the Council of Florence, and the assumed basis when Protestants on trial were charged with denying the change in the elements at this point, has never had conciliar or papal sanction to be required as *de fide*. In fact, the very existence of Eastern rites under the Roman aegis would preclude such a requirement

ringing of bells has advertised that the requested effect has already happened!

However, this aphorism blurred a vital distinction. For two rites to have an identical pattern of effecting consecration in no way implies that they have a common understanding of what consecration effects; and where Anglicans have held to a '1662' doctrine of effecting consecration by recitation of the dominical words, that has in no way implied that they have flirted with doctrines of transubstantiation or kindred beliefs.

Once the whole EP is viewed as consecratory, some readjustment of the ceremonial becomes desirable.[45] But an unresolved run-on from the principle concerns supplementary consecration. Various texts for this are included in the rites here, sometimes located at the end of the distribution of communion (which is when the provision is needed), sometimes in an appendix. There has been a slow move away from 1662's repetition of the narrative (or half of it) towards viewing supplementary consecration as in some way extending the context of the original consecration so that new elements brought into it are safely treated as consecrated. The reasoning is explicit in the section at the end of **CNI/1**. The tendency is nevertheless to guard the Church's flank by repeating the words of institution within the formula. One fascinating exception is **Ire3**, which offers two alternatives, of which the first is to add more *'silently'*. This is most consistent with the concept of bringing new elements into an existing context, and incidentally allows the distribution to continue without interruption.[46]

Analysis of the Prayer

There are three main sensitive features of the structure of the EP: the narrative of institution (henceforward the 'narrative'), the anamnesis, and the epiclesis.

(i) The narrative

The narrative has lost much of its fixed form. It can be with different wording in two successive prayers in the same rite. Jesus may be 'at supper with his friends', his purpose may be to 'celebrate the freedom of your people', and similar informal wording is often found.

However, as the emphasis comes off the narrative as being a set of rubrics which, when followed, provide a reliable form of consecration, that change re-establishes its role as a warrant text. When the narrative is read, that conveys assurance within the great thanksgiving that this is the Lord's Supper which the Church is providing. It incidentally fulfils the Lambeth Quadrilateral insistence that the sacrament must include the invariable use of the Lord's own words of institution.

This nevertheless allows a variant. The Quadrilateral does not state *where* the Lord's words must come, and in one liturgy in this volume it can come outside the eucharistic prayer. In North India and Bangladesh, when the various denominations came together

---

45 Curiously, one of the few places where heavy rubrics about manual acts remain in the rites here is in the **Amer4** prayers, repeating the pattern of **Amer2-2** from the 1979 BCP. These are in a footnote on page 95, and are faithfully copied in the texts drafted with an eye to the USA in **Braz3** and **HK3**.

46 It was expounded this way by the Church of England Doctrinal Commission in 1970, and was thus incorporated in **Eng3** when it went in draft form to the General Synod. But it was stamped upon, not least with the assistance of Michael Ramsey.

in 1970, one non-Anglican tradition was reading the narrative in advance of beginning the eucharistic action, as a warrant text. This has been preserved as an option, and in **CNI1** the narrative is then omitted from the EP itself, so that to use it this way gives the final blow to any suggestion that the narrative is consecratory – the taking of the bread and wine and giving thanks are yet to come; and it is itself simply and visibly a warrant text.

However, another trend which is visible may lead to a minor side-path which itself leads to something more serious. In **Scot2** in 1982 the narrative reported Jesus as having said, 'This is my body: it is broken for you'. There was not much precedent for this, though it was in the *textus receptus* for 1 Cor. 11.24 (and is thus in the King James Version at that verse); and Cranmer, although he must have been aware of it, either because he doubted its authenticity or because he was not particularly interested in the actual breaking of the bread (it is wholly lacking in 1552), never wished this text upon us. Little would hang on it in itself, but we should note where the path leads.

Various rites now have this reading in the narrative: each of the **Scot2A** EPs, **Wal4** EP5 (borrowed from **Scot2**), **Amer4** EP3, **Ken**, **SAfr3** EP4, **NZ2A**. The issue is not so much whether this reading is compatible with 'not a bone of him shall be broken' (John 19.36), as to whether it brings into the breaking of the bread the notion that it is somehow a dramatization of the cross. This is reinforced by an oddity of history, also under suspicion of having its roots in the King James Version. A number of texts here (**Amer4** Form 4, **Bangl** EP2 and most of the **NZ6** ones) expound the use of the bread and wine as being to 'show forth' the death or the sacrifice of Christ. There must be a suspicion that such language derives from the King James Version of 1 Cor. 11.26: 'As often as ye eat this bread and drink this wine, ye do shew the Lord's death till he come'. But Paul was not writing about dramatization – his verb is *kataggellete*, 'you proclaim'.[47] The Lord's death is articulated at the Lord's Supper, but it is not dramatized; and the breaking of the bread is far better expounded in terms of 1 Cor. 10.17 (indeed it is not in view in 1 Cor. 11.26). And the sense that the side-path might lead somewhere serious is underlined by attempts to provide a parallel to it in the pouring of wine. The scriptural narratives have no mention of Jesus pouring wine, but the dramatizing instinct starts to discover it – as with 'broken bread and wine outpoured' in **EngCW1A** EP E, or in different ways in **SAfr5** Second EP of Creation and in **CSI1**, or with this straight invention, 'Jesus then took the wine, gave thanks and poured it out to speak to us of the pouring out of his blood' (**SAfr5** First prayer of season of creation). To stick with the many sharing one bread gives a sense of proportion to the breaking of bread, whereas the quest for dramatization takes us on the wrong track for a mistaken reason.

(ii) Anamnesis

The anamnesis sets out the Church's understanding of how it fulfils Jesus' command: 'Do this in remembrance of me'. Cranmer wrote 1549 against a background of the Roman text 'Wherefore, O Lord, we . . . being mindful [of Jesus' death, resurrection and ascension] . . . do offer unto thy excellent majesty . . . a pure victim, a holy victim, an undefiled victim, the holy bread of eternal life, and the cup of eternal salvation.'

---

47 'Shewing' and 'shewing forth' in Tudor English could readily mean 'articulating' (as in 'Our mouth shall shew forth thy praise') in a way which is not the obvious meaning of 'show forth' today.

So 1549 (in complicated language) had 'we . . . do celebrate and make here . . . the memorial which thy Son hath willed us to make.' Cranmer includes not a hint of offering, but also is reticent about how to obey Jesus' command. He will simply say 'Whatever Jesus willed is what we are doing here'. But in 1552 he was wholly clear that the command is to eat and drink, and so much so that he removed the spoken anamnesis and put the physical distribution of communion in its place – doing in fact what he reckoned Jesus had told him to do.[48]

With the return to traditionally shaped EPs, the form of an anamnesis became quite critical in the 1960s and 1970s. What verb could best encapsulate the Church's response to Jesus' command? In England, **Eng2**, in 1967, after a dispute, limped on with that 1549 stopgap, 'We make the memorial'. The answer came with an element of breakthrough, when **Eng3**, in its initial 1971 report form, had 'With this bread and this cup we celebrate his perfect sacrifice made once for all upon the cross'. The word 'celebrate' had been rare in 1662, and when used it had simply meant to perform or execute a BCP service. This use had in turn allowed the word 'celebrant' to be imported from Roman circles (and in time the highly questionable 'concelebrant'!). But now the congregation would 'celebrate', and they would celebrate the mighty acts of God; and this use of 'celebrate', with the works of redemption as its object, proved irenic and acceptable.[49]

In some rites the offering of the elements to God has run on. One oddity has been in the Scottish Episcopal Church rites, where the offering came into the eucharist in the 18th century.[50] **Scot2** had in its anamnesis (and the new prayers here, **Scot2A**, follow it):

> 'Made one with him, we offer you these gifts
> and with them ourselves,
> a single, holy, living, sacrifice.'

And this, at its lowest, provides a complex exegetical problem; indeed it may well read that, as we have been united with Christ in this 'single, holy, living, sacrifice' (which is a long way from Rom. 12.1–2), and as we are offering that sacrifice with or by means of the gifts, we are, at least implicitly, offering Christ in his sacrifice to the Father. But without this complication, yet with the example of the Roman canon already affecting rites in the early 20th century, the concept of offering the gifts to God got a renewed boost in the post-Dix era, when it was thought that we had the *Apostolic Tradition* of Hippolytus as a rule of thumb to imitate (note, for example, the very Hippolytan **Jap1**, **EP2**). More recently, both the credentials of the document and the degree of authority to be attributed to 'the early church' have come into question.[51] But unless

---

48 For further on this see Colin Buchanan, *What did Cranmer Think he was Doing?* (Grove Liturgical Study 7, 2nd ed, Grove Books, Bramcote, 1982).

49 It had precedent elsewhere, and its scholarly roots were well written up by Paul Bradshaw in 'Celebration' in Ronald Jasper (ed.), *The Eucharist Today: Studies on Series 3* (SPCK, 1974).

50 See the anamnesis in the 1764 text in the right-hand column in the chart on page 28.

51 The reassessment of the document is in Paul F. Bradshaw, Maxwell E. Johnson and L. Edward Phillips, *The Apostolic Tradition: A Commentary* (Fortress, Minneapolis, 2002). The issue of the authority of 'the early church' was posed especially by Lambeth 1958 saying 'It was Cranmer's aim . . . to recover as much as possible of the character of the worship of what he called the "Primitive Church" . . . but [he lacked the evidence we have today as to what the early Church did]' (2.80). This analysis begs a whole series of questions.

challenged, the texts that say we obey Christ's command by offering the elements to God have tended to run on; and perhaps, with the diminution of any conviction that the elements have been transubstantiated during the narrative, that offering may not be as controversial as it once was.[52] But like the offering of the elements to God at the preparation of the table, it would still need, and has not achieved, a cogent biblical rationale. The elements are God's gifts to us, not ours to him.

More immediately, a glance through the pages of this volume will show that 'celebrate' has come to stay. Over half the rites have adopted it in at least one prayer. It is linked on occasion to 1 Cor. 5.7–8 (where Paul has the evocative *heortazo*). Over the whole range we celebrate Jesus' birth and life among us as well as his death, resurrection and ascension, his gift of the Spirit, and more specific benefits to believers also. Here is a verb of true rejoicing and a genuine bonding with the event to be commemorated.

But the linear descendant of the pioneering **Eng3**, that is, EP A in **EngCW1A**, has had the humiliation of being robbed of 27 years of its glory and being rewarded with, yes, the regressive 'we . . . make the memorial'.

(iii) Epiclesis

'Epiclesis' always needs defining. The most useful bounding of its meaning is to confine its use to a petition that (by some means) the bread and wine here, over which we are giving thanks, should be, or become, or be 'for us', the body and blood of Christ, or that we by receiving them should be partakers of the body and blood of Christ. Such use is not dependent upon mention of the Holy Spirit (though that is frequent), nor is it bound up with any particular theory about what consecration effects (though that may be implied by the different forms of the epiclesis). Two classic, somewhat polarized, historic examples from Anglicanism will illustrate some of the possible range of such prayers:

1552/1662	Scottish 1764
	⟦narrative of institution⟧ . . . in remembrance of me. Wherefore, O Lord and heavenly Father, according to the institution of thy dearly beloved Son our Saviour Jesus Christ, we thy humble servants do celebrate and make here before thy divine majesty, with these thy holy gifts, which we now offer unto thee, the memorial thy Son hath commanded us to make; rendering unto thee most hearty thanks for the innumerable benefits procured unto us by the same.
Hear us, O merciful Father, we beseech thee; and grant that we, receiving these thy creatures of bread and wine, according to thy Son our Saviour Jesus Christ's holy institution, in remembrance of his death and passion, may be partakers of his most blessed body and blood; Who in the same night that he was betrayed . . . ⟦continues with narrative of institution⟧	And we most humbly beseech thee, O merciful Father, to hear us, and of thy almighty goodness vouchsafe to bless and sanctify, with thy word and Holy Spirit, these thy gifts and creatures of bread and wine, that they may become the body and blood of thy most dearly beloved Son.

---

52 A rare phenomenon is the third EP in **SAfr3**, where two different options for that central transitive verb are provided.

1552 is, of course, the text of Cranmer's developed receptionism. 1764 is the connoisseur text of the semi-underground Jacobite Scottish Episcopalians, who were using their enforced obscurity to refine their text, still Cranmerian in style and in some kind of descent from 1549 and 1637, yet in accordance with their understanding of the ancient use of Jerusalem.[53]

The contrasts are far-reaching:

1. They are in different positions in the prayer – 1552 in the western position (i.e. that of the Roman Catholic 'Hanc igitur'); 1764 in the eastern position.
2. 1552 has no mention of the Holy Spirit; 1764 views the Holy Spirit (with the 'word', an echo of 1549) as operating to bring about consecration.
3. 1552 is a petition for the benefits of communion to come from the action of giving and receiving the elements; 1764, in the starkest way imaginable, is a petition that the elements should be converted into the body and blood of Christ, without any reference to possible recipients.[54]

I have given a warning on page 25 above that identifying what, liturgically, effects consecration does not of itself identify what consecration effects.

These contrasts take us some way in analysis, and in some ways set outer limits within which the epiclesis is usually to be found.[55] However, some side-questions emerge from each of the contrasts.

With reference to the position of the epiclesis, once a full eucharistic prayer is being drafted, the western position still leaves open a question about a petition after the anamnesis for fruitful reception – often therefore called a 'second epiclesis' – and this (as in, for example, **EngCW1A** EP B) may well include an invocation of the Spirit onto the people.

With reference to the mention of the Spirit, rites have been generally moving in the direction of explicitly invoking the Spirit.[56] However, the ways of invoking the Spirit display a great range. Consider the following:

Western

(a) 'Send your Holy Spirit that broken bread and wine outpoured may be for us the body and blood of your Son' (**EngCW1A**, EP E)
(b) 'Pour out your refreshing Spirit on us
    as we remember him in the way he commanded,
    through these gifts of your creation' (**Ken**)
(c) 'May the Holy Spirit sanctify this bread and wine we offer with thanksgiving that it may be for us the body and blood of Christ' (**Kor3**)

---

53 While much was owed to English nonjurors, the crucial Scottish contribution came from Thomas Rattray's *The Ancient Liturgy of the Church of Jerusalem* (1744).

54 Dowden says it is 'without precedent or parallel' (*The Scottish Communion Office 1764*, 2nd edn, Oxford University Press, 1922, p. 165). I quote it for its starkness in illustration, not for any supposed appropriateness for use.

55 David Kennedy's book, *Eucharistic Sacramentality in an Ecumenical Context: The Anglican Epiclesis* (Ashgate, Aldershot, 2008), takes all but the most recent texts here into its purview, and provides a study at considerable depth.

56 'Invoking the Spirit' means in almost all cases asking the Father that the Spirit should in some way be operative. However, in **Ire3** EP 3 the Spirit is addressed directly in the second person.

Eastern

(a) 'Send your Holy Spirit upon us and upon these gifts of bread and wine that they may be to us the Body and Blood of your Christ' (**Amer4**, EP3)
(b) 'to send your Holy Spirit upon these gifts
and sanctify them that they may be
the sacrament of the body of Christ,
and his blood of the new covenant' (**Braz2**)
(c) 'Breathe your Holy Spirit,
the wisdom of the universe,
upon these gifts that we bring to you:
this bread, this cup' (**Can5** EP S1)

The third contrast was really a contrast in end-points – does the petition look for an effect on the elements (even if still 'out there') or upon the recipients in and through receiving the elements? The middle way here has been to use the dative – that they may be 'for us' the body and blood of Christ, and that may be understood as looking to either of the two end-points. But alongside that middle way there has also been a trend not to be specific at all about the elements being or becoming the body and blood of Christ. The last example above, from **Can5**, illustrates this tendency.

Are there, then, general trends? In relation to the position of the epiclesis in the EP, the pendulum has swung somewhat in the eastern direction (splendidly dignified as the 'Trinitarian structure'). Anglicans have generally been constrained by a combination of the western character of 1662, the great weight placed upon it by western anglo-catholics (including the great emphasis on ceremonial surrounding the narrative), and by the reluctance of Gregory Dix to make this part of his package (he questioned Hippolytus' text at this point). But the continued Scottish/American tradition from the 18th century kept it alive as authentic in Anglicanism, and fashions have thereafter swayed to and fro. Probably **CSI** had a growing influence from 1950 onwards, and the advocacy of Tom Talley, and the general underwriting given by IALC-5, have helped to move the Communion in that direction. Curiously, some provinces now have a mixture of western and eastern uses, not least the United States (the 'star-trek' EP in **Amer3-3** (see **LAL**), now found in **Braz2**, is surprisingly western), but also Southern Africa (traditionally wholly western but now with eastern instances in **SAfr5**); and England went eastern in most of its new EPs in **EngCW1A**, almost without discussion. Whether western anglo-catholics can be at ease using an eastern text remains a question.

If this is not such a serious matter of division as in the past, can the same be said for the other contrasts? It has become wholly fashionable at least to mention the Holy Spirit, but still that is not invariably followed. But sending or pouring the Spirit upon the elements continues to be somewhat controversial; while invoking the Spirit to change the elements, almost without qualification, seems to be such a fading usage as hardly to require questioning. For the record we note one classic run-on of the genre in **Mel2** Alternative Great Thanksgiving 1 (i.e. for children), in the western position:

'We ask you to send your Holy Spirit
to make this bread and this wine
become the body and blood of Christ.'

Here there is no hint of 'for us'. But such a case is rare, and the general trend is for rites that ask for the Spirit to come upon the action, and thus to enable us to eat the body of Christ and drink his blood. That may leave many questions unanswered, but it locates the end-point of the petition in the distribution, in the eating and drinking.

Just as the persuasion that consecration is by thanksgiving overall has lightened concerns about the narrative, so it may be that, although there is usually a determination to have an epicletic component in each EP, consecration is not closely identified with it, and the provinces are the freer in the forms they provide for it. Indeed, not only are there EPs where the epiclesis does not quite name the body and blood of Christ; there are signs of EPs where it is hard to find any hint of an epiclesis at all – see, for example, **Jap1** EP 2, or **NZ6** alternative Great Thanksgiving C.

The fraction, distribution and post-communion

There is little changed from previous decades in the handling of these features of the new rites. The use of a separated fraction is almost universal (**Cong** still has it in the narrative in all three EPs), and its significance (while a little under pressure to be a supposed dramatization of the passion[57]) is generally well anchored in 1 Cor. 10.17. There has been some return to using Humble Access as a last approach to the table, and that is where it started in 1548. The distribution looks clean and is generally unprescriptive about posture for communicants, let alone about architectural features like rails. And the post-communion varies between a single prayer and dismissal, and built-up features of prayers which trace the benefits of communion (and give insights into particular understandings of the sacrament, and also of mission). Each of these stages may well have related music, anthems, songs or hymns in the foreground or in the background of the action – and the actual character of particular celebrations may be hard to gather without more information about the three-dimensional features of the actual use of the rites.

And the future?

The rites gathered in this volume appear to have a strong family structural resemblance both in overall shape and in the textual range of their EPs. On the other hand, there is clearly visible a steep decline from single fixed mandatory texts, and the textual range, as between rites as well as between options in any one rite, is ever-widening. Indeed, the great range of choice already introduced shows signs of leading on to a freedom first of all to vary liturgical material at will, and then to write (or extemporize) even EPs at will. If this proves to be the case, then the once-projected title for this volume – *Terminal Anglican Liturgies* – may have had a tongue-in-cheek prophetic credibility to it.

---

57 See page 26.

B. Britain and Ireland (with Spain and Portugal)

3. The Church of England

In the Church of England Rite A and Rite B were authorized as 'alternative services', and contained within the Alternative Service Book (ASB), with an initial currency from 1980 to 31 December 1990. They were contained in **LAL**, coded as **EngA** and **EngB**, and **EngA** quite quickly proved out of date in relation to inclusive language. Yet after the 1985 elections to General Synod, the report *The Worship of the Church* recommended a renewal of that licence for a further ten years, and Synod duly voted that extension in 1986. This led to a remit to the new Liturgical Commission, appointed in early 1986, to work towards replacing the ASB services by 2000.[58] They had to take into account not only inclusive language, but also the judgement of the report of the Archbishops' Commission on 'Urban Priority Areas', *Faith in the City* (Church House Publishing, 1985), that the ASB was too weighty in both its language and its format to be a sensible working tool in socially and educationally deprived areas. The previous Commission had gone over in 1982 to working solely with inclusive language in drafting the rites of *Lent – Holy Week – Easter* (published in its 'commended by the House of Bishops' form in 1986), and the expectation that the language would be changed in any revision of **EngA** was reinforced by the new Commission's early report, *Making Women Visible* (CHP, 1987). The first results were in a report, *Patterns for Worship* (CHP, 1989), which provided for a 'Rite C', in which the structure was all-important, and a great variety of liturgical materials was provided to supply each category in the structure. There were four eucharistic prayers, all fairly innovative. None of them had a consecratory epiclesis in a western (pre-narrative) position, and prayer A arguably lacked one in the eastern position also. Prayer B drew upon an imaginative (but never authorized) draft of the Roman Catholic International Commission for English in the Liturgy (ICEL), a prayer which used some feminine imagery about God. Prayers B and C prayed that the Spirit would 'show' the elements to be the body and blood of Christ, which proved controversial. Prayer D was a very much shortened prayer of a more **EngA** type. Prayers A and (optionally) C concluded with the sanctus. *Patterns* was debated in General Synod in early 1990 and its eucharistic provision ran into trouble.[59]

---

58 An account of the process through to 2000, from the standpoint of the secretary of the Commission, is told in David Hebblethwaite, *Liturgical Revision in the Church of England 1984–2004: The Working of the Liturgical Commission* (Alcuin/GROW Joint Liturgical Study 57, Grove Books, Cambridge, 2004). A less official report is in Colin Buchanan, *Taking the Long View: Three and a Half Decades of General Synod* (Church House Publishing, 2006), pp. 77–81.

59 See David Kennedy, *Eucharistic Sacramentality*, pp. 153–157, for fuller analysis.

The rest of *Patterns* went ahead to be 'commended' by the House of Bishops, but the eucharistic prayers were to become a separate special case.

The Commission worked over the prayers and brought four to the House of Bishops in January 1992. They were told to go away and do better. They returned in January 1994 with four revised prayers. The House of Bishops asked the Synod in July whether the members would like the four to be introduced. The Synod said 'Let it be five', and the Bishops then started the authorization processes in November with but two (and without declaring any reason why two were chosen and the others left). Trevor Lloyd from the Commission introduced the two, and explained the eastern place for a consecratory epiclesis – a point of principle not previously expounded in any official document, yet an enormous change for the Church of England. The prayers went to a Revision Committee; the Revision Committee increased the number to six; they came to a Revision Stage in Synod in July 1995; no motion to refer the texts back was even proposed; and the six prayers thus headed uncontroversially for final approval. However, the timetable had been skewed by the House of Bishops' delays; a new Synod was elected that Autumn without having followed the earlier stages; and in February 1996 the six prayers failed to get the necessary two-thirds majority in one of the Houses of Synod, the House of Laity.[60]

The Commission, with a firm eye on the year 2000, had to start again quickly. Because alternative eucharistic prayers were being considered on their own, the Commission had already started a process to see through General Synod a eucharistic rite without eucharistic prayers, and it was now to devise a new set of eucharistic prayers to follow their own separate synodical route, with a view to being joined with the framework of the rite at final approval. The Synod had meanwhile accepted as a principle that traditional language rites should accompany contemporary ones in the proposed Books.

The new eucharistic prayers produced by the Commission began by turning the four eucharistic prayers of **EngA** into three, labelled A to C – the previous second prayer being elided, but in such a way as to leave some traces inserted into the first prayer. Thus the genuinely new were the second three, D–F: D was fairly child-friendly, built round an echo of the chorus of a Christian hymn 'Blessed assurance' – viz. 'This is my story, this is my song . . . '; E had a groundplan like the first three, and with them had scope for extended seasonal prefaces; and F drew at some length upon eastern sources. In the progress through Synod two more prayers were added, G being a reversion to the prayer drawn from the ICEL text of the 1980s, and H, after some struggle, being a more actively responsive prayer.[61] All eight came together with the rest of the liturgical rite and were authorized on 1 March 2000, to come into use on Advent Sunday that year.

---

60 The six prayers, along with an historical explanation and with the coaching material on providing child-friendly eucharists which had been intended to be authorized with the prayers, and therefore fell with them, are published in Colin Buchanan and Trevor Lloyd, *Six Eucharistic Prayers as Proposed in 1996* (Grove Worship Series 136, Grove Books, Cambridge, 1996).

61 I have written up the process of bringing prayer H into the rite in *Prayer H: An Unauthorized Account*, originally published in the *Ushaw Library Bulletin and Liturgical Review* no. 13 (September 2000), but also readily available as an offprint.

Alongside this rite, **EngCW1A**, in line with the policy supported by Synod, there were authorized a traditionalized version of it (though with only two eucharistic prayers), **EngCW1B**, a very slightly adapted version of 1662 (intended to be 'as currently used'), **EngCW2B**, and a modernized, that is, 'contemporary', version of 1662, **EngCW2A**. Some contemporary propers (as, for example, collects) were to be used with **EngCW1A** and **EngCW2A**, whereas other supplementary materials (such as prayers at the preparation of the table) obviously belong with **EngCW1A** and **EngCW1B**. All were bound in together in the main *Common Worship* hardback Book.

In 2010 the House of Bishops released for preliminary trial use two eucharistic prayers specifically for use where a good number of children were present. Comment was collected and the Liturgical Commission returned slightly adapted prayers to the House of Bishops. They were due to begin their synodical journey (which will almost certainly involve changes of text) in July 2011.

An appendix to this chapter provides part of the 1986 recommendations about an agape eucharist.

'ORDER ONE' IN THE CHURCH OF ENGLAND'S *COMMON WORSHIP: SERVICES AND PRAYERS FOR THE CHURCH OF ENGLAND* BOOK, 2000 (EngCW1A)

⟦The Structure page with which the rite begins is viewed as foundational. The lining is original. The numbering is editorial.⟧

The Order for the Celebration of Holy Communion also called The Eucharist and the Lord's Supper

⟦The title, and the elements listed here are applicable to all four rites: General Notes and A Form of Preparation, which includes Veni, Creator Spiritus, A short Exhortation, The Commandments, Summary of the Law, The Comfortable Words, The Beatitudes, Silence for Reflection, Confession, and Absolution⟧

Order One ⟦EngCW1A⟧

Structure

The people and the priest
- *greet each other in the Lord's name*
- *confess their sins and are assured of God's forgiveness*
- *keep silence and pray a Collect*
- *proclaim and respond to the word of God*
- *pray for the Church and the world*
- *exchange the Peace*
- *prepare the table*
- *pray the Eucharistic Prayer*
- *break the bread*
- *receive communion*
- *depart with God's blessing*

The Gathering
1. ⟦*Hymn, *Invocation of the name of the Trinity⟧

THE GREETING
2. ⟦Greeting⟧

PRAYER OF PREPARATION
3. *Almighty God, to whom . . . ⟦CF 1⟧ . . . Christ our Lord. Amen.

PRAYERS OF PENITENCE
4. ⟦*Commandments, *Beatitudes, *Comfortable Words, *Summary of the Law⟧
   ⟦Invitation to Confession⟧
   ⟦One of two congregational confessions or Kyries (ELLC 2)⟧

5. Almighty God, who forgives . . . ⟦CF 2⟧ . . . Christ our Lord. **Amen.**

GLORIA IN EXCELSIS
6. *Glory to God . . . ⟦ELLC 3⟧ . . . God the Father. Amen.
   God's people] his people

THE COLLECT
7. ⟦Collect⟧

The Liturgy of the Word

READINGS
8. ⟦One or *two readings, with *proclamation and response following; and with psalm or canticle after the first; *hymns and songs between readings⟧

GOSPEL READING
9. ⟦Gospel; *acclamation before, announcement and response before, proclamation and response after⟧

10. SERMON ⟦The heading alone provides for the Sermon⟧

THE CREED
11. *On Sundays and Principal Holy Days an authorized translation of the Nicene Creed is used, or on occasion the Apostles' Creed ⟦ELLC 4⟧ or an authorized Affirmation of Faith may be used (see pages . . .).*
    We believe in one God . . . ⟦ELLC 5⟧ . . . world to come. Amen.
    incarnate of] incarnate from
    became truly human] was made man
    [and the Son]] OMIT BRACKETS

PRAYERS OF INTERCESSION
12. ⟦Forms are in an appendix but others may be used. Two sets of versicles and responses and an ending are here.⟧

The Liturgy of the Sacrament

THE PEACE
13. *The president may introduce the Peace with a suitable sentence, and then says*
    The peace of the Lord be always with you
    and also with you.

    These words may be added
    Let us offer one another a sign of peace.
    All may exchange a sign of peace.

PREPARATION OF THE TABLE
TAKING OF THE BREAD AND WINE

14. *A hymn may be sung.*

15. *The gifts of the people may be gathered and presented.*

16. *The table is prepared and bread and wine are placed upon it.*

17. *One or more of the prayers at the preparation of the table may be said* [see §46 below].

18. *The president takes the bread and wine.*

THE EUCHARISTIC PRAYER

19. *An authorized Eucharistic Prayer is used (pages . . .)*
    [The eucharistic prayers, labelled A–H, are appended to the rite as 'Eucharistic Prayers for use in Order One'. In the rite there is here a page of cue words introducing congregational responses and acclamations. They purport erroneously to enable congregations to respond aright in any of the eight prayers, but the page is omitted here.]

THE LORD'S PRAYER

20. As our Saviour taught us, so we pray
    Our Father in heaven . . . [ELLC 1] **. . . now and for ever. Amen.**
       Save us from the time of trial and] Lead us not into temptation but
    (or)
    Let us pray with confidence as our Saviour has taught us.
    Our Father, who art . . . [modified traditional text] **. . . ever and ever. Amen.**

BREAKING OF THE BREAD

21. *The president breaks the consecrated bread*

22. We break this bread . . . [CF 8(a)] **. . . in one bread.**
    (or)
    Every time we eat . . . [CF 8(b)] **. . . until he comes.**

23. *The Agnus Dei may be used as the bread is broken.*
    Lamb of God . . . [ELLC 8(b)] **. . . grant us peace.**
    (or)
    Jesus, Lamb of God . . . [ELLC 8(a)] **. . . grant us peace.**

GIVING OF COMMUNION

24. *The president says one of these invitations to communion*
    Draw near with faith . . . [CF 9(a)] **. . . with thanksgiving.**
    (or)
    Jesus is the Lamb . . . [CF 9(b)] **. . . shall be healed.**
    (or)
    God's holy gifts . . . [CF 9(c)] **. . . God the Father.**
    or, *from Easter Day to Pentecost*
    Christ our passover is sacrificed for us.
    Therefore let us keep the feast. Alleluia.

25. *One of these prayers may be said before the distribution*
    We do not presume . . . [CF 3(a)] **. . . he in us. Amen.**
    (or)
    Most merciful Lord . . . [CF 3(b)] **. . . in your kingdom. Amen.**

26. *The president and people receive communion. Authorized words of distribution are used and the communicant replies.* **Amen.**

27. *During the distribution hymns and anthems may be sung.*

28. *If either or both of the consecrated elements are likely to prove insufficient, the president returns to the holy table and adds more, saying the words on page . . .* [i.e. §47 below]

29. *Any consecrated bread and wine which is not required for purposes of communion is consumed at the end of the distribution or after the service.*

PRAYER AFTER COMMUNION

30. *Silence is kept.*

31. *The Post Communion or another suitable prayer is said.*

32. *All may say one of these prayers*
Almighty God . . . [CF 11(a)] **. . . praise and glory. Amen.**
(or)
Father of all . . . [CF 11(b)] **. . . Christ our Lord. Amen.**

The Dismissal

33. *A hymn may be sung.*

34. *The president may use the seasonal blessing or another suitable blessing (or)*
The peace of God . . . [CF 12(a)] . . . with you always. **Amen.**

35. **Go in peace . . .** [CF 12(b)] **. . . name of Christ. Amen.**
(or)
Go in the peace of Christ.
Thanks be to God.
[From Easter to Pentecost 'Alleluia alleluia' may be added to both versicle and response]

36. *The ministers and people depart.*

37. [Appendix] **Eucharistic Prayers for Use in Order One**

   [Guidance re finding and using Proper Prefaces]

   [Each eucharistic prayer begins with this dialogue

   The Lord is here . . . [ELLC 6 and CF 5] . . . **give thanks and praise.**

   and that is not reproduced in the edited texts which follow.

   In Prayers A and B an opening rubric before the dialogue says
   If an extended Preface (pages . . .) is used, it replaces all words between the opening dialogue and the Sanctus.

   Each prayer is followed by a rubric stating that the Lord's Prayer (§20) comes next.]

38. *Prayer A*

It is indeed right,
it is our duty and our joy,
at all times and in all places
to give you thanks and praise,
holy Father, heavenly King,
almighty and eternal God,
through Jesus Christ your Son our Lord.
The following may be omitted if a short Proper Preface is used.

For he is your living Word.
through him you have created all things
    from the beginning,
and formed us in your own image.
[To you be glory and praise for ever.]

Through him you have freed us from the
    slavery of sin,
giving him to be born of a woman and to
    die upon the cross;
you raised him from the dead
and exalted him to your right hand on
    high.
[To you be glory and praise for ever.]

Through him you have sent upon us
your holy and life-giving Spirit,
and made us a people for your own
    possession.
[To you be glory and praise for ever.]

Short Proper Preface, when appropriate.

Therefore with angels and archangels,
and with all the company of heaven,
we proclaim your great and glorious name,
for ever praising you and *saying*:
Holy, holy . . . [[ELLC 7]] . . . **in the highest.**
[Blessed is . . . [[ELLC 8]] . . . **in the highest.]**

Accept our praises, heavenly Father,
through your Son, our Saviour Jesus Christ,
and as we follow his example and obey
    his command,
grant that by the power of your Holy Spirit
these gifts of bread and wine
may be to us his body and his blood;

who, in the same night that he was
    betrayed,
took bread and gave you thanks;
he broke it and gave it to his disciples,
    saying:

Take, eat; this is my body which is given
    for you;
do this in remembrance of me.
[To you be glory and praise for ever.]

In the same way, after supper
he took the cup and gave you thanks;
he gave it to them, saying:
Drink this, all of you;
this is my blood of the new covenant,
which is shed for you and for many for the
    forgiveness of sins.
Do this, as often you drink it,
in remembrance of me.
[To you be glory and praise for ever.]

Therefore, heavenly Father,
we remember his offering of himself
made once for all upon the cross;
we proclaim his mighty resurrection and
    glorious ascension;
we look for the coming of your
    kingdom,
and with this bread and this cup
we make the memorial of Christ your
    Son our Lord.
One of these four acclamations is used
[Great is the . . . [[CF 6(a)]] . . . **come again.**
[Praise to you . . . [[CF 6(b)]] . . . **in glory.**
[Christ is the bread . . . [[CF 6(c)]] . . . **in**
    glory.
[Jesus Christ . . . [[CF 6(d)]] . . . **of the world.**

Accept through him, our great high
    priest,
this our sacrifice of thanks and praise,
and as we eat and drink these holy gifts
in the presence of your divine majesty,
renew us by your Spirit,
inspire us with your love
and unite us in the body of your Son,
Jesus Christ our Lord.
[To you be glory and praise for ever.]

Through him, and with him, and in him,
in the unity of the Holy Spirit,
with all who stand before you in earth
    and heaven,
we worship you, Father almighty,
in songs of everlasting praise:
Blessing and honour . . . [[CF 7]] . . . **ever**
    and ever. Amen.

39. *Prayer B*

Father, we give you thanks and praise
through your beloved Son, Jesus Christ,
    your living Word,
through whom you have created all
    things,
who was sent by you in your great
    goodness to be our Saviour.

By the power of the Holy Spirit he took
    flesh;
as your Son, born of the blessed Virgin,
he lived on earth and went about among
    us;
he opened wide his arms for us on the
    cross;
he put an end to death by dying for us;
and revealed the resurrection by rising to
    new life;
so he fulfilled your will and won for you
    a holy people.

Short Proper Preface, when appropriate
Therefore with angels and archangels,
and with all the company of heaven,
we proclaim your great and glorious name,
for ever praising you and *saying*:
Holy, holy . . . ⟦ELLC 7⟧ . . . in the highest.
[Blessed is . . . ⟦ELLC 8⟧ . . . in the highest.]
Lord, you are holy indeed, the source of
    all holiness;
grant that by the power of your Holy
    Spirit,
and according to your holy will,
these gifts of bread and wine
may be to us the body and blood of our
    Lord Jesus Christ;

who, in the same night that he was
    betrayed,
took bread and gave you thanks;
he broke it and gave it to his disciples,
    saying:
Take, eat; this is my body which is given
    for you;

do this in remembrance of me.

In the same way, after supper
he took the cup and gave you thanks;
he gave it to them, saying:
Drink this, all of you;
this is my blood of the new covenant,
which is shed for you and for many for
    the forgiveness of sins.
Do this, as often you drink it,
in remembrance of me.

One of these four acclamations is used
⟦CF 6(a), 6(b), 6(c) and 6(d) as in Prayer A⟧

And so, Father, calling to mind his death
    on the cross,
his perfect sacrifice made once for the
    sins of the whole word;
rejoicing in his mighty resurrection and
    glorious ascension,
and looking for his coming in glory,
we celebrate this memorial of our
    redemption.
As we offer you this our sacrifice of praise
    and thanksgiving,
we bring before you this bread and this
    cup
and we thank you for counting us worthy
to stand in your presence and serve you.

Send the Holy Spirit on your people
and gather into one in your kingdom
all who share this one bread and one cup,
so that we, in the company of [*N and*] all
    the saints,
may praise and glorify you for ever,
through Jesus Christ our Lord;

by whom, and with whom, and in whom,
in the unity of the Holy Spirit,
all honour and glory be yours, almighty
    Father,
for ever and ever.
Amen.

40. *Prayer C*

It is indeed right . . . [as in Prayer A above]
    . . . Jesus Christ our Lord.

Short Proper Preface, when appropriate
[or, when there is no Proper Preface
For he is our great high priest,
who has loosed us from our sins
and has made us to be a royal priesthood
    to you,
our God and Father.]

Therefore with angels . . . [as in Prayer A
    above] . . . and *saying*:
Holy, holy . . . [ELLC 7] . . . in the highest.
[Blessed is . . . [ELLC 8] . . . in the highest.]

All glory be to you, our heavenly Father,
who, in your tender mercy,
gave your only Son our Saviour Jesus
    Christ
to suffer death upon the cross for our
    redemption;
who made there by his one oblation of
    himself once offered
a full, perfect and sufficient sacrifice,
    oblation and satisfaction for the sins of
    the whole world;
he instituted, and in his holy gospel
    commanded us to continue,
a perpetual memory of his precious death
    until he comes again.

Hear us, merciful Father, we humbly pray,
and grant that, by the power of your Holy
    Spirit,
we, receiving these gifts of your creation,
    this bread and this wine,
according to your Son our Saviour Jesus
    Christ's holy institution,
in remembrance of his death and passion,
may be partakers of his most blessed
    body and blood;

who, in the same night that he was
    betrayed,
took bread and gave you thanks;
he broke and gave it to his disciples,
    saying:

Take, eat; this is my body which is given
    for you;
do this in remembrance of me.

In the same way, after supper
he took the cup and gave you thanks;
he gave it to them, saying:
Drink this, all of you:
this is my blood of the new covenant,
which is shed for you and for many for
    the forgiveness of sins.
Do this, as often as you drink it,
in remembrance of me.

One of these four acclamations is used
[CF 6(a), 6(b), 6(c) and 6(d) as in Prayer A]

Therefore, Lord and heavenly Father,
in remembrance of the precious death and
    passion,
the mighty resurrection and glorious
    ascension
of your dear Son Jesus Christ,
we offer you through him this our
    sacrifice of praise and thanksgiving.

Grant that by his merits and death,
and through faith in his blood,
we and all your Church may receive
    forgiveness of our sins
and all other benefits of his passion.
Although we are unworthy, through our
    manifold sins,
to offer you any sacrifice,
yet we pray that you will accept this
the duty and service that we owe.
Do not weigh our merits, but pardon our
    offences,
and fill us all who share in this holy
    communion
with your grace and heavenly blessing:

through Jesus Christ our Lord,
by whom, and with whom, and in whom,
in the unity of the Holy Spirit,
all honour and glory be yours, almighty
    Father,
for ever and ever.
Amen.

41. *Prayer D*

Almighty God, good Father to us all,
your face is turned towards your world.
In love you gave us Jesus your Son
to rescue us from sin and death.
Your Word comes out to call us home
   to the city where angels sing your praise.
We join with them in heaven's song:
Holy, holy . . . ⟦ELLC 7⟧ . . . in the highest.
[Blessed is . . . ⟦ELLC 8⟧ . . . in the highest.]

Father of all, we give you thanks
   for every gift that comes from heaven.

To the darkness Jesus came as your
   light.
With signs of faith and words of hope
he touched untouchables with love and
   washed the guilty clean.

This is his story.
This is our song:
Hosanna in the highest.

The crowds came out to see your Son,
   yet at the end they turned on him.
On the night he was betrayed
he came to table with his friends
   to celebrate the freedom of your people.

This is his story.
This is our . . . ⟦as above⟧ . . . in the highest.

Jesus blessed you, Father, for the food;

he took bread, gave thanks, broke it and
   said:
This is my body, given for you all.
Jesus then gave thanks for the wine;
he took the cup, gave it and said:
This is my blood, shed for you all
   for the forgiveness of sins.
Do this in remembrance of me.

This is our story.
This is our . . . ⟦as above⟧ . . . in the highest.

Therefore, Father, with this bread and
   this cup
we celebrate the cross
on which he died to set us free.
Defying death he rose again
and is alive with you to plead for us and
   all the world.

This is our story.
This is our . . . ⟦as above⟧ . . . in the highest.

Send your Spirit on us now
that by these gifts we may feed on Christ
   with opened eyes and hearts on fire.

May we and all who share this food
offer ourselves to live for you
and be welcomed at your feast in heaven
   where all creation worships you,
Father, Son and Holy Spirit.
Blessing and honour . . . ⟦CF 7⟧ . . . for
ever and ever. Amen.

42. *Prayer E*

Here follows an extended Preface (pages . . .) or the following

Father, you made the world and love
   your creation.
You gave your Son Jesus Christ to be our
   Saviour.
His dying and rising have set us free
   from sin and death.
And so we gladly thank you,
with saints and angels praising you and
   saying:
Holy, holy . . . [[ELLC 7]] . . . in the highest.
[Blessed is . . . [[ELLC 8]] . . . in the highest.]

We praise and bless you, loving Father,
through Jesus Christ, our Lord;
and as we obey his command,
send your Holy Spirit,
that broken bread and wine outpoured
may be for us the body and blood of
   your dear Son.

On the night before he died he had
   supper with his friends
and, taking bread, he praised you.
He broke the bread, gave it to them and
   said:
Take, eat: this is my body which is given
   for you;
do this in remembrance of me.

When supper was ended he took the cup
   of wine.
Again he praised you, gave it to them
   and said:

Drink this, all of you;
this is my blood of the new covenant,
which is shed for you and for many for
   the forgiveness of sins.
Do this, as often as you drink it, in
   remembrance of me.

So, Father, we remember all that Jesus
   did,
in him we plead with confidence his
   sacrifice made once for all upon the
   cross.

Bringing before you the bread of life and
   cup of salvation,
we proclaim his death and resurrection
until he comes in glory.

One of these four acclamations is used
[[CF 4(a), 4(b), 4(c) and 4(d) as in Prayer A]]

Lord of all life,
help us to work together for that day
when your kingdom comes
and justice and mercy will be seen in all
   the earth.

Look with favour on your people,
gather us in your loving arms
and bring us with [*N and*] all the saints
to feast at your table in heaven.

Through Christ, and with Christ, and in
   Christ,
in the unity of the Holy Spirit,
all honour and glory are yours, O loving
   Father,
for ever and ever. **Amen.**

43. *Prayer F*

You are worthy of our thanks and praise
Lord God of truth,
for by the breath of your mouth
you have spoken your word,
and all things have come into being.

You fashioned us in your image
and placed us in the garden of your
  delight.
Though we chose the path of rebellion
you would not abandon your own.

Again and again you drew us into your
  covenant of grace.
You gave your people the law and taught
  us by your prophets
to look for your reign of justice, mercy
  and peace.

As we watch for the signs of your
  kingdom on earth,
we echo the song of the angels in
  heaven,
evermore praising you and *saying*:
Holy, holy . . . [[ELLC 7]] . . . in the highest.
[Blessed is . . . [[ELLC 8]] . . . in the highest.]

Lord God, you are the most holy one,
enthroned in splendour and light,
yet in the coming of your Son Jesus Christ,
you reveal the power of your love
made perfect in our human weakness.
[Amen. Lord, we believe.]

Embracing our humanity,
Jesus showed us the way of salvation;
loving us to the end,
he gave himself to death for us;
dying for his own,
he set us free from the bonds of sin,
that we might rise and reign with him in
  glory.
[Amen. Lord, we believe.]

On the night he gave up himself for us
  all
he took bread and gave you thanks;
he broke it and gave it to his disciples,
  saying:
Take, eat; this is my body which is given
  for you;
do this in remembrance of me.
[Amen. Lord, we believe.]

In the same way, after supper
he took the cup and gave you thanks;
he gave it to them, saying:
Drink this, all of you; this is my blood of
  the new covenant,
which is shed for you and for many for
  the forgiveness of sins.
Do this, as often as you drink it, in
  remembrance of me.
[Amen. Lord, we believe.]

Therefore we proclaim the death that he
  suffered on the cross,
we celebrate his resurrection, his
  bursting from the tomb,
we rejoice that he reigns at your right
  hand on high
and we long for his coming in glory.
[Amen. Come, Lord Jesus.]

As we recall the one, perfect sacrifice of
  our redemption,
Father, by your Holy Spirit let these gifts
  of your creation
be to us the body and blood of our Lord
  Jesus Christ;
form us into the likeness of Christ
and make us a perfect offering in your
  sight.
[Amen. Come, Holy Spirit.]

Look with favour on your people
and in your mercy hear the cry of our
  hearts.
Bless the earth,
heal the sick,
let the oppressed go free
and fill your Church with power from on
  high.
[Amen. Come, Holy Spirit.]

Gather your people from the ends of the
  earth
to feast with [*N and*] all your saints
at the table in your kingdom,
where the new creation is brought to
  perfection
in Jesus Christ our Lord;

by whom, and with whom, and in whom,
in the unity of the Holy Spirit,
all honour and glory be yours, almighty
  Father,
for ever and ever. **Amen.**

44. *Prayer G*

Blessed are you, Lord God,
our light and our salvation;
to you be glory and praise for ever.

From the beginning you have created all
   things
and all your works echo the silent music
   of your praise.
In the fullness of time you made us in
   your image,
the crown of all creation.

You give us breath and speech, that with
   angels and archangels
and all the powers of heaven
we may find a voice to sing your praise:
Holy, holy . . . ⟦ELLC 7⟧ . . . in the highest.
[Blessed is . . . ⟦ELLC 8⟧ . . . in the highest.]

How wonderful the work of your hands,
   O Lord.
As a mother tenderly gathers her
   children,
you embraced a people as your own.
When they turned away and rebelled
your love remained steadfast.

From them you raised up Jesus our
   Saviour, born of Mary,
to be the living bread
in whom all our hungers are satisfied.

He offered his life for sinners,
and with a love stronger than death
he opened wide his arms on the cross.

On the night before he died
he came to supper with his friends
and, taking bread, he gave you thanks.
He broke it and gave it to them, saying:
Take, eat; this is my body which is given
   for you;
do this in remembrance of me.

At the end of supper, taking the cup of
   wine,
he gave you thanks, and said:

Drink this, all of you; this is my blood of
   the new covenant,
which is shed for you and for many for
   the forgiveness of sins.
Do this, as often as you drink it, in
   remembrance of me.
One of these four acclamations is used
⟦CF 6(a), 6(b), 6(c) and 6(d) as in Prayer A⟧

Father, we plead with confidence
his sacrifice made once for all upon the
   cross;
we remember his dying and rising in
   glory,
and we rejoice that he intercedes for us
   at your right hand.

Pour out your Holy Spirit as we bring
   before you
these gifts of your creation;
may they be for us the body and blood of
   your dear Son.

As we eat and drink these holy things in
   your presence,
form us in the likeness of Christ,
and build us into a living temple to your
   glory.

[Remember, Lord, your Church in every
   land.
Reveal her unity, guard her faith,
and preserve her in peace . . .]

Bring us at the last with [*N and*] all the
   saints
to the vision of your eternal splendour
for which you have created us;
through Jesus Christ, our Lord,
by whom, with whom, and in whom,
with all who stand before you in earth
   and heaven,
we worship you, Father almighty, in
   songs of everlasting praise:
Blessing and . . . ⟦CF 7⟧ . . . and ever. Amen.

45. *Prayer H*

It is right to praise you, Father, Lord of
all creation;
in your love you made us for yourself.

When we turned away
you did not reject us,
but came to meet us in your Son.
**You embraced us as your children
and welcomed us to sit and eat with you.**

In Christ you shared our life
that we might live in him and he in us.
**He opened his arms of love on the cross
and made for all the perfect sacrifice for
sin.**

On the night he was betrayed,
at supper with his friends
he took bread, and gave you thanks;
he broke it, and gave it to them, saying:
Take, eat; this is my body which is given
for you;
do this in remembrance of me.
**Father, we do this in remembrance of him:
his body is the bread of life.**

At the end of supper, taking the cup of
wine
he gave you thanks, and said:
Drink this, all of you; this is my blood of
the new covenant,
which is shed for you for the forgiveness
of sins;
do this in remembrance of me.
**Father, we do this in remembrance of him:
his blood is shed for all.**

As we proclaim his death and celebrate his
rising in glory,
send your Holy Spirit that this bread and
this wine
may be to us the body and blood of your
dear Son.
**As we eat and drink these holy gifts,
make us one in Christ, our risen Lord.**

With your whole Church throughout the
world
we offer you this sacrifice of praise
and lift our voice to join the eternal song
of heaven:
Holy, holy . . . ⟦ELLC 7⟧ . . . in the highest.

46. ⟦Appendix⟧ *PRAYERS AT THE PREPARATION OF THE TABLE* ⟦designed for **EngCW1A,**
though placed after all four rites⟧
 1–3. ⟦Related to money⟧

4. Blessed are you . . . ⟦CF 4(a)⟧ . . . **Blessed be God for ever.**
    offer] set before you

   Blessed are you . . . ⟦CF 4(b)⟧ . . . **Blessed be God for ever.**
    offer] set before you

5. Be present, be present . . . ⟦CF 4(c)⟧ . . . the breaking of the bread. **Amen.**

6. As the grain once scattered in the fields
   and the grapes once dispersed on the hillside
   are now reunited on this table in bread and wine,
   so, Lord, may your whole Church soon be gathered together
   from the corners of the earth
   into your kingdom. **Amen.**

7.   Wise and gracious God,
     you spread a table before us;
     nourish your people with the word of life
     and the bread of heaven. **Amen.**

8.   *In this prayer, the texts for single voice need not be spoken by the president. It will sometimes be appropriate to ask children to speak them.*
     With this bread that we bring
     we shall remember Jesus.

     With this wine that we bring
     we shall remember Jesus.

     Bread for his body,
     wine for his blood,
     gifts from God to his table we bring.
     We shall remember Jesus.

9–12. ⟦General, not overtly sacramental⟧

47. ⟦Appendix⟧ *SUPPLEMENTARY CONSECRATION* ⟦intended for all four **EngCW** rites⟧
     If either or both of the consecrated elements are likely to prove insufficient, the president returns to the holy table, and adds more, saying these words
     Father, having given thanks over the bread and cup
     according to the institution of your Son Jesus Christ,
     who said,
     'Take, eat; this is my body'
     [*and/or* 'Drink this; this is my blood'],
     we pray that by the power of your Holy Spirit
     this *bread/wine* also
     may be to us his *body/blood*
     to be received in remembrance of him.

     ⟦a similar form follows in traditional language⟧

'ORDER ONE IN TRADITIONAL LANGUAGE' IN THE CHURCH OF ENGLAND'S *COMMON WORSHIP: SERVICES AND PRAYERS FOR THE CHURCH OF ENGLAND* BOOK, 2000 (EngCW1B)

⟦The lining is original. The numbering is editorial, and matches that in **EngCW1A**, from which this rite differs by being in 'traditional' language, but in other respects mirrors it, except where noted below.⟧

The Gathering

1.   ⟦*Hymn, *Invocation of the name of the Trinity⟧

THE GREETING

2.   ⟦Greeting⟧

PRAYER OF PREPARATION

3.   ***Almighty God, unto whom** . . . ⟦CF 1, but 'traditional'⟧ . . . **Christ our Lord. Amen.**

PRAYERS OF PENITENCE
4. [[*Commandments, *Beatitudes, *Comfortable Words, *Summary of the Law]]

   [[Invitation to confession, one of two congregational confessions or Kyries]]

5. Almighty God, who forgives . . . [[CF 2]] . . . Christ our Lord. **Amen.**

GLORIA IN EXCELSIS
6. *Glory be to God on high . . . [[ELLC 3, but 'traditional']] . . . **God the Father. Amen.**

THE COLLECT
7. [[Collect]]

The Liturgy of the Word

READINGS
8. [[One or *two readings, with proclamation and response following; and with psalm or canticle after the first; *hymns and songs between readings]]

GOSPEL READING
9. [[Gospel; *acclamation, announcement and response before, proclamation and response after]]

10. *SERMON* [[The heading alone provides for the Sermon]]

THE CREED
11. [[On Sundays and Principal Holy Days –'*on occasion the Apostles' Creed or an authorized Affirmation of Faith may be used (see pages . . .)'*]]
   I believe in one God . . . [[ELLC 5, but 'traditional']] . . . **world to come. Amen.**
   [and the Son]] OMIT BRACKETS

PRAYERS OF INTERCESSION
12. [[Forms are in an appendix but others may be used. Two sets of versicles and responses and an ending are here.]]

The Liturgy of the Sacrament

THE PEACE
13. *The president may introduce the Peace with a suitable sentence and then says*
   The peace of the Lord be always with you
   and with thy spirit.

   These words may be added
   Let us offer one another a sign of peace.
   All may exchange a sign of peace.

PREPARATION OF THE TABLE
TAKING OF THE BREAD AND WINE
14. *A hymn may be sung.*

15. *The gifts of the people may be gathered and presented.*

16. *The table is prepared and bread and wine are placed upon it.*

17. *One or more of the prayers at the preparation of the table may be said* [[see §46 on pages 46–7 above]].

18. *The president takes the bread and wine.*

THE EUCHARISTIC PRAYER

19. *One of the following Eucharistic Prayers is used: Prayer A below, or Prayer C on page ...*
    [i.e. immediately following Prayer A.]
    [Prayer A from **EngCW1A**, on page 39 above, but in 'traditional' language]
    [Prayer C from **EngCW1A**, on page 41 above, but in 'traditional' language]

THE LORD'S PRAYER

20. Let us pray with confidence as our Saviour has taught us.
    Our Father, who art ... [modified traditional text] ... ever and ever. Amen.
    (or)
    As our Saviour taught us, so we pray
    Our Father in heaven ... [ELLC 1] ... now and for ever. Amen.
    Save us from the time of trial and] Lead us not into temptation but

BREAKING OF THE BREAD

21. *The president breaks the consecrated bread*

22. We break this bread ... [CF 6(a)] ... **in one bread.**
    (or)
    Every time we eat ... [CF 6(b)] ... **until he comes.**

23. *The Agnus Dei may be used as the bread is broken.*
    O Lamb of God, that takest ... [ELLC 8(b), but 'traditional'] ... grant us thy peace.

GIVING OF COMMUNION

24. *The president says one of these invitations to communion*
    Draw near with faith ... [CF 9(a)] ... **with thanksgiving.**
    (or)
    Jesus is the Lamb ... [CF 9(b), but 'traditional'] ... **my soul shall be healed.**
    (or)
    God's holy gifts ... [CF 9(c)] ....**God the Father.**

    or, from Easter Day to Pentecost
    Christ our passover is sacrificed for us.
    Therefore let us keep the feast. Alleluia.

25. *This prayer may be said before the distribution*
    We do not presume ... [CF 3(a), but 'traditional'] ... he in us. Amen.

26. *The president and people receive communion. Authorized words of distribution are used and the communicant replies.* **Amen.**

27. *During the distribution hymns and anthems may be sung.*

28. [Rubric providing for supplementary consecration, as directed in an appendix – §47 on page 47 above]

29. *Any consecrated bread and wine which is not required for purposes of communion is consumed at the end of the distribution or after the service.*

PRAYER AFTER COMMUNION

30. *Silence is kept.*

31. *The Post Communion, or this or another suitable prayer is said.*
    [Prayer of thanksgiving, the second post-communion prayer in 1662]

32. *All may say this prayer*
    Almighty God ... [CF 11(a), but 'traditional'] ... thy praise and glory. Amen.

The Dismissal

33. *A hymn may be sung.*

34. *The president may use the seasonal blessing or another suitable blessing (or)*
    The peace of God . . . ⟦CF 12(a)⟧ . . . with you always. **Amen.**

35. Go in peace . . . ⟦CF 12(b)⟧ . . . **name of Christ. Amen.**
    (or)
    Go in the peace of Christ.
    Thanks be to God.
    ⟦From Easter to Pentecost 'Alleluia alleluia' may be added to both versicle and response⟧

36. *The ministers and people depart.*

'ORDER TWO' IN THE CHURCH OF ENGLAND'S *COMMON WORSHIP: SERVICES AND PRAYERS FOR THE CHURCH OF ENGLAND* BOOK, 2000 (EngCW2B)

⟦The lining is original. The numbering is editorial. The text is 1662 with small adjustments, such as the insertion of hymns and the provision of cross-headings.⟧

Order Two

Structure

The people and the priest
- *prepare for worship*
- *hear and respond to the commandments of God*
- *keep silence and pray a Collect*
- *proclaim and respond to the word of God*
- *prepare the table*
- *pray for the Church and the world*
- *confess their sins and are assured of God's forgiveness*
- *praise God for his goodness*
- *pray the Consecration Prayer*
- *receive communion*
- *respond with thanksgiving*
- *depart with God's blessing*

Order Two

1. *A hymn may be sung.*

THE LORD'S PRAYER
2. Our Father, which art . . . ⟦1662 text⟧ . . . deliver us from evil. Amen.

PRAYER OF PREPARATION
3. Almighty God, unto whom . . . ⟦CF 1, but 'traditional'⟧ . . . Christ our Lord. **Amen.**

THE COMMANDMENTS

4. ⟦Ten Commandments with 1662 responses, or Summary of the Law with response, or Kyries (ELLC 2)⟧

5. *The Collect for the Sovereign may be said*
   ⟦First of the two 1662 Prayers for the monarch⟧

THE COLLECT

6. ⟦Collect⟧

EPISTLE

7. ⟦One or *two readings, with announcement at the beginning and 'Here endeth . . .' at the end. A psalm may be used after the Old Testament and a hymn after the readings⟧

GOSPEL

8. ⟦Gospel; announcement and *response before, *proclamation and *response after⟧

THE CREED

9. *The Creed is used on every Sunday and Holy Day and may be used on other days also.*
   I believe in one God . . . ⟦1662 text⟧ . . . **world to come. Amen.**
   Banns of marriage may be published and notices given.

10. SERMON ⟦The heading alone provides for the Sermon⟧

OFFERTORY

11. *One of the following or another sentence of Scripture is used*
    ⟦Matt. 5.16; Matt. 6.19; 1 Chron. 29.14; 1 John 3.17⟧

12. *A hymn may be sung.*

13. *The gifts of the people may be gathered and presented.*

14. *The priest places the bread and wine upon the table.*

INTERCESSION

15. *Brief biddings may be given.*
    Let us pray for the whole state . . . ⟦1662 'Church militant'⟧ . . . and advocate. **Amen.**
16. *The priest may read the Exhortation (page . . .) or one of the other Exhortations in* **The Book of Common Prayer**

INVITATION TO CONFESSION

17. Ye that do truly . . . ⟦as 1662⟧ . . . upon your knees.

CONFESSION

18. **Almighty God** . . . ⟦as 1662, but said congregationally⟧ . . . **Christ our Lord. Amen.**

ABSOLUTION

19. Almighty God . . . ⟦as 1662, but *'you' 'your'* italicized⟧ . . . Jesus Christ our Lord. **Amen.**

THE COMFORTABLE WORDS

20. Hear what comfortable words our Saviour Christ saith unto all that truly turn to him.
    ⟦Matt. 11.28; John 3.16; 1 Tim. 1.15; 1 John 2.1, 2⟧

PREFACE

21. *The priest and the people praise God for his goodness.*
    The Lord be with you
    and with thy Spirit.
    Lift up . . . ⟦dialogue, preface (rubric re proper prefaces), sanctus (in bold type for congregational participation, text as 1662)⟧ . . . **most high. [Amen.]**

    These words may also be used
    Blessed is he that cometh . . . ⟦ELLC 8⟧ . . . **in the highest.**

22. We do not presume . . . [[as 1662, traditional form of CF 3(a)]] . . . he in us. **Amen.**

THE PRAYER OF CONSECRATION
23. *The priest, standing at the table, says the Prayer of Consecration*
    Almighty God, our heavenly Father . . . [[as 1662, including five manual acts]] . . . of me. **Amen.**
    The following may be used
    O Lamb of God that takest . . . [[ELLC 8(b), but 'traditional']] . . . **grant us thy peace.**

GIVING OF COMMUNION
24. *The priest and people receive communion. To each is said*
    The body of our Lord . . . [[CF 10(a), with 'thee'/'thy' for 'you'/'yours']] . . . with thanksgiving.
    The blood of our Lord . . . [[CF 10(b), with 'thee'/'thy' for 'you'/'yours']] . . . be thankful.
    Or, when occasion requires, these words may be said once to each row of communicants, or to a convenient number within each row.
25. *If either or both of the consecrated elements are likely to prove insufficient, the priest returns to the holy table and adds more, saying the words on page . . . [[i.e. §47 on page 47 above]]*
26. *What remains of the consecrated bread and wine which is not required for purposes of communion is consumed now or at the end of the service.*

THE LORD'S PRAYER
27. *The priest may say*
    As our Saviour Christ hath commanded and taught us, we are bold to say
    Our Father, which art . . . [[1662 text]] . . . **for ever and ever. Amen.**

PRAYER AFTER COMMUNION
28. *The priest says either the Prayer of Oblation or the Prayer of Thanksgiving*
    Prayer of Oblation
    O Lord and heavenly Father . . . [[as 1662]] . . . world without end. **Amen.**
    Prayer of Thanksgiving
    Almighty and everliving God . . . [[as 1662]] . . . world without end. **Amen.**

GLORIA IN EXCELSIS
29. **Glory be to God on high** . . . [[as 1662]] . . . **God the Father. Amen.**

THE BLESSING
30. The peace of God, which passeth . . . [[CF 12(a)]] . . . always. **Amen.**
    Spirit] Ghost

31. *A hymn may be sung*

[[After the end of the rite come the Third Exhortation and the Proper Prefaces from 1662]]

'ORDER TWO IN CONTEMPORARY LANGUAGE' IN THE CHURCH OF ENGLAND'S *COMMON WORSHIP: SERVICES AND PRAYERS FOR THE CHURCH OF ENGLAND* BOOK, 2000 (EngCW2A)

[The lining is original. The numbering is editorial, and repeats that of **EngCW2B** above. The text is 1662 in contemporary language, with variants such as the insertion of hymns and the provision of cross-headings.]

Order Two in Contemporary Language

1. *A hymn may be sung.*

2. *The Lord's Prayer may be said.*

PRAYER OF PREPARATION

3. Almighty God, to whom . . . [CF 1] . . . Christ our Lord. **Amen.**

THE COMMANDMENTS

4. [Ten Commandments with 1662 responses, or Summary of the Law with response, or Kyries (ELLC 2)]

5. *The Collect for the Sovereign may be said*
   [First of the two 1662 Prayers for the monarch]

THE COLLECT

6. [Collect]

READINGS

7. [One or *two readings, *proclamation and response at the end of each. A psalm may be used after the first reading and *hymns and songs between the readings]

GOSPEL

8. [Gospel; *acclamation, announcement and response before, *proclamation and *response after]

THE CREED

9. *On Sundays and Principal Holy Days an authorized translation of the Nicene Creed is used, or on occasion the Apostles' Creed* [ELLC 4] *or an authorized Affirmation of Faith may be used (see pages . . .).*
   We believe in one God . . . [ELLC 5] . . . **world to come. Amen.**
   incarnate of] incarnate from
   became truly human] was made man
   [and the Son]] OMIT BRACKETS

10. *SERMON* [The heading alone provides for the Sermon]

OFFERTORY

11. *One of the following or another sentence of Scripture is used* [Matt. 5.16; Matt. 6.19; 1 Chron. 29.14; 1 John 3.17]

12. *A hymn may be sung.*

13. *The gifts of the people may be gathered and presented.*

14. *The president places the bread and wine upon the table.*

PRAYERS OF INTERCESSION

15. [Rubrics re forms elsewhere in the Book, with suggested concerns, and versicles and responses]

PRAYERS OF PENITENCE

16. *A minister reads this shorter exhortation*
    [contemporary text of brief summary of Long Exhortation of 1662]

INVITATION TO CONFESSION

17. *A minister uses a seasonal invitation to confession or these or other suitable words*
You then, who truly . . . ⟦contemporary version of 1662⟧ . . . humble confession to
Almighty God.

CONFESSION

18. *Either of these forms, or form 2 on page . . . may be used*
Almighty God . . . ⟦1662 in contemporary language, said congregationally⟧ . . . **Christ
our Lord. Amen.**
(or)
Father eternal . . . ⟦from EngA⟧ . . . **children of light. Amen.**

ABSOLUTION

19. Almighty God . . . ⟦contemporary version of 1662⟧ . . . Jesus Christ our Lord. Amen.

THE COMFORTABLE WORDS

20. Hear what words of comfort our Saviour Christ says to all who truly turn to him.
⟦Matt. 11.28; John 3.16; 1 Tim. 1.15; 1 John 2.1, 2⟧

PREFACE

21. *The priest and the people praise God for his goodness.*
Lift up your hearts . . . ⟦ELLC 6⟧ . . . **give thanks and praise.**
It is indeed right,
it is our duty and our joy,
at all times and in all places
to give you thanks and praise,
holy Father, heavenly King,
almighty and eternal God.

A Proper Preface may follow here (see Note . . .).

Therefore with angels and archangels,
and with all the company of heaven,
we proclaim your great and glorious name,
for ever praising you and *saying*:
Holy, holy, holy . . . ⟦ELLC 7⟧ . . . **Hosanna in the highest.**

PRAYER OF HUMBLE ACCESS

22. *One of these prayers is said*
We do not presume . . . ⟦CF 3(a)⟧ . . . and he in us. **Amen.**
(or)
Most merciful Lord . . . ⟦CF 3(b)⟧ . . . in your kingdom. **Amen.**

THE PRAYER OF CONSECRATION

23. *The president, standing at the table, says the Prayer of Consecration*
Almighty God, our heavenly Father,
who, in your tender mercy,
gave your only Son our Saviour Jesus Christ
to suffer death upon the cross for our redemption;
who made there by his one oblation of himself once offered
a full, perfect and sufficient sacrifice, oblation and satisfaction for the sins of the
whole world:

he instituted, and in his holy gospel commanded us to continue,
a perpetual memory of his precious death until he comes again.

Hear us, merciful Father, we humbly pray,
and grant that we receiving these gifts of your creation, this bread and this wine,
according to your Son our Saviour Jesus Christ's holy institution,
in remembrance of his death and passion,
may be partakers of his most blessed body and blood;

who in the same night that he was betrayed,
took bread and gave you thanks; *Here the president takes the paten.*
he broke it and gave it to his disciples, saying: *Here the president breaks the bread.*
Take, eat; this is my body which is given for you; *Here the president lays a hand on all the bread.*
do this in remembrance of me.
In the same way, after supper he took the cup; *Here the president takes the cup.*
and when he had given thanks; he gave it to them, saying:
Drink this, all of you: this is my blood of the new covenant,
which is shed for you and for many
for the forgiveness of sins. *Here the president is to lay a hand on every vessel in which there is wine to be consecrated.*

Do this, as often as you drink it,
in remembrance of me.
Amen.

GIVING OF COMMUNION

24. *The priest and people receive communion. To each is said*
The body of our Lord . . . [CF 10(a)] . . . with thanksgiving.
The blood of our Lord . . . [CF 10(b)] . . . be thankful.
Or, when occasion requires, these words may be said once to each row of communicants, or to a convenient number within each row.

25. *If either or both of the consecrated elements are likely to prove insufficient, the priest returns to the holy table and adds more, saying the words on page . . . [i.e. §47 on page 47 above]*

26. *What remains of the consecrated bread and wine which is not required for purposes of communion is consumed now or at the end of the service.*

THE LORD'S PRAYER

27. As our Saviour taught us, so we pray
Our Father in heaven . . . [ELLC 1] . . . and for ever. Amen.
Save us from the time of trial and] Lead us not into temptation but
(or)
Let us pray with confidence as our Saviour has taught us.
Our Father, who art . . . [modified traditional text] . . . ever and ever. Amen.

PRAYER AFTER COMMUNION

28. *The president says one of the following prayers or the prayer on page . . . [a contemporary form of the 1662 post-communion Prayer of Thanksgiving]*
Lord and heavenly Father . . . [contemporary form of 1662 Prayer of Oblation] . . . and ever. **Amen.**
(or)
Father of all . . . [CF 11(b)] . . . Christ our Lord. **Amen.**

GLORIA IN EXCELSIS

29. Glory to God in the highest . . . ⟦ELLC 3⟧ . . . **God the Father. Amen.**
    God's people] his people
    Or another song of praise may be used.

THE BLESSING
    The president may use a seasonal blessing or another suitable blessing, or
30. The peace of God . . . ⟦CF 12(a)⟧ . . . always. **Amen.**

31. *A hymn may be sung.*

THE AGAPE IN THE CHURCH OF ENGLAND'S *LENT – HOLY WEEK –*
EASTER SERVICES (1986)(EngAgape)

⟦Services in *Lent – Holy Week – Easter* (SPCK, 1986) were 'commended' by the House of Bishops, and the section headed 'THE AGAPE WITH THE HOLY COMMUNION' was partly a short essay with a brief history of the agape leading into coaching as to how the eucharist – then Rite A (**EngA**) – could be lawfully celebrated within the context of a larger meal. This did not necessarily have to be within the season concerned. The section then concluded with this suggested outline order.⟧

The following order may be found suitable (the numbers are of ASB Rite A) or the meal may follow the eucharist.

1	Sentence
2	Greeting
	The introductory part of the meal.
3–8	Prayers of Penitence
11	Collect
12–18	The Ministry of the Word
	The main course of a simple meal may be taken here.
20–21	The Intercession
30–31	The Peace
	The people may move about as they exchange the Peace.
	The second course may be taken here.
32–35	The Preparation of the Gifts
38–45	The Eucharistic Prayer and Communion
	The consecrated bread and wine may be passed reverently round the tables or the communicants may move to a central point.
50–56	After Communion

4. The Scottish Episcopal Church

The Scottish Episcopal Church's first steps in revision of its eucharistic rite were provided by reordered forms of the 1929 liturgy (Scot, published in LiE), published in 'grey bookies' in 1966 (ScotR, published in MAL) and in 1970 (ScotRR, shown in summary in FAL). Forms in modern language followed in 1977 (the 'orange bookie') and in 1982 (the 'blue bookie'), and these, labelled Scot1 and Scot2, were presented in LAL.[62] A feature of Scot1 which was eliminated in Scot2 was the provision of congregational recitation of two major paragraphs of the eucharistic prayer. Thus Scot2 had, unusually for Anglican liturgies, no acclamations or other responsive or congregational material from the sanctus through to the amen, but this apparent omission was, it seems, occasioned by different congregations wanting to say different parts congregationally – but the deliberate abstention from rubrics or guidance left this unadvertised in the blue bookie.

A need was felt for a variety of eucharistic prayers, and in 1989 four alternative ones drafted by the Liturgy Committee were authorized for experimental use for five years by the College of Bishops. Then in 1995, the convenor of the Committee proposed to the Synod that the texts be referred to the dioceses with a view to becoming definitive. Some minor improvements were made, the dioceses approved the texts, and in 1996 the General Synod amended the relevant Canon in order to incorporate the four prayers into the existing Scot2. These were then inserted at §18 into a new printing of the blue bookie. The existing eucharistic prayer became Prayer I; and the balance of its sacramental theology, expressed particularly from the narrative onwards, was preserved by reproducing that second part of its text *verbatim* in Prayers II, III and IV. These prayers were chiefly designed (and labelled) to give emphasis to seasons of the year, perhaps because Scot2 provided no proper prefaces. However, Prayer V was less tied to existing forms and was boldly creative.

The printings continued some elements of pre-inclusive language characteristic of the early 1980s. In 2010 the College of Bishops 'offered . . . as an interim measure' some permissive changes to make it more fully inclusive, largely following the ELLC models at relevant points in the Gloria in Excelsis, the Nicene Creed and the Opening Dialogue. They also noted that 'The Faith & Order Board has instructed the Liturgy Committee to prepare a new Eucharistic Liturgy'. This process has begun, but is unlikely to be concluded for some years.

---

62 A variant from ecumenical texts in Scot2 was missed in LAL. In the eleventh line of the Nicene Creed, the traditional 'of one substance with the Father' was retained in preference to 'of one Being with the Father'.

ALTERNATIVE EUCHARISTIC PRAYERS to SCOTTISH LITURGY 1982 (Scot2), 1996 (Scot2A)

⟦These eucharistic prayers all come within §18 of **Scot2** in its 1996 'blue bookie' form. Prayer I is the single eucharistic prayer of **Scot2** shown in **LAL**. Prayers II, III, and IV reproduce prayer I from the narrative of institution onwards. That common part is shown here once in Prayer II below, and is not repeated for Prayers III and IV. The marginal commentary on each section of the prayer in Prayer I (see **LAL**) is repeated for each of the new prayers, except that Prayer V has no penultimate 'Prayer of Petition'. Prayer V is wholly distinctive. The lining is original.⟧

Eucharistic Prayer II: Anticipation (*Suitable for Advent*)

The Lord . . . ⟦ELLC 6⟧ . . . **him thanks and praise.**

Worship and praise belong to you, God our maker.
Out of nothing, you called all worlds to be,
and still you draw the universe to its fulfilment.
Dawn and evening celebrate your glory
till time shall be no more.

In Christ your Son
the life of heaven and earth were joined,
sealing the promise of a new creation,
given, yet still to come.

Taught by your Spirit,
we who bear your threefold likeness
look for the City of Peace
in whose light we are transfigured
and the earth transformed.

As children of your redeeming purpose
who await the coming of your Son,
we offer you our praise,
with angels and archangels
and the whole company of heaven
singing the hymn of your unending glory:
**Holy, holy . . . ⟦ELLC 7⟧ . . . in the highest.
Blessed is . . . ⟦ELLC 8⟧ . . . in the highest.**

Glory and thanksgiving be to you,
most loving Father.
In Jesus you showed us yourself.
Our hope is built on him,
the first, the last, the living one.
Obedient, even to accepting death,
he opened the gate of glory
and calls us now to share the life of heaven.

Before he was given up to suffering and death,
alight with the vision of a feast
that heralded a kingdom yet to come,
at supper with his disciples
he took bread and offered you thanks.
He broke the bread,
and gave it to them, saying:
'Take, eat.
This is my Body: it is broken for you.'
After supper, he took the cup,
he offered you thanks,
and gave it to them saying:
'Drink this, all of you.
This is my Blood of the new covenant;
it is poured out for you, and for all,
that sins may be forgiven.
Do this in remembrance of me.'

We now obey your Son's command.
We recall his blessed passion and death,
his glorious resurrection and ascension;
and we look for the coming of his Kingdom.
Made one with him, we offer you these gifts
and with them ourselves,
a single, holy, living sacrifice.

Hear us, most merciful Father,
and send your Holy Spirit upon us
and upon this bread and this wine,
that, overshadowed by his life-giving power,
they may be the Body and Blood of your Son,
and we may be kindled with the fire of your love
and renewed for the service of your Kingdom.

Help us, who are baptized into the
  fellowship of Christ's Body
to live and work to your praise and glory;
may we grow together in unity and love
until at last, in your new creation,
we enter into our heritage
in the company of the Virgin Mary,
the apostles, and prophets,
and of all our brothers and sisters
living and departed.

Through Jesus Christ our Lord,
with whom and in whom,
in the unity of the Holy Spirit,
all honour and glory be to you,
Lord of all ages,
world without end.
Amen.

Eucharistic Prayer III: Returning to God (Suitable for Lent and Passiontide)

The Lord be with . . . [[ELLC 6]] . . . **him
  thanks and praise.**

Worship and praise belong to you,
maker of light and darkness.
Your wisdom draws beauty from chaos,
brings a harvest out of sorrow
and leads the exiles home.

In Christ your Son enemies are reconciled,
debts forgiven
and strangers made welcome.

Your Spirit frees us
to live as sons and daughters
in our Father's house.

We who by Christ's power
follow the way of the Cross
sharing the joy of his obedience,
now offer you our praise,
with angels and archangels,
and the whole company of heaven

singing the hymn of your unending glory:
**Holy, holy . . . [[ELLC 7]] . . . in the highest.
Blessed is . . . [[ELLC 8]] . . . in the highest.**

Glory and thanksgiving be to you,
most loving Father,
for Christ in whom the world is
  reconciled.
Lifted on the Cross,
his suffering and forgiveness
spanned the gulf our sins had made.
Through that dark struggle
death was swallowed up in victory
that life and light might reign.

Before he was given up to suffering and
  death,
recalling the night of Israel's release,
the night in which the sons of Egypt died,
your Chosen one, himself the First-Born,
freely offered his life.
At supper with his disciples . . . [[then as Pr
  II]]

Eucharistic Prayer IV: New Life, The Lord, The Spirit (*Suitable from Easter Day to Pentecost*)

The Lord be with . . . ⟦ELLC 6⟧ . . . **him
thanks and praise.**

Worship and praise belong to you, Author
  of all being.
Your power sustains, your love restores,
  our broken world.
You are unceasingly at work,
from chaos bringing order
and filling emptiness with life.

Christ, raised from the dead,
proclaims the dawn of hope.
He lives in us that we may walk in light.

Your Spirit is fire in us,
your breath is power
to purge our sin
and warm our hearts to love.

As children of your redeeming purpose,
freed by him who burst from the tomb
and opened the gate of life,
we offer you our praise,
with angels and archangels
and the whole company of heaven,
singing the hymn of your unending glory;
**Holy, holy . . . ⟦ELLC 7⟧ . . . in the highest.
Blessed is . . . ⟦ELLC 8⟧ . . . in the highest.**

Praise and thanksgiving be to you, Lord
  of all,
for by the Cross eternal life is ours
and death is swallowed up in victory.
In the first light of Easter
glory broke from the tomb
and changed the women's sorrow into joy.
From the Garden the mystery dawned
that he whom they had loved and lost
is with us now
in every place for ever.

Making himself known in the breaking of
  the bread,
speaking peace to the fearful disciples,
welcoming weary fishermen on the shore,
he renewed the promise of his presence
and of new birth in the Spirit
who sets the seal of freedom on your sons
  and daughters.

Before he was given up to suffering and
  death,
recalling the night of Israel's release,
the night in which slaves walked free
at supper with his disciples. ⟦then as in Pr II⟧

Eucharistic Prayer V

The Lord be with you . . . [[ELLC 6]] . . .
him thanks and praise.

Worship and praise belong to you, Father,
in every place and at all times.
You made us,
all the people of the world
and everything that is.

You give us the daylight.
Your Word lights up our minds.
Jesus was born among us
to be light in our darkness.

Your Spirit lives in us
so that we can look at the world with your
eyes.

One day we will be with you in heaven,
but already we laugh with the saints and
angels,
and sing their joyful song:
**Holy, holy, holy . . . [[ELLC 7]] . . . in the
highest.
Blessed is he . . . [[ELLC 8]] . . . in the
highest.**

Father, you never forget us or turn away
from us,
even when we fail you.
You sent your Son Jesus
who gave his life for us.
He healed those who were sick,
cared for those who were poor,
and cried with those who were sad.
He forgave sinners
and taught us to forgive.

For all your love we give you thanks
in the way that Jesus showed us.

On the night before he died
while he was having supper with his
friends,
he took bread and offered you thanks.
He broke the bread,
and gave it to them, saying:
'Take, eat.
This is my Body: it is broken for you.'
After supper he took the cup,
he offered you thanks,
and gave it to them saying:
'Drink this, all of you.
This is my Blood of the new covenant;
it is poured out for you, and for all,
that sins may be forgiven.
Do this in remembrance of me.'

So, as we do what he told us,
we open our hearts to him;
we remember how he died and rose again
to live now in us.

Together with him we offer you these gifts:
in them we give you ourselves.

Send your Holy Spirit on us and on this
bread and this wine,
that they may be the Body and Blood of
Christ,
and that, sharing your life,
we may travel in your company to our
journey's end.

With all your people
we give you thanks and praise
through the Son and in the Spirit
now and for ever.
Amen.

5. The Church in Wales

The Church in Wales provided a complete hardback BCP in 1984 in both English and Welsh. The English text of the eucharist in it was published in **LAL** as **Wal1**. Uniquely among English-language liturgies compiled after 1970, in this BCP God was consistently addressed as 'thou', and the grammar and literary style in a somewhat inconsistent way reflected this. However, there was also authorized, in booklet form for experimental purposes, a 'Modern English Liturgy', and this was also published in **LAL** (**Wal2**).

A new Standing Liturgical Advisory Commission was appointed in 1987, and they, working in both languages, drafted a new eucharistic rite. This moved on from the 'fourfold' structure publicized by Gregory Dix, and exhibited two main headings only for the eucharistic action – 'The Thanksgiving' (in which the 'taking' preceded the eucharistic prayer by simple rubric) and 'The Communion' (in which the fraction was similarly presented in low profile as the preliminary to the main action, reception). It included as an alternative 'An Outline Order for the Holy Eucharist'. The whole rite was entitled 'An Alternative Order for the Holy Eucharist' and was authorized by the Governing Body in 1993, and published in 1994. It is labelled here as **Wal3**.

Wal3 passed into widespread use, and on the basis of such wide experience it was revised by the Standing Commission. The work was completed in 2003, and while the 1994 text was only slightly affected (one instance being the final elimination from the rubrics of masculine pronouns for the priest), there were now added three further eucharistic prayers, one of which was lifted almost verbatim from **Scot2**, and the other two of which were specifically designated for use when significant numbers of children would be present, one for under-7s, and one for 7–11s. The provision of these two prayers was thought to be the first such official authorization within the Anglican Communion.[63] The revised rite was passed overwhelmingly by the Governing Body in 2004 and became an official part of 'The Book of Common Prayer for use in the Church in Wales' (and thus dropped the adjective 'alternative'). It was published as a separate substantial book, with lectionary and a wide range of seasonal and optional material included as appendices. The 1984 rite (**Wal1**) was printed at the back, to enable those who clung to the traditional text to use the new Book and gain the advantage of the three-year lectionary and the appended material. The main 2004 rite is presented here in its English text as **Wal4** and the Outline Order as **Wal5**, each with **Wal3** of 1994 shown by *apparatus*.

---

63 See the discussion on page 23 above.

THE CHURCH IN WALES, AN ORDER FOR THE HOLY EUCHARIST, 2004
(Wal4)

[A structure document introduces the rite, providing the wide-canvas enumeration which is followed in the main text and shown here below. There are then 18 opening Notes and eight 'Guidelines for the Celebration of the Eucharist with Children'. The lining here is original.]

An Order for The Holy Eucharist

1 THE GATHERING
Wal3 ADDS OF THE PEOPLE

A hymn, psalm or anthem may be sung.

(STAND)
In the name of the Father, and of the Son and of the Holy Spirit. **Amen.**
Wal3: the Father . . . Spirit] God: Father, Son and Holy Spirit

Grace and peace be with you
and keep you in the love of Christ.
Or in Eastertide: Alleluia! Christ is risen. **He is risen indeed. Alleluia!**

Either [a prayer for strength and light] *or* [a variant on CF 1]
(KNEEL)
The Kyries or another section from Appendix I pages . . ., may be used.
Lord, have mercy . . . [ELLC 2, English responsive form] . . . **Lord, have mercy.**

Silence
[Corporate confession]
[Absolution, with similarities to CF 2]

GLORIA IN EXCELSIS *(STAND)*
Glory to God . . . [ELLC 3] . . . **glory of God the Father. Amen.**
God's people] his people

THE COLLECT OF THE DAY
Let us pray.

2 THE PROCLAMATION OF THE WORD
[One or two readings, with announcement before each and *acclamation and response after, and a *psalm, hymn or song following each.]

THE GOSPEL *(STAND)*
[Gospel reading with announcement and response before and acclamation and response after.]

THE SERMON *(SIT)*

AN AFFIRMATION OF THE FAITH *(STAND)*

THE NICENE CREED
We believe . . . [ELLC 4] . . . **world to come. Amen.**
was incarnate of . . . fully human] by the power of the Holy Spirit, he became incarnate from the
Virgin Mary, and was made man
[and the Son]] OMIT BRACKETS
The Apostles' Creed (Appendix II, page . . .) may be used instead of the Nicene Creed.
Wal3 OMITS

3 THE INTERCESSION
Wal3: *INTERCESSION*] *PRAYERS OF THE CHURCH*

⟦Prayers composed for the occasion (with suggested cued responses) or a Litany form from Appendix III or any of the Shorter Litanies from Morning or Evening Prayer. These directions vary slightly from those in **Wal3**.⟧

One of the following prayers may then be said
Either
We do not presume . . . ⟦CF 3(a)⟧ . . . he in us. Amen.
        that our sinful bodies . . . through his most precious blood, and] OMIT

or
Lord Jesus Christ,
you draw and welcome us,
emptied of pride and hungry for your grace,
to this your kingdom's feast.
Nowhere can we find the food
for which our souls cry out,
but here, Lord, at your table.
Invigorate and nourish us, good Lord,
that in and through this bread and wine
your love may meet us
and your life complete us
in the power and glory of your kingdom. Amen.
        Wal3: THIS PRAYER IS IN APPENDIX III WITH THE RUBRIC ABOVE WORDED
        ACCORDINGLY

4 THE PEACE

A sentence of Scripture from Appendix V may be read.
        Wal3: V] IV (pages . . .)
The peace of the Lord be with you always.
And also with you.

A sign of peace may be exchanged.
A hymn, psalm or anthem may be sung.
When a collection is taken it is brought to the priest.

5 THE THANKSGIVING

The priest takes the bread and the cup
        Wal3: *When the gifts have been prepared, the priest takes the bread and the cup into his hands.*

Either the priest may say
We celebrate together the gifts and grace of God.
We take this bread,
we take this wine
to follow Christ's example
and obey his command.
Or the priest may praise God for his gifts in these words (not to be used with Eucharistic Prayer 1)
Blessed are you . . . ⟦CF 4(a) and (b)⟧ . . . become our spiritual drink.
Blessed be God for ever.
        IN Wal3 THE ALTERNATIVES COME IN THE OPPOSITE ORDER AND REFERENCE IS MADE
        TO APPENDIX V FOR CF 4, FROM WHICH ONLY THE RESPONSE IS PRINTED IN THE
        MAIN TEXT

One of the following Eucharistic Prayers is used.
⟦In **Wal3** this rubric follows the next heading. Note that **Wal3** variants on each eucharistic prayer are on page 65⟧

VARIATIONS IN THE EUCHARISTIC PRAYERS

〚The 1994 **Wal3** textual variations from **Wal4** in the eucharistic prayers are shown together here to enable the actual **Wal4** prayers to be set out cleanly each on a single page〛

Eucharistic Prayer 1

Wal3: Lord . . . universe] Lord God of the universe TWICE
creating us male and female, and] male and female you created us
give you thanks for your Son, Jesus Christ] thank you for the gift of your Son
THE RUBRIC IN THE NEXT LINE IS OMITTED AND THE PRAYER RUNS ON
AS A WHOLE
You gave him to be] OMIT
He was born of the Virgin Mary and] born of Mary, he
suffering death] died
You raised him] and rose
THE RUBRIC ABOUT A PROPER PREFACE IS OMITTED
We give you thanks for the living hope . . . **Hosanna in the Highest**] OMIT
Loving Father . . . Christ took] We thank you that our Lord Jesus Christ, on the night
before he died, took
After supper] And after supper
made once . . . ascension] once for all on the cross, his resurrection and ascension
for us] OMIT

Eucharistic Prayer 2

Wal3: and in the fullness . . . the Saviour;] you sent your Son to be the Saviour; in the
fullness of time
in remembrance of me] to remember me TWICE
poured out . . . forgiveness of sins] shed for you
[Let us . . . faith:]] OMIT
recalling . . . resurrection] recalling now Christ's death and resurrection

Eucharistic Prayer 3

Wal3: **Blessed is he . . . the highest**] IN SQUARE BRACKETS
[Let us proclaim . . . faith.]] [*The deacon or priest may say:* Let us proclaim . . . **glory.**]

Eucharistic Prayer 4

Wal3: *Either* For . . . *or*] OMIT
eternal life] everlasting life
All praise . . . he in us] We acclaim you, holy Father, glorious in power.
You created all things and formed us in your own image;
but all have sinned and fall short of your glory.
We thank you that you gave your only Son for our salvation:
to be made man, to die on the cross and to rise again.
Sanctify . . . gifts to us] Send your Holy Spirit on these gifts to make them holy,
of our Saviour] of your Son our Saviour
As he has . . . for ever and ever] We ask you to accept our sacrifice of thanks and praise.
As we now proclaim his death and resurrection
we offer to you these your gifts,
this bread and this cup.
May we who receive them
be united by your Spirit
in peace and love with all your faithful people.
To you, almighty Father,
through your Son Jesus Christ our Lord,
in the power of your Holy Spirit,
be all honour and glory
now and for ever.

The Lord be with you . . . . ⟦ELLC 6 and
  CF 5⟧ . . . **our thanks and praise.**

Blessed are you, Lord our God, King of the
  universe:
you bring forth bread from the earth.
Blessed be God for ever.

Blessed are you, Lord our God, King of the
  universe:
you create the fruit of the vine.
Blessed be God for ever.

Wheat and grape, this bread and wine,
are part of the riches of your earth.
**You are worthy, O Lord our God,
to receive glory and honour and praise,
for you created all things
and by your will they have their being.**

We thank you, Father,
that you formed us in your own image,
creating us male and female,
and loving us even when we rebelled
  against you.
Above all we give you thanks for your
  Son, Jesus Christ.

The following is omitted if a proper preface is used
You gave him to be the Saviour of the
  world.
He was born of the Virgin Mary
and lived on earth in obedience to you,
suffering death on the cross for our sins.
You raised him from the dead in glory;
through him you sent the Spirit as he had
  promised.

*A proper preface may be inserted here
(Appendix VI).*
We give you thanks for the living hope
You have given us in Jesus Christ our
  Lord,
whom we praise with our lips and in our
  lives, *saying/singing:*
Blessed is . . . ⟦ELLC 8⟧ . . . **in the highest.**

Loving Father,
we praise you that, on the night before he
  died,
our Lord Jesus Christ took bread and gave
  you thanks,
he broke it and gave it to his disciples,
  saying,
Take, eat; this is my body which is given
  for you:
do this in remembrance of me.

After supper he took the cup, gave you
  thanks
and, giving it to his disciples, said,
Drink from this, all of you;
this is my blood of the new covenant,
shed for you and for many for the
  forgiveness of sins:
do this as often as you drink it
in remembrance of me.

Therefore, with these holy gifts
we celebrate his offering of himself made
  once for all on the cross,
we rejoice in his glorious resurrection and
  ascension,
and we look for his coming again:
Christ has . . . ⟦CF 6(a)⟧ . . . **come in glory.**

Father, accept this offering of our duty and
  service,
this memorial of Christ your Son our
  Lord.
Send your Holy Spirit on us and on these
  your gifts
that they may be for us the body and
  blood of your Son.
Grant that we who eat this bread and
  drink of this cup
may, with the hosts of angels and all the
  company of heaven,
proclaim the glory of your name
and join in their unending hymn of praise:
Holy, holy . . . ⟦ELLC 7⟧ . . . **in the highest.**

Silence

The Lord be with you . . . [[ELLC 6 and CF 5]] . . . **our thanks and praise.**

True and living God, the source of life for all creation,
you have made us in your own image.
Always and everywhere we give you thanks
through Jesus Christ our Lord.

The following is omitted when a proper preface is used.
In your love for us
and in the fullness of time
you sent your Son to be the Saviour;
the Word was made flesh,
he lived among us and we have seen his glory.
For our sins and the sins of all the world
he suffered death on the cross.
You raised him to life in triumph
and exalted him in glory.
Through him you send your Holy Spirit
upon your Church
and make us your people.

A proper preface may be inserted here (Appendix VI).
Therefore, with angels and archangels
and with all the company of heaven
we praise your glorious name:
Holy, holy . . . [[ELLC 7]] . . . in the highest.
Blessed is . . . [[ELLC 8]] . . . in the highest.

Blessed are you, almighty God,
because on the night he was betrayed
the Lord Jesus took bread,
and when he had given you thanks,
he broke it, gave it to his disciples and said,
Take, eat; this is my body

which is given for you:
do this in remembrance of me.
In the same way, after supper he took the cup;
when he had given you thanks
he gave it to them and said,
Drink this, all of you;
this cup is the new covenant in my blood
poured out for you and for many
for the forgiveness of sins:
do this as often as you drink it
in remembrance of me.
[Let us proclaim the mystery of faith:]
Christ has . . . [[CF 6(a)]] . . . come in glory.

Therefore, loving God,
recalling now the sacrifice of Christ your Son
once for all upon the cross
and the triumph of his resurrection,
we ask you to accept this our sacrifice of praise.

Send your Holy Spirit on us and on these gifts
that we may be fed with the body and blood of your Son
and be filled with your life and goodness.
Unite us in Christ and give us your peace
that we may do your work and be his body in the world.

Through him, with him, in him,
in the unity of the Holy Spirit
all honour and glory are yours,
almighty Father,
for ever and ever.
Amen.

Silence

The Lord be with you . . . [[ELLC 6 and CF 5]] . . . **our thanks and praise.**

It is indeed right,
it is our duty and our joy
at all times and in all places to give you
thanks and praise,
holy Father, heavenly King, almighty,
everlasting God,
through Jesus Christ your only Son our
Lord.

The following is omitted when a proper preface is used.
He is your eternal Word:
through him you created the universe
and formed us men and women in your
own image.
You sent him to be our Saviour,
born of Mary through the power of the
Spirit.
Upon the cross he opened wide his arms of
mercy,
embracing us in perfect love,
destroying the power of evil, suffering and
death.
On the first day of the week you raised
him from the dead
and opened to us the gate of everlasting
life.
Through him you have given us your holy
and life-giving Spirit,
and made us your own sons and
daughters.

A proper preface may be inserted here (Appendix VI).
Therefore with angels and archangels
and with all the company of heaven
we proclaim your great and glorious name,
for ever praising you and saying:
Holy, holy . . . [[ELLC 7]] . . . **in the highest.**
Blessed is . . . [[ELLC 8]] . . . **in the highest.**

Hear us, heavenly Father,
through Jesus Christ your Son our Lord.
Through him accept our sacrifice of praise,
and grant that, by the power of your
Spirit,
these gifts of bread and wine may be for us
his body and his blood;
who in the same night that he was
betrayed
took bread and gave you thanks;
he broke it and gave it to his disciples,
saying,
Take, eat; this is my body which is given
for you.
Do this in remembrance of me.
In the same way, after supper,
he took the cup and gave you thanks;
he gave it to them, saying,
Drink from this, all of you;
for this is my blood of the new covenant
which is shed for you and for many
for the forgiveness of sins.
Do this, as often as you drink it,
in remembrance of me.

[Let us proclaim the mystery of faith:]
Christ has . . . [[CF 6(a)]] . . . **come in glory.**

Therefore, Father,
remembering the saving death and
resurrection of your Son,
we offer to you in thanksgiving this bread
and this cup, your gifts to us,
and we thank you for counting us worthy
to stand in your presence and serve you.

Send your Holy Spirit upon all of us
who share this bread and this cup.
Strengthen our faith, make us one
and welcome us and all your people into
the glorious kingdom of your Son.
Through him, with him, in him,
in the unity of the Holy Spirit,
all honour and glory are yours,
almighty Father,
for ever and ever.
Amen.

Silence

The Lord be with you . . . .⟦ELLC 6 and CF 5⟧ . . . **our thanks and praise.**

It is indeed right, it is our duty and our joy
at all times and in all places
to give you thanks, holy Father,
all-powerful and everliving God,
through Jesus Christ our Lord:

*A proper preface may be inserted here
(Appendix VI); otherwise, on Sundays:*
Either
For he is our great high priest
who has freed us from our sins
and has made us a royal priesthood
serving you, our God and Father.

Or
Who by his death
has destroyed death
and by his rising to life again
has restored to us eternal life.

And so with the hosts of angels and all the
   company of heaven
we proclaim the glory of your name
and join in their unending hymn of praise:
Holy, holy . . . ⟦ELLC 7⟧ . . . **in the highest.**
Blessed is . . . ⟦ELLC 8⟧ . . . **in the highest.**

All praise and thanks to you, true and
   living God,
Creator of all things, Giver of life.
You formed us in your own image;
but we have marred that image and fall
   short of your glory.
We give you thanks
that you sent your Son to share our life;
you gave him up to death that the world
   might be saved,
and you raised him from the dead
that we might live in him and he in us.

Sanctify with your Spirit this bread and
   wine, your gifts to us
that they may be for us the body and
   blood of our Saviour Jesus Christ.

On the night he was betrayed, he took
   bread,
and when he had given thanks
he broke it and gave it to his disciples,
   saying,
Take, eat; this is my body which is given
   for you:
do this in remembrance of me.
In the same way after supper he took the
   cup,
and when he had given thanks
he gave it to them, saying,
Drink from this, all of you,
for this is my blood of the new covenant
which is shed for you and for many
for the forgiveness of sins:
do this as often as you drink it
in remembrance of me.

[Let us proclaim the mystery of faith:]
Christ has . . . ⟦CF 6(a)⟧ . . . **come in glory.**

As he has commanded us, Father,
we remember Jesus Christ, your Son.
Proclaiming his glorious death,
rejoicing in his resurrection,
and waiting for him to come in glory
we bring to you this bread, this cup.

Accept our sacrifice of thanks and praise.
Restore and revive your people,
renew us and all for whom we pray
with your grace and heavenly blessing,
and at the last receive us with all your
   saints
into that unending joy promised by your
   Son, Jesus Christ our Lord.

Through him, with him, in him,
in the unity of the Holy Spirit
all honour and glory are yours, almighty
   Father,
for ever and ever.
Amen.

Silence

The Lord be with you . . . [[ELLC 6 and CF 5]] . . . **our thanks and praise.**

Worship and praise belong to you, Father,
in every place and at all times.
All power is yours.
You created the heavens and established
   the earth;
you sustain in being all that is.
In Christ your Son our life and yours
are brought together in a wonderful
   exchange.
He made his home among us that we
   might for ever dwell in you.
Through your Holy Spirit
you call us to a new birth in a creation
   restored by love.
As children of your redeeming purpose we
   offer you our praise,
with angels and archangels and the
   company of heaven,
singing the hymn of your unending glory:
Holy, holy . . . [[ELLC 7]] . . . **in the highest.**
Blessed is . . . [[ELLC 8]] . . . **in the highest.**

Glory and thanksgiving be to you, most
   loving Father,
for the gift of your Son born in human
   flesh.
He is the word existing beyond time,
both source and final purpose,
bringing to wholeness all that is made.
Obedient to your will he died upon the
   cross.
By your power you raised him from the
   dead.
He broke the bonds of evil and set your
   people free
to be his body in the world.

On the night when he was given up to
   death,
knowing that his hour had come,
having loved his own, he loved them to the
   end.
At supper with his disciples
he took bread and offered you thanks.
He broke the bread, and gave it to them,
   saying:
Take, eat.
This is my body: it is broken for you.

After supper, he took the cup,
he offered you thanks, and gave it to them
   saying:
Drink this all of you.
This is my blood of the new covenant;
it is poured out for you, and for all, that
   sins may be forgiven.
Do this in remembrance of me.
[Let us proclaim the mystery of faith:]
Christ has . . . [[CF 6(a)]] . . . **come in glory.**

We now obey your Son's command.
We recall his blessed passion and death,
his glorious resurrection and ascension;
and we look for the coming of his
   Kingdom.
Made one with him, we offer you these
   gifts
and with them ourselves, a single, holy,
   living sacrifice.

Hear us, most merciful Father,
and send your Holy Spirit upon us
and upon this bread and wine,
that, overshadowed by his life-giving
   power,
they may be the body and blood of your
   Son,
and we may be kindled with the fire of
   your love
and renewed for the service of your
   Kingdom.

Help us, who are baptized into the
   fellowship of Christ's body
to live and work to your praise and glory;
may we grow together in unity and love
until at last, in your new creation,
we enter into our heritage
in the company of the Virgin Mary,
the apostles and prophets,
and of all our brothers and sisters living
   and departed,
through Jesus Christ our Lord.

Through him, with him, in him,
in the unity of the Holy Spirit
all honour and glory are yours, almighty
   Father,
for ever and ever.
Amen.

Silence

70

[[This prayer 5, new in **Wal4** in 2004, is the original eucharistic prayer I from **Scot2** with minor amendments to conform to general Church in Wales practice as follows:

Location	Change
Opening dialogue	The Lord be with you . . . [[ELLC 6 and CF 5]] . . . **our thanks and praise.**
Acclamations	. . . of me.
after narrative of institution	[Let us proclaim the mystery of faith:]
	Christ has . . . [[CF 6(a)]] . . . **come in glory.**
Doxology	Through him, with him, in him,
	in the unity of the Holy Spirit
	all honour and glory are yours, almighty Father,
	for ever and ever.
	Amen.]]

EUCHARISTIC PRAYER 6
Suitable for use when a significant number of children under 7 years is present.

The Lord be with you . . . [[ELLC 6 and CF 5]] . . . **our thanks and praise.**

Thank you, Father,
for making us and our wonderful world.
Wherever we are in your world,
we should always thank you,
through Jesus, your Son.

[Jesus lived as one of us;
Jesus died on the cross for us;
Jesus is alive because you gave him life again;
Jesus is with us now.]

So, with the angels and everyone in heaven,
we *say/sing* together:
Holy, holy . . . [[ELLC 7]] . . . **in the highest.**
Blessed is . . . [[ELLC 8]] . . . **in the highest.**

Great and wonderful Father,
we remember when Jesus had supper with his friends
the night before he died,
he took the bread;
he thanked you, broke it, gave it to his friends and said:
Take this and eat it – this is my body, given for you.
Do this to remember me.
After supper, Jesus took the cup of wine;
he thanked you, gave it to his friends and said:

All of you drink from this cup, because this is my blood –
the new promise of God's love:
Do this every time you drink it
to remember me.

Together we remember that Jesus is always with us and *say/sing*:
Christ has . . . [[CF 6(a)]] . . . **come in glory.**

So loving Father,
remembering how dearly Jesus loves us,
we should love him too.
Send your Holy Spirit, gentle as a dove,
on us and on these gifts,
so that, with everyone who eats and drinks this bread and wine,
the body and blood of Jesus,
we may be full of your life and goodness.
Help us all to walk hand in hand with Jesus
and live our lives for him.

All honour and glory belong to you, Father,
through Jesus, your Son,
with the Holy Spirit:
one God, for ever and ever.
Amen.

Silence

71

EUCHARISTIC PRAYER 7

Suitable for use when a significant number of 7–11 year-olds is present.
In place of the Proper Preface [Through him you made us . . .], three or four children may each
read out a brief sentence of thanksgiving for the love of God in Christ.

The Lord be with you . . . [[ELLC 6 and
CF 5]] . . . **our thanks and praise.**

It is always right,
wherever we are,
to thank you and to praise you,
God our Father and King for ever,
through Jesus Christ, your Son.

[Through him you made us and the
whole universe.
When your Holy Spirit came to Mary,
Jesus was born as one of us.
He loved us so much that he died for us;
on the first Easter Day you raised him
to life;
and death and evil were conquered for
ever.
At Pentecost, you gave the Holy Spirit,
as Jesus promised,
to help us to live as your children.]

So here on earth,
with the angels and archangels
and with everyone in heaven
we praise your name and *say/sing*:
Holy, holy . . . [[ELLC 7]] . . . **in the highest.**
Blessed is . . . [[ELLC 8]] . . . **in the highest.**

Father in heaven,
listen to the prayer we make in Jesus'
name;
through the Holy Spirit's power, gentle as
a dove,
may this bread and this wine be for us
Jesus' body and blood.

Father, we remember
when Jesus had supper with his friends
the night before he died,
he took the bread;

he thanked you, broke it, gave it to his
friends and said:
Take this and eat it – this is my body,
given for you.
Do this to remember me.
After supper, Jesus took the cup of wine;
he thanked you, gave it to his friends and
said:
All of you drink from this cup, because
this is my blood –
the new promise of God's love:
Do this every time you drink it
to remember me.

Together we remember that Jesus is always
with us and *say/sing*:
Christ has . . . [[CF 6(a)]] . . . **come in glory.**

Father, as we remember your Son, Jesus
Christ,
who died on the cross and rose again,
we offer you these and all the gifts you
freely give to us.
Send your Holy Spirit to be with us
and all who share this bread and drink
from this cup.
Help us to trust you,
bring us closer together and welcome us,
with all your people,
into Jesus' glorious kingdom.

All honour and glory belong to you,
Father,
through Jesus, your Son,
with the Holy Spirit:
one God, for ever and ever.
Amen.

Silence

72

Either	*Or*
Let us pray with confidence to the Father:	As our Saviour taught us, we boldly pray:
Our Father in heaven . . . ⟦ELLC 1⟧ . . . and for ever. Amen.	**Our Father who . . . ⟦'modified traditional text'⟧ . . . ever and ever. Amen.**

6 THE COMMUNION

The priest breaks the bread
We break this bread . . . ⟦CF 6(a)⟧ . . . **in one bread.**
> because] for

Or
Every time . . . ⟦CF 6(b)⟧ . . . **until he comes.**
> drink this] drink of this
> **Wal3** OMITS CF 6(b)

This anthem may be used here or during the communion.
Either **Jesus, Lamb of God . . . ⟦ELLC 8(a)⟧ . . . give us your peace.**
Or **Lamb of God . . . ⟦ELLC 8(b)⟧ . . . grant us peace.**
> sin] sins THREE TIMES

One of the following invitations
God's holy gifts . . . ⟦CF 7(c)⟧ . . . **God the Father.**
> **Wal3**: God's holy gifts . . . people] The gifts of God for the people of God
Or Jesus is the Lamb of God . . . ⟦CF 7(b)⟧ . . . **I shall be healed.**
> Blessed] Happy
Or Come, let us receive the body and blood of our Lord Jesus Christ, given for us, and feed on him in our hearts by faith with thanksgiving.

The priest and people receive the communion.
The sacrament is administered with these words
> The body of Christ keep you in eternal life. **Amen.**
Or The body of Christ, the bread of life. **Amen.**
Or The body of Christ. **Amen.**

> The blood of Christ keep you in eternal life. **Amen.**
Or The blood of Christ, the true vine. **Amen.**
Or The blood of Christ. **Amen.**

Non-communicants may be given a blessing.
> **Wal3**: *given a blessing] blessed with these or similar words:* The Lord Jesus bless you. **Amen.**

A form for additional consecration is provided in Appendix VII, page . . . ⟦i.e. on page 75 below⟧

After the communion, an appropriate sentence of Scripture from the Proclamation of the Word may be read.

Silence is kept.

A hymn may be sung.

Any consecrated bread and wine which is not to be reserved for purposes of communion is consumed.
> **Wal3**: *to be reserved] required*

7 THE SENDING OUT
> **Wal3**: *SENDING OUT] Dismissal of the People*

Give thanks to the Lord for he is gracious:
his love is everlasting.

A post-communion prayer and/or one of the following prayers is used:

Wal3:   *A post-communion] Another suitable*
              is] may be

We thank you, Father,
for feeding us with the body and blood of your Son
in this holy sacrament,
through which we are assured of the hope of eternal life.
We offer ourselves to you as a living sacrifice.
Keep us in the fellowship of his body, the Church,
and send us out in the power of your Spirit
to live and work to your praise and glory. Amen.

Or

Generous God,
you have fed us at your heavenly table.
Kindle us with the fire of your Spirit
that when the Lord comes again
we may shine as lights before him,
who is alive and reigns
in glory for ever. Amen.

Wal3: who is alive . . . ever] who lives and reigns with you,
                            in the unity of the Holy Spirit,
                            one God, now and for ever

Or

Eternal God,
comfort of the afflicted and healer of the broken,
you have fed us at the table of life and hope;
teach us the ways of gentleness and peace,
that all the world may acknowledge
the kingdom of your Son,
Jesus Christ our Lord. Amen.

Wal3 OMITS

Or

God of truth,
we have seen with our eyes
and touched with our hands the bread of life.
Strengthen our faith
that we may grow in love for you
and for each other,
through Jesus Christ, our risen Lord. Amen.

The Lord be with you.
And also with you.

An appropriate dismissal (Appendix VIII, pages . . .) may be added.
Go in peace to love and serve the Lord.
In the name of Christ. Amen.
⟦From Easter to Pentecost 'Alleluia alleluia' may be added to both versicle and response⟧

8 APPENDICES

I   ⟦The Commandments, Summary of the Law, Words of Assurance and Kyries (including seasonal options in expanded forms to express confession)⟧
        Wal3 OMITS SUMMARY OF THE LAW

II   ⟦Creeds: The Apostles' Creed (slightly varied from ELLC 4) and a short Trinitarian alternative⟧
        Wal3 OMITS, AND NUMBERS THE NEXT APPENDIX AS 'II'

III   ⟦Intercessions: three forms of suggested alternatives⟧
        Wal3 THIS IS 'II' AND APPENDIX III IS THE ALTERNATIVE PRAYER OF APPROACH FROM §3 READING 'KINGDOM' IN LINE 3

IV   ⟦Concluding collects: three forms⟧
        Wal3 OMITS, AND NUMBERS THE NEXT APPENDIX 'IV'

V   ⟦Sentences for the Peace: 11 General and 17 (13 in 1994) Seasonal and Proper forms⟧
        Wal3: THIS IS 'IV' AND APPENDIX V IS PRAYERS AT THE PREPARATION OF THE GIFTS WITH CF 4

VI   ⟦Proper Prefaces: 35 forms (26 in 1994)⟧

VII *Form for additional consecration*
    Holy Father, hear the prayer and thanksgiving which we offer through Jesus Christ our Lord, who took *bread (and) the cup* and said: This is my *body (and this is my) blood*. We also take this *bread (and) wine* and pray that by your Word and Spirit it may be for us the sacrament of the *body (and) blood* of Christ. **Amen.**

VIII ⟦Dismissals *'For optional use between the final responses, with or without a blessing'*: 8 General and 18 Seasonal forms⟧

THE CHURCH IN WALES, AN OUTLINE ORDER FOR THE HOLY EUCHARIST, 2004 (**Wal5**)

⟦The numbering here is original, and matches that in **Wal4**⟧

1 *We Gather in the Lord's Name*

2 *We Share God's Peace*
   Grace and peace be with you from God our Father and the Lord Jesus Christ.
   And also with you.

3 *We Proclaim the Word of God*
   Bible readings, including a Gospel. The people should respond to the Word.

4 *We Pray with the Church*
   After the prayers, the people are called to silence and repentance.
   ⟦Short congregational confession and presidential absolution⟧
   The act of repentance may be used in section 2 above.

5 *We Offer Thanksgiving*
   The gifts are presented. The priest takes the bread and wine.
   One of the EUCHARISTIC PRAYERS ⟦i.e. in **Wal4**⟧ *is used and then all say the Lord's Prayer.*

6   *We Share the Gifts*
    The priest breaks the bread.
    ⟦Words of distribution as in **Wal4**⟧

7   *We Go in God's Strength*
    Concluding prayer, [blessing] and dismissal.
    The following may be used
    Blessed be God who calls us together.
    Praise the Lord who makes us one people.

    Blessed be God who forgives our sin.
    Praise the Lord who gives hope and freedom.

    Blessed be God whose word is proclaimed.
    Praise the Lord who is revealed as love.

    Blessed be God whose grace is abundant.
    Praise the Lord for all we shall be.

    Accept, O Lord, our thanks and praise.
    Our hands were empty until you filled them.

    We will serve the Lord.
    In the name of Christ. Amen.

Notes for the Outline Order
⟦10 general notes concerning preparation of people and elements, silence, posture, hymnody etc., nos 1 and 9 are printed here⟧

1   *This order is not intended for use at principal celebrations of the Eucharist on Sundays and festivals but for occasional use.* ⟦In **Wal3** this Note precedes the Order⟧

9   *At the priest's discretion, the consecrated bread and wine may be shared by being passed around by the communicants (standing); if so, care needs to be taken that the elements may be passed around simply and reverently. The Christian name of each communicant may be used at the administration. Consecrated bread and wine not required for communion is consumed after the Sharing (6) or immediately after the service.*

6. The Church of Ireland

The Church of Ireland from 1967 onwards provided 'alternative' services, a category reflecting the continued currency of the 1926 Book of Common Prayer, in which the eucharist was the Irish version of 1662 (**Ire**). This derived from the 1878 rite, but still only differed by a hair's breadth from 1662 itself. The first alternative eucharistic rite in 1967 (**IreR**) retained the 'thou' form of address to God, and many other features of **Ire**, but altered the shape of the rite in line with the general trend, and with an eye to **CSI**. It was followed in 1972 by a thoroughly revised alternative (**Ire1**). This rite, still in booklet form, took the language into a 'you' form of address to God and drew heavily upon the international texts recommended by ICET. The eucharistic prayer in it, when re-touched by the Liturgical Advisory Committee in 1980, involved too great a departure from 1662 emphases for it to be welcomed in all parts of the Church, and it was initially defeated in the House of Laity in General Synod, but later accepted in conjunction with the main eucharistic prayer from the 1978 *An Australian Prayer Book* (**Aus5**) being added as an alternative to it. In this form the rite (**Ire2**) was included in the 1984 slim hardback collection of alternative services, the *Alternative Prayer Book*, and was presented in **LAL**. This Book gave stability and medium-term continuity to the alternative rites, and its currency ran for 20 years. However, it had been compiled without reference to the inclusive language issue, and was probably the last major revision in the English language to be produced and authorized without such concerns being incorporated; and to that extent it had an element of being outdated even before it began.

For various cumulative reasons the General Synod accepted in 1997 and endorsed in 1998 a proposal for a complete new Book of Common Prayer. The proposal envisaged the traditional language services being included alongside the modern ones, and thus the 1926 BCP would be totally superseded. The Liturgical Advisory Committee duly worked to this plan, and a complete new Book was approved in General Synod on 15 May 2003, to be authorized from the following year as *The Book of Common Prayer 2004*. The Book contains in 'Holy Communion One' a version of the 1926 text, **Ire**, in order to retain the legality of the rite when the 1926 Book was itself being superseded. The Preface to the Book says that the Committee has in its new services specifically looked to the guidance given by the various Statements of the IALC, which in the case of Holy Communion was the Dublin Statement of IALC-5 in 1995. The modern service, Holy Communion Two (**Ire3**), reflects this guidance. It is specifically interesting for having in its three eucharistic prayers forms from three distinct provenances, indeed from three different countries. Prayer 1 is directly descended from **IreR**, **Ire1** and **Ire2**, retaining in the post-sanctus the weighty emphasis upon the cross from the 1662 tradition, following the Church of South India in the anamnesis by responding to

Jesus' command to 'do this' by duly affirming 'we do as Christ your Son commanded', and transferring the receptionist epiclesis to follow the anamnesis in the form of a prayer for fruitful participation. Prayer 2 came into the *APB* from Australia in 1984 (shown in **LAL** as **Aus5**), as described above, and it has a receptionist epiclesis prior to the narrative of institution. It continued virtually unchanged in 2004, but with the acclamations ('Christ has died' etc.) moved down one paragraph to follow the anamnesis. Prayer 3 is a responsive prayer, overtly drawn from the pattern of Prayer H in **EngCW1A** (see page 46 above), yet diverging from that prayer. This divergence came not from retouching its finished form, but from reworking the draft that had lain before the Church of England's General Synod in November 1999; and from that point of divergence it has been developed into a Trinitarian shape unique to **Ire3**.[64]

HOLY COMMUNION ONE FROM THE CHURCH OF IRELAND
THE BOOK OF COMMON PRAYER 2004

⟦'Holy Communion One' deliberately retains the text and structure of **Ire**. There is a minimal allowance for small changes in the lapse of time since 1878/1926, the most notable variants from **Ire** being:

(a) The opening and closing rubrics have been removed and a minimal set of '*General Directions for Public Worship*' come after the Calendar and Lectionary in the BCP 2004, and these include §14, headed '*At the Holy Communion*'. The 'Directions' here are to cover Holy Communion One and Holy Communion Two, and apart from requiring consumption of consecrated bread and wine remaining at the end of the service, have little in common with the rubrics in **Ire**. The 'Black Rubric' or Declaration on Kneeling does, however, appear at the end of Holy Communion One.

(b) The Lord's Prayer, at both occurrences, is in the 'modified traditional' form.

(c) The Offertory Sentences (which are wholly about almsgiving) are in an appendix and include a new series of seasonal sentences.

(d) The Long Exhortations form a second appendix.

(e) The Prayer of Humble Access is printed in bold type for congregational recitation.

(f) A 'Post-communion prayer' is permitted after the Gloria in Excelsis.⟧

---

64 The process, beginning in the Church of England but then translated into the Church of Ireland, is reported in close detail in Kevin J. Moroney, 'The Church of Ireland's Eucharistic Prayer 3: Revision and Analysis', in *Studia Liturgica* vol. 39 no. 2 (2009) pp. 171–84.

HOLY COMMUNION TWO FROM THE CHURCH OF IRELAND
THE BOOK OF COMMON PRAYER 2004 (Ire3)

[[*The Book of Common Prayer 2004* is printed in two colours.
The numbering is editorial. The lining is original.]]

THE CELEBRATION OF
THE HOLY COMMUNION
ALSO CALLED THE LORD'S SUPPER OR THE EUCHARIST

The Gathering of God's People

1. *THE GREETING*
   [[Greetings, *sentence of scripture, *presiding minister's introduction]]

2. *THE COLLECT FOR PURITY*
   Almighty God, to whom . . . [[CF 1]] . . . Christ our Lord. Amen.
   or another suitable opening prayer

3. *PENITENCE*
   The prayers of penitence may take place at this point or before or after the Intercession.
   [[The Commandments or the Beatitudes (from an appendix) or the Summary of the Law
   printed here, with call to confession, congregational confession, absolution (like CF 2), or
   penitential sentences with Kyrie response in English (ELLC 2)]]

4. *GLORIA IN EXCELSIS* [[omission or variation permitted]]
   Glory to God . . . [[ELLC 3]] . . . glory of God the Father. Amen.

5. *THE COLLECT OF THE DAY*
   [[rubric re reading of the collect]]

Proclaiming and Receiving the Word

6. *THE FIRST READING is normally from the Old Testament* [[*proclamation and response
   at end]]

7. *THE PSALM* 'Glory to the Father' *may be omitted*

8. *THE SECOND READING is from the New Testament* [[*proclamation and response at
   end]]

9. *THE GRADUAL A canticle, psalm, hymn, anthem or acclamation may be sung*

10. *Stand THE GOSPEL READING* [[announcement and response at beginning, proclamation
    and response at end]]

11. *THE SERMON is preached here or after the Creed*

12. *THE NICENE CREED* [[to be used on Sundays and principal holy days with permission
    to omit on other days]]
    We believe . . . [[ELLC 5]] . . . world to come. Amen.
      of the Holy Spirit and] by the Holy Spirit of
      and became fully human] and was made man
      [and the Son]] OMIT BRACKETS

The Prayers of the People

13. [[Directions for topics and forms and leaders of intercessions, *concluding with the Lord's
    Prayer (ELLC 1)]]
    *If the Lord's Prayer is used at this point in the service, it is not used after the Great
    Thanksgiving.*
    If the Penitence [[at §3 above]] comes at this point in the service it may be followed by

14. *THE PRAYER OF HUMBLE ACCESS*
We do not presume ... ⟦CF 3(a)⟧ ... he in us. Amen.

15. *THE PEACE*[65]
The presiding minister introduces the Peace with these or other similar words:
Christ is our peace.
He has reconciled us to God in one body by the cross.
We meet in his name and share his peace.
or
Jesus said, A new commandment ... that you also love one another. *John 13.34*
or
If you forgive others ... neither will your Father forgive your sins. *Matthew 6.14–15*
followed by:
The peace of the Lord be always with you
and also with you.

It is appropriate that the congregation share with one another a sign of peace.
It may be introduced with these words:
Let us offer one another a sign of peace.

Celebrating at the Lord's Table

16. *The table may be prepared by a deacon or lay people.*
The gifts of money may be brought forward and presented.

17. *AT THE PREPARATION OF THE TABLE*
The bread and wine shall be placed on the table for the communion if this has not already
been done, and one of the following may be said:
Be present, be present, ... ⟦CF4(c)⟧ ... of bread. **Amen.**

Wise and gracious God,
you spread a table before us;
nourish your people with the word of life,
and the bread of heaven. **Amen.**

How can I repay the Lord
for all the benefits he has given to me?
I will lift up the cup of salvation
and call upon the name of the Lord.
I will fulfil my vows to the Lord
in the presence of all his people.   *Psalm 116.12–14*

Lord, yours is the greatness
and the power and the glory
and the victory and the majesty;
for all things come from you
and of your own we give you.

18. *THE TAKING OF THE BREAD AND WINE*
Stand
The bishop or priest who presides takes the bread and wine and may say
Christ our passover has been sacrificed for us
therefore let us celebrate the feast.

---

65 ⟦This section comes, unusually, within the intercessions, rather than as part of the ministry of the sacrament.⟧

19. THE GREAT THANKSGIVING

One of the following Eucharistic Prayers is said by the presiding minister:

Prayer 1

The Lord is here . . . ⟦ELLC 6 and CF 5⟧
. . . **our thanks and praise.**

Father, almighty and everliving God,
at all times and in all places
it is right to give you thanks and praise

*When there is a Proper Preface it follows here
(pages . . .)*

And so with all your people,
with angels and archangels,
and with all the company of heaven;
we proclaim your great and glorious name,
for ever praising you and saying:
**Holy, holy . . . ⟦ELLC 7⟧ . . . in the highest!
Blessed is . . . ⟦ELLC 8⟧ . . . in the highest!**

Blessed are you, Father,
the creator and sustainer of all things;
you made us in your own image,
male and female you created us;
even when we turned away from you,
you never ceased to care for us,
but in your love and mercy you freed us
    from the slavery of sin,
giving your only begotten Son to become
    man
and suffer death on the cross to redeem us:
he made there the one complete and all-
    sufficient sacrifice
for the sins of the whole world:
he instituted,
and in his holy Gospel commanded us to
    continue,
a perpetual memory of his precious death
until he comes again.

On the night that he was betrayed he took
    bread;
and when he had given thanks to you, he
    broke it,

and gave it to his disciples, saying, Take,
    eat,
this is my body which is given for you.
Do this in remembrance of me.

In the same way, after supper he took the
    cup;
and when he had given thanks to you,
he gave it to them, saying, Drink this, all
    of you,
for this is my blood of the new covenant
which is shed for you and for many
for the forgiveness of sins.
Do this, as often as you drink it,
in remembrance of me.

Therefore, Father, with this bread and this
    cup
we do as Christ your Son commanded:
**we remember his passion and death,
we celebrate his resurrection and
    ascension,
and we look for the coming of his kingdom.**

Accept through him, our great high priest,
this our sacrifice of praise and
    thanksgiving;
and as we eat and drink these holy gifts,
grant by the power of the life-giving Spirit
that we may be made one in your holy
    Church
and partakers of the body and blood of
    your Son,
that he may dwell in us and we in him:

Through the same Jesus Christ our Lord,
by whom, and with whom, and in whom,
in the unity of the Holy Spirit,
**all honour and glory are yours, Almighty
    Father,
for ever and ever. Amen.**

⟦NB: This prayer repeats §24a of **Ire2** (§20 of **Aus5**) in **LAL**, with the same seasonal prefaces at the same places, but with the acclamations (CF 6(a)) moved one paragraph lower down⟧

The Lord is here . . . ⟦ELLC 6 and CF 5⟧
   . . . **our thanks and praise.**

All glory and honour, thanks and praise
be given to you at all times and in all
   places,
Lord, holy Father, true and living God,
through Jesus Christ our Lord.

For he is your eternal Word
through whom you have created all things
from the beginning
and formed us in your own image.

In your great love you gave him
to be made man for us and to share our
   common life.

In obedience to your will
your Son our Saviour offered himself as a
   perfect sacrifice,
and died on the cross for our redemption.
Through him you have freed us from the
   slavery of sin
and reconciled us to yourself, our God and
   Father.

For he is our great high priest
whom you raised from death
and exalted to your right hand on high
where he ever lives to intercede for us.

Through him you have sent upon us
your holy and life-giving Spirit
and made us a royal priesthood
called to serve you for ever.

Therefore with angels and archangels
and with all the company of heaven
we proclaim your great and glorious name,
for ever praising you and saying:
Holy, holy . . . ⟦ELLC 7⟧ . . . **in the highest.**

Merciful Father, we thank you
for these gifts of your creation, this bread
   and this wine,
and we pray that we who eat and drink
   them

in the fellowship of the Holy Spirit
in obedience to our Saviour Christ
in remembrance of his death and passion
may be partakers of his body and his
   blood,

who on the night he was betrayed took
   bread;
and when he had given you thanks
he broke it, and gave it to his disciples,
   saying,
Take, eat. This is my body which is given
   for you;
Do this in remembrance of me.
After supper, he took the cup,
and again giving you thanks
he gave it to his disciples, saying;
Drink from this, all of you.
This is my blood of the new covenant
which is shed for you and for many
for the forgiveness of sins.
Do this, as often as you drink it, in
   remembrance of me.

Father, with this bread and this cup,
we do as our Saviour has commanded:
we celebrate the redemption he has won
   for us;
we proclaim his perfect sacrifice
made once for all upon the cross,
his mighty resurrection and glorious
   ascension;
and we look for his coming
to fulfil all things according to your will.
Christ has . . . ⟦CF 6(a)⟧ . . . **come again.**

Renew us by your Holy Spirit,
unite us in the body of your Son,
and bring us with all your people
into the joy of your eternal kingdom;
through Jesus Christ our Lord,
with whom and in whom,
by the power of the Holy Spirit,
we worship you, Father almighty,
in songs of never-ending praise:
Blessing . . . ⟦CF 7⟧ . . . **are yours for ever
   and ever. Amen.**

The Lord is here . . . [ELLC 6 and CF 5]
. . . **our thanks and praise.**

Father, Lord of all creation;
we praise you for your goodness and your
love.
When we turned away you did not reject
us.
You came to meet us in your Son,
welcomed us as your children
and prepared a table where we might feast
with you.

In Christ you shared our life
that we might live in him and he in us.
**He opened wide his arms upon the cross
and, with love stronger than death,
he made the perfect sacrifice for sin.**

Lord Jesus Christ, our redeemer,
on the night before you died
you came to table with your friends.
Taking bread, you gave thanks, broke it
and gave it to them saying:
Take, eat; this is my body which is given
for you;
Do this in remembrance of me.
**Lord Jesus, we bless you:
you are the bread of life.**

At the end of supper
you took the cup of wine, gave thanks,
and said:

Drink this, all of you; this is my blood of
the new covenant
which is shed for you and for many for the
forgiveness of sins;
do this in remembrance of me.
**Lord Jesus, we bless you:
you are the true vine.**

Praise to you, Lord Jesus . . . [CF 6(b)] . . .
come in glory.

Holy Spirit, giver of life,
come upon us now;
may this bread and wine be to us
the body and blood of our Saviour Jesus
Christ.
**As we eat and drink these holy gifts,
make us, who know our need of grace,
one in Christ, our risen Lord.**

Father, Son and Holy Spirit, Blessed
Trinity:
with your whole church throughout the
world
we offer you this sacrifice of thanks and
praise
and lift our voice to join the song of
heaven,
for ever praising you and saying:
Holy, holy . . . [ELLC 7] . . . in the highest.

Thanks be to you, our God, for your gift
beyond words.
Amen. Amen. Amen.

20. *THE LORD'S PRAYER*
As our Saviour Christ has taught us, so we pray
Our Father in heaven . . . [ELLC 1] . . . for ever. Amen.
Save us from the time of trial and] Lead us not into temptation but
or
As our Saviour Christ has taught us, we are bold to say
Our Father, who art . . . [modified traditional text] . . . and ever. Amen.

21. *THE BREAKING OF THE BREAD*
    *The presiding minister (who may be assisted by the deacon) breaks the consecrated bread
    in preparation for the Communion.*
    The bread which . . . ⟦CF 8(a)⟧ . . . **for we all share in the one bread.**
        Though we are many, we] We being many

22. *THE COMMUNION*
    Draw near ⟦CF 9(a)⟧ . . . with thanksgiving.
        Eat and drink in remembrance] Remember
    or
    The gifts of God for the people of God, **Jesus** . . . ⟦CF 9(c)⟧ . . . **the glory of God the
      Father.**
    or
    Jesus Christ is the Lamb of God who has taken away . . . ⟦CF 9(b)⟧ . . . **I shall be
      healed.**
        Blessed] Happy

    The presiding minister and people receive communion.
    The minister who gives the bread and wine says
    The body of our Lord Jesus Christ . . . ⟦CF 10(a)⟧ . . . with thanksgiving.
        everlasting] eternal
    The blood of our Lord Jesus Christ . . . ⟦CF 10(b)⟧ . . . be thankful.
        everlasting] eternal
    or
    The body of Christ keep you in eternal life.
    The blood of Christ keep you in eternal life.
    or
    The body of Christ given for you.
    The blood of Christ shed for you.
    and the communicant replies **Amen.**

    *The following anthem may be sung after the Breaking of the Bread or during the
    Communion:*
    Jesus, Lamb of God . . . ⟦ELLC 9(a)⟧ . . . **grant us peace.**
    or
    Lamb of God, you take away . . . ⟦ELLC 9(b)⟧ . . . **grant us peace.**

    Other hymns or anthems may be sung.

23. *THE GREAT SILENCE*
    *When all have received communion, the presiding minister, other ministers and people
    keep silence for reflection.*

Going out as God's People

24. *A hymn may be sung here or before the Dismissal.*

25. *PRAYER AFTER COMMUNION*
    The appropriate Post Communion Prayer (pages . . .), or the following may be said:
    Father of all . . . ⟦CF 11(b)⟧ . . . Christ our Lord. **Amen.**

26. **Almighty God** . . . ⟦CF 11(a)⟧ . . . **praise and glory. Amen.**
        with the body] with the spiritual food of the body

27. **DISMISSAL**

The presiding minister may say the seasonal blessing, or another suitable blessing, or
The peace of God . . . ⟦CF 12(a)⟧ . . . Jesus Christ our Lord;
ending:
and the blessing . . . ⟦CF 12(a)⟧ . . . be with you and remain with you always. **Amen.**

A minister says
Go in peace . . . ⟦CF 12(b)⟧ . . . **name of Christ. Amen.**

From Easter Day to Pentecost
Go in the peace of the Risen Christ. Alleluia! Alleluia!
Thanks be to God. Alleluia! Alleluia!

28. *Appendix*

A. *COMMANDMENTS AND BEATITUDES* ⟦texts with responses⟧

B. *SEASONAL VARIATIONS* ⟦Penitential Kyries, Introduction to the Peace, Preface and Blessing, for Advent, Christmas, Epiphany, Lent, Passiontide and Holy Week, Easter, Ascension, Pentecost, Trinity Sunday, Transfiguration and some Saints Days⟧

C. *FORMS OF INTERCESSION*

D. *WHEN THE CONSECRATED ELEMENTS ARE INSUFFICIENT*
If either of the consecrated elements is insufficient, the presiding minister adds further bread or wine, silently, or using the following words:
Father,
having given thanks over the bread and cup
according to the institution of your Son Jesus Christ,
who said, Take, eat, this is my body
and/or
Drink this, this is my blood.

We pray that this bread/wine also may be to us his body/blood,
to be received in remembrance of him.

7. Spain and Portugal

The Spanish Reformed Episcopal Church (known as the I.E.R.E.) and the Portuguese Lusitanian Church are two fairly small non-provincial dioceses which originated from breakaways from the Roman Catholic Church in the wake of Vatican I. From the start they looked for episcopal ministrations from Anglican provinces, and from 1956 onwards have had a continuity of duly consecrated bishops themselves. In 1980 they became officially part of the Anglican Communion under the metropolitical care of the Archbishop of Canterbury. Each church had from its early days a nineteenth-century eucharistic rite in their respective vernaculars (**Span1** and **Port1**), and each provided a more modern rite in the twentieth century (**Span2** in 1984, **Port2** in 1969). The four rites – two nineteenth-century, two modern – were published in English alongside **LAL**, in Colin Buchanan (ed.), *The Liturgies of the Spanish and Portuguese Reformed Episcopal Churches* (Grove Liturgical Study 43, Grove Books, 1985) (**LS43**). The I.E.R.E has started trial use of a revised eucharistic text, but it has not reached its final form or been authorized.

In Portugal the Lusitanian Church adopted a new eucharistic liturgy in 1991, drawing heavily upon **EngA**. The rite was authorized in Portuguese; and it is an unofficial English-language text which is edited for inclusion here as **Port3**

THE MODERN EUCHARISTIC RITE OF THE LUSITANIAN CHURCH (Port3)

⟦The translation here is largely that of Bishop Fernando Soares, partly also of the editor assisted by Francis Zanger. The numbering and lining here are editorial⟧

⟦*Gathering*⟧

1. *A hymn may be sung*

2. *The Priest and people greet one another*
   The grace of our Lord Jesus Christ, the love of the Father and the fellowship of the Holy Spirit be always with you.
   Blessed be God
   who gathered us in the love of Christ.

   Holy God . . . ⟦Trisagion⟧ . . . **Have mercy upon us.**

3. *COLLECT FOR PURITY*
   Almighty God, to whom . . . ⟦CF 1⟧ . . . **Christ our Lord. Amen.**

4. *PENITENCE*
   ⟦Summary of the Law, invitation to confession, confession, absolution (CF 2), all as in **EngA**⟧

5. *THE COLLECT*
   Let us pray

The Ministry of Word

6. ⟦Readings from New Testament and the Gospel, with proclamation and responses⟧

7. *Homily*

8. *Deacon:* Let us proclaim the faith once delivered to the saints
   We believe in one God . . . ⟦ELLC 5⟧ . . . world to come. Amen.
   was incarnate of . . . fully human] **by the power of the Holy Spirit, he became incarnate of the
   Virgin Mary, and was made man**
   [and the Son]] OMIT BRACKETS

The Intercession

9. ⟦A responsive form, based on **EngA**⟧

Eucharistic Liturgy

10. *THE PEACE*
    Christ is our peace.
    He has reconciled us to God in one body by the cross.
    We meet in his name and share his peace.

    The peace of the Lord be always with you.
    The love of Christ has united us.

    Let us offer one another a sign of peace.

11. *The offerings of the people may be collected while the following* CANTICLE *may be sung*
    **Yours, Lord, is the greatness, the power,
    the glory, the splendour, and the majesty;
    for everything in heaven and on earth is yours.
    All things come from you,
    and of your own do we give you.**

12. *THE TAKING OF THE BREAD AND WINE*
    Blessed be you, Lord God of the universe,
    for the bread and wine which we receive from your goodness,
    fruits of the earth and the work of women and men which we are presenting you:
    it will become for us the Bread of Life and the Wine of Salvation.
    Blessed be God for ever.

13. *THE THANKSGIVING*
    The Lord is here. **His Spirit is with us** . . . ⟦CF 6⟧ . . . **him thanks and praise.**
    '1 EUCHARISTIC PRAYER'
    It is indeed right . . . ⟦As the Second Eucharistic Prayer in **EngA**⟧ . . . living temple to
    your glory.
    **Through Jesus Christ our Lord,
    by whom, and with whom, and in whom,
    in the unity of the Holy Spirit,
    all honour and glory be yours, almighty Father,
    now and for ever. Amen.**
    Let us proclaim the mystery of faith] This is the mystery of faith

II EUCHARISTIC PRAYER

Father, it is our duty and our salvation to
   give you thanks
always and everywhere,
through your well-loved Son, Jesus Christ.

He is your Word, through whom you have
   made the universe,
and he is the Saviour, whom you sent to
   redeem us.
By the power of the Holy Spirit,
he became incarnate and was born of the
   Virgin Mary.
For love of us, he stretched out his arms
   upon the cross,
put an end to death and revealed the
   resurrection.
Thus, he fulfilled your will,
and won for you a holy people.
A Proper Preface follows

Therefore we join our voice with the
   angels and the saints,
and proclaim your glory as we sing
Holy, holy . . . ⟦ELLC 7⟧ . . . in the highest.
   are full of] proclaim
Blessed is . . . ⟦ELLC 8⟧ . . . in the highest.

The congregation may kneel or remain standing.

Lord, you are holy indeed;
and are the fount of all holiness.
Sanctify these gifts, pouring over them
   your Spirit,
that they will be changed for us
into the Body and Blood of our Lord Jesus
   Christ.

Before he was handed over to death,
a death he voluntarily accepted,
Jesus took the bread, gave thanks to you,
   broke it, and gave it to his disciples,
   saying:
Take and eat;
this is my body which is given for you.
Do this in remembrance of me.

In the same way, at the end of supper,
he took the cup,
gave you thanks and delivered it to his
   disciples, saying:
Take this and drink of it, all of you;
this is the cup of my blood,
the blood of a new and eternal covenant,

shed for you and for all people.
for the forgiveness of sins;
do this as often as you drink it,
in remembrance of me.

Let us proclaim the mystery of faith
Christ has . . . ⟦CF 6(a)⟧ . . . come again.
Or
Lord, by your cross . . . ⟦CF 6(b)⟧ . . . of the
   world.

Now we celebrate the memorial of his
   death and resurrection,
as we offer to you, Father, the bread of life
   and the cup of salvation.
We give you thanks
that you have admitted us to your presence
   and that we may serve you.

Grant that we, who share in the body and
   blood of Christ,
may be joined together in unity by the
   Holy Spirit.
Watch over, Lord, your Church dispersed
   through all the world.
Make us grow in love,
all united to our Bishop N. and with the
   clergy.
Remember our brothers and sisters
who have entered into rest in the hope of
   resurrection;
that they, and all who have left this world,
may rejoice in the light of your presence.

Have mercy, Lord, upon us all;
make us worthy to share in life eternal,
with Mary, the Virgin mother of God
   incarnate,
with the apostles, and with all the saints
   and martyrs
who through the ages have been obedient
   to your will.
Grant us the grace, in union with them,
to adore you and give you glory for ever,
through your Son, Jesus Christ, our Lord.
Through Christ, with Christ and in Christ,
in the unity of the Holy Spirit,
to you be given, God the almighty Father,
all honour and all glory,
now and for ever. Amen.

III EUCHARISTIC PRAYER

Truly it is our duty and our joy
to give you thanks, holy Father,
through Jesus Christ, your Son,
through him you have created us in your
    own image,
you have freed us from the power of sin
    and death,
and, through the gift of the Holy Spirit,
have formed us as a people for yourself.

Therefore, with the angels and saints,
we sing with joy:
Holy, holy . . . [[ELLC 7]] . . . in the highest.
    are full of] proclaim
Blessed is . . . [[ELLC 8]] . . . in the highest.

The congregation may kneel or remain standing.

Father, accept our praises,
through your Son, our Lord Jesus Christ,
and grant that, by the power of the Holy
    Spirit,
these gifts of bread and wine
may become for us his Body and his
    Blood.

Jesus, in the same night in which he was
    betrayed,
took the bread, gave thanks to you, broke
    it,
and gave it to his disciples, saying:
Take and eat;
this is my body which is given for you;
do this in remembrance of me.

In the same way, at the end of supper,
he took the cup,

he gave you thanks and delivered it to his
    disciples, saying:
Take this and drink of it, all of you;
this is the cup of my blood,
the blood of a new and eternal covenant,
shed for you and for all people
for the forgiveness of sins;
do this as often as you drink it,
in remembrance of me.

This is the mystery of faith
Christ has . . . [[CF 6(a)]] . . . come again.

Therefore, Father,
remembering his saving death,
proclaiming his resurrection and ascension,
and looking for his return in glory,
we celebrate, with this bread and this cup,
his one perfect sacrifice.

Accept, through Jesus Christ,
this our sacrifice of thanksgiving and
    praise;
and grant that we, in eating this bread and
    drinking this cup,
may be renewed by your Spirit
and may each conform ourselves more to
    his likeness.

Through Christ, with Christ and in Christ,
in the unity of the Holy Spirit,
to you be given, God the almighty Father,
all honour and all glory,
now and for ever. Amen.

14. As our Saviour taught us, so we pray
    Our Father in heaven . . . ⟦ELLC 1⟧ . . . for ever. Amen.
        Save us from the time of trial and] Lead us not into temptation but

THE BREAKING OF THE BREAD
15. We break this bread . . . ⟦CF 8(a)⟧ . . . **in the one bread.**

16. **Lamb of God, you take away . . . ⟦ELLC 9(b)⟧ . . . grant us peace.**

17. *THE COMMUNION*
    Draw near with faith . . . ⟦CF 9(a)⟧ . . . with thanksgiving.
    We do not presume . . . ⟦CF 3(a)⟧ . . . he in us. Amen.
        our sinful bodies . . . and that] OMIT

18. *While the celebrants take communion the Congregation may sing the following HYMN*

After Communion

19. Let us pray
    Almighty God, we thank you . . . ⟦CF 11(a)⟧ . . . praise and glory. Amen.

THE DISMISSAL
20. *The Priest may say the BLESSING*
    The Spirit of truth lead you into all truth,
    give you grace to confess that Jesus Christ is Lord,
    and to proclaim the word and works of God;
    and the blessing of God,
    the Father, the Son, and the Holy Spirit,
    be among you, and remain with you always.
    Amen.

21. *The Deacon may dismiss the Congregation*
    Go in peace to love . . . ⟦CF 12(b)⟧ . . . **name of Christ. Amen.**

C. North America

8. The Anglican Church of Canada

In the Anglican Church of Canada, *The Book of Alternative Services* (*BAS*), the modern hardback worship book approved in principle by General Synod, and finally edited by the Worship and Doctrine Committee and authorized by the National Executive Committee, was published in 1985. It provided services 'alternative' to those in the 1962 BCP, the traditional, 1662-type, service book of the Church, the eucharistic rite in which was published in **LiE** as **Can**. The eucharistic text in the *BAS* was available in duplicated form just in time for its inclusion in **LAL** in 1985 as **Can4**, with the 1981 *Third Canadian Order*, **Can3**, shown by *apparatus*.

While the *BAS*, as a definitive hardback worship book, would clearly last for decades, the General Synod in 1995 called for the creation of 'eucharistic prayers reflecting a Reformed theological conscience and eucharistic prayers inclusive in language and images'.[66] The Faith, Worship and Ministry Committee took wide consultations and proposed three prayers to General Synod in 1998, specifically intended to meet these criteria, as alternatives to the prayers in **Can4**. In the light of the synodical debate small changes were made, initially by Synod itself and finally by the Committee. In 2001 the Committee published the texts (along with supplementary non-sacramental liturgical material) in *Eucharistic Prayers, Services of the Word, and Night Prayer* (ABC, Toronto), and in this publication printed the three eucharistic prayers within the whole text of **Can4** (save its eucharistic prayers), in order that the new prayers might be used within a whole rite with ease from a single booklet.

---

66 This is a quotation from the Introduction to *Eucharistic Prayers, Services of the Word, and Night Prayer* (ABC, Toronto, 2001), the report that resulted from the Synod initiative reported above.

EUCHARISTIC PRAYERS SUPPLEMENTARY TO *THE BOOK OF ALTERNATIVE SERVICES* OF THE ANGLICAN CHURCH IN CANADA (Can5)

⟦In each prayer the lining is original.⟧

Supplementary Eucharistic Prayer 1 (S1)

The Lord be . . . ⟦ELLC 6⟧ . . . **and praise.**

⟦Alternatives to lines 1,4,5 and 6:

May God be with you.

We lift them up to God.
Let us give thanks to God our Creator.
It is right to offer thanks and praise.⟧

Holy God, Lover of creation,
we give you thanks and praise
for in the ocean of your steadfast love you
　　bear us
and place the song of your Spirit in our
　　hearts.

When we turn from your love and defile
　　the earth,
You do not abandon us.
Your Spirit speaks through Huldah and
　　Micah,
through prophets, sages, and saints in
　　every age,
to confront our sin
and reveal the vision of your new creation.

Joining in the song of the universe
we proclaim your glory saying (singing):
Holy, holy . . . ⟦ELLC 7⟧ . . . **in the highest.**
Blessed is the One . . . ⟦ELLC 8⟧ . . . **in the
　　highest.**

Gracious God,
in the fullness of time you sent Jesus the
　　Christ
to share our fragile humanity.
Through Jesus' life, death, and resurrection
you open the path from brokenness to
　　health,
from fear to trust, from pride and conceit
to reverence for you.

Rejected by a world
that could not bear the Gospel of life,
Jesus knew death was near.

His head anointed for burial
by an unknown woman,
Jesus gathered together those who loved
　　him.
He took bread, gave thanks to you, broke
　　it
and gave it to his friends,
saying, 'Take and eat:
this is my body which is given for you.
Do this for the remembrance of me.'

After supper, Jesus took the cup of wine,
gave you thanks,
and said 'Drink this all of you,
this is my blood of the new covenant
which is shed for you and for many.
Whenever you drink it,
do this for the remembrance of me.'
And now we gather at this table
in response to his commandment,
to share the bread and cup of Christ's
　　undying love,
and to proclaim our faith.
Christ has died . . . ⟦CF 6(a)⟧ . . . **come
　　again.**

Breathe your Holy Spirit,
the wisdom of the universe,
upon these gifts that we bring to you:
this bread, this cup,
ourselves, our souls and bodies,
that we may be signs of your love for all
　　the world
and ministers of your transforming
　　purpose.

Through Christ, with Christ, and in
　　Christ,
in the unity of the Holy Spirit,
all glory is yours, Creator of all,
and we bless your holy name for ever.
Amen.

Supplementary Eucharistic Prayer 2 (S2)

The Lord . . . [[CF 6]] . . . **thanks and praise.**

[[Alternatives to lines 1,4,5 and 6 as S1 opposite]]

Eternal God, Source of all being,
we give you thanks and praise
for your faithful love.
You call us into friendship
with you and one another
to be your holy people,
a sign of your presence in the world.

When those we trust betray us,
unfailingly you remain with us.
When we injure others,
you confront us in your love
and call us to the paths of righteousness.
You stand with the weak,
and those, broken and alone,
whom you have always welcomed home,
making the first last, and the last first.
Therefore we raise our voices
with angels and archangels,
forever praising you and saying (singing):
Holy, holy . . . [[ELLC 7]] . . . in the highest.
Blessed is the One . . . [[ELLC 8]] . . . in the
highest.

Blessed are you, O Holy One:
When Hagar was driven into the
  wilderness
you followed her and gave her hope.
When Joseph was sold into bondage,
you turned malice to your people's good.
When you called Israel out of slavery,
you brought them through the wilderness
into the promised land.
When your people were taken into exile
you wept with them by the river of
  Babylon
and carried them home.
Restore us, O God, let your face shine!

At the right time you sent your Anointed
  One
to stand with the poor,
the outcast, and the oppressed.
Jesus touched lepers, and the sick, and
  healed them.

He accepted water from a woman of
  Samaria
and offered her the water of new life.
Christ knew the desolation of the cross
and opened the way for all humanity
into the redemption of your reconciling
  love.

On the night he was betrayed,
Jesus, at supper with his friends,
took bread, gave you thanks, broke the
  bread,
gave it to them, and said, 'Take and eat:
this is my body which is given for you.
Do this for the remembrance of me.'

After supper he took the cup of wine,
and when he had given thanks,
he gave it to them,
and said, 'Drink this, all of you:
this is my blood of the new covenant
which is shed for you and for many
for the forgiveness of sins.
Whenever you drink it,
do this for the remembrance of me.'

Loving and Holy One,
recalling Christ's death and resurrection,
we offer you these gifts,
longing for the bread of tomorrow
and the wine of the age to come.
Therefore we proclaim our hope.
Dying you . . . [[CF 6(b)]] . . . come in glory.

Pour out your Spirit on these gifts
that through them you may sustain us
in our hunger for your peace.
We hold before you
all whose lives are marked by suffering,
our sisters and brothers.
When we are broken and cast aside,
embrace us in your love.
Restore us, O God, let your face shine!

Through Christ, with Christ, and in Christ
in the unity of the Holy Spirit,
all honour and glory are yours,
O source of all life,
now and forever.
Amen.

The Lord be . . . ⟦ELLC 6⟧ . . . **and praise.**

It is indeed right to thank you and praise
    you,
holy and gracious God,
creator of all things,
ruler of heaven and earth, sustainer of life,
for you are the source of all goodness,
rich in mercy and abounding in love;
you are faithful to your people in every
    generation,
and your word endures for ever.

Therefore with angels and archangels,
with the fellowship of saints
and the company of heaven,
we glorify your holy name,
evermore praising you and singing,
Holy, holy . . . ⟦ELLC 7⟧ . . . **in the highest.**
Blessed is . . . ⟦ELLC 8⟧ . . . **in the highest.**

We praise you, merciful Father,
not as we ought, but as we are able,
because in your tender love
you gave the world your only Son,
in order that the world might be saved
    through him.
He made you known by taking the form of
    a servant,
healing the sick, liberating the oppressed,
reaching out to the lost.

Betrayed, reviled, and nailed to the cross,
he confronted the power of sin
and disarmed it for ever.
In his offering of himself,
he became the perfect and sufficient
    sacrifice
for the sins of the whole world.
Redeemed by Christ,
we have been adopted as your children;
by your pardon
you have made us worthy to praise you.

On the night he was betrayed,
Jesus, at supper with his friends,

took bread, gave you thanks, broke the
    bread,
gave it to them, and said, 'Take and eat:
this is my body which is given for you.
Do this for the remembrance of me.'

After supper he took the cup of wine,
and when he had given thanks,
he gave it to them,
and said, 'Drink this all of you:
this is my blood of the new covenant
which is shed for you and for many
for the forgiveness of sins.
Whenever you drink it,
do this for the remembrance of me.'

In obedience to him and with grateful
    hearts
we approach your holy table,
remembering our Saviour's sacrifice,
and rejoicing in his victory.
Confident in his sovereign purpose,
we declare our faith.
Christ has . . . ⟦CF 6(a)⟧ . . . **come again.**

Send your Holy Spirit on us
that as we receive this bread and this cup
we may partake of the body and blood
of our Lord Jesus Christ,
and feed on him in our hearts
by faith with thanksgiving.

May we be renewed in his risen life,
filled with love,
and strengthened in our will to serve
    others;
and make of our lives, we pray,
a pure and holy sacrifice, acceptable to
    you,
knitting us together as one in your Son
    Jesus Christ,
to whom, with you and the Holy Spirit,
be all honour and glory, now and forever.
Amen.

The option **'Blessed is the One who comes in the name of the Lord'** *may be used if approved by the Ordinary.*

9 The Episcopal Church (The United States of America)

The 1979 BCP of the Episcopal Church in the USA contained three eucharistic rites, reproduced in **LAL** and coded as **Amer1-1**, **Amer2-2** and **Amer3-3**. The 1979 Book itself remains as the definitive liturgical provision of the Church. However, the General Convention of 1985 encouraged the Standing Liturgical Commission to begin work on both adapting **Amer2-2** and writing new alternative eucharistic rites. The 'adaptation' process did not prove viable, but proposals for two 'supplemental' eucharistic prayers were published in *Supplemental Liturgical Texts: Prayer Book Studies 30* (Church Hymnal Corporation, 1989). Debate on these texts led the committee to develop these two eucharistic prayers and to add a third, and to attach two further ones modelled on those provided in **Amer3-3** for the 1991 General Convention. The General Convention steered the third of the new prayers into oblivion, but the other proposals were then published in *Supplemental Liturgical Materials* with encouragement to give the 'materials' trial use. The 1994 General Convention encouraged further development. Thus in 1997 the Commission brought a large report to the General Convention, the Convention accepted the materials, and they were published as *Enriching Our Worship* (Church Publishing Inc., 1998). The introduction to the report points out that the supplemental eucharistic prayers may be used in the context of either **Amer2-2** or **Amer3-3**, but their use is subject to episcopal permission.

The presentation continues the format of the 1979 BCP, including the term 'Celebrant' for the president of the eucharist, the insistent use of 'forth', the lack of distinctive typeface for congregational parts (save for the capitalized bold '**AMEN**'at the end of each eucharistic prayer, and some use of italicized text to provide responses to versicles) and the detailed provision given prior to the narrative of institution for specific manual acts to be used within the narrative.[67]

---

67 The rubric, repeating that in **Amer2-2**, reads as follows: '*At the following words concerning the bread, the Celebrant is to hold it, or lay a hand upon it; and at the words concerning the cup, to hold or place a hand upon the cup and any other vessel containing wine to be consecrated.*' It occurs in this form in each of the five eucharistic prayers here, save the third (§14), where its omission may be accidental.

THE HOLY EUCHARIST IN THE EPISCOPAL CHURCH (USA)
ENRICHING OUR WORSHIP 1998 (Amer4)

[The rite is presented as a single order, though the materials can in fact be treated as separate resources to be used as alternatives within **Amer2-2** or **Amer3-3**. As far as the eucharistic prayers, the form of the rite is a presentation of simple headings, with a minimal provision under each heading to supplement what was presented in **Amer2-2** or **Amer3-3**. The numbering here is editorial. The lining is original.]

The Holy Eucharist

1. *OPENING ACCLAMATIONS*
    [Five alternatives of versicle and response, the Easter one as in **Amer2-2**]

2. *SONG OF PRAISE*
    [Reference to the rubric from **Amer2-2** re Gloria in Excelsis (ELLC 3) and to other canticles within *Enriching Worship* and the 1979 Book of Common Prayer.]

3. *SALUTATION*
    [The Salutation ('God be with you.' / '**And also with you.**') has a separate heading, but leads into the Collect.]

4. *COLLECT OF THE DAY*
    [10 optional collects are printed, and in 'low' seasons any of these may replace the Collect in the 1979 BCP.]

5. *LESSONS*
    [Alternative announcements to the readings are provided.]

6. *GOSPEL ANNOUNCEMENT*
    The Holy Gospel of our Saviour Jesus Christ according to _____

7. *NICENE CREED*
    We believe in one God . . . [ELLC 5] . . . **world to come. Amen.**

8. *PRAYERS OF THE PEOPLE*
    This book contains no forms for the Prayers of the People. [Instead it provides some coaching as to how to use the existing provision in **Amer2-2**, and some models as to how to vary from it.]

9. *CONFESSION OF SIN*
    [A new form of corporate confession]

10. *ABSOLUTION*
    [Absolution varied by two words from that in **Amer2-2**]

11. *THE PEACE*
    The peace of Christ be always with you.
    And also with you.

The Lord be . . . ⟦ELLC 6⟧ . . . **and praise.**

It is truly right, and good and joyful,
to give you thanks, all-holy God,
source of life and fountain of mercy.

The following Preface may be used at any time.
You have filled us and all creation with
    your blessing
and fed us with your constant love;
you have redeemed us in Jesus Christ
and knit us into one body.
Through your Spirit you replenish us
and call us to fullness of life.
In place of the preceding, a Proper Preface from
the Book of Common Prayer may be used.

Therefore, joining with Angels and
    Archangels
and with the faithful of every generation,
we lift our voices with all creation as we
    sing (say):
Holy, holy . . . ⟦ELLC 7⟧ . . . **in the highest.**
Blessed is the one who . . . ⟦ELLC 8⟧ . . . **in**
    the highest.

Blessed are you, gracious God,
creator of the universe and giver of life.
You formed us in your own image
and called us to dwell in your infinite love.
You gave the world into our care
that we might be your faithful stewards
and show forth your bountiful grace.

But we failed to honour your image
in one another and in ourselves;
we would not see your goodness in the
    world around us;
and so we violated your creation,
abused one another,
and rejected your love.
Yet you never ceased to care for us,
and prepared the way of salvation for all
    people.

Through Abraham and Sarah
you called us into covenant with you.
You delivered us from slavery,
sustained us in the wilderness,
and raised up prophets
to renew your promise of salvation.
Then, in the fullness of time,
you sent your eternal Word,

made mortal flesh in Jesus.
Born into the human family,
and dwelling among us,
he revealed your glory.
Giving himself freely to death on the cross,
he triumphed over evil,
opening the way of freedom and life.

⟦Rubric – see footnote 67 on page 95⟧

On the night before he died for us,
our Saviour Jesus Christ took bread,
and when he had given thanks to you,
he broke it, and gave it to his friends, and
    said:
'Take, eat:
This is my Body which is given for you.
Do this for the remembrance of me.'
As supper was ending, Jesus took the cup
    of wine,
and when he had given thanks,
he gave it to them, and said:
'Drink this, all of you:
This is my Blood of the new Covenant,
which is poured out for you and for all
for the forgiveness of sins.
Whenever you drink it,
do this for the remembrance of me.'

Therefore we proclaim . . . ⟦CF 6(a)⟧ . . .
    come again.

Remembering his death and resurrection,
we now present to you from your creation
this bread and this wine.
By your Holy Spirit may they be for us
the Body and Blood of our Saviour Jesus
    Christ.
Grant that we who share these gifts
may be filled with the Holy Spirit
and live as Christ's Body in the world.
Bring us into the everlasting heritage
of your daughters and sons,
that with [_____ and] all your saints,
past, present, and yet to come,
we may praise your Name for ever.

Through Christ and with Christ and in
    Christ,
in the unity of the Holy Spirit,
to you be honour, glory and praise,
for ever and ever. **AMEN.**

The Lord be . . . ⟦ELLC 6⟧ . . . **and praise.**

We praise you and we bless you, holy and
  gracious God,
source of life abundant.
From before time you made ready the
  creation.
Your Spirit moved over the deep
and brought all things into being:
sun, moon, and stars;
earth, winds, and waters;
and every living thing.
You made us in your image,
and taught us to walk in your ways.
But we rebelled against you, and wandered
  far away;
and yet, as a mother cares for her children,
you would not forget us.
Time and again you called us
to live in the fullness of your love.

And so this day we join with Saints and
  Angels
in the chorus of praise that rings through
  eternity,
lifting our voices to magnify you as we
  sing (say):
Holy, holy . . . ⟦ELLC 7⟧ . . . **in the highest.**
Blessed is the one . . . ⟦ELLC 8⟧ . . . **in the
  highest.**

Glory and honour and praise to you, holy
  and living God.
To deliver us from the power of sin and
  death
and to reveal the riches of your grace,
you looked with favour upon Mary, your
  willing servant,
that she might conceive and bear a son,
Jesus the holy child of God.
Living among us, Jesus loved us.
He broke bread with outcasts and sinners,
healed the sick, and proclaimed good news
  to the poor.
He yearned to draw all the world to
  himself
yet we were heedless of his call to walk in
  love.
Then, the time came for him to complete
  upon the cross

the sacrifice of his life,
and to be glorified by you.

⟦Rubric – see footnote 67 on page 95⟧

On the night before he died for us,
Jesus was at table with his friends.
He took bread, gave thanks to you,
broke it, and gave it to them, and said:
'Take, eat:
This is my Body, which is given for you.
Do this for the remembrance of me.'
As supper was ending, Jesus took the cup
  of wine.
Again, he gave thanks to you,
gave it to them, and said:
'Drink this, all of you:
This is my Blood of the new Covenant,
which is poured out for you and for all
for the forgiveness of sins.
Whenever you drink it,
do this for the remembrance of me.'

Now gathered at your table, O God of all
  creation,
and remembering Christ, crucified and
  risen,
who was and is and is to come,
we offer you our gifts of bread and wine,
and ourselves, a living sacrifice.

Pour out your Spirit upon these gifts
that they may be the Body and Blood of
  Christ.
Breathe your Spirit over the whole earth
and make us your new creation,
the Body of Christ given for the world you
  have made.

In the fullness of time bring us
with [_____ and] all your saints,
from every tribe and language and people
  and nation,
to feast at the banquet prepared
from the foundation of the world.

Through Christ and with Christ and in
  Christ,
in the unity of the Holy Spirit,
to you be honour, glory, and praise,
for ever and ever. **AMEN.**

The Lord be . . . [ELLC 6] . . . **and praise.**

All thanks and praise
are yours at all times and in all places,
our true and loving God;
through Jesus Christ, your eternal Word,
the Wisdom from on high by whom you
    created all things.
You laid the foundations of the world
and enclosed the sea when it burst from
    the womb;
You brought forth all creatures of the
    earth
and gave breath to humankind.

Wondrous are you, Holy One of Blessing,
all you create is a sign of hope for our
    journey;
And so as the morning stars sing your
    praises
we join with the heavenly beings and all
    creation
as we shout with joy:
Holy, holy . . . [ELLC 7] . . . **in the highest.**
Blessed is the one . . . [ELLC 8] . . . **in the**
    highest.

[In two columns: one has '**he who**' not 'the one
who'.]

Glory and honour are yours, Creator of
    all,
your Word has never been silent;
you called a people to yourself, as a light
    to the nations,
you delivered them from bondage
and led them to a land of promise.
Of your grace, you gave Jesus
to be human, to share our life,
to proclaim the coming of your holy reign
and give himself for us, a fragrant offering.

Through Jesus Christ our Redeemer,
you have freed us from sin,
brought us into your life,
reconciled us to you,
and restored us to the glory you intend for
    us.

We thank you that on the night before he
    died for us

Jesus took bread,
and when he had given thanks to you, he
    broke it,
gave it to his friends and said:
'Take, eat, this is my Body, broken for
    you.
Do this for the remembrance of me.'

After supper Jesus took the cup of wine,
said the blessing, gave it to his friends and
    said:
'Drink this, all of you:
this cup is the new Covenant in my Blood,
poured out for you and for all
for the forgiveness of sin.
Do this for the remembrance of me.'

And so, remembering all that was done
    for us:
the cross, the tomb, the resurrection and
    ascension,
longing for Christ's coming in glory,
and presenting to you these gifts
your earth has formed and human hands
    have made,
we acclaim you, O Christ:
Dying, you . . . [CF 6(b)] . . . **Christ Jesus,**
    come in glory!

Send your Holy Spirit upon us
and upon these gifts of bread and wine
that they may be to us
the Body and Blood of your Christ.
Grant that we, burning with your Spirit's
    power,
may be a people of hope, justice and love.

Giver of Life, draw us together in the Body
    of Christ,
and in the fullness of time gather us
with [blessed _____, and] all your people
into the joy of our true eternal home.

Through Christ and with Christ and in
    Christ,
by the inspiration of your Holy Spirit,
we worship you our God and Creator
in voices of unending praise.
Blessed are you now and for ever. AMEN.

15. FORMS FOR THE EUCHARISTIC PRAYER

*For use with the Order for Celebrating the Holy Eucharist ⟦i.e. **Amer3-3**⟧ on pages . . . of the Book of Common Prayer. In keeping with the rubrics governing the use of the Order, these forms are not intended for use at the principal Sunday or weekly celebration of a congregation.*

Form A

The Lord be . . . ⟦ELLC 6⟧ . . . **and praise.**

The Celebrant gives thanks to God for the created order, and for God's self-revelation to the human race in history;

Recalls before God, when appropriate, the particular occasion being celebrated;

If desired, incorporates or adapts the Proper Preface of the Day.

If the Sanctus is to be included, it is introduced with these or similar words

And so we join the saints and angels in proclaiming your glory, as we sing (say),
Holy, holy . . . ⟦ELLC 7⟧ . . . in the highest.
Blessed is the one . . . ⟦ELLC 8⟧ . . . in the highest.

The Celebrant now praises God for the salvation of the world through Jesus Christ.

And so, we offer you these gifts.
Sanctify them by your Holy Spirit
to be for your people the Body and Blood of Christ.

⟦Rubric – see footnote 67 on page 95⟧
On the night before he died for us,
our Saviour Jesus Christ took bread,
and when he had given thanks to you,
he broke it, and gave it to his friends, and said:
'Take, eat:
This is my Body which is given for you.
Do this for the remembrance of me.'

As supper was ending, Jesus took the cup of wine,
and when he had given thanks,
he gave it to them, and said:
'Drink this, all of you:
This is my blood of the new Covenant,
Which is poured out for you and for all for the forgiveness of sins.
Whenever you drink it,
do this for the remembrance of me.'

The Celebrant may then introduce, with suitable words, a memorial acclamation by the people.

We now celebrate, O God, the memorial of Christ our Saviour.
By means of this holy bread and cup,
we show forth the sacrifice of Christ's death,
and proclaim the resurrection,
until Christ comes in glory.

Gather us by this Holy Communion
into one body in the Risen One,
and make us a living sacrifice of praise.
Through Christ and with Christ and in Christ,
in the unity of the Holy Spirit,
to you be honour, glory, and praise,
for ever and ever. **AMEN.**

[This Form is identical to Form A until the end of the sanctus and benedictus qui venit. It omits the next three lines in Form A and goes straight from 'The celebrant now praises . . .' to the rubric before the narrative of institution. It then continues:]

. . . the remembrance of me.'

The Celebrant may then introduce, with suitable words, a memorial acclamation by the people.

Remembering now the suffering and death
and proclaiming the resurrection and
  ascension
of Jesus our Redeemer,
we bring before you these gifts.

Sanctify them by your Holy Spirit
to be for your people the Body and Blood
  of Christ.

The Celebrant then prays that all may receive the benefits of Christ's work, and the renewal of the Holy Spirit.

The Prayer concludes with these or similar words

Through Christ and with Christ and in
  Christ,
in the unity of the Holy Spirit,
to you be honour, glory and praise,
for ever and ever. **AMEN.**

16. *FRACTION ANTHEMS*

   Any of the following, or a Fraction Anthem from the Hymnal 1982, S167–S172, may be said or sung in place of the anthem 'Christ our Passover' (BCP, p. . . . [Amer 2–2, no. 68]).
   We break . . . [CF 8(a)] . . . for we all share in the one bread.
   Though we are many, we] **We who are many are**

   God of promise, you have prepared a banquet for us.
   Happy are those who are called to the Supper of the Lamb.

   This is the true bread which comes down from heaven and gives life to the world.
   Whoever eats this bread will live for ever.

   Lamb of God . . . [ELLC 9(b)] . . . grant us peace.
   sin] sins THREE TIMES

17. *POSTCOMMUNION PRAYER*

God of abundance,
you have fed us
with the bread of life and cup of salvation;
you have united us
with Christ and with one another;
and you have made us one
with all your people in heaven and on
  earth.
Now send us forth
in the power of your Spirit
that we may proclaim your redeeming love
  to the world
and continue for ever
in the risen life of Christ our Saviour.
  Amen.

Or
Loving God,
we give you thanks
for restoring us in your image
and nourishing us with spiritual food
in the Sacrament of Christ's Body and
  Blood.
Now send us forth
a people, forgiven, healed, renewed;
that we may proclaim your love to the
  world
and continue in the risen life of our Christ
  our Saviour. Amen.

18. *BLESSINGS*
   [Five innovative optional blessings follow.]

[*Enriching our Worship* continues with eight pages of Notes and nine of musical settings for the texts.]

D. Central and South America

10. The Anglican Churches of Mexico and of the Central American Region

Mexican Anglicanism began in the nineteenth century through an independent growth of Christians separating from the Church of Rome. In 1875 they entered into intercommunion with the Protestant Episcopal Church in the USA, and American bishops conducted confirmations and ordained clergy for the Church. It became in 1893 'The Mexican Episcopal Church' and it adopted a Mexican Prayer Book, called *The Book of Provisional Offices*, in 1894. Its chief source was an earlier Spanish translation of the American 1789 BCP, but it was also influenced by the eucharistic rite of the Spanish Reformed Episcopal Church (**Span1**), a church which had had a somewhat parallel history to the Mexican Episcopal Church. However, the American Church established a 'missionary district' in Mexico in 1904, nominally only to oversee English-speaking congregations; and the Mexican Episcopal Church, which had sought in vain for decades to have a duly consecrated bishop, asked to join the missionary district. It was canonically integrated in 1906 and, becoming part of PECUSA, it had to relinquish *The Book of Provisional Offices* and adopt the American 1892 services, which had apparently been very poorly translated. In due course the 1928 rite (**Amer**) was also initially rendered poorly into Spanish, until a new translation was made in 1949. In more recent times the 1979 BCP, containing **Amer1-1**, **Amer2-2** and **Amer3-3**, was published in a definitive Spanish text from the start, and consequently took its place in the Mexican dioceses. By 1989 there were five dioceses, and in 1995 they were released from the American Church to form a separate province of the Anglican Communion. The 1979 American eucharistic rites have remained in use, but they are viewed as not only adaptable, but also as in some sense provisional, until the province can devise its own, perhaps more visibly inculturated and Mexican, forms of worship.

The Anglican Church of the Central American Region (IARCA) was formed from Province IX of the Episcopal Church (USA), and gained its autonomy in 1998. It is almost entirely Spanish-speaking and continues to use **Amer1-1**, **Amer2-2** and **Amer3-3** from the Spanish version of the Episcopal Church's 1979 BCP.

The extra-provincial diocese of Cuba has a diocesan rite, composed in Spanish, derived in part from **Amer2-2** and authorized in 1989.

11. The Province of the West Indies

The Church in the Province of the West Indies had a soft-back collection of *Revised Services* in use from 1980. The services in it did not replace 1662, but were authorized for 'Trial Use'. The eucharistic rite in it was a descendant of the experimental rite which had been in use since 1959, **WInd**, which was published in **LiE**. The 1980 rite, which offered a choice of three eucharistic prayers and, of course, used a modern style of English, addressing God as 'you', was published as **WInd1** in **LAL**. Subsequently, the provincial authorities have worked to provide a complete new BCP, one to supersede 1662, and give a comprehensive set of services in a hardback book for the Province. The Book is dated St Andrew's Day 1995.

The eucharistic rite within the book, **WInd2**, offers more options than **WInd1**, but in content and style (and often actual wording) follows it closely.

THE EUCHARISTIC RITE IN *THE BOOK OF COMMON PRAYER* (1995) OF THE CHURCH IN THE PROVINCE OF THE WEST INDIES (WInd2)

⟦The numbering is editorial. The capitalization is original. The lining is original in eucharistic prayers A, B, C, and E, but is mostly editorial elsewhere.⟧

THE HOLY EUCHARIST

1. *CONCERNING THE CELEBRATION* ⟦General instructions for the celebration, including provision for distribution of communion from the reserved sacrament⟧

2. *THE PREPARATION* ⟦*psalm or hymn, opening sentences, responsive greeting, *corporate affirmation of reason for gathering (as **WInd1** § 4), *Collect for Purity (CF 1 with tiny changes), *Kyries, *Gloria in Excelsis (ELLC 3), and collect of the day⟧

3. *THE MINISTRY OF THE WORD* ⟦readings from Old Testament (or Apocrypha), New Testament, and Gospels, with *psalms, hymns or canticles between, sermon, *Nicene Creed (retaining its **WInd1** form and without *Filioque*) or Apostles' Creed (in its **WInd1** form)⟧

4. *THE PRAYERS* ⟦Forms A–H follow, almost identical to those in **WInd1** §§ 16–24, and then six 'concluding collects' to provide one to conclude whichever form is used⟧

5. *ACT OF PENITENCE*
   The President shall introduce the Act of Penitence
   ⟦Citing of 1 John 1.8–9, silence and a call to confess, then two forms of confession, one as in **WInd1** §26, with absolution (CF 2 without the relative clause)⟧

6. *THE GREETING OF PEACE*
   One of the following forms shall be said
   Form A   We are the body of Christ. By the one Spirit we were all baptized into one Body, and have all been made to drink of the one Spirit.
   Let us then pursue the things that make for peace and build up the common life.

   Form B   If you are offering your gift at the altar, and there remember that your brother has something against you.
   Leave your gift there before the altar and go;
   first be reconciled to your brother, and then come and offer your gift.

   Form C   The Kingdom of God is justice, peace and joy, inspired by the Holy Spirit.
   They who thus serve Christ are acceptable to God and approved by others.

   The President shall then greet the congregation.
   The peace of the Lord be always with you.
   And also with you.

   The President and people shall greet one another in the name of the Lord.

7. *THE PRESENTATION OF THE OFFERINGS*
   When the offerings are presented at the altar, either 'A' or 'B' shall be said
   A.   Through your goodness, Lord, we have this bread and wine to offer,
        the fruit of the earth and work of human hands.
        They will become our spiritual food.
        All things come from you, O Lord,
        and of your own do we give you.
        Blessed be God for ever. Amen.

   B.   **Father, we offer you these gifts which you have given us;**
        this bread, this wine, this money.
        With them we offer ourselves, our lives and our work,
        to become through your Holy Spirit a reasonable, holy, and lively sacrifice.
        As this bread and wine become the Body and Blood of Christ,
        so may we and all your people become channels of your love;
        through the same Christ our Lord. Amen.

8. *THE EUCHARISTIC PRAYER*
   The President shall indicate which form of the Eucharistic Prayer, including Proper Prefaces, shall be used.
   The Lord be with you . . . ⟦ELLC 6⟧ . . . **give God thanks and praise.**
        to the Lord] up to the Lord

   It is right, and a good and joyful thing,
   always and everywhere to give you thanks,
   Father almighty, everlasting God:

   The Proper Preface follows: ⟦17 Proper and 3 Common Prefaces⟧

   Therefore we praise you,
   joining our voices with angels and archangels
   and with all the company of heaven,
   who forever sing this hymn to proclaim the glory of your Name:
   Holy, holy, holy Lord . . . ⟦ELLC 7⟧ . . . in the highest.
   Blessed is He who comes . . . ⟦ELLC 8⟧ . . . in the highest.

   One of the forms A, B, C, D, or E shall now be used.

A

All Holy and glorious Father,
our Creator God,
we give you thanks
because in your loving wisdom
you brought all things into being,
and are truly worthy of praise
from every creature you have made.

Again and again
we have turned away from you;
yet in every age your steadfast love
has called us to return,
to live in union with you:
for it is your eternal purpose
to put new life into all things
and make them holy.

Through your Son Jesus Christ
who took our human nature upon Him:
you have redeemed the world
from the bondage of sin:
and by the power of the Holy Spirit
you have gathered a people to yourself,
to make known in every place
His perfect offering which He made
to the glory of your Name.

Hear us, therefore, Father,
through your Son, Jesus Christ our Lord;
and grant that these gifts of bread and
    wine may be unto us His Body and Blood.

For, on the night He was betrayed
He took bread,
and when He had given thanks to you,
He broke it and gave it to His disciples
and said: 'Take this, and eat it:
This is my Body which is given for you.
Do this for the remembrance of me.'

And after supper
He took the cup of wine:
and when He had given thanks,
He gave it to them and said:
'Drink this, all of you:
This is my Blood of the New Covenant,
which is shed for you and for many
for the forgiveness of sins.
Whenever you drink it,
do this for the remembrance of me.'

Let us proclaim the mystery of our faith.
One of the following Acclamations shall be said:
Christ has . . . ⟦CF 6(a)⟧ . . . come again.

Or
Jesus is Lord.
He has reconciled us to Himself:
Christ makes all things new.
Or
Christ is Lord.
Through His death
we were made children of God:
He is our hope of glory.

And so, Heavenly Father,
rejoicing in His Holy Incarnation;
His Blessed Passion and His Perfect
    Sacrifice
made once for all upon the Cross;
His Mighty Resurrection from the dead;
His Glorious Ascension into heaven;
and looking for His Coming in glory;
we offer to you this Bread and this Cup.

We pray that you will accept this sacrifice
    of praise and thanksgiving;
and grant that all who eat and drink of the
    Body and Blood
of your Son, our great High Priest,
may be renewed by your Holy Spirit,
and be one Body, one Spirit, in Him.

Let faith and love increase in us.
Unite us with all Bishops,
all other ministers of your Word and
    Sacraments,
and with the whole people of God,
living and departed,
whom you have made for yourself.

Confirm us in holiness,
that we may be found ready to join the
    company
of the Blessed Virgin Mary, the Holy
    Apostles,
and all your saints,
when our Lord Jesus Christ comes again:
Forever giving you thanks and praise
through Him from whom all good things
    do come.

With Him and in Him and through Him
by the power of the Holy Spirit,
we worship you, Father Almighty,
with all who stand before you in earth and
    heaven,
in songs of everlasting praise:
Blessing and . . . ⟦CF 7⟧ . . . and ever. Amen.

B

Holy and gracious Father,
all creation rightly gives you praise.
All life, all holiness, comes from you
through your Son, Jesus Christ our Lord,
whom you sent to share our human
    nature,
to live and die as one of us, to reconcile us
    to you,
the God and Father of all.

We therefore bring you these gifts,
and we ask you to make them holy by the
    power of your Spirit,
that they may become the Body and Blood
    of your Son,
our Saviour Jesus Christ,
who offered Himself in obedience to your
    will,
the Perfect Sacrifice for all mankind.

On the night He was betrayed
He took bread,
and when He had given thanks to you,
He broke it and gave it to His disciples
    and said:
'Take this, and eat it:
This is my Body which is given for you.
Do this for the remembrance of me.'

After supper He took the cup of wine:
and when He had given thanks, He gave it
    to them and said:
'Drink this, all of you:
This is my Blood of the New Covenant,
which is shed for you and for many for the
    forgiveness of sins.
Do this, whenever you drink it,
for the remembrance of me.'

One of the following Acclamations shall be said:

**When we eat . . . ⟦CF 8(b)⟧ . . . the death
of Christ until he comes again.**

Or

Christ has . . . ⟦CF 6(a)⟧ . . . come again.

Or

**Christ Jesus is Lord.
He has set us free from the law of sin
    and death:
In His name alone is our salvation.**

Father, calling to mind the death your
    Son
endured for our salvation;
His glorious Resurrection and Ascension;
His continual intercession for us in
    heaven;
and looking for His coming again in
    glory
we offer you, in thanksgiving,
this holy and life-giving sacrifice.

Look with favour on your Church's
    offering,
and grant that we who eat and drink these
    holy gifts
may be filled with your Holy Spirit
and become one body in Christ,
and serve you in unity, constancy and
    peace.

May He make us a perpetual offering to
    you and enable us,
in communion with blessed Mary
and the whole company of heaven,
to share in the inheritance of your Saints.

With Him, and in Him, and through Him,
by the power of the Holy Spirit, we
    worship you,
Father Almighty, with all who stand
    before you
in earth and heaven in songs of
    everlasting praise:
Blessing . . . ⟦CF 7⟧ . . . and ever. Amen.

C

We give thanks to you Lord our God,
for the goodness and love you have made
   known to us in creation;
in calling Israel to be your people;
in your Word spoken through the
   prophets;
and above all in the Word made flesh,
Jesus your Son.
For in these last days you sent Him
to be incarnate from the Virgin Mary,
to be the Saviour and Redeemer of the
   world.

In Him you have delivered us from evil,
and made us worthy to stand before you.
In Him, you have brought us out of error
   into truth,
out of sin into righteousness, out of death
   into life.

For, on the night that He was betrayed
He took bread,
and when He had given thanks to you,
He broke it and gave it to His disciples
and said: 'Take this, and eat it:
This is my Body which is given for you.
Do this for the remembrance of me.'

And after supper
He took the cup of wine:
and when He had given thanks,
He gave it to them and said:
'Drink this, all of you:
This is my Blood of the New Covenant,
which is shed for you and for many
for the forgiveness of sins.

Whenever you drink it,
do this for the remembrance of me.'

Therefore, Father, according to His
   command:
We remember His death.
We proclaim His resurrection.
We await His coming in glory.

And we offer our sacrifice of praise
and thanksgiving to you, Lord of all,
presenting to you, from your creation,
this bread and this wine.

We pray you, gracious God,
to send your Holy Spirit upon these gifts
that they may be the sacrament of
the Body of Christ and His Blood of the
   New Covenant.
Unite us to your Son in His Sacrifice
that we, made acceptable in Him,
may be sanctified by the Holy Spirit.

In the fullness of time,
reconcile all things in Christ,
and make them new,
and bring us to that city of light
where you dwell with all your sons and
   daughters;
through Jesus Christ our Lord,
the firstborn of all creation,
the head of the Church,
and the author of our salvation:

By whom, and with whom, and in whom,
in the unity of the Holy Spirit,
all honour and glory are yours,
Almighty Father, now and ever.
Amen.

D

All glory, praise and thanksgiving be unto
  you,
O Lord, Holy Father, Almighty,
  Everlasting God,
you created the world and all mankind,
and of your tender mercy gave your only
  Son Jesus Christ
to take our nature upon Him,
and to suffer death upon the cross, for our
  redemption.

He made there, by His own oblation of
  Himself once offered
a full, perfect, and sufficient sacrifice,
  oblation and satisfaction
for the sins of the whole world:
and He instituted, and in His holy Gospel
  commanded us to continue,
a perpetual memory of His precious death,
until His coming again.

Hear us, O merciful Father, we most
  humbly beseech you;
and be pleased to accept, bless and sanctify
these gifts and creatures of bread and wine,
that they may be for us the Body and Blood
of your Son, our Saviour Jesus Christ.

For, on the night He was betrayed
He took bread, and when He had given
  thanks to you,
He broke it and gave it to His disciples
  and said:
'Take this, and eat it:
This is my Body which is given for you.
Do this for the remembrance of me.'

And after supper He took the cup of wine:
and when He had given thanks,
He gave it to them and said:
'Drink this, all of you:
This is my Blood of the New Covenant,
which is shed for you and for many
for the forgiveness of sins.
Whenever you drink it,
do this for the remembrance of me.'

In faith we acclaim You, O Christ
Dying You . . . ⟦CF 6(b)⟧ . . . **Christ Jesus,
  come in glory.**

Now, therefore, O Lord and heavenly
  Father,

we your servants with all your holy
  people,
having in remembrance the blessed
  passion, mighty resurrection,
and glorious ascension of your beloved
  Son,
do offer unto your Divine Majesty
this Bread of eternal life
and this Cup of everlasting salvation,
rendering thanks to you for the wonderful
  redemption
which you have made possible for us in
  Him.

And we beseech you O Father, to accept
  upon your heavenly altar
this sacrifice of praise and thanksgiving;
and to grant that by the merits and death
  of your Son Jesus Christ,
and through faith in His blood,
we and all your whole Church may obtain
  remission of our sins
and all other benefits of His passion.

And we pray that by the power of your
  Holy Spirit
all who shall be partakers of this holy
  Communion
may be filled with your grace and heavenly
  benediction,
and be numbered in the glorious company
  of your Saints.

And here we offer and present unto you O
  Lord,
ourselves, our souls and bodies,
to be a reasonable, holy and lively
  sacrifice.

And although we are unworthy to offer
  unto you any sacrifice,
yet we beseech you to accept this,
our bounden duty and service,
not weighing our merits but pardoning our
  offences:

Through Jesus Christ our Lord,
by whom, and with whom, and in whom,
in the unity of the Holy Spirit,
all honour and glory be unto you,
O Father Almighty, throughout all ages,
world without end.
Amen.

E

Sovereign Lord and Father,
to you be glory and praise for ever.
In your boundless wisdom
you brought creation into being;
In your great love you fashioned
us in your image;
In your tender compassion
you sent your Son, Jesus Christ, our
　　Saviour,
to share our human nature;
In the power of the Holy Spirit,
He overcame the power of sin and death
and brought your people to new birth
as first fruits of your new creation.

On the night that He was betrayed
He took bread,
and when He had given thanks to you,
He broke it and gave it to His disciples
and said: 'Take this, and eat it:
This is my Body which is given for you.
Do this for the remembrance of me.'

And after supper
He took the cup of wine:
and when He had given thanks,
He gave it to them and said:
'Drink this, all of you:
This is my Blood of the New Covenant,
which is shed for you and for many
for the forgiveness of sins.

Whenever you drink it,
Do this for the remembrance of me.'

Therefore, Father, according to the
　　command
of your dearly beloved Son
We remember His death.
We proclaim His resurrection.
We await His coming in glory.

And we offer you, Father,
our sacrifice of thanks and praise.
Send your Holy Spirit on these gifts of
　　bread and wine
that they may become the Body and Blood
　　of your Son,
Jesus, our Lord and Redeemer.
As we partake of this holy food of new
　　and unending life,
may your Holy Spirit establish us as a
　　royal priesthood
with the Blessed Virgin Mary,
St N and all your sons and daughters
who share in your eternal inheritance:
Through Jesus Christ our Lord.
With Him and in Him and through Him,
by the power of the Holy Spirit,
we worship you, Father Almighty,
with all who stand before you
in earth and heaven,
in songs of everlasting praise.
Blessing and . . . ⟦CF 7⟧ . . . ever. Amen.

9. *THE LORD'S PRAYER*
   As our Saviour has taught us, so we pray:
   Our Father in heaven . . . ⟦ELLC 1⟧ . . . and forever. Amen.

10. *THE BREAKING OF THE BREAD*
    One of the following forms shall be used:
    We break this bread . . . ⟦CF 8(a)⟧ . . . **in one bread.**
    or
    God of promise, You have prepared a Banquet for us
    Happy are those who are called to the supper of the Lamb.
    or
    This is the true bread which comes from heaven
    Whoever eats this bread will live forever.

    The Agnus Dei may follow here.

11. *THE COMMUNION*
    The Invitation   *One of the following forms shall be used:*

    Form A
    My brothers and sisters in Christ, draw near and receive . . . ⟦CF 9(a)⟧ . . . with
        thanksgiving.
    Grant gracious Lord, that we so eat the flesh of your dear Son, Jesus Christ,
    and drink His blood,
    that we may evermore dwell in Him and He in us. Amen.
        the body of our Lord Jesus Christ] His body
        Eat and drink in remembrance] Remember

    Form B
    The Gifts of God for the People of God.
    Our souls will feast and be satisfied,
    and we will sing glad songs of praise to Him.

    Form C
    Draw near and receive the Body and Blood of our Saviour Jesus Christ with faith and
        thanksgiving.
    We do not presume . . . ⟦CF 3(a)⟧ . . . dwell in Him, and He in us.
        merciful Lord] most merciful Father
        in your manifold and great mercies] only in your boundless mercy
        worthy so much as] even worthy
        the same Lord . . . have mercy] the Lord ever the same, ever merciful
        Grant us therefore . . . so to eat] Grant therefore, Lord of grace and love, that we may so eat
        to drink] drink
        that our sinful . . . and that we] that with bodies and souls made clean from every stain of sin we

    The Agnus Dei may follow here.
    Either **Lamb of God . . . ⟦ELLC 9(b)⟧ . . . grant us peace.**
    or **Jesus, Lamb of God . . . ⟦ELLC 9(a)⟧ . . . us your peace.**

    During the administration, the Ministers say to each communicant:
    The Body of Christ given for you.
    The Blood of Christ shed for you.
    and the communicant replies, each time: **Amen.**

12. THE DISMISSAL

Post Communion

One of the following shall be used:

Almighty Father,
we thank you for feeding us
with the Body and Blood
of your Son Jesus Christ.
May we who share His Body
live His risen life:
we who drink His cup
bring life to others;
we upon whom the Spirit shines
give light to the world.
Help us to continue in faithful witness
to your Word,
so we and all your children shall be free,
and the whole earth live to praise your
    Name,
through Christ our Lord. Amen.

or

Almighty and everliving God,
we thank you for feeding us
with the spiritual food
of the most precious Body and Blood
of your Son our Saviour Jesus Christ;
and for assuring us in these holy mysteries;
that we are living members
of the Body of your Son,
and heirs of your eternal kingdom.
And now Father, send us out
to do the work you have given us to do,
to love and serve you as faithful witnesses
of Christ our Lord.
To Him, to you, and to the Holy Spirit,
be honour and glory, now and for ever.
Amen.

or

Eternal God and Heavenly Father,
we thank you for feeding us
with the Body and Blood
of your Son Jesus Christ.
Send us now into the world in peace,
and grant us strength and courage
to love and serve you
and all persons in you,
with gladness and singleness of heart,
through your Son Jesus Christ our Lord.
Amen.

Dismissal

The President (or the Bishop, if present) may say this Blessing or a Seasonal Blessing:
The Blessing of God Almighty . . . ⟦CF 12(a)⟧ . . . with you always. **Amen.**

⟦20 Seasonal Blessings⟧
Notices and Banns may be given.

A hymn may be sung.

Go in peace and serve . . . ⟦CF 12 (b)⟧ . . . **In the name of Christ. Amen.**

13. *WHEN THE CONSECRATED ELEMENTS ARE INSUFFICIENT*

If either or both of the consecrated elements are likely to prove insufficient, the President returns to the holy table and adds more, with these words:

Either Having given thanks to you, Father, over the bread and the cup according to the institution of your Son, Jesus Christ, on the night that he was betrayed; we pray that you will accept the praise and thanksgiving we offer through Him who said, 'Take, eat; this is my Body (*and/or* 'Drink this; this is my Blood'), grant that this bread/wine also may be to us His Body/Blood and be received in remembrance of Him.

Or Hear us, O merciful Father, and with your Word and Holy Spirit, bless and sanctify these gifts of bread and wine, that they also may be unto us the Body and Blood of your dearly beloved Son, Jesus Christ, and be received in remembrance of Him.

12. The Episcopal Church of Brazil

The Portuguese-speaking Province of Brazil separated from the Episcopal Church of the United States of America in 1965, and produced its own revisions of the eucharistic rites of its parent church in 1967 (**Braz**, published in **MAL**) and 1972 (**BrazR**, published in **FAL**). A further revision was advertised as under way in the early 1980s, and in **LAL** it was anticipated that a revised rite would take its place in a complete new Prayer Book, expected in 1986. In the event the new Book, *Libro de Oração Comun*, was synodically authorized and published in 1988. It contained two eucharistic rites, shown here as **Braz1** and **Braz2**, and also a separate provision of additional alternative eucharistic prayers, here labelled **Braz3**.

'RITO 1' FROM THE PROVINCE OF BRAZIL'S BOOK OF COMMON PRAYER, 1988 (Braz1)

[The translation from Portuguese is by the editor. The numbering and lining are editorial.]

Liturgia da Proclamação da Palavra de Deus e Celebração da Santa Comunhão

PREPARATION
  1. *The officiant, or another liturgical minister designated by him, may say*:
     Come, let us celebrate with praise and thanksgiving the sacrament of the new and eternal covenant, which reminds us of the Last Supper, and tells out the death and victory of the Lord, and his living presence through the holy mysteries of his body and blood, and the way of his people, which our Lord proclaimed: for he is the living bread which comes down from heaven; whoever eats this bread will live for ever.

  2. *A psalm or hymn may be sung or said.*

  3. Blessed be God, Father, Son, and Holy Spirit
     Blessed be his kingdom, now and for ever.
     [Other versicles and responses for special occasions]

  4. *COLLECT FOR PURITY*
     Almighty God, to whom ... [CF 1] ... Christ our Lord. Amen.

  5. *The officiant may begin the Penitential Order here, or it can come after the Intercessions and before the Greeting of Peace. A deacon or other minister may recite the Ten Commandments.*

PENITENTIAL ORDER
  6. *DECALOGUE* [The text with the responses as in 1662]
     or the officiant may say:

     THE SUMMARY OF THE LAW [Standard text]

7. *KYRIE*
   Lord, have mercy . . . ⟦ELLC 2⟧ . . . Lord, have mercy.

8. *CONFESSION*
   Let us humbly confess our sins to almighty God.
   Or
   You who are truly and sincerely repentant for your sins, are in love with your
   neighbour, and are resolved to lead a new life, walking in the ways of the Lord;
   draw near with faith, make your confession to almighty God, and trusting in his
   forgiveness, receive this holy sacrament.
   All kneeling, they may keep some moments for recollection in silence.
   ⟦Congregational confession⟧

   The presbyter, or the bishop when present, says:
   Almighty God, our heavenly Father, who of his great mercy promises forgiveness to
   all those who with true repentance and living faith turn to him, pardon and deliver
   . . . ⟦CF 2⟧ . . . life eternal; through Jesus Christ, our Saviour.
   Amen.

LITURGY OF THE WORD

9. *COLLECT OF THE DAY*
   The Spirit of the Lord be with you.
   And also with you.
   or
   The Lord is here.
   His Spirit is with us.
   The officiant says the collect of the day and/or of the season.
   Amen.

10. *LECTIONS*
    *All seated, readings appropriate to the day are made from the Old Testament and the
    Epistle, which are announced as follows:*
    ⟦Form of announcement, and of acclamation and response following each reading;
    provision to omit one reading, and to have a psalm or hymn, or silence, after each reading⟧

    *All standing, the deacon, when present, or another officiating minister, reads the Gospel,
    saying:*
    ⟦Form of announcement and response and of acclamation and response at the end⟧

    A hymn may be sung.

11. *SERMON*

12. ⟦Rubric concerning use, and omission, of Nicene and Apostles' Creeds⟧

    NICENE CREED
    I believe in one God . . . ⟦ELLC 5⟧ . . . **world to come. Amen.**
      We] I   FIVE TIMES
      [and the Son]] OMIT BRACKETS

    or APOSTLES' CREED
    I believe in God . . . ⟦ELLC 4⟧ . . . **life everlasting. Amen.**

13. INTERCESSIONS *(Prayer of the Faithful)*
⟦Rubrics outlining topics for intercessions, with reference to possible use of forms later in the Prayer Book, and of authorized litanies, extempory prayers, and silence.⟧

Then the Penitential Order may be used.

14. *Then there may be a welcome of visitors and the greeting of peace may be used.*

GREETING OF PEACE
The peace of the Lord be always with you.
And also with you.

CELEBRATION OF HOLY COMMUNION

15. OFFERTORY
The celebrant may begin the Offertory with the following sentence, or one from page . . .
⟦*i.e. later in the Book*⟧, *or even other Scriptures.*
Let us present to the Lord the offerings of our life and labour.

A hymn or psalm may be sung during the Offertory.

The members of the congregation bring up the offerings of bread, wine, money and other goods to hand them over to the deacon or other minister. All stand while the offerings are presented and placed upon the altar.

16. GREAT THANKSGIVING[68] PRAYER
*Alternative Eucharistic Prayers are to be found on pages . . . and . . . ⟦i.e. **Braz3** below⟧.*

Standing up, the celebrant, whether bishop or presbyter, facing the people, says or sings:

---

68 ⟦The Portuguese word is, of course, 'Eucaristica', but in English 'Great Thanksgiving' is a regular title which 'Great Eucharistic Prayer' is not.⟧

The Spirit of the Lord be with you.
And also with you.

or

The Lord is here
His Spirit is with us . . . [ELLC 6] . . . It is right and just to do so.

It is indeed right and just,
reasonable and for our salvation,
that we should at all times and in all places
give you thanks, O almighty Father,
creator of heaven and earth.

A Proper Preface is said or sung from page . . .

Therefore with angels and archangels,
and with all the multitude of heaven
who never cease to proclaim your glory,
we joyfully praise your name:
Holy, holy, holy . . . [ELLC 7] . . . Glory be given to you, O Lord most high.
Blessed is he . . . [ELLC8] . . . the highest.

The people standing or kneeling, the Celebrant continues:
All glory and thanksgiving be given to you,
O God the Father of infinite power and love,
for the whole of creation, and for us,
your workmanship made in your own image;
and because, when we had fallen into sin,
in your mercy you sent to assist us
your only Son Jesus Christ,
who for our redemption took upon himself human nature
and suffered the death of the cross;
and because, by his one oblation of himself,
he made a perfect, complete and sufficient sacrifice
for the sins of the whole world.

The Lord Jesus, on the night in which he was betrayed,
took bread and, when he had given thanks,
broke it and gave it to his disciples, saying:

'Take, eat, this is my body, which is given for you;
do this in remembrance of me.'

And after supper, he took the cup,
and, when he had given thanks,
he gave it to them, saying,
'Drink this, all of you,
for this is my blood of the new covenant,
which is poured out for you and for many,
for the forgiveness of sins.
Do this, as often as you drink it,
in remembrance of me.'

Your death, Lord, we tell out.
Your resurrection we proclaim.
And your coming we await.
Come, Lord Jesus.

Therefore, O Father, following the command of your Son,
we commemorate, until he comes,
his life, passion, death, resurrection and ascension,
giving you thanks for the innumerable benefits
which we have received through him.

And here, O Lord, we present to you the offering of ourselves.
We humbly ask that you will accept
our sacrifice of praise and thanksgiving,
and be pleased to bless and sanctify this bread and wine,
in order that we, clothed in your grace and heavenly blessing,
may be united, with Christ and your Holy Spirit,
by the mediation of the same, your Son, our Saviour,
through whom and with whom, in the unity of the Holy Spirit,
all honour and glory be to you, O Father almighty,
for ever and ever.
Amen.

17. As Christ the Saviour has taught us, so we are bold to say:
   Our Father in heaven . . . [ELLC 1] . . . for ever. Amen.
      Save us . . . trial and] Lead us not into temptation, but

18. *BREAKING OF BREAD*
   The celebrant then breaks the consecrated bread, keeping some moments of silence, after which he says:
   The bread which we break is a sharing in the body of Christ,
   and the cup which we bless is a sharing in the blood of Christ.
   So we, though we are many, are one single body.

19. *The greeting of peace may be done here, if it has not been done earlier.* [As at §14 above]

20. *There may be said or sung the following (or another appropriate hymn):*
    Lamb of God . . . [ELLC 9(b)] . . . **grant us your peace.**
       sin] sins THREE TIMES
    Or this prayer
    We do not presume . . . [CF 3(a)] . . . he in us. **Amen.**

21. COMMUNION
    The celebrant receives the holy communion and then distributes it for eating or drinking, saying as he gives the bread:
    The body of our Lord . . . [CF 10(a)] . . . to eternal life. And be thankful. **Amen.**
    When he gives the cup:
    The blood of our Lord . . . [CF 10(b)] . . . to eternal life. And be thankful. **Amen.**
    The celebrant may then consume the bread and wine which remain.

22. *AFTER COMMUNION*
    Let us pray.
    Almighty and eternal God, with all our heart we give you thanks,
    because, in these holy mysteries, you have deigned
    to nourish us with the body and blood of your Son Jesus Christ,
    and to keep us in his mystical body,
    which is the blessed company of all the faithful,
    making us members of his eternal kingdom.
    We ask you, O Father, that, assisted by your grace,
    we may continue in your holy church,
    and do all the good works that you have prepared for us;
    through Jesus Christ our Lord,
    who lives and reigns in the unity of the Holy Spirit,
    one God, for ever and ever. Amen.
    Or
    Almighty God, we thank you . . . [CF 11(a)] . . . **praise and glory. Amen.**

23. *On festival days, the following hymn is said or sung, but it is omitted during Lent, Advent and Memorial services; however, in place of Gloria in Excelsis some appropriate hymn may be substituted.*

    GLORIA IN EXCELSIS
    Glory to God . . . [ELLC 3] . . . **God the Father. Amen.**

24. *BLESSING*
    The celebrant, or the bishop when present, adds the following blessing, or another one on pages . . .
    The blessing of God Almighty, Father, Son and Holy Spirit, be with you and remain with you for ever. **Amen.**

    Notices may be given here. A hymn or psalm may be sung.

25. *DISMISSAL*
    It is the privilege of the deacon, when present, to do the dismissal.
    Go in the peace of Christ. Be bold and strong in the witness of the gospel among men. Serve the Lord with cheerfulness.
    In the power of the Holy Spirit.
    Alleluia!

'RITO 11' FROM THE PROVINCE OF BRAZIL'S BOOK OF COMMON PRAYER, 1988 (Braz2)

[The translation from Portuguese is by the Editor.
The numbering and lining are editorial.]

THE WORD OF GOD

1. *A hymn, psalm or antiphon may be sung.*

2. *The people standing, the officiant says:*
   Blessed be God, Father, Son and Holy Spirit.
   Blessed be his kingdom, now and for ever. Amen.
   [Seasonal variants follow]

3. *The officiant may say:*
   Almighty God, to whom . . . [CF 1] . . . through Jesus Christ, our Lord. **Amen.**

4. *When it is appointed, the following hymn or another hymn of praise may be said or sung, all standing.*
   GLORIA IN EXCELSIS
   Glory to God in the highest . . . [ELLC 3] . . . **God the Father. Amen.**

5. *On other occasions, the Kyries may be sung or said:*
   KYRIES
   Lord, have mercy on us . . . [ELLC 2 in Portuguese] . . . **on us. Lord, have mercy on us.**

6. COLLECT OF THE DAY. *The officiant says to the people:*
   The Lord be with you.
   And also with you.
   Or
   The Lord is here.
   His Spirit is with us.
   The officiant says the Collect of the Day and/or the Collect of the season.

READINGS

7. *The people sitting, one or two appointed readings are used* [with announcement preceding and acclamation and response following each]

   A period of silence may be used. A hymn, psalm or canticle can be sung after the readings.

   All standing, a deacon or presbyter reads the Gospel [announcement and response preceding and acclamation and response following]

8. *A hymn may be sung.*

9. SERMON

10. *On Sundays and principal feasts, there is sung or said the Nicene Creed (or the Apostles' Creed), all standing; on days appointed for baptism, unless there is no candidate for the same, the Baptismal Covenant may be used, on page . . ., in place of the Nicene Creed.*
    NICENE CREED
    We believe in one God . . . [ELLC 5] . . . **world to come. Amen.**
    [and the Son]] OMIT BRACKETS

    or this
    APOSTLES' CREED
    I believe in God . . . [ELLC 4] . . . **life everlasting. Amen.**

11. INTERCESSIONS *(Prayer of the faithful)*
[Rubrics outlining topics for intercessions, with reference to possible use of forms later in the Prayer Book, and of authorized litanies, extemporary prayers, and silence.]

12. *CONFESSION OF SINS*
The confession can be made here, if it has not been made earlier. On occasion the confession may be omitted.
The deacon or officiant says:
Let us confess our sins to God.
[Congregational confession and absolution by the presbyter or bishop follow]

13. *GREETING OF PEACE*
Here visitors may be introduced and received with welcomes. All standing, the celebrant says to the people:
The peace of the Lord be always with you.
And also with you.

CELEBRATION OF HOLY COMMUNION

14. OFFERTORY
The celebrant begins the offertory with the following sentence, or with another sentence from page . . .
Let us present to the Lord the offerings of our life and labour.

During the offertory a hymn or psalm may be sung. Members of the congregation bring offerings of bread, wine, money and other offerings, and hand them over to the deacon or celebrant. The people standing, the offerings are presented and placed upon the altar.

15. GREAT THANKSGIVING[69] PRAYER
Alternative Eucharistic Prayers are to be found on page . . . [i.e. **Braz3** below].

Standing up, the celebrant, whether bishop or presbyter, facing the people, says or sings:

The Spirit of the Lord be with you.
And also with you. *or*
The Lord is here . . . [ELLC 6 with CF 5]
. . . right and just to do so.

It is indeed right and just,
for our salvation and joy,
that at all times and in all places
we should give thanks to you,
O almighty Father, creator of heaven and earth.
The Proper Preface on pages . . . is sung or said.

Therefore, with angels and archangels
and all the company of heaven,
we do not cease to proclaim your glory,
joyfully praising your name:
Holy, holy, holy . . . [ELLC 7] . . . Glory be given to you, O Lord most high.
Blessed is he . . . [ELLC 8] . . . the highest.

People standing or kneeling, the Celebrant continues:
We give you thanks, O blessed God,

for showing us your goodness and love in creation,
for calling Israel to be your people,
for your word sent out by means of your prophets,
and, above all, for your Word made flesh,
your Son, Jesus.

For at the right time, you sent him
to take on human flesh,
to be born of the Virgin Mary,
and to become the Saviour and Redeemer of the world.
So you have freed us from evil,
and made us worthy to stand before you.
So you have led us from error to the truth,
from sin to righteousness,
from death to life.

Jesus Christ, our Lord,
in the night before his death for us
took bread, and, having given thanks to you,
broke it and gave to his disciples, saying:

---

69 [See footnote 68 on page 116 above.]

'Take and eat, this is my body,
which is given for you.
Do this in remembrance of me.'
And after supper, he took the cup,
and, having given thanks to you,
he gave it to them, saying:
'Drink this, all of you,
for this is my blood of the new covenant,
which is poured out for you and for many,
for the forgiveness of sins.
Do this, whenever you drink it,
in remembrance of me.'

Therefore, O Father, in line with his
 command;
We tell out his death.
We proclaim his resurrection.
We await his glorious coming.

And we offer you, O Lord of all,
our sacrifice of praise and thanksgiving,
and, from your own creation,
present to you this bread and this wine.
And we ask you, O gracious Lord,
to send your Holy Spirit upon these gifts
and sanctify them that they may be
the sacrament of the body of Christ,

and his blood of the new covenant.
Let your Holy Spirit descend on us, O
 Lord.
Send us your Holy Spirit, O Lord.

Make us with your Son a single sacrifice,
that we may be accepted through him,
and be sanctified by the Holy Spirit.
In the fullness of time
make us all the possession of your Christ,
we pray you,
and bring us to your heavenly kingdom,
in the company (of ___and) of all your
 saints,
that we may be accounted in your eternal
 inheritance
as your sons and your daughters.

Through Jesus Christ, our Lord,
the firstborn of all creation,
the head of the church, the author of our
 salvation.
Through Christ, with Christ and in Christ,
in the unity of the Holy Spirit,
all honour and glory be given to you,
O Father almighty, now and for ever.
Amen.

16. As Christ, the Saviour, has taught us, now we are bold to say:
 Our Father in heaven . . . ⟦ELLC 1⟧ . . . for ever. Amen.

17. *BREAKING OF BREAD*
 The celebrant continues with the breaking of the consecrated bread.

 A moment of silence is kept.

 There may be sung or said:
 (Alleluia.) Christ our passover is sacrificed for us.
 Therefore, let us keep the feast. (Alleluia).
 In Lent the Alleluia is omitted.

18. *Facing the people, the celebrant says the following words of invitation to the Supper of the
 Lord (or other words from the Scriptures):*
 The gifts of God for the people of God.
 Whoever eats of me shall never hunger; and whoever drinks of me shall never thirst.
 (John 6.35)

19. *The ministers receive the sacrament in both kinds and immediately minister them to the
 people with the following words:*
 The body (or blood) of our Lord Jesus Christ keep you in eternal life. (**Amen**).
 Or with these words:
 The body of Christ, the bread of heaven. (**Amen**).
 The blood of Christ, the cup of salvation. (**Amen**).
 The sacrament may be administered by intinction.
 During the administration of communion, hymns, psalms or antiphons may be sung.
 *When necessary, the celebrant consecrates more bread and/or wine, with the formula on
 page . . .*

20. AFTER COMMUNION

Let us pray.
O eternal God and heavenly Father,
you have graciously accepted us as living members
of your Son, our Saviour Jesus Christ,
and you have fed us with spiritual food
in the sacrament of his body and blood.
Send us now into the world in peace,
and grant us strength and courage
to love and serve you
with cheerfulness and singleness of heart,
through Jesus Christ our Lord.
Amen.

21. BLESSING

The bishop when present, or the celebrant, may add the following blessing, or another on pages . . .
The blessing of God Almighty, Father, Son and Holy Spirit, be with you and remain with you for ever. **Amen.**

A hymn or psalm may be sung or said.

22. DISMISSAL

The deacon, or the celebrant, dismisses the people with these words:
Go in the peace of Christ. Be bold and strong in the witness of the gospel among men. Serve the Lord with cheerfulness.
In the power of the Holy Spirit. Alleluia!

'ORAÇÕES EUCARÍSTICAS ALTERNATIVAS' FROM THE PROVINCE OF BRAZIL'S BOOK OF COMMON PRAYER, 1988 (Braz3)

[[The two alternative prayers appear to be available for use with either of the preceding rites. The translation from Portuguese is by the Editor, in the case of Prayer A confirmed by its dependence upon the 'star trek' eucharistic prayer from **Amer2-2**, and confirmed for Prayer B by the bilingual rite provided by the bishops of Brazil for the 1998 Lambeth Conference. The numbering and lining are editorial.]]

Oração Eucarística A

1. *The celebrant, whether bishop or presbyter, facing the people, sings or says:*

The Spirit of the Lord be with you . . .
[[ELLC 6 with CF 5]] . . . **It is right and just to do so.**

Facing the Holy Table, the celebrant continues:
God of all power, Lord of the Universe,
you are worthy to receive glory and praise.
Glory to you, Lord, from now and for ever.

At your command all things came to exist:
the vast expanse of inter-stellar space,
galaxies, suns, the planets in their courses,
and this fragile earth, our island home.
By your will all things were created and came to exist.

From the primal elements you brought
forth the human race,
and blessed us with memory, reason and
skill.
You gave us dominion over the creation.
But we betrayed your trust and rebelled
against you
and turned against each other.
**Lord, have mercy upon us, for we are
sinners in your sight.**

Yet again and again you called on us to
return.
Through prophets and sages you revealed
your righteous law.

And, in the fullness of time, you sent your
    only Son,
born of a woman, to fulfil your will
and be for us the way of freedom and
    peace.
By his blood he reconciled us,
By his wounds we are made whole.

Therefore we praise you, joining with the
    heavenly chorus,
with prophets, apostles and martyrs,
and with all those in every generation
who with hope have trusted you,
to proclaim with them your glory
in unceasing voice:
Holy, holy . . . [[ELLC 7]] . . . in the highest.
Blessed is he . . . [[ELLC 8]] . . . the highest.

And so, Father, we, who have been
    redeemed by your Son
and made the people of the new covenant
by water and the Holy Spirit,
now bring before you these gifts of bread
    and wine.
Sanctify them by your Holy Spirit,
that they may be the body and blood
of Jesus Christ our Lord.
In the night in which he was betrayed
Jesus took bread and blessed it,
broke it and gave it to his friends, saying:
'Take, eat; this is my body which is given
    for you.
Do this in remembrance of me.'

After supper Jesus took a cup of wine,
gave thanks and said: 'Drink this, all of
    you;
this is my blood of the new covenant
which is poured out for you and for many
for the forgiveness of sins.
As often as you drink it,
do this in remembrance of me.'

Remembering now his work of redemption
and offering you this sacrifice of praise and
    thanksgiving,
We celebrate his death and resurrection,
as we await the day of his coming.

Lord God of our Fathers,
God of Abraham, Isaac and Jacob,
God and Father of our Lord Jesus Christ,
open our eyes to see the works of your
    hand
in the world about us.
Make us come to your Table
seeking strength for your service,
not simply our own satisfaction,
and renewal of our lives, not simply
    pardon.
Let the grace of this holy communion
make us one body and one spirit in Christ
that we may work to transform the
    kingdoms of this world
into the kingdom of our Lord Jesus Christ.
Risen Lord, reveal yourself to us
in the breaking of the bread.

Accept our prayers and praises, Father,
through Jesus Christ, our high priest,
to whom with you and the Holy Spirit,
your church gives adoration, honour and
    glory,
from generation to generation.
Amen.

2. As Christ, the Saviour, has taught us, now we are bold to say:
    Our Father in heaven . . . [[ELLC 1]] . . . for ever. Amen.

3. *The celebrant continues with the breaking of the bread.*

    A moment of silence is kept. There may be sung or said:
    (Alleluia.) Christ, our Passover is sacrificed for us.
    Therefore, let us celebrate the feast. (Alleluia.)

    In Lent, the Alleluia is omitted. Other antiphons may be used also.

4. *The celebrant may say the following words of invitation to the Lord's Supper:*
    The gifts of God for the people of God.
    Whoever eats of me shall never hunger; and whoever drinks of me shall never thirst.
    (John 6.35)

5. COMMUNION

6. *AFTER COMMUNION*
Let us pray
O eternal God . . . ⟦as §20 in **Braz2**⟧ . . . **Jesus Christ our Lord. Amen.**

7. *BLESSING* ⟦as §21 in **Braz2**⟧

8. *DISMISSAL* ⟦as §22 in **Braz2**⟧

Oração Eucarística B

9. *Standing, the celebrant, whether bishop or presbyter, facing the people, sings or says:*

The Spirit of the Lord be with you . . .
  ⟦ELLC 6 with CF 5⟧ . . . **It is right and**
just to do so.
here] among us

It is truly right to glorify you, Father,
and to give you thanks;
for you alone are God, living and true,
dwelling in light inaccessible
from before time and for ever.

Fountain of life and source of all goodness,
you made all things and fill them with
  your blessing;
you created them to rejoice
in the splendour of your radiance.

Countless throngs of angels stand before
  you
to serve you night and day;
and, beholding the glory of your presence,
they offer you unceasing praise.
With them, giving expression to every
  creature under heaven,
we acclaim and glorify you,
and proclaim your Name, as we sing/say:
Holy, holy . . . ⟦ELLC 7⟧ . . . in the highest.
Blessed is he . . . ⟦ELLC 8⟧ . . . the highest.

We acclaim you, holy Lord, glorious in
  power.
Your mighty works reveal your wisdom
  and your love.
You formed us in your own image,
giving the whole world into our care,
so that, in obedience to you, our Creator,
we might rule and serve all your creatures.
When our disobedience took us far from
  you,
you did not abandon us to the power of
  death.
In your mercy you came to our help,
so that in seeking you we might find you.

Again and again you called us into
  covenant with you,
and through the prophets you taught us to
  hope for salvation.

Father, you have loved the world so much
that in the fullness of time
you sent your Son to be our Saviour.
Incarnate by the Holy Spirit, born of the
  Virgin Mary,
he lived as one of us, yet without sin.
To the poor he proclaimed the good news
of salvation;
to prisoners, freedom; to the sorrowful,
joy.

To fulfil your purpose Jesus gave himself
  up to death;
and, rising from the grave, destroyed
  death,
and made the whole creation new.
And, that we might live no longer for
ourselves,
but for him who died and rose for us,
he sent the Holy Spirit,
to accomplish his work in the world,
and to complete the sanctification of all
who believe.
When the hour had come for him to be
  glorified
by you, his heavenly Father,
having loved his own who were in the
  world,
he loved them to the end.

At supper with them he took bread,
and when he had given thanks to you,
he broke it, and gave it to his disciples,
and said: 'Take, eat: This is my Body,
which is given for you.
Do this for the remembrance of me.'
After supper he took the cup of wine,

gave thanks, and gave it to them, saying:
'Drink this, all of you:
this is my blood of the new covenant,
which is shed for you and for many
for the forgiveness of sins.
Whenever you drink it,
do this for the remembrance of me.'

Therefore, Father, we now celebrate
this memorial of our redemption.
Recalling Christ's death
and his descent among the dead,
proclaiming his resurrection and
   ascension,
awaiting his coming in glory;
and offering to you,
from what you have given us,
this bread and this cup.
We praise you and we bless you,
we give thanks to you,
and we pray to you, Lord our God.

Lord, we pray that your Holy Spirit
may descend upon us
and may by your mercy
sanctify and consecrate these holy gifts
that they may be for your holy people
the bread of life and the cup of salvation,
the body and blood of your Son Jesus
   Christ.
Grant that all who share this bread and
   this cup
may become one body and one spirit,
a living sacrifice in Christ,
to the praise of your name.

Remember, Lord, your one holy catholic
   and apostolic church,

redeemed by the blood of your Christ.
Reveal her unity, make her lively in your
   faith,
maintain her peace, and strengthen her in
   your service.
[Remember (*NN*) and all other ministers,
   especially (*NN*).]
(Remember all your people,
and those who seek your truth.)
(Remember _____.)
[Remember all who have died in the peace
   of Christ (*NN*),
and those whose faith is known to you
   alone.
Bring them into your presence,
the place of eternal joy and light.]

And grant that we may find our
   inheritance with the saints,
[with the Blessed Virgin Mary,
with patriarchs, prophets, apostles and
   martyrs, (and with *NN*)]
and with all who have found favour with
   you in ages past.

We praise you in union with them
and give you glory through your Son Jesus
   Christ our Lord.

Through Christ, and with Christ, and in
   Christ,
all honour and glory are yours,
Almighty God and Father,
in the unity of the Holy Spirit now and for
   ever.
Amen.

⟦The service continues with §§10–16 in the identical form to §§2–8 on pages 123–4 above⟧

13. The Anglican Church of the Southern Cone of South America

At and after the formation of the Province of the Southern Cone in 1983 there was no provision made for a provincial liturgical usage. **LAL** records the continuing use of the 1973 Chile Liturgy (**ChilR**, published in **FAL**) in most dioceses. However, after ten years a provincial eucharistic liturgy was produced in Spanish, though it has visible English-language antecedents in **EngA**. In 1993 it was approved for use in the province by the Bishops and the Provincial Executive Council, and made available in booklet form. There is a minimum of rubrical directions. There exist various English-language translations with different numbering.

THE PROVINCIAL EUCHARIST OF THE ANGLICAN CHURCH OF THE SOUTHERN CONE OF SOUTH AMERICA 1993 (SouCon)

〚The text is edited here from a semi-official English-language translation with careful reference to the Spanish text. The numbering is original. The lining is partly original, partly editorial.〛

Holy Communion
The Lord's Supper Holy Eucharist

INTRODUCTION

1. *WELCOME AND GREETING*
   In the name of the Lord, the presbyter who presides gives the congregation a welcome and greeting using this or another greeting from the letters of Saint Paul.
   May God our Father and the Lord Jesus Christ pour upon you his grace and peace.
   Praise to his name, now and for ever. Amen.

2. *COLLECT FOR PURITY*
   Almighty God, to whom . . . 〚CF 1〛 . . . through Christ our Lord. Amen.

3. *CONFESSION OF SIN AND ABSOLUTION*
   This may be taken here or below (§10).

4. *PRAISE AND WORSHIP*
   Praise and worship of God in spontaneous form or in the traditional form of the hymn 'Glory to God in the highest'.
   Glory to God . . . 〚ELLC 3〛 . . . the glory of God the Father. Amen.

5. *COLLECT OF THE DAY*

PROCLAMATION OF THE WORD

6. **BIBLICAL READINGS**
   Then one or two biblical readings from the Old or New Testament.

   ⟦A response may follow each reading⟧

   Between the readings hymns, psalms, songs or alleluias may be sung.
   Then comes the reading of the Holy Gospel. ⟦An acclamation preceding and following it⟧

7. **SERMON**

8. **THE NICENE CREED**
   We believe in one God . . . ⟦ELLC 5⟧ **. . . world to come. Amen.**
   became truly human] was made man
   [and the Son]] OMIT BRACKETS

9. **INTERCESSION AND THANKSGIVING**
   Intercessions and thanksgivings are made, especially for the church, the world, the local
   community and for specific people according to their need. ⟦Versicle and petition to close
   each petition⟧

10. **CONFESSION OF SIN AND ABSOLUTION**
    ⟦Congregational confession, ministerial absolution and congregational absolution of the
    minister⟧

11. **PRAYER OF ACCESS TO THE TABLE**
    This prayer may be used in preparation for communion.
    Oh merciful Lord, we do not venture to draw near to this your table,
    trusting in our own righteousness,
    but in your divine grace.
    We are not even worthy
    to pick up the crumbs that fall to the ground.
    We trust not in our merits, but in your compassion.
    Grant us, therefore, heavenly Father,
    so to receive this bread and this cup,
    that we might be participants by faith
    in the body and blood of your beloved Son, Jesus Christ,
    and that we might live in him, and he in us. Amen.

12. **THE PEACE**
    Christ is our peace.
    He has reconciled us to God in one body through the cross.
    We meet in his name and share his peace.

    The peace of the Lord be always with you.
    And with your spirit.

MINISTRY OF THE SACRAMENT

13. **PREPARATION OF THE HOLY TABLE**

The Lord be with you.
And with your spirit.
Let us lift up . . . [[ELLC 6]] . . . **give thanks
and praise.**
Receive all honour and glory, thanks and
praise,
at all times and in all places,
Lord, holy Father, living and true God,
through Jesus Christ our Lord.

For he is your eternal Word;
through him you have created all things
from the beginning,
and formed us in your own image.
In your great love you handed him over
to become man for our sakes
and to share our common life.
In obedience to your will,
he offered himself to become a perfect
sacrifice
and died upon the cross for our
redemption.
Through him you have freed us from the
slavery of sin
and reconciled us to you, our God and
Father.
He is our great High Priest whom you
raised from death
and exalted to your right hand in heaven,
where he ever lives to intercede for us.
Through him you have sent us your Holy
Spirit, Giver of life,
and have made us into a royal priesthood
called to serve you for ever.
A seasonal preface may be used.

So we join with angels and archangels,
with the patriarchs, prophets and apostles,
and with the whole church in heaven and
on earth, in endless song:
**Holy, holy, holy is the Lord, the God of the
universe.**
Heaven and earth . . . [[ELLC 7]] . . . highest.

And now, Father, we thank you for these
gifts of your creation,
this bread and this wine,
and we ask that, through the activity of
your Holy Spirit,

we who eat and drink
in obedience to our Saviour Jesus Christ,
might share in his body and blood,
and obtain unity in him
and with each other in peace and love.

*The celebrant takes the bread into his hands and
says*
For in the night when he was betrayed, he
took bread;
and when he had given you thanks he
broke it,
and gave it to his disciples, and said:
'Take, eat.
This is my body given up for you.
Do this in remembrance of me.'

The celebrant takes the cup into his hands and says
After supper he took the cup and again
gave you thanks;
he gave it to his disciples and said:
'Drink of it, all of you.
This is my blood of the new covenant,
poured out for you and for many
for the forgiveness of sins.
Whenever you drink it, do so in
remembrance of me.'
With this bread and this cup
**we proclaim Christ's death until his
coming in glory.**

As we thank you, Father, for the gift of
your Son,
we proclaim his passion and death,
his resurrection and ascension,
his pouring out of the Holy Spirit
and his presence with his people.
Renew us by the same Spirit
so that we might be united in the body of
your Son
and serve you as a royal priesthood in the
joy of your eternal kingdom.

Receive our praises, almighty Father,
through Jesus Christ our Lord,
with whom and in whom,
by the power of the Holy Spirit,
we worship you with songs of everlasting
praise:
**Blessing, honour, glory . . . [[CF 7]] . . . and
ever. Amen.**

15. *THE PRAYER 'OUR FATHER'*
    ⟦No text is printed here⟧

16. *THE BREAKING OF THE BREAD*
    We break this bread . . . ⟦CF 8(a)⟧ . . . **in one bread.**

17. *THE COMMUNION*
    The gifts of God for the people of God.
    Following the invitation to participate, the sacrament is administered using these words
    The body of Christ [which was given . . . ⟦CF 10(a)⟧ . . . with thanksgiving]. **Amen.**
    The blood of Christ [which was shed . . . ⟦CF 10(b)⟧ . . . be thankful]. **Amen.**

    Then all that remains of the consecrated bread and wine is consumed.

CONCLUSION

18. *WORSHIP AND THANKSGIVING*
    *After Communion there may be a time of worship and thanksgiving with or without song;
    a time of openness to the Holy Spirit and the manifestations of his supernatural gifts.*

19. *POST-COMMUNION PRAYER*
    **Eternal God and heavenly Father,
    in your goodness you have received us
    as the living body of your Son, our Saviour Jesus Christ;
    you have fed us with spiritual food
    in the sacrament of his body and blood.
    Now, Lord, in gratitude we offer you our lives
    as a living sacrifice consecrated to your service.
    Send us into the world in peace;
    clothe us with strength and valour
    to love and to serve you with joy and sincerity of heart,
    through Christ our Lord. Amen.**

20. *BLESSING AND DISMISSAL*
    The peace of God . . . ⟦CF 12(a)⟧ . . . with you always. **Amen.**

    Brothers and sisters, rise, let us go and serve the Lord.
    Amen. We will serve the Lord. Alleluia.

    Or there may be said
    Go in peace to love and serve the Lord.
    Thanks be to God.

E. Africa

14. The Church of Nigeria
(Anglican Communion)

The dioceses of Nigeria separated from the Province of West Africa and were constituted as the Province of Nigeria in 1979. The only lawful eucharistic rite at that time was the 1662 service of Communion. In 1983 the Province authorized its own experimental eucharistic liturgy, largely modelled on **EngA**, and printed as **Nig** in **LAL**. The Province aimed to provide a complete Nigerian Book of Common Prayer, and the project was addressed by the Church of Nigeria Liturgical Commission chaired by Bishop Gideon Olajide, Bishop of Ibadan. The Commission worked on revising and enriching the eucharistic rite from 1991 to 1996, and it was then accepted by the House of Bishops, ratified by General Synod, and incorporated into the large hardback Book of Common Prayer of the Church of Nigeria (Anglican Communion). Its authorization and publication in English paved the way for translation into the major languages of the country, and the 1996 rites have only replaced 1662 as translations have become available. The eucharistic rite is presented here under the code **Nig1**.

Whereas **Nig** closely resembled **EngA**, **Nig1** has moved on a little in terms both of inculturation and of providing alternatives, though the text overall reads as still deeply western in language and thought-forms. Some encouragement of Nigerian ways is provided at the Peace (§14) and the Preparation of the Gifts (§15). The range of alternatives includes five forms of intercession, and no fewer than 46 proper prefaces. The main interest, however, lies with the addition of a second eucharistic prayer. This draws heavily upon **CSI**, and in the process provides an epiclesis subsequent to the narrative of institution and the anamnesis.

THE EUCHARIST IN THE 1996 BOOK OF COMMON PRAYER OF THE CHURCH OF NIGERIA (ANGLICAN COMMUNION) (Nig1)

[The numbering here is original to the rite, except nos 31–33, which are editorial. The lining is mostly original. The capitalization is original]

THE HOLY EUCHARIST

DIRECTIONS

[17 opening notes provide guidance for the rite. The first provides principles for using the rite as 'chief service' even without a priest, and facilitates lay leadership and lay participation in such an 'Ante Communion' service. Further notes give directions concerning the structure of the rite, the parts of presbyters, deacons and lay persons, banns of marriage, the disposal of alms, the vesture of ministers and the nature of the elements.]

THE PREPARATION

1. *A hymn may be sung*
   An appropriate sentence may be used (See Appendix III)

2. [Versicles and responses of greeting]

3. *COLLECT FOR PURITY: (Standing)*
   Almighty God, to whom . . . [CF 1] . . . Christ our Lord. Amen.

4. *GLORIA IN EXCELSIS (may be said or sung)*
   Glory be to God in the highest . . . [ELLC 3] . . . God the Father. Amen.
   God's people] his people

ACT OF PENITENCE

The Decalogue or else the Summary of the Law shall be said or sung on Sundays. At other times, instead thereof, the Kyrie Eleison or the Trisagion may be sung or said.

5 (a) *THE COMMANDMENTS*
   [Old Testament Commandments with New Testament interpretation, 1662 congregational responses]
   or
   (b) *SUMMARY OF THE LAW*
   [Jesus' Summary of the Law with 1662 final congregational response]
   or
   (c) *KYRIE ELEISON*
   [The Kyries (ELLC 2) in two alternative responsive threefold patterns]
   or
   (d) *TRISAGION*
   [The Trisagion]

6. [Exhortation to penitence, with a brief lead-in or one or more of the Comfortable Words]

7. [Further lead-in to confession with congregational confession and presidential absolution (CF 2)]

8. *Then follows the Collect for the Day.* [With salutation]
   Let us pray. *(The President says the Collect)*

9. *THE MINISTRY OF THE WORD (Congregation sits)*
   [Provision for Old Testament, Psalm and New Testament Readings with proclamation and responses]

10. [Provision for a *Gradual Canticle or Hymn, and for the Gospel (with *procession) and responses]

11. *Congregation sits.* THE SERMON

12. *Congregation stands.* THE NICENE CREED
    We believe . . . ⟦ELLC 5⟧ . . . world to come. Amen.
    For us] For us men
    was incarnate . . . truly human] **by the power of the Holy Spirit He became incarnate of the Virgin Mary and was made man**
    [and the Son]] OMIT BRACKETS

13. *THE INTERCESSION*
    ⟦Five varying forms of intercession, with permission to use other forms instead⟧

14. *THE MINISTRY OF THE SACRAMENT*
    All stand: The President says either the following or other suitable words:

    ### THE PEACE

Christ is our peace.	*or*	We are the body of Christ.
He has reconciled us to God		In the one Spirit we were all baptized
in one body by the cross.		into one body.
We meet in His name and share His		Let us then pursue all that makes for
peace.		peace and builds up our common life.

    The Peace of the Lord be always with you.
    And also with you.
    Let us offer one another a sign of peace.

    And all may exchange a sign of peace; African fraternal or traditional embrace or traditional handshake or double handclasp.

    ### THE PREPARATION OF THE GIFTS

15. *A Hymn or lyrics or choruses with or without musical accompaniment and dancing may follow as the Bread and Wine are brought by the representatives of the congregation to the Deacon or President. The people dance forward to give their offerings. People stand as the offerings are presented and placed on the Holy Table.*

16. *Ceremonial washing of hands may take place here. These words may be said as water is poured on the fingers.*
    I wash my hands in innocence, O Lord,
    that I may go about your altar
    and lift up the voice of thanksgiving. **Amen.**

    The President takes the Bread and Cup into his hands and places them on the Holy Table. At the offering of the Bread

    Blessed are you . . . ⟦CF 4(a)⟧ . . . bread of life. **Blessed be God for ever.**
    At the offering of the Cup

    Blessed are you . . . ⟦CF 4(b)⟧ . . . become our spiritual drink. **Blessed be God for ever.**

17. *Then the President takes the offering in his hand and says with the people:*
    Yours, Lord, is the greatness, the power,
    the glory, the splendour, and the majesty,
    for everything in heaven and earth is Yours.
    All things come from You, and of Your own do we give You.
    Or
    Accept, we pray You, O Lord, these gifts
    which we here bring to You as the token of our love and gratitude;
    and grant that they may be so wisely used,
    that by them the work of Your Church may be prospered
    and Your kingdom enlarged; for the glory of Jesus Christ our Saviour. **Amen.**

18. *THE EUCHARISTIC PRAYER, THE TAKING OF THE BREAD AND CUP AND THE GIVING OF THANKS*

Eucharistic Prayer 1

(Congregation remains standing) (The President faces the congregation and sings or says):

The Lord be with you . . . ⟦ELLC 6⟧ . . .
give Him thanks and praise.

It is indeed right:
it is our duty and our joy
at all times and in all places
to give You thanks and praise
Holy Father, heavenly King,
Almighty and eternal God
through Jesus Christ Your only Son our
    Lord,
for He is Your living word,
through Him You have created all things
from the beginning,
and formed us in Your own image.
Through Him You have freed us
from the slavery of sin,
giving Him to be born as man
and to die upon the cross;
You raised Him from the dead
and exalted Him to your right hand on
    high,
through Him You have sent upon us
Your Holy and Life-giving Spirit,
And made us a people for Your own
    possession.

Proper Prefaces ⟦directions re Proper Prefaces⟧

Therefore with angels and archangels
and with all the company of heaven,
we proclaim Your great and glorious
    name,
for ever praising You and saying:
Holy, Holy . . . ⟦ELLC 7⟧ . . . in the highest.
This ANTHEM may also be used ⟦responsively⟧:
Blessed is he . . . ⟦ELLC 8⟧ . . . the highest.

(The congregation may kneel)
Accept our praises, heavenly Father,
    through
Your Son our Saviour Jesus Christ:
and as we follow his example
and obey his command,
grant that by the power of Your Holy
    Spirit
these gifts of bread and wine
may be to us His Body and Blood:

Who in the same night that he was
    betrayed,
took bread and gave You thanks,
He broke it and gave it to His disciples
saying: 'Take, eat, this is my body
which is given for you:
do this in remembrance of me.'
In the same way, after supper
He took the cup and gave You thanks.
He gave it to them,
saying: 'Drink this, all of you;
this is my blood of the new covenant,
which is shed for you and for many
for the forgiveness of sins.
Do this as often as you drink it,
in remembrance of me.'

Therefore we proclaim the mystery . . .
    ⟦CF 6(a)⟧ . . . **come again.**

Therefore, heavenly Father,
we remember His offering of Himself
made once for all upon the cross:
we proclaim His mighty resurrection
and glorious ascension.
As we look for His coming in glory,
we celebrate with this bread and this cup
His one perfect sacrifice.

Accept through Him,
our great High Priest
this our sacrifice of thanks and praise:
and as we eat and drink these holy gifts
in the presence of Your divine Majesty,
renew us by Your Spirit,
inspire us with Your love,
and unite us in the body of Your Son,
Jesus Christ our Lord.
Through Him, and with Him, and in Him,
by the power of the Holy Spirit
with all who stand before You
on earth and in heaven,
we worship You, Father Almighty,
in songs of everlasting praise.
Blessing and . . . ⟦CF 7⟧ . . . ever. Amen.

Silence may be kept

(Congregation remains standing) (The President faces the congregation and sings or says):

The Lord be with you . . . [ELLC 6] . . . **It is meet and right so to do.**

It is very meet, right,
and our bounden duty,
that we should at all times,
and in all places,
give thanks to You, O Lord,
Holy Father, Almighty and Everlasting God.

(Then follows this Preface, or another Preface proper to the season)

Through Jesus Christ Your Son our Lord
through whom You did create the heaven
   and the earth
and all that is in them,
and did make man in Your Own image,
and when he had fallen into sin,
did redeem him to be the first fruit
of a new creation.
Therefore with angels and archangels
and with all the company of heaven,
we laud and magnify Your glorious name;
evermore praising You, and saying:
Holy, holy, holy, Lord God of hosts,
Heaven and earth are full of Your glory,
glory be to You, O Lord most high.
Blessed is He that has come
and is to come in the name of the Lord,
Hosanna in the highest.

Truly holy, truly blessed are You,
O heavenly Father,
who of Your tender love towards mankind
did give Your only Son Jesus Christ
to take our nature upon Him
and to suffer death upon the cross
for our redemption;
who made there,
by His one oblation of Himself once offered,
a full, perfect, and sufficient sacrifice,
oblation and satisfaction,
for the sins of the whole world:
and did institute
and in His gospel command us
to continue,
a perpetual memory of His
precious death,
until His coming again,
who, in the same night that He was betrayed,
took bread,
and when He had given thanks,
He broke it,
and gave it to His disciples saying,

'Take, eat,
this is my body which is given for you:
do this in remembrance of me.'
Likewise after supper
He took the Cup,
and, when He had given thanks,
He gave it to them, saying,
'Drink this all of you,
for this is my blood of the new covenant,
which is shed for you and for many
for the remission of sins:
do this, as often as you shall drink it,
in remembrance of me.'
Amen, Your death,
O Lord, we commemorate,
Your resurrection we confess,
and Your second coming we await.
Glory be to You, O Christ.

Wherefore, O Father,
having in remembrance
the precious death and passion,
and glorious resurrection and
ascension of Your Son our Lord,
we Your servants do this in remembrance
   of Him,
as He had commanded,
until His coming again,
giving thanks to You for the perfect
redemption which You have wrought for us
   in Him.
We give thanks to You, we praise You,
we glorify You, O Lord our God.

And we most humbly pray You,
O merciful Father,
to sanctify with Your Holy Spirit,
us and Your own gifts of bread and wine,
that the bread which we break
may be the communion of the body of Christ
and the cup which we bless may be the
communion of the blood of Christ.
Grant that being joined together in Him,
we may all attain to the unity of the faith,
and may grow up in all things
unto Him who is the Head,
even Christ, our Lord,
by Whom and with Whom
in the unity of the Holy Spirit
all honour and glory be unto You,
O Father Almighty, world without end.
Amen.

Silence may be kept.

19. *The President breaks the consecrated bread, saying:*

   (A) The bread which we break, is it not the communion of the Body of Christ?

   He then lays his hand on the cup and says:
   The cup which we bless, is it not the communion of the Blood of Christ?
   Though we are many, we are one body, because we share in one Bread.

   Or (B) We break this bread . . . ⟦CF 8(a)⟧ . . . we share in one Bread.
   Either here or during the distribution, one of the following anthems shall be said:

   Lamb of God . . . ⟦ELLC 9(b)⟧ . . . **grant us peace.**
   sin] sins THRICE
   or
   Jesus, Lamb of God . . . ⟦ELLC 9(a)⟧ . . . the world: give us Your peace.

20. *PRAYER OF HUMBLE ACCESS (All kneeling)*
   We do not presume . . . ⟦CF 3(a)⟧ . . . He in us. Amen.
   this your table] Your table
   our sinful . . . and that] OMIT

21. *THE DISTRIBUTION OF THE EUCHARISTIC ELEMENTS*
   Before the distribution, the President says:
   Draw near . . . ⟦CF 9(a)⟧ . . . heart by faith with thanksgiving.

   Or
   Holy things belong to Holy people.
   If any is holy, let him come;
   If any is not, let him repent.
   The Lord is here.
   There is one holy,
   One Lord Jesus Christ
   to the glory of God the Father,
   blessed for ever. Amen.

22. *The President and people receive communion. At the distribution the Minister says to each communicant:*
   The body of Christ keep you in eternal life.
   The blood of Christ keep you in eternal life.
   or
   The Body of Christ.
   The Blood of Christ.

   The communicant replies each time
   Amen.

   and then receives.

23. *During the distribution lyrics or hymns may be sung.*

24. *If either or both of the consecrated elements be likely to prove insufficient, the President himself returns to the holy table and adds more, saying these words:*

(for bread)
Our Saviour, Christ,
in the same night He was betrayed,
took bread and gave You thanks:
He broke it and gave it to His disciples
saying: 'Take, eat: this is my body
which is given for you:
do this in remembrance of me.'

(for wine)
In the same way, after supper,
He took the cup and gave You thanks,
He gave it to them,
saying: 'Drink this all of you,
this is my blood of the new covenant,
which is shed for you and for many
for the forgiveness of sins.
Do this in remembrance of me.'

Or

(for bread)
Father, giving thanks over the bread and the
  cup
according to the institution of Your Son
  Jesus Christ,
who said: 'Take, eat: this is my body',
we pray that this bread also may be to us
  His Body,
to be received in remembrance of Him.

(for wine)
Father, giving thanks over the bread and
  the cup
according to the institution of Your Son
  Jesus Christ,
who said: 'Drink this; this is my blood',
we pray that this wine also may be to us
  His Blood
to be received in remembrance of Him.

25. *A Hymn may be sung. (Here any consecrated bread and wine which is not required for purposes of communion is consumed.)*

AFTER COMMUNION

Appropriate sentence may be said here.

26. As our Saviour taught us, so we pray.
    Our Father in Heaven . . . [[ELLC 1]] . . . for ever. Amen.
    Save us from the time of trial and] Lead us not into temptation but

27. *Either or both of the following prayers or other suitable prayer is said.*
    Father of all . . . [[CF 11(b)]] . . . Christ our Lord. **Amen.**
    Or **Almighty God, we thank you . . . [[CF 11(a)]] . . . praise and glory. Amen.**

28. *The President may say this or an alternative Blessing:*
    The peace of God . . . [[CF 12(a)]] . . . with you always. **Amen.**

29. *A hymn may be sung as the Ministers are processing out.*

30. Go in peace . . . [[CF 12(b)]] . . . of Christ. **Amen.**
    Or Go in the peace . . . [[CF 12(c)]] . . . be to God.

31. *APPENDIX I*

PROPER PREFACES
  [[46 Proper Prefaces]]

32. *APPENDIX II*

EXHORTATIONS
  [[Three Long Exhortations taken from 1662]]

33. *APPENDIX III*

SENTENCES
  [[A scriptural sentence for each Sunday of the year and for other Holy Days]]

15. The Anglican Church of Congo

The first separate Anglican organization in Congo came with the formation of the diocese of Boga in 1972, within the Province of Uganda.[70] Burundi, Rwanda and Zaire separated from Uganda in 1980 to form a new Province, and further separation led to the Province of Zaire in 1992. Swahili is the common tongue in the east of the country, and Swahili translations of English rites had been provided for Boga diocese in 1973, and again, in a larger bound Prayer Book, in 1984. In 1992 the new Province addressed the provision of provincial liturgy, first by an expeditious editing and republishing of the 1984 Book, but second by setting in train the preparation of a completely new Book.[71] Representatives of the Province took part in the Kanamai Consultation on African Culture and Anglican Liturgy in 1993, and that participation assisted the task within Congo. In the process a new eucharistic rite was compiled and was authorized as part of the 1998 BCP. The rite has three eucharistic prayers, the first conserving much of the **EngA** tradition, the second having a greater emphasis upon creation and dispensing with a first epiclesis, and the third having all the appearance of 'blue sky' thinking among the compilers.

HOLY COMMUNION FROM THE PROVINCE OF THE ANGLICAN CHURCH OF CONGO *BOOK OF COMMON PRAYER*, 1998 (Cong)

⟦The translation from Swahili is by Ian Tarrant, a compiler of the rite.
The numbering and lining are original.⟧

TEACHING ⟦Two pages of teaching about Holy Communion⟧

INSTRUCTIONS

⟦Ten notes concern preparation, the roles of presbyter and deacon, the use of the Commandments, the actions of the president and posture of the people during the eucharistic prayer, the elements to be used and the persons to distribute them. One explains that material marked with an asterisk (*) is always optional, and material marked with a cross (†) is optional except at the main Sunday service. Another directs that during each of the eucharistic prayers, where the five manual acts are indicated by references, the presbyter should at (a) take the plate into his hands, at (b) break the bread, at (c) lay his hand on all the bread, at (d) take the cup into his hands, and at (e) lay his hand on each cup or bottle of wine.⟧

---

70 The nation was called Zaire, the term naturally used at the same time for church organization, until 1998, when, following a revolution, the nation became 'Congo', and church bodies followed suit.

71 The story of the creation of the 1998 Congo Book of Common Prayer is told in Ian Tarrant, *Anglican Swahili Prayer Books* (Alcuin/GROW Joint Liturgical Study 62, SCM-Canterbury, 2006).

HOLY COMMUNION *or* THE LORD'S SUPPER

1. *At the entry of the ministers a psalm or hymn is sung.*

2.† *The verse of the day is read.*

3. *The presbyter welcomes the people with these words:*
   The Lord be with you.
   And also with you.
   From Easter to Pentecost, the presbyter says: Alleluia! Christ is risen. **He is risen indeed. Alleluia!**

4.† *All kneel and say one of the following prayers:*
   (a) **Almighty God . . . ⟦CF 1⟧ . . . Christ our Lord. Amen.**
   Or
   (b) **Almighty God,**
   you bring to light things hidden in darkness,
   and know the shadows of our hearts:
   by your Spirit,
   cleanse us, revive us and renew us,
   that we may walk in the light,
   and glorify your name,
   through Jesus Christ, the light of the world. Amen.

5.† *The TEN COMMANDMENTS or OUR LORD'S SUMMARY OF THE LAW are read by a minister who stands, while the congregation remains kneeling.*
   (a)† ⟦The Ten Commandments with New Testament matching verses, and congregational responses⟧
or (b)† ⟦Our Lord's Summary of the Law with congregational response⟧

6. *A presbyter reads two or more of these verses:*
   Hear the words of comfort our Saviour Jesus Christ says to all who truly turn to him:
   ⟦Matt. 11.28; John 3.16; 1 Tim. 1.15; 1 John 2.1 as in 1662⟧

7. ⟦Exhortation to silence, then call to confession and congregational confession⟧

8. *The presbyter declares the remission of sins.*
   Almighty God . . . ⟦CF 2⟧ . . . Jesus Christ our Lord. **Amen.**

9.† *Gloria is said or sung.*
   Glory to God . . . ⟦ELLC 3⟧ . . . glory of God the Father. Amen.

RECEIVING THE WORD OF GOD

10. *The presbyter says the COLLECT OF THE DAY* ⟦with prior greeting⟧

11. *Two or three passages from the Holy Scriptures are read, the last being the Gospel.*

12. *All sit. A passage from the OLD TESTAMENT is read* ⟦proclamation before and versicle and response after⟧

13.* *A psalm or hymn may be said or sung.*

14. *All sit. A passage from the NEW TESTAMENT is read* ⟦proclamation before and versicle and response after⟧

15.* *A psalm or hymn may be said or sung.*

16. *All stand. A passage from a GOSPEL is read* ⟦proclamation and response before and after⟧

17. *SERMON*
    The sermon may be followed by short prayers, a song, or silence.

18.† *All stand. THE NICENE CREED*
We believe in one God . . . ⟦ELLC 5⟧ . . . world to come. Amen.[72]
> For us] For us people
> was incarnate . . . human] **by the power of the Holy Spirit he became incarnate of the Virgin Mary and was made human**
> [and the Son]] OMIT BRACKETS

THE PRAYERS OF THE CHURCH

19.† ⟦The three forms include provision for extemporary prayer by the congregation⟧

20. *THE LORD'S PRAYER.* Let us pray;
as our Saviour commanded and taught us, we are bold to say:
Our Father . . . ⟦ELLC 1⟧ . . . and for ever. Amen.

THE PEACE OF THE LORD

21.† *All stand. Before greeting the people, the presbyter says one of these introductions (chosen according to the season or the theme of the service):*
⟦1 Cor. 12.13 with Rom. 14.9; Eph. 2.16; Isa. 9.6–7; John 14.27; Gal. 5 22–23, 25⟧

The peace of the Lord be always with you
And also with you.

The presbyter may say:
In the love of Christ, let us give one another peace.

The people greet each other.

THE FEAST OF THE LORD'S TABLE

22. *The presbyter prepares the bread and wine on the Holy Table, while the people sing a hymn, and give their offerings. The presbyter prays over the offerings. The presbyter says the EUCHARISTIC PRAYER: 22a or 22b or 22c.* ⟦The references to manual acts in the narrative of institution are explained in opening Instructions on page 138.⟧

---

72 ⟦A footnote gives an explanation of 'katolika'.⟧

22a.

The Lord be with you . . . ⟦ELLC 6⟧ . . . **It is good and right so to do.**

Indeed, it is best for us, it is our duty and our joy,
at all times and in all places, to thank you O Lord,
Holy Father, almighty and eternal God,
through Jesus Christ, your only Son our Lord.
For he is your living Word,
through him you have created all things from the beginning,
and formed us in your own image.
Through him you have saved us from the slavery of sin,
giving him a human birth, to die upon the cross,
and to rise again for us.
Through him you have made us your own people,
exalting him to your right hand in glory;
and through him you have sent us your Holy Spirit of life.

⟦Seasonal inserts are printed for major festivals and holy days.⟧

Therefore with angels and archangels, and with all the company of heaven,
we exalt and praise your holy name.
We praise you forever, saying:
Holy, holy, holy . . . ⟦ELLC 7⟧ . . . **Glory be to you, O Lord in heaven.**
Blessed is . . . ⟦ELLC 8⟧ . . . **in the highest.**

Accept our praises, O heavenly Father,
through your Son, our Saviour Jesus Christ,
and as we receive this bread and this cup as your Son commanded us,
may we be partakers of his body and blood.
On the same night that he was betrayed he took bread[a]

and, after giving you thanks, he broke it[b]
and gave it to his disciples, saying,
'Take, eat, this is my Body[c] which is given for you;
do this in remembrance of me.'
In the same way, when they had eaten,[d]
he took the cup;
and after giving you thanks,
he gave it to them, saying,
'Drink this all of you,
for this[e] is my Blood of the New Covenant,
which is shed for you and for many,
for the forgiveness of sins;
do this, as often as you drink it,
in remembrance of me.'

Christ has . . . ⟦CF 6(a)⟧ . . . **come again.**

Indeed, heavenly Father,
with this bread and this cup we do this in remembrance of him.
We show and proclaim his perfect sacrifice made once for all on the cross;
we proclaim his resurrection from the dead,
and his ascension into heaven;
and we wait for his coming in glory.

Accept through him, our high priest,
this our sacrifice of praise and thanks,
and as we eat and drink these holy gifts,
in the presence of your majesty,
renew us by your Spirit,
inspire us with your love,
and unite us in the body of your Son.

With him and through him,
by the power of the Holy Spirit,
with all who stand before you in earth and heaven,
we worship you, Father Almighty, now and forever.
Blessing and . . . ⟦CF 7⟧ . . . **ever. Amen.**

or 22b.

The Lord be with you ... ⟦ELLC 6⟧ ... **It
is good and right so to do.**

Indeed, it is our joy to thank you,
O heavenly Father, for you created all
    things:
the stars, sun, moon, and this world;
hill and valley, forest and field, river and
    lake,
and all that dwell in them.
You created human beings,
making them more intelligent and
    powerful than all the animals;
and you chose one nation to know more
    of you.
We give you thanks,
because when people scorned your will,
you called them to return to your ways,
by filling the prophets with your Holy
    Spirit,
to be witnesses to your righteousness and
    power.

With the words that the prophet Isaiah
    heard in the temple,
we join with the angels and archangels,
and all the host of heaven,
praising you forever, and saying,
**Holy, holy, holy ... ⟦ELLC 7⟧ ... Glory be
to you, O Lord in heaven.**
Blessed is he ... ⟦ELLC 8⟧ ... the highest.

We give you thanks, O loving Father,
for you sent your Son,
to be born as man,
to show us your likeness,
and to save people of all nations,
by dying for our sake on the cross.

On the same night that he was betrayed he
    took bread.[(a)]
and, after giving you thanks, he broke it[(b)]
and gave it to his disciples, saying,
'Take, eat,[(c)] this is my Body
which is given for you;
do this in remembrance of me.'
In the same way, when they had eaten,[(d)]
he took the cup; and after giving you
    thanks,
he gave it to them, saying,
'Drink this all of you,
for this is my blood[(e)] of the new Covenant,
which is shed for you and for many,
for the forgiveness of sins;
do this, as often as you drink it,
in remembrance of me.'

Christ has ... ⟦CF 6(a)⟧ ... come again.

We give you thanks, because you fulfilled
    his promise,
by sending us the Helper, the Holy Spirit,
so that the Good News of your love
might be known throughout the world.

And now, as we do this in remembrance
    of Jesus,
grant, by the power of your Spirit,
that we may be partakers of his Body and
    his Blood.
Renew us through your Spirit,
that together with your worldwide church,
we may serve our neighbours in your love,
draw all people to you,
and reveal your glory,
Father Almighty, now and forever:
Blessing and ... ⟦CF 7⟧ ... ever. Amen.

or 22c.

Almighty Father,
You are with us at all times and in all
    places;
we lift our hearts and voices to glorify
    your name:
We praise your holy name!

Holy and perfect God,
source of righteousness and truth:
you are light, there is no darkness in you,
and you hate all sin.
We praise your holy name!

You are the one who loves even us sinners:
you seek to gather your lost children
    beneath your wings;
time and again you call us back to you.
We praise your holy name!

You sent your Son,
to be born of the Virgin Mary,
to be human like us, but without sin,
and you filled him with your Holy Spirit.
**Thanks be to Jesus Christ, he came to save
    us!**

He humbled himself to be the servant of
    all:
he healed, he taught, he drew near to those
    whom others rejected.
For the sake of our salvation, he died on
    the cross,
rose from the dead, and ascended into
    heaven.
**Thanks be to Jesus Christ, he came to save
    us!**

Before his death, at table with his disciples:
he took bread,[(a)] gave you thanks, broke it,[(b)]
and gave it to them, saying:

'Take, eat,[(c)] this is my Body which is given
    for you.'
Afterwards he took the cup,[(d)] gave you
    thanks,
and gave it to them, saying:
'This is my blood[(e)] of the new Covenant
which is shed for you and for many,
for the forgiveness of sins.
Do this, in remembrance of me.'
**Thanks be to Jesus Christ, he came to save
    us!**

He did not leave his friends like orphans,
for your Holy Spirit came to comfort them,
to sanctify them, and to empower them.
Father, we praise your name forever,
because your Spirit gives us life, unity and
    strength.
May your Holy Spirit be with us every day!

Today as we do this in remembrance of
    Christ,
through the power of your Spirit
may this bread be to us his body,
and this wine be to us his blood,
so that our hearts be made clean,
and we may be ready to obey your will.
May your Holy Spirit be with us every day!

Revive your church,
that it might be salt, yeast and light in the
    world,
bearing witness to your holiness and love,
while we wait for Christ's return in glory.
May your Holy Spirit be with us every day!

We will worship you, Holy God,
without ceasing, on earth and in heaven,
forever and ever.
Alleluia, alleluia, alleluia! Amen.

23. Let us prepare to receive the Lord's meal:
    We do not presume . . . ⟦CF 3(a)⟧ . . . he in us. Amen.
      that our sinful bodies . . . most precious blood and] OMIT

24. Draw near with faith, receive this holy sacrament of the body and blood of Christ as
    we remember that he died for our sake, and feed on him in our hearts by faith with
    thanksgiving.

    The presbyter and other ministers receive the bread and the wine.

25.* *The minister distributing the bread may say:*
    The body of our Lord Jesus Christ . . . ⟦CF 10(a)⟧ . . . with thanksgiving.

    And the minister distributing the wine may say:
    The blood of our Lord Jesus Christ . . . ⟦CF 10(b)⟧ . . . and give thanks.

26. *Then the ministers distribute the bread and wine to the people, using the words of 26a, 26b or 26c. While the people are receiving, silence should be kept at first, but later prayerful songs may be sung.*

26a *Those distributing the bread and wine say to each person:*
The body of Christ. *or* The blood of Christ.
And each one receiving replies: **Amen.**

OR

26b *For the bread:*
Take this and eat remembering that Christ died for you, and give thanks.
For the cup:
Drink this, remembering that Christ's blood was shed for you, and give thanks.

OR

26c *For the bread:* The body of Christ, the bread of heaven.
For the cup: The blood of Christ, the cup of salvation.
And each one receiving replies: **Amen.**

27.* *If the consecrated bread and/or wine is finished before everybody has received, the Presbyter adds more, saying these words:*
Merciful Father, as we remember your Son, who gave his body and blood for our sake, grant that
. . . as we eat this bread we may be partakers of his body;
. . . (and) as we drink this wine we may be partakers of his blood;
through the power of the Holy Spirit. **Amen.**

28. *If consecrated bread and wine are left over, they are consumed by the Presbyter and other communicants whom he invites, straightaway, or after the Blessing, with reverence.*

THE GOING OUT OF THE PEOPLE OF GOD

29. *All say one of these prayers:*
Almighty God, we thank you . . . ⟦CF 11(a)⟧ . . . **your praise and glory. Amen.**
    Send us out] Send us out into the world
    OR **Father of all** . . . ⟦CF 11(b)⟧ . . . **through Christ our Lord. Amen.**
    met us in your Son and brought us home] sent us your Son to bring us home
    hope you have set before us] hope of salvation

30.* *An appropriate sentence may be said.*

31.† *The Presbyter, or the Bishop if present, says the Peace and Blessing, or a seasonal blessing.*
The Peace of God . . . ⟦CF 12(a)⟧ . . . with you always. **Amen.**

Or: ⟦Nine seasonal blessings⟧

32. *A minister dismisses the people with these words:*

In the season of Easter	*Or*
The Lord be with you.	*At other times:*
And with your spirit.	The Lord be with you.
Go in peace to love and serve the	**And with your spirit.**
Lord. Alleluia!	Go in peace to love and serve the Lord.
In the name of Christ. Alleluia! Amen.	**In the name of Christ. Amen.**

33.* *Closing hymn.*

16. The Anglican Church of Kenya

The Church of the Province of Kenya in the 1970s authorized in its *Modern English Services* a modern-English version of 1662 (see **LAL** p. 204). However, the issue of true inculturation became very live in the 1980s, and a new departure came when in 1986 the Provincial Board of Theological Education (PBTE), chaired by Bishop David Gitari, recommended the production of a Kenyan service of Holy Communion. After an unadventurous draft, drawn largely from **EngA,** was criticized by the worship committee of St Andrew's Institute for Theology and Development, Kabare, the same committee found itself asked to revise the draft. Instead they produced in June 1987 an almost completely new service, written in English, but without any inbuilt dependence upon western models. This was circulated in duplicated form and aroused interest both inside Kenya and beyond it.[73] The worldwide circulation was increased through the discussion at the Partners in Mission Consultation in Kenya in February 1988, and the eucharistic prayer was published in England as an example of inculturation in Africa.[74] The structure had some residual resemblances to 1662, as the preparation of the Table was followed by the penitential section, the breaking of the bread came within the narrative of institution, and the Gloria in Excelsis came after communion. An option of sharing the Peace also came just before the Blessing. But the most imaginative features were in the wording, not least in the opening dialogue to the eucharistic prayer. Where the 1987 text differed more than minimally from the 1989 revised rite it is shown by *apparatus* below.

The Provincial Synod asked the PBTE to revise the draft rite. Some structural changes were made, and some minor textual ones. One wholly unparalleled alteration was needed in the new form of blessing. The notion of Christians sending their troubles 'to the setting sun' apparently caused disquiet in the western parts of the country (where local inhabitants imagined themselves to be targeted), and a more overtly Christian solution was devised. The rite was published as *A Kenyan Service of Holy Communion* (Uzima Press, 1989) and went through several printings in booklet form, some containing slight textual variations. It continued to attract worldwide interest and was used for the opening service of the 1998 Lambeth Conference. It was then incorporated into the Anglican Church of Kenya (as the Province was now titled) Book, *Our Modern Services* (Uzima, 2002), the comprehensive set of Kenyan rites edited by Joyce Karuri

---

73 The story of the first production of the 1987 draft and its subsequent revision and authorization in 1989 is told in Graham Kings and Geoff Morgan, *Offerings from Kenya to Anglicanism: Liturgical Texts and Contexts Including 'A Kenyan Service of Holy Communion'* (Alcuin/GROW Joint Liturgical Study 50, Grove Books, Cambridge, 2001). For the later stages of inclusion in *Our Modern Services*, see also Joyce Karuri's introductory essay in that Book, pp. 299–307.

74 See Phillip Tovey, *Inculturation: The Eucharist in Africa* (Alcuin/GROW Joint Liturgical Study 7, Grove Books, Bramcote, 1988) pp. 44–5.

and published as a single Book on the day David Gitari retired as primate. Since then the primary task has been to provide it in local languages – initially in Swahili, but following that in over 40 tribal tongues. In the event, after a poor Swahili version was produced in 2003, the translation work stalled for some years, and the definitive Swahili version was only published in December 2010. Versions in other languages are still to follow.

THE SERVICE OF HOLY COMMUNION FROM *OUR MODERN SERVICES* *ANGLICAN CHURCH OF KENYA* (2002) (Ken)

⟦The numbering is original to the rite save for §39 and it varies from 1987; much of the lining is editorial⟧

NOTES
⟦Six opening notes concerning posture, hymnody, provision of the elements and consumption of the remains⟧

SCRIPTURE SENTENCES FOR USE IN SECTION 2
⟦Nine appropriate sentences, three of them seasonal⟧

ORDER OF SERVICE
1. *At the entry the people stand and a hymn is announced.*

2. *The minister reads a scripture sentence.*

3. *The minister welcomes the people using these or other appropriate words:*
   ⟦Five versicles and responses, with three additional ones for each of Christmas, Easter and Pentecost⟧

4. *The people kneel. One of the following prayers for purity is said by all:*
   Either
   Almighty God,
   you bring to light
   things hidden in darkness,
   and know the shadows of our hearts;
   cleanse and renew us by your Spirit,
   that we may walk in the light
   and glorify your name,
   through Jesus Christ,
   the Light of the world. Amen.
   Or
   Almighty God . . . ⟦CF 1⟧ . . . **Christ our Lord. Amen.**

5. *THE COMMANDMENTS*
   People remain kneeling. Then follows the reading of the Ten Commandments, or the New Testament interpretation of the Law, or the Summary of the Law.
   ⟦Ten Commandments with responses similar to 1662⟧
   Or
   THE NEW TESTAMENT INTERPRETATION OF THE LAW
   This section may be shared by two leaders: one to read the Old Testament version and the other, the New Testament rendering of the law.

6. ⟦Old Testament commandments with New Testament interpretative verses and congregational responses largely as in **EngA**⟧

or SUMMARY OF THE LAW

7. ⟦Jesus' Summary of the Law with congregational response⟧

THE GLORIA AND 'KYRIE ELEISON' (LORD HAVE MERCY)
Either version of the GLORIA may be sung or said:
   1987: BOTH VERSIONS COME AFTER §34
We stand to glorify the Lord.

Either

8. *This first version of the GLORIA may be accompanied by regular clapping.*
Glory to the Father
Glory to the Son
Glory to the Spirit
For ever Three in One
Be glorified at home
Be glorified in church
Be glorified in Kenya
Be glorified in Africa
Be glorified on earth
Be glorified in heaven
Glory to the Father
Glory to the Son
Glory to the Spirit
For ever Three in One
Alleluia
Amen.
   1987: IN LINES 5 AND 6 AND IN LINES 9 AND 10 THE TWO LINES COME IN INVERTED
   ORDER

Or this version

9. **Glory to God . . . ⟦ELLC 3⟧ . . . God the Father. Amen.**
   God's people] his people

Or during Lent only

10. *During Lent the petitions 'Lord have Mercy' are recommended instead of the Gloria. At other seasons, the Gloria is used.*
Lord have mercy . . . ⟦ELLC 2, threefold in English⟧ . . . **Lord have mercy.**

People remain standing. Prayer for the Day, introduced with these or other appropriate words:

11. As we stand, let us pray the prayer appointed for today.

MINISTRY OF THE WORD

People sit. Not more than three passages from scripture are read, the last of which is always the Gospel.

12. *The Old Testament:* ⟦Announcement, responses, *silence, *choir item⟧

13. *The Epistle:* ⟦Announcement, response⟧

14. *Silence may be kept. Hymn.*

15. *The Gospel.* ⟦All standing, announcement, proclamation at the end, response⟧

16. *Silence may be kept. Hymn.*

17. *Sermon.*

18. *THE NICENE CREED, introduced with the words:*
We stand together with Christians throughout the centuries, and throughout the world today, to affirm our faith in the words of the Nicene Creed.
We believe in one God . . . [[ELLC 5]] . . . world to come. Amen.
was incarnate . . . truly human] by the power of the Holy Spirit he became incarnate of the Virgin Mary and was made man
[and the Son]] OMIT BRACKETS

INTERCESSIONS

Prayerful songs may be sung between the intercessions. People may be encouraged to join in open prayer. The leading of the intercessions may be shared among the people.

Let us pray.
People sit or kneel.

EITHER – this Litany
19   [[Litany of intercession]]

OR – these Prayers of Intercession
20.   [[Prayer for the Church with versicles and responses]]

PRAYERS OF PENITENCE

People remain kneeling

21.   [[Call to confession, including Luke 9.23–24 and Matt. 11.28]]

22.   [[Congregational confession]]

23.   [[Absolution]]

24.   **Thank you, Father, for forgiveness;
we come to your table as your children,
not presuming but assured,
not trusting ourselves but your Word;
we hunger and thirst for righteousness,
and ask for our hearts to be satisfied
with the body and blood of your Son,
Jesus Christ the righteous. Amen.**

MINISTRY OF THE SACRAMENT

25.   **Sharing of Peace**
People stand
The peace of the Lord be always with you.
And also with you.
Let us offer one another a sign of peace.

People greet each other with a handshake or other appropriate gestures.
1987 HAS THE PEACE BEFORE THE BLESSING (§35)

26.   *The Holy Table is prepared for communion. A hymn is sung, during which the offering is collected. Presiding minister and his assistants may wash hands. If there is no offertory the minister moves directly to section 27. Where there is offertory, the minister and people may respond in the following or other appropriate manner:*
All things come from you, O Lord.
And of your own have we given you.
1987 OMITS

148

PRAYER OF THANKSGIVING

People remain standing

27. We remain standing for thanksgiving and remembrance.

Is the Father with us? **He is.**
Is Christ among us? **He is.**
Is the Spirit here? **He is.**
This is our God.
Father, Son and Holy Spirit.
We are his people.
We are redeemed.
Lift up your hearts . . . [ELLC 6] . . . **him thanks and praise.**

It is right and our delight
to give you thanks and praise,
great Father, living God, supreme over the world.
Creator, Provider, Saviour and Giver.
From a wandering nomad you created your family;
for a burdened people you raised up a leader;
for a confused nation you chose a king;
for a rebellious crowd you sent your prophets.
In these last days you have sent us your Son,
your perfect image, bringing your kingdom,
revealing your will, dying, rising, reigning,
remaking your people for yourself.
Through him you have poured out your Holy Spirit,
filling us with light and life.

Special thanksgivings shall be said at this point when appropriate (Sections 39–47)

Therefore with angels, archangels,
faithful ancestors and all in heaven,
we proclaim your great and glorious name,
forever praising you and saying:
Holy, holy . . . [ELLC 7] . . . in the highest.

THE BREAKING OF BREAD IS AT SECTION 29

The presiding minister performs the traditional actions of taking the bread and the cup.
People remain standing

Almighty God, owner of all things,
we thank you for giving up your Son
to die on the cross
for us who owe you everything.
Pour your refreshing Spirit on us
as we remember him in the way he commanded,
through these gifts of your creation.
On the same night that he was betrayed
he took bread and gave you thanks;
he broke it and gave it to his disciples, saying.
'Take, eat, this is my body
which is given for you;
Do this in remembrance of me.'
Amen. His body was broken for us.

In the same way, after supper
he took the cup and gave you thanks;
he gave it to them saying:
'Drink this, all of you,
this is my blood of the new covenant,
which is shed for you and for many,
for the forgiveness of sins.
Do this as often as you drink it,
in remembrance of me.'
Christ has . . . [CF 6(a)] . . . come again.

We are brothers and sisters through his blood.
We have died together,
we will rise together,
we will live together.

Therefore, heavenly Father, hear us
as we celebrate this covenant with joy,
and await the coming of our Saviour, Jesus Christ.
He died in our place,
making a full atonement for the sins of the whole world,
the perfect sacrifice, once and for all.
You accepted his offering
by raising him from death
and granting him great honour
at your right hand on high.
Amen. Jesus is Lord.

This is the feast of victory.
The lamb who was slain has begun his reign. Alleluia.

[the 1987 variants are at the head of the next page]

1987:   This is our God] Now who is our God?
         We are . . . **redeemed**] And who are we? **His faithful people**
         Provider] Allocator
         poured out your Holy] sent upon us your life-giving
         light and life] energy and light
         faithful ancestors and all] Christian ancestors
         The presiding . . . cup] *During the words of institution, the presiding minister performs the*
                              traditional actions of taking the bread and breaking it etc.
         Almighty God, owner] Owner
         Christ has died . . . come again] OMIT
         We are brothers] **Amen. We are brothers**
         our Saviour Jesus Christ] our Brother

THE COMMUNION
People kneel

28. As our Saviour taught us, we are bold to pray:
    Our Father in heaven . . . ⟦ELLC 1⟧ . . . for ever. Amen.
      Save us . . . trial and] Lead us not into temptation but
      1987: hallowed] holy
          Save us . . . trial and] Do not bring us to the test but

29. We break this bread . . . ⟦CF 8(a)⟧ . . . **for we all share one bread.**
    The cup of blessing which we bless
    is a sharing in the blood of Christ.
    Draw near with faith and receive.
    Christ is the host and we are his guests.
    Christ is alive for ever.
    We are because he is.
      1987 HAS NO BREAKING OF BREAD HERE AND NO USE OF CF 8(a)

The celebrant and his assistants receive the bread and wine.

The congregation is led by the choir in a musical recitation of the Agnus Dei.
Lamb of God . . . ⟦ELLC 9(b)⟧ . . . **Give us your peace.**

*The celebrant then holds the bread, and one of his assistants holds the wine and they
declare to the people:*

30. *Minister* The body of our Lord Jesus Christ which was broken for you, keep your
    body and soul in eternal life. Take and eat this in remembrance that Christ died for
    you, and feed on him in your hearts, by faith, with thanksgiving.
    Assistant The blood of our Lord Jesus Christ, which was shed for you, keep your body
    and soul in eternal life.
    Drink this, in remembrance that Christ's blood was shed for you and be thankful.
      1987 PLACES THIS BEFORE THE LORD'S PRAYER (§28)

31. *As the bread and wine are distributed, the minister or his assistant may say to each
    communicant:*
    Minister The body of Christ keep you in eternal life.
    Assistant The blood of Christ keep you in eternal life.

Each time, the communicant replies, **Amen,** *and then receives.*

*If the bread and wine are used up they are replaced by more from the Holy Table without
any additional prayers.*
Reconsecration is necessary only if the bread and wine on the Holy Table run out.

During Communion prayerful songs may be sung.

AFTER COMMUNION

The congregation may observe a brief moment of silence.
People stand. One of the following prayers is said.

Either

32. Almighty God, eternal Father, we have sat at your feet,
    learnt from your word, and eaten from your table.
    We give you thanks and praise for accepting us into your family.
    Send us out with your blessing
    to live and to witness for you in the power of your Spirit,
    through Jesus Christ, the First Born from the dead.
    Amen.

    > 1987: eternal Father] our Great Elder
    >   the First Born from the dead] your First Born

or

33. God Most High, we thank you for welcoming us,
    teaching us and feeding us.
    We deserve nothing from you
    but in your great mercy, you have given us everything
    in your Son Jesus Christ.
    We love you and give ourselves to you
    to be sent out for your work;
    grant us your blessing, now and for ever.
    Amen.

or

34. O God of our ancestors, God of our people,
    before whose face the human generations pass away;
    we thank you that in you we are kept safe for ever,
    and that the broken fragments of our history
    are gathered up in the redeeming act of your dear Son,
    remembered in this holy sacrament of bread and wine.
    Help us to walk daily in the Communion of saints,
    declaring our faith in the forgiveness of sins
    and the resurrection of the body.
    Now send us out in the power of your Holy Spirit
    to live and work for your praise and glory.
    Amen.

    > 1987: OMIT

    1987 PROVIDES HERE BOTH VERSIONS OF *GLORIA* FROM §§8 AND 9 ABOVE
    FOLLOWED BY THE PEACE FROM §25 ABOVE

THE BLESSING
    One of the following two blessings may be used.

    Either
35. *People accompany their first three responses with a sweep of the arm towards the cross*
    behind the Holy Table, and their final response with a sweep towards heaven.
        1987: *cross . . . Table*] *towards the West end of the Church*
                heaven] *the East end*
    All our problems,
    we send to the cross of Christ.
    All our difficulties,
    we send to the cross of Christ.
    All the devil's works,
    we send to the cross of Christ.
    All our hopes,
    we set on the risen Christ.
    Christ the Sun of righteousness shine upon you
    and scatter the darkness from before your path;
    and the blessing . . . ⟦CF 12(a)⟧ . . . always. **Amen.**
        the Father . . . Holy] Father, Son, and Holy
        1987: **cross of Christ**] **setting sun THREE TIMES**
                risen Christ] **risen Son**

    or/and
36. Let us pray.
    People kneel or sit.
    The peace of God . . . ⟦CF 12(a)⟧ . . . always. **Amen.**

DISMISSAL
37. *One of the following may be used.*
    Either
    Go in peace . . . ⟦CF 12(b)⟧ . . . **of Christ. Amen.**
    or
    Go out into the world, rejoicing in the power of the Spirit.
    Thanks be to God.
    or
    Jesus said 'As the Father has sent me, even so I send you'. Go forth in peace.
    Thanks be to God.
        1987 OMITS THIS SECTION

38. *Recessional Hymn*

39. **APPENDIX TO SERVICE OF HOLY COMMUNION**
    ⟦Special Thanksgivings, to be inserted before 'Therefore with angels', for nine occasions
    during the year, with a choice between two different texts for each of Advent, Christmas,
    Easter Day, Ascension Day and Pentecost⟧

17. The Anglican Church of Tanzania

The Province of Tanzania was formed in 1970, and quickly set about providing a provincial eucharistic rite which would bring together the anglo-catholic southern dioceses with the evangelical northern ones. The rite was compiled in Swahili, and was authorized from 1973. It was published as **Tan** in an English translation in **FAL** in 1975. After three years' use, the text was marginally revised by the Provincial Liturgical and Theological Committee, and was authorized and published in 1977. The alterations made in the text are summarized on one page in **LAL**, and the 1977 text is labelled **TanR**. **TanR** was published in an English translation in 1980, and was included in a collected volume of authorized services in 1986. The Province then created a drafting committee of five members to work on a revision of the services, and they delegated specific rites to separate sub-groups before drawing all the work into a unity in the years 1990–92. The revised Book, again compiled in Swahili and not published in any English translation, was duly authorized and was published in 1995.[75] The Book states that the revisers have drawn upon various liturgical resources, including for the eucharist both the previous rites in Tanzania and **EngA**. The eucharistic rite, **Tan1**, has not moved far beyond **Tan** and **TanR**, and still represents at every sensitive point the careful crafting of its predecessors in order to provide a single unitive rite for a province originally evangelized by two starkly contrasting forms of Anglicanism.

THE HOLY COMMUNION FROM THE ANGLICAN CHURCH OF TANZANIA BOOK OF COMMON PRAYER (1995)(Tan1)

[The numbering is original. The lining is editorial. The translation of the eucharistic prayer (§§23–24) is taken from the translation of Ian Tarrant, while the rest of the rite is drawn from the earlier translation of **Tan** by Roger Bowen, checked against the more official English translation published in 1980, and updated here by Roger Bowen for the 1995 text.]

GATHERING

1. *At the entry of the ministers, the people standing, a hymn or psalm is sung.*

2. In the name of the Father and of the Son and of the Holy Spirit. **Amen.**

3. [Our Lord's Summary of the Law, or a shortened form of the Ten Commandments]

4. [Kyries (ELLC 2) in Swahili]

5. [Exhortation to confession and congregational confession]

6. [Absolution]

---

75 Some detail of the processes is given in Esther Mombo's chapter 'Anglican Liturgies in Eastern Africa' in Heffler and Shattuck, *The Oxford Guide to the Book of Common Prayer*, p. 280, and in Ian Tarrant, *Anglican Swahili Prayer Books*, pp. 8 and 15–16.

7. *The people standing, then is said the Glory:*
   Glory to God in the highest . . . ⟦ELLC 3⟧ . . . to the glory of God the Father. Amen.

8. The Lord be with you:
   And with your spirit.
   Let us pray

COLLECT OF THE DAY

9. *The people sit*

PROCLAIMING THE WORD OF GOD

10. *READING – The Old Testament (if being used)* ⟦announcement preceding and versicle and response following⟧

11. *PSALM*

12. *READING – THE EPISTLE (if being used)* ⟦announcement preceding and versicle and response following⟧

13. *The people stand*

14. *A HYMN OR PSALM is sung*

15. *THE GOSPEL* ⟦with proclamation and response preceding and versicle and response following⟧

16. *SERMON (A hymn may be sung before the Sermon)*

17. *THE NICENE CREED is said or sung:*
    We believe in one God . . . ⟦ELLC 5⟧ . . . world to come. Amen.
    [and the Son]] OMIT BRACKETS

18. *INTERCESSIONS* ⟦a form with versicle and response after each paragraph, but permission to use other forms⟧

19. *ANNOUNCEMENTS*

20. *As the hymn is sung, Bread and Wine are placed ready. The Offering is received here. When the Minister receives the Offering, he may use these words:*

21. Yours, Lord, is the greatness, the power, the glory,
    the splendour and the majesty;
    for everything in heaven and earth is yours.
    All things come from you, and of your own have we given you.
    We ask you to receive and to bless these offerings
    and your people who have offered them to you,
    through Jesus Christ our Lord. **Amen.**

22. *GREETING OF PEACE*
    The peace of the Lord be always with you.
    And with your spirit.

    (The president and the people may give one another the greeting of peace)

23. The Lord be with you.
And with your spirit . . . ⟦ELLC 6⟧ . . . It is right and fitting for us.

It is indeed fitting and right for us,
also our duty and joy, at all times and in all places,
that we thank you, holy Lord, Almighty Father,
everlasting God, through Jesus Christ our Lord.

This line is replaced by a longer text on Trinity Sunday

We praise you for the whole world
which you made and sustain through him,
for the order of your creation,
and for your many gifts of grace.
Above all it is fitting, for us who have fallen,
to praise you for your love,
that you even gave your Son Jesus Christ,
to take our human nature,
that he might overcome sin and death and set us free,
to become heirs of your kingdom.

These last three lines are replaced by alternative texts for Advent, Christmas, Epiphany, Lent, Passiontide, Easter, Ascension, and Pentecost.

O Father, we praise you for your Holy Spirit,
who assures us that in baptism
you have sealed us to be your own,
so that we may proclaim your wonderful works.
Therefore with angels and prophets,
with apostles and martyrs,
and with the whole company of heaven,
we glorify and praise you forever,
saying (or singing):
Holy, holy, holy . . . ⟦ELLC 7⟧ . . . glory be to you, O Lord most high.
Blessed is he . . . ⟦ELLC 8⟧ . . . the highest.

24 *All kneel*
Glory be to you, O heavenly Father,
who in your great mercy gave your only Son Jesus Christ,
that all who believe in him might have eternal life.
Hear us, O merciful Father, we beseech you,
that we, as we receive this bread and this cup,
as your Son commanded us,

may be partakers of his Body and Blood.
In the same night in which he was betrayed,
he took bread,
and having thanked you and glorified you,
broke it and gave it to his disciples saying:
Take eat, this is my body which is given for you.
Do this in remembrance of me.
Likewise after eating he took the cup, and gave thanks,
and gave it to them saying:
Drink of this, all of you.
For this is my blood of the New Covenant,
which is shed for you and for many for the forgiveness of sins.
Do this every time you drink it,
in remembrance of me.
O Father, his death we proclaim,
his resurrection we affirm,
his return we await.
Glory be to you, Lord.

Therefore, O Father, with this bread and this cup,
we do this for the remembrance
commanded by your Son Jesus Christ.
We proclaim his death as a perfect sacrifice,
which he made for us on the cross once for all,
and we celebrate the redemption he made for us.
We thank you, O Father, for his mighty resurrection,
and his ascension into heaven,
where he is always interceding for us.
And we look forward to his coming again in glory.

And accept us in him, we pray,
that we may be filled with your Holy Spirit,
that we might be united in your Church,
which you have gathered from all the ends of the earth;
through him and in him, in the unity of the Holy Spirit,
all honour and glory be to you, Father, God Almighty.
Blessing and thanksgiving and power
be to our God for ever and ever.
Amen.

25. As our Lord Jesus Christ has commanded and taught us, we are bold to say or to sing:
Our Father in heaven . . . ⟦ELLC 1⟧ . . . **now and for ever. Amen.**

26. *The people say or sing:*
Lamb of God . . . ⟦ELLC 9(b)⟧ . . . **grant us peace.**

27. The bread which we break is a sharing in the Body of Christ.
There is one bread, and we who are many are one Body
because we all share in that one bread.

28. *Then may be said:*
We do not presume . . . ⟦CF 3(a)⟧ . . . **he in us. Amen.**
that our sinful bodies . . . through his most precious blood] that we sinners may be cleansed in body
and spirit

29. Let us draw near with faith . . . ⟦CF 9(a)⟧ . . . with thanksgiving.

30. *The minister receives Holy Communion. When communicating the people, the minister says:*
The body of Christ keep you unto eternal life. **Amen.**
The blood of Christ keep you unto eternal life. **Amen.**

31. *If the consecrated elements run out before all have communicated, the Minister is to consecrate more. In consecrating the bread he begins, 'In the same night . . .' In consecrating the wine he begins: 'Likewise . . .'*

32. *When the people have communicated, the remains of the Sacrament are to be reverently consumed here or at the end of the service. It is fitting for a short silence to be kept.*

DISMISSAL

33. *The people standing the minister says:*
Let us give thanks to God.

34. *The minister and people say or sing:*
⟦Verses from Psalm 103 set out responsively as in **Tan** in 1973⟧

35. *The minister and people say:*
Almighty God, we thank you . . . ⟦CF 11(a)⟧ . . . **praise and glory. Amen.**

36. ⟦Various forms of blessing⟧

37. Our Lord Jesus Christ said, 'As the Father sent me, so I send you.' Go in peace.
Thanks be to God.

38. *A hymn may be sung as the congregation leaves.*

18. The Anglican Church of Southern Africa

The Anglican Church of Southern Africa includes six countries on the continent of Africa, with three British island colonies in the South Atlantic. Its constitution entrenches 1662. However, the Provincial Synod authorized an alternative Book in 1950, and this was published in 1954 and became the dominant use. It included the eucharistic rite which had been first authorized in 1929 and was reprinted in **LiE** as **Afr**. The Province's first experimental rite in contemporary English came in 1969 (**SAfr1**, published in **FAL**), and this was followed by a revision of it, **SAfr2**, in the liturgical collection *Liturgy 1975*, and this rite was also published in **FAL**.[76] From then on, there developed a plan to return to a complete hardback Prayer Book, and this was duly completed and authorized. It was published in 1989 initially in six of the many languages of the Church. It did not supersede 1662 or the 1954 Book, so its title is *An Anglican Prayer Book*, indicating that it is an alternative to those Books.

The eucharist in it, presented here as **SAfr3**, has four eucharistic prayers; the first is a slight revision of the first in **SAfr2**, with the words 'present before you' removed; the second is heavily dependent upon **EngA**; and the third and fourth have a strongly Hippolytan character. Of these the third one has been drawn from the Roman rite, so that it has a first epiclesis before the narrative, and includes intercessions later, and the fourth has borrowed more directly from translations of Hippolytus, with overt dependence upon Eucharistic Prayer 2 in **Can4** of 1985. It thus has only the bare post-anamnesis epiclesis of Hippolytus, without any petition anywhere that the bread and wine may in any sense be the body and blood of Christ. This latter prayer, however, has the interesting (and rarely encountered) device of alternative words at the critical point within the anamnesis, and to that extent provides a variant from the stark 'we offer' of Hippolytus himself. The changes in the first and fourth prayers were designed to enable their wider use within the Province.

There follows in the 1989 Book an 'Alternative Order for Celebrating the Eucharist', which is for when a 'freer form' is desired. It requires the specific permission of the bishop for its use, and it is not to be used at the principal Sunday services. It is presented here as **SAfr4**, and it has a stripped-down eucharistic prayer, drawn almost exclusively from the second prayer in **SAfr3**.

The years since 1989 have been largely devoted to rendering the whole 1989 Book into all the leading languages of the Province and getting them published and distributed. However, the Synod of Bishops has approved further eucharistic prayers, and these were published in the Province's *Worship Resource Manual* in 2009. These have in most cases specific themes, and they are presented here as **SAfr5**.

---

76 The text shown was edited from a duplicated document of the Liturgical Committee before the published work was ready, and the text proved to have more tiny errors than other texts (see the **FAL** corrigendum sheet).

THE HOLY EUCHARIST FROM *AN ANGLICAN PRAYER BOOK* OF THE PROVINCE OF SOUTHERN AFRICA (1989) (SAfr3)

[The numbering here is original, and an early note in the Book indicates that bracketed numbers are optional. The lining is largely editorial.]

Preface

[The Book has a page of teaching about the eucharist]

General Rubrics

[Five rubrics concerning presidency, silence, sentences of scripture, hymnody, and welcomes and the giving of notices]

INTRODUCTION

1. The Lord be with you.
   And also with you.
2. [At Easter: 'Alleluia! Christ is risen. **He is risen indeed. Alleluia.**' precedes the greeting]
3. [Rubric re omission of §§4 and 5 in Lent and Advent and on weekdays, and re replacement of §5 with a canticle or hymn]

4. Praise the Lord.
   Praise him, you servants of the Lord.
   Blessed be God, Father, Son and Holy Spirit.
   Blessed be his Name, now and for ever.
5. **Glory to God** . . . [ELLC 3] . . . **God the Father. Amen.**
   God's people] his people
6. *The Minister may introduce The Collect for Purity by saying*
   Let us pray
7. **Almighty God** . . . [CF 1] . . . **through Christ our Lord.**
   hidden] hid
(8). Lord have mercy . . . [ELLC 2 in English] . . . **Lord, have mercy.**

PENITENCE

9. *Sections 10–14 are used here or after the Sermon, or before the Peace at section 43.*
10. *At least on Ash Wednesday and the five Sundays following, the Ten Commandments (section 104) are said. At other times the following may be said.* [The Lord's Summary of the Law]
11. [Call to confession]
12. *Silence may be kept.*
13. [Corporate confession]
14. [Absolution – near to CF 2]

THE COLLECT OF THE DAY

15. Let us pray   *The Priest says the Collect and the people respond*   **Amen.**

THE WORD OF GOD

16. *The Gospel is always read.* [Rubrics about when and whether to have one or two readings, psalm and hymn or canticle before it]
17. [The first reading with announcement before and proclamation and response following]
18. *The appointed psalm follows.*
19. [The second reading with proclamation and response following]
20. *A canticle or hymn follows.*
21. *The Gospel* [announcement and response before it and proclamation and response after it]
22. *The Sermon* [rubric re occasions to omit it, permitting it to follow the Creed, and citing §9]

THE NICENE CREED

23. *The Creed is said at least on Sundays, other Great Festivals and Festivals.*

24. **We believe in one God . . . ⟦ELLC 5⟧ . . . world to come. Amen.**
    became truly human] **was made man**
    [and the Son]] OMIT BRACKETS

25. *The Apostles' Creed (section 22 of the Offices ⟦ELLC 4⟧) may be used instead of the Nicene Creed.*

26. *The Sermon (and Penitence) may follow.*

THE PRAYERS

27. *The Prayers of the Church are offered in one of the four forms following.*

28–42. ⟦Four forms of prayer; the last permits use of any forms and the congregation may be invited to join in them⟧

43. *The Penitence (sections 10–14) follows if it has not already been used.*

THE PEACE

44. *A sentence taken from one of the readings or the Gospel, or another appropriate verse of Scripture, may be said (see section 106).*

45. The peace of the Lord be with you always.
    Peace be with you.

46. *The Peace is given according to local custom.*

THE PRESENTATION OF GIFTS

47. *Alms, and other gifts for the church and the poor, may be presented here or after sections 49–50. One of the following prayers may be said.*

48. Yours, Lord, is the greatness, the power,
    the glory, the splendour and the majesty;
    for everything in heaven and on earth is yours.
    All things come from you,
    and of your own do we give you.
    Amen.
    or
    Source of all life, the heaven and earth are yours,
    yet you have given us dominion over all things.
    Receive the fruits of our labour offered in love;
    in the name of Jesus Christ our Lord.
    Amen.

THE TAKING OF THE BREAD AND WINE

49. *The bread and wine are placed on the holy table. The following prayers may be said.*

50. *At the taking of the bread*
    Blessed are you . . . ⟦CF 4(a)⟧ . . . for us it becomes the bread of life.
    Blessed be God for ever.

    At the taking of the wine
    Blessed are you . . . ⟦CF 4(b)⟧ . . . for us it becomes the cup of salvation.
    Blessed be God for ever.

THE GREAT THANKSGIVING

51. *A choice of four Eucharistic Prayers follows. A fifth Eucharistic Prayer is provided for optional use in* **An Alternative Order** *(sections 92–102)* ⟦SAfr4⟧.

52. The Lord be with you . . . ⟦ELLC 6⟧
 . . . **him thanks and praise.**

It is right and indeed our duty and joy,
Lord and heavenly Father, God almighty
 and eternal,
always and everywhere to give thanks
through Jesus Christ, your only Son our
 Lord;

53. *Section 54 may be omitted when a Proper
Preface is used, except when Proper Preface 27 is
used.*

54. Because through him you have created
 everything from the beginning
and formed us in your own image;
Through him you delivered us from the
 slavery of sin,
when you gave him to be born as man,
to die on the cross and to rise again for us;
Through him you claimed us as your own
 people
when you enthroned him in heaven,
and through him sent out your Holy Spirit,
 the giver of life;

55. *The Proper Preface follows here (see section 103)*

56. Therefore with angels and archangels,
and with all the company of heaven,
we acclaim you and declare the greatness
 of your glory;
we praise you now and for ever, saying:
Holy, holy . . . ⟦ELLC 7⟧ . . . **in the highest.**
Blessed is . . . ⟦ELLC 8⟧ . . . **in the highest.**
Hear us, through your Son Christ our
 Lord;
through him accept our offering of thanks
 and praise,
and send your Holy Spirit upon us
and upon these gifts of bread and wine
so that they may be to us his body and his
 blood.

For on the night that he was betrayed
he took bread, and when he had given you
 thanks,
he broke it, and gave it to his disciples
 saying,

'Take this and eat; this is my body which
 is given for you;
do this in remembrance of me.'

So too after supper he took the cup,
and when he had given you thanks,
he gave it to them saying,
'Drink of it all of you;
for this is my blood of the new covenant,
which is shed for you and for many
for the forgiveness of sins;
whenever you drink it,
do this in remembrance of me.'

57. *Here may be said*
So we proclaim the mystery . . . ⟦CF 6(a)⟧
 . . . **will come again.**
Or
So we acclaim the victory of Christ
Dying you . . . ⟦CF 6(b)⟧ . . . **come in glory.**

Holy Father, with these your gifts,
we your people celebrate before you
the one perfect sacrifice of Christ our
 Lord,
his rising from the dead
and his ascending to the glory of heaven.

Gracious Lord, accept us in him,
unworthy though we are,
so that we who share in the body and
 blood of your Son
may be made one with all your people of
 this and every age.

Grant that as we await the coming of
 Christ our Saviour
in the glory and triumph of his kingdom,
we may daily grow into his likeness;
with whom, and in whom, and through
 whom,
by the power of the Holy Spirit,
all glory and honour to be given to you,
almighty Father,
by the whole company of earth and
 heaven,
throughout all ages, now and for ever.
Amen.

The service continues with the Lord's Prayer at 77.

59. The Lord be with you . . . ⟦ELLC 6 and CF 5⟧ . . . **him thanks and praise.**

It is indeed right, it is our duty and our joy,
at all times and in all places,
to give you thanks and praise,
holy Father, heavenly King, almighty and eternal God,
through Jesus Christ your only Son our Lord;

60. *Section 61 may be omitted when a Proper Preface is used, except when Proper Preface 27 is used.*

61. For he is your living Word,
through him you have created all things from the beginning,
and formed us in your own image.

Through him you have freed us from the slavery of sin,
giving him to be born as man
and to die upon the cross;
you raised him from the dead
and exalted him to your right hand on high.

Through him you have sent upon us
your holy and life-giving Spirit,
and made us a people for your own possession.

62. *The Proper Preface follows here (see section 103)*

63. Therefore with angels and archangels,
and with all the company of heaven,
we proclaim your great and glorious Name,
for ever praising you and saying:
Holy, holy . . . ⟦ELLC 7⟧ . . . **in the highest.**
This Anthem may also be used
Blessed is . . . ⟦ELLC 8⟧ . . . **in the highest.**

64. Accept our praises, heavenly Father,
through your Son our Saviour Jesus Christ;
and as we follow his example and obey his command,
grant that by the power of your Holy Spirit

these gifts of bread and wine
may be to us his body and his blood;

Who in the same night that he was betrayed
took bread and gave you thanks;
he broke it and gave it to his disciples, saying,
'Take, eat; this is my body
which is given for you.
Do this in remembrance of me.'
In the same way, after supper he took the cup,
and gave you thanks;
he gave it to them, saying,
'Drink this, all of you;
this is my blood of the new covenant,
which is shed for you and for many,
for the forgiveness of sins.
Do this, as often as you drink it,
in remembrance of me.'

65. *Here may be said*
Christ has . . . ⟦CF 6(a)⟧ . . . **come again.**

Therefore, heavenly Father, we remember his offering of himself
made once for all upon the cross,
and proclaim his mighty resurrection and glorious ascension.
As we look for his coming in glory,
we celebrate with this bread and this cup his one perfect sacrifice.

Accept through him, our great high priest,
this our sacrifice of thanks and praise;
and as we eat and drink these holy gifts
in the presence of your divine majesty,
renew us by your Spirit,
inspire us with your love,
and unite us in the body of your Son, Jesus Christ our Lord.

Through him, and with him, and in him,
by the power of the Holy Spirit,
with all who stand before you in earth and heaven,
we worship you, Father almighty, in songs of everlasting praise:
Blessing and . . . ⟦CF 7⟧ . . . **ever. Amen.**

The service continues with the Lord's Prayer at 77.

THE THIRD EUCHARISTIC PRAYER

67. The Lord be with you . . . [ELLC 6]
. . . **him thanks and praise.**

Father, it is our duty and our salvation,
always and everywhere to give you thanks
through your beloved Son, Jesus Christ.

68. *Section 69 may be omitted when a Proper
Preface is used, except when Proper Preface 27 is
used.*

69. He is the Word through whom you
  made the universe,
the Saviour you sent to redeem us.
By the power of the Holy Spirit
he took flesh and was born of the Virgin
  Mary.
For our sake he opened his arms on the
  cross;
he put an end to death and revealed the
  resurrection.
In this he fulfilled your will
and won for you a holy people.

70. *The Proper Preface follows here (see section
103)*

71. And so we join the angels and the saints
in proclaiming your glory as we say:
**Holy, holy . . . [ELLC 7] . . . in the highest.
Blessed is . . . [ELLC 8] . . . in the highest.**

Lord, you are holy indeed, the fountain of
  all holiness.
Let your Spirit come upon these gifts
to make them holy,
so that they may become for us the body
  and blood of Christ.

Before he was given up to death,
a death he freely accepted,
he took bread and gave you thanks.
He broke the bread,
gave it to his disciples, and said:
'Take this, all of you, and eat it:
this is my body which will be given up for
  you.'
When supper was ended he took the cup.
Again he gave you thanks and praise,
gave the cup to his disciples and said:
'Take this, all of you, and drink from it:
this is the cup of my blood,
the blood of the new and everlasting
  covenant.

It will be shed for you and for all
so that sins may be forgiven.
Do this in memory of me.'

72. *Here may be said*
So we proclaim the mystery of faith
Christ has . . . [CF 6(a)] . . . come again.
Or
Dying you . . . [CF 6(b)] . . . come in glory.
Or
When we eat . . . [CF 6(c)] . . . in glory.
Or
Lord, by your . . . [CF 6(d)] . . . the world.

73. In memory of his death and
  resurrection,
we offer you, Father,
this life-giving bread, this saving cup.

We thank you for counting us worthy
to stand in your presence and serve you.
May all of us who share in the body and
  blood of Christ
be brought together in unity by the Holy
  Spirit.

Lord, remember your Church throughout
  the world;
make us grow in love,
together with N our bishop, and all the
  clergy.

Remember our brothers and sisters
who have gone to their rest
in the hope of rising again;
bring them and all the departed
into the light of your presence.

Have mercy on us all;
make us worthy to share eternal life
with Mary, the virgin mother of God,
with the apostles, and with all the saints
who have done your will throughout the
  ages.

May we praise you in union with them,
and give you glory through your Son, Jesus
  Christ.

Through him, with him, in him,
in the unity of the Holy Spirit,
all glory and honour is yours,
almighty Father, for ever and ever.
Amen.

The service continues with the Lord's Prayer at 77.

74. The Lord be with you . . . ⟦ELLC 6⟧
. . . him thanks and praise.

We give you thanks and praise, almighty
  God,
through your beloved Son, Jesus Christ,
our Saviour and Redeemer.
He is your living Word
through whom you have created all things.

By the power of the Holy Spirit
he took flesh of the Virgin Mary
and shared our human nature.
He lived and died as one of us,
to reconcile us to you, the God and Father
  of all.

In fulfilment of your will
he stretched out his hands in suffering,
to bring release to those who place their
  hope in you;
and so he won for you a holy people.

He chose to bear our griefs and sorrows,
and to give up his life on the cross,
that he might shatter the chains of the evil
  one,
and banish the darkness of sin and death.
By his resurrection he brings us into the
  light of your presence.

Now with all creation we raise our voices
to proclaim the glory of your name:
Holy, holy . . . ⟦ELLC 7⟧ . . . **in the highest.**
Blessed is . . . ⟦ELLC 8⟧ . . . **in the highest.**

Holy and gracious God, accept our praise,
through your Son our Saviour Jesus Christ;

who on the night he was handed over to
  suffering and death,
took bread and gave you thanks, saying,
'Take, and eat: this is my body which is
  broken for you.'
In the same way he took the cup, saying,
'This is my blood which is shed for you.
When you do this, you do it in memory of
  me.'

75. *Here may be said*
So we proclaim the mystery of faith
Christ has . . . ⟦CF 6(a)⟧ . . . **come again.**

76. Remembering, therefore, his death and
  resurrection,
we *offer/bring before* you this bread and
  this cup,
giving thanks that you have made us
  worthy
to stand in your presence and serve you.

We ask you to send your Holy Spirit
upon the offering of your holy Church.
Gather into one all who share in these
  sacred mysteries,
filling them with your Holy Spirit
and confirming their faith in the truth,
that together we may praise you
and give you glory
through your Servant, Jesus Christ.

All glory and honour are yours,
Father and Son, with the Holy Spirit
in the holy Church, now and for ever.
Amen.

THE LORD'S PRAYER

77. As Christ has taught us we are bold to say
    Our Father in heaven . . . ⟦CF 1⟧ . . . for ever. Amen.

78. *The traditional form of the Lord's Prayer may be used instead of 77 (see p. . . . ⟦i.e. opening note⟧).*

THE BREAKING OF THE BREAD

79. *The Priest breaks the consecrated bread, saying*
    The bread which we break
    is it not a sharing of the body of Christ?
    We, who are many, are one body
    for we all partake of the one bread.

(80) **Jesus, Lamb of God . . . ⟦ELLC 9(a)⟧ . . . grant us peace.**
    or **Lamb of God, you take away . . . ⟦ELLC 9(b)⟧ . . . grant us peace.**
    This may be said after 82 during the distribution of the elements.

THE COMMUNION

(81) **We do not presume . . . ⟦CF 3(a)⟧ . . . he in us.**
    that our sinful . . . precious blood and] OMIT

82. Draw near and receive . . . ⟦CF 9(a)⟧ . . . with thanksgiving.
    Eat and drink . . . died for you and] OMIT

83. *The Priest and people receive the sacrament.*

84. The body of Christ (given for you) **Amen.**
    The blood of Christ (shed for you) **Amen.**
    or
    The body of our Lord Jesus Christ keep you in eternal life. **Amen.**
    The blood of our Lord Jesus Christ keep you in eternal life. **Amen.**

85. *After the people have received, a period of silence may be kept.*

    What remains of the consecrated bread and wine which is not required for the purposes of communion is consumed either here or at the end of the service.

CONCLUSION

86. Give thanks to the Lord for he is gracious.
    His mercy endures for ever.

87. Almighty and eternal God,
    we thank you for feeding us in these holy mysteries
    with the body and blood of your Son our Saviour Jesus Christ;
    and for keeping us by your grace in the Body of your Son,
    the company of all faithful people.
    Help us to persevere as living members of that holy fellowship,
    and to grow in love and obedience according to your will;
    through Jesus Christ our Lord,
    who lives and reigns with you and the Holy Spirit,
    one God, now and for ever.
    Amen.

88. **Father almighty**
    we offer ourselves to you
    as a living sacrifice
    in Jesus Christ our Lord.
    Send us out into the world
    in the power of the Holy Spirit
    to live and work
    to your praise and glory.

89. The peace of God . . . ⟦CF 12(a)⟧ . . . always. **Amen.**

90. Go in peace . . . ⟦CF 12(b)⟧ . . . **name of Christ. Amen.**
    ⟦In Easter season 'Alleluia Alleluia' is added to versicle and response⟧

THE CONSECRATION OF ADDITIONAL ELEMENTS

91. *If the consecrated bread and wine do not suffice, the Priest consecrates more of either or*
    both by saying
    Hear us, heavenly Father, and with your Word and Holy Spirit bless and sanctify this
    bread/wine that it, also, may be the sacrament of the precious *body/blood* of your Son
    Jesus Christ our Lord, who took *bread/the cup* and said, 'This is my *body/blood*'.
    Amen.

    Or else he may consecrate more of both kinds, saying again the words of one of the Euchar-
    istic Prayers, from after the Sanctus up to but not including the Acclamation.

'AN ALTERNATIVE ORDER FOR CELEBRATING THE EUCHARIST' FROM *AN ANGLICAN PRAYER BOOK* OF THE PROVINCE OF SOUTHERN AFRICA (1989) (SAfr4)

⟦The numbering continues from SAfr3. The lining is largely editorial.⟧

92. *On informal occasions when a freer form of service is desired, the following rite is used. The*
    permission of the Bishop is required. The rite is not for use at the principal Sunday service.

    It requires special preparation by the Priest and participants.

93. *The service includes the following*

    GATHERING IN THE LORD'S NAME

    OFFERING OF PRAISE AND PENITENCE

    PROCLAMATION OF THE WORD OF GOD AND RESPONSE TO IT
    These sections may include readings, dance, and other art forms, comment, discussion and
    silence. A reading from a Gospel is always included.

    PRAYERS FOR THE WORLD AND THE CHURCH

    THE PEACE

    THE PREPARATION OF THE TABLE, AND THE BREAD AND WINE

    THE GREAT THANKSGIVING

94. *The Great Thanksgiving is made in the following form. One of the four Eucharistic Prayers*
    in sections 52–76 may be substituted for it. The form below may also be used at other cele-
    brations of the Eucharist when desired.

95. The Lord be with you . . . ⟦ELLC 6
and CF 5⟧ . . . **him thanks and praise.**

It is indeed right, it is our duty and our
joy,
to give you thanks, holy Father,
through Jesus Christ our Lord.
Through him you have created us in your
image;
through him you have freed us from sin
and death;
through him you have made us your own
people
by the gift of the Holy Spirit.

96. *Here may be said*
Holy, holy . . . ⟦ELLC 7⟧ . . . **in the highest.**
Blessed is . . . ⟦ELLC 8⟧ . . . **in the highest.**

97. Hear us, Father,
through Christ your Son our Lord;
and grant that by the power of your Holy
Spirit
these gifts of bread and wine
may be to us his body and his blood.

Who in the same night that he was
betrayed,
took bread and gave you thanks;
he broke it and gave it to his disciples,
saying, 'Take, eat; this is my body
which is given for you;
do this in remembrance of me.'

In the same way, after supper he took the
cup
and gave you thanks;
he gave it to them, saying,
'Drink this, all of you;
this is my blood of the new covenant,
which is shed for you and for many
for the forgiveness of sins.
Do this as often as you drink it,
in remembrance of me.'

98. *Here may be said*
So we proclaim the mystery of faith
Christ has . . . ⟦CF 6(a)⟧ . . . **come again.**

99. Therefore, Father,
proclaiming his saving death and
resurrection
and looking for his coming in glory,
we celebrate with this bread and this cup
his one perfect sacrifice.

Accept through him, our great high priest,
this our sacrifice of thanks and praise,
and grant that we who eat this bread and
drink this cup
may be renewed by your Spirit
and grow into his likeness.

Through Jesus Christ our Lord,
by whom, and with whom and in whom,
all honour and glory be yours,
Father, now and for ever.
Amen.

100. *Then follow*

   THE LORD'S PRAYER

   THE BREAKING OF THE BREAD

   THE SHARING OF THE GIFTS OF GOD
   *The bread and wine of the Eucharist are shared reverently. When all have received, any of
   the sacrament remaining is consumed.*

101. *The service concludes with*

   THE GIVING OF THANKS

102. *When a common meal is part of the celebration, it follows here.*

---

103. ⟦Proper Prefaces⟧
104. ⟦The Ten Commandments⟧
105. ⟦Sentences⟧
106. ⟦Introductions to the Peace⟧

ADDITIONAL EUCHARISTIC PRAYERS AUTHORIZED BY THE SOUTHERN AFRICA SYNOD OF BISHOPS, 2005–2008 (SAfr5)

[The numbering and much of the lining are editorial. The dates given are the years of authorization, but the order is that provided in the *Worship Resource Manual*.]

1. EUCHARISTIC PRAYER WITH CHILDREN (2006)

This service is for use in parishes where children have been admitted to receive Holy Communion.
[Some text here is spoken by '*Children*', in distinction from '*Celebrant*' and '*All*', and it is shown here in ***bold italic***.]

The Lord be . . . [ELLC 6] . . . **him thanks and praise.**

Why do we give thanks and praise at this table?
We give thanks for all that God has done for us.
God the Father created the heavens,
the earth and everything in them;
and created us in his own image.
Let us give thanks and praise.
Christ our Lord became human like us, and died to save us.
Let us give thanks and praise.
God sent the Holy Spirit to gather us together as the people of God.
Let us give thanks and praise.
So come let us join together to worship this God who loves us.
(All sing)   **Holy, holy . . . [ELLC 7] . . . in the highest.**
            Blessed is . . . [ELLC 8] . . . in the highest.

We praise you Father
that before Jesus our Saviour suffered and died,
he gave us this holy meal to share
and told us to continue it until he comes again.

Why do we eat bread together at this table?
On the night before he died, Jesus took bread.
After giving thanks, he broke it, and gave it to his disciples saying,
'Take, eat. This is my body, given for you.
Do this in remembrance of me.'

Why do we drink from the cup together at this table?
In the same way after supper Jesus took the cup,
saying, 'This cup is God's new covenant sealed with my blood,
poured out for you for the forgiveness of sins.
Do this in remembrance of me.'

What do we remember at this table?
We remember the Father's gracious love for us,
Christ's death and resurrection for us,
and the Spirit's tender care for us.
Let us proclaim the mystery of faith:
(All sing) **Christ has died . . . [CF 6(a)] . . . will come again.**

Merciful Father, pour out your Holy Spirit
on us and on these gifts of bread and wine.
In eating and drinking together
may we be made one with Christ and with one another.
Amen.

2. EUCHARISTIC PRAYER FOR ANY OCCASION (2005)

The Lord be . . . ⟦ELLC 6⟧ . . . **him thanks and praise.**

Loving God, the source of all,
we thank you and praise you
with our lips and with our lives,
that you have created us and all things
   through your word,
you welcome and accept our prayer and
   praise.
You are worthy, our Lord and God,
to receive glory and honour and power,
for you created all things
and through your will they have their being.

For the goodness of creation
and glory of redemption, we praise you.
For the law of holiness, inviting our
   obedience,
and for the call of prophets, rebuking our
   disobedience,
we praise you.
We praise and adore you.

You made us in your image,
and you sent your Son
to take upon him our flesh and to die for us
in order that we might no longer be slaves
   to sin
but that we might rise to life with him.
We praise and adore you.

With all that is, seen and unseen,
we sing this song of creation
as we adore and praise you forever.
Holy, holy . . . ⟦ELLC 7⟧ . . . in the highest.
Blessed is . . . ⟦ELLC 8⟧ . . . in the highest.

Holy God, holy and mighty, holy and
   immortal
you we praise and glorify.
You we worship and adore.

Holy God, in your time Mary, daughter of
   your people,
conceived at your word
and from her you brought for us the
   Messiah.
You we honour and acclaim.

The Lord Jesus, your chosen Son,
on the night when he was betrayed

took bread, and when he had given thanks,
he broke it and said:
'This is my body that is for you.
Do this in remembrance of me.'
In the same way after supper
he took the cup, saying:
'This cup is the new covenant in my blood.
Do this, as often as you drink it,
in remembrance of me.'

As often as we eat this bread and drink the
   cup,
we proclaim the Lord's death until he
   comes.
Christ has . . . ⟦CF 6(a)⟧ . . . come again.

Holy God, holy and merciful, holy and
   forgiving,
with this bread and cup we remember him
who is the first born of your new creation.
We remember his life lived for others,
we remember his death and resurrection
   which renews the face of the earth.
We await his coming again,
with the world made perfect through your
   wisdom,
and when all sin and sorrow will be no
   more.
Amen. Come Lord Jesus.

Holy God, holy and compassionate,
holy and exalted,
send down upon us and upon this meal
   your Holy Spirit,
by whose breath we are revived for life,
by whose fire we are roused to love.
Enfold in your arms all who share this
   holy food.
Nurture in us the fruits of the Spirit,
that we may be a living tree,
sharing your bounty with all the world.
Amen. Come Holy Spirit.

This sacrifice of praise and thanksgiving
we offer you, Father, through Jesus Christ
   our Lord and Saviour,
in the unity of the Holy Spirit,
as with one voice we worship and glorify
   your name:
Blessing . . . ⟦CF 7⟧ . . . and ever. Amen.

The Lord be . . . ⟦ELLC 6⟧ . . . **him thanks and praise.**

Almighty God, good Father to us all,
your face is ever turned towards your
    world.
In love you created us in your own image,
yet in disobedience we continue to distort
    that image.
In love you gave us Jesus your Son
to rescue us from sin and death,
yet in disobedience we continue to try to
    earn our salvation.
In love you poured out your Spirit
to empower a community of faith,
yet in disobedience we continue to live
    selfishly in our own strength.
Into the darkness, Jesus came as your light.
With signs of faith and words of hope
he touched untouchables with love
and washed the guilty clean.

He accepted the way of the cross
that we might know the way of salvation.

Father of all, we give you thanks
for every gift that comes from heaven.
We do not always understand them,
we do not always accept them,
we cannot always appreciate them.
As we stand at the foot of the cross today,
we can only wonder at the depth of your
    love,
and bow down and worship.

He accepted the way of the cross
that we might know the way of salvation.

The crowds came out to see your Son,
yet at the end they turned on him.
In Gethsemane he asked that you might
    take this cup from him,

yet willingly he surrendered to your will
    for our sake.

He accepted the way of the cross
that we might know the way of salvation.

On the night that he was betrayed
he came to table with his friends
to celebrate the freedom of your people.
Jesus blessed you, Father, for the food;
he took bread, gave thanks, broke it and
    said:
This is my body, given for you all.
Jesus then gave thanks for the wine;
he took the cup, gave it and said:
This is my blood, shed for you all
for the forgiveness of sins.
Do this in remembrance of me.

He accepted the way of the cross
that we might know the way of salvation.

Therefore, Father, with this bread and this
    cup
we celebrate the cross
on which he died to set us free.
Defying death he rose again
and is alive with you
to plead for us and for all the world.
Send your Spirit on us now
that by these gifts we may feed on Christ
with eyes wide open and hearts on fire.

He accepted the way of the cross
that we might know the way of salvation.

May we and all who share this food
offer ourselves to live for you
and be welcomed at your feast in heaven
where all creation worships you,
Father, Son and Holy Spirit,
now and for ever.
Amen.

The Lord be . . . ⟦ELLC 6⟧ . . . **give thanks and praise.**

It is right to praise you, Lord of all creation;
in your love you made us for yourself.
When we turned away you did not reject us,
but came to meet us in your Son.
You embraced us as your children
and welcomed us to sit and eat with you.

In Christ you shared our life
that we might live in him and he in us.
He opened his arms of love upon the cross
and made for all the perfect sacrifice for sin.
He put an end to death, revealed the resurrection,
and in the power of the Holy Spirit made us your own people.

On the night he was betrayed,
at supper with his friends he took bread and gave you thanks;
he broke it and gave it to them, saying:
Take, eat; this is my body which is given for you;
do this in remembrance of me.
We do this in remembrance of him:
his body is the bread of life.

At the end of supper, taking the cup of wine,
he gave you thanks, and said:
Drink this, all of you;
this is my blood of the new covenant,
which is shed for you for the forgiveness of sins;
do this in remembrance of me.

We do this in remembrance of him:
his blood is shed for all.

On the day that he rose from the tomb
he walked and talked with disciples
on the road to Emmaus,
but they were kept from recognizing him;
as he shared supper with them in their home,
he again took bread, blessed and broke it,
and gave it to them.
Their eyes were opened
and he revealed himself to them
in the breaking of the bread,
and they recognized him.
We do this in remembrance of him:
his risen life revealed in the breaking of the bread.

So we proclaim the mystery . . . ⟦CF 6(a)⟧
. . . **will come again. Alleluia.**

As we proclaim his death
and celebrate his rising in glory,
send your Holy Spirit
that this bread and this wine
may be to us the body and blood of your dear Son.
As we eat and drink these holy gifts,
send your Spirit upon us,
and make us one in Christ,
our risen Lord. Alleluia.

With your whole Church throughout the world
we offer you this sacrifice of praise
and lift our voice to join the eternal song of heaven:
Holy, holy . . . ⟦ELLC 7⟧ . . . in the highest.
Blessed is . . . ⟦ELLC 8⟧ . . . in the highest.

*The Lord be . . . [[ELLC 6]] . . . them to God
Let us praise and magnify
the God of all of Creation
We sing to the Creator
with songs of creation.
Let us give thanks to God, Creator, Lover,
and Sustainer of the universe,
Let us rejoice
in our Maker, Sustainer and Reconciler.*

God of power and might,
you spoke the Word
and all that is in heaven and on the earth,
all things, came to be.
Your Spirit hovered over the primal
elements,
and you brought forth life in forms
innumerable,
including this fragile earth, and us
amongst its inhabitants.

As our past is in you,
so our hope for the future rests with you.
As we have turned from your way,
so we turn again to the warmth of your
love.
Through you all things are brought to new
life.

Specific Proper Preface to be inserted here

So with all creation, we raise our voices
to proclaim your great and glorious name:
Holy, holy . . . [[ELLC 7]] . . . in the highest.
Blessed is . . . [[ELLC 8]] . . . in the highest.

In the night that Jesus was betrayed,
he took bread, gave thanks and broke it
to speak to us of the breaking of his body
upon the cross.
He gave the bread to his friends and said:
Take and eat, for this is my body
which is given for you.
Do this in remembrance of me.

Jesus then took the wine,
gave thanks and poured it out
to speak to us of the pouring out of his
blood.

He gave the wine to his friends saying:
This is my blood of the new covenant,
shed for you and for all creation
for the forgiveness of sins.
Every time you drink of the wine,
do this in remembrance of me.

So we proclaim the mystery . . . [[CF 6(a)]]
. . . **will come again.**

Therefore, remembering the reconciliation
of all creation
achieved by the death and resurrection of
our Lord Jesus Christ,
we offer you this bread and this wine.
Let his perfect sacrifice reconcile us with
you,
with one another and with all of creation.
In the power of your grace
make us ministers of your reconciling love.

In Christ life once broken,
spilt and buried, sprang to life again.
Now, as we wait with confidence for his
coming again,
keep alive in us the new life and
reconciliation
he won for us.
Make one what is broken,
restore what is spilled
and renew all creation
in the resurrection of Jesus Christ.

Send upon this bread and wine,
upon us and all creation,
the life-giving Spirit
who first moved upon the waters of the
deep.
Stir up in us what is creative,
redeem what is destructive.

Unite us with you in the body of your Son
by whom, with whom and in whom,
in the unity of your Creative Spirit,
with all that has been, is,
and will be in your universe,
we stand before you and worship you,
God of all, in songs of everlasting praise,
Blessing and . . . [[CF 7]] . . . ever. Amen.

. . . [[Alternative opening dialogue: The Lord . . . [[ELLC 6 with 'up to' for 'to']] . . . you
thanks and praise.]]
*The Sanctus and Benedictus can be said or sung in any of the languages normally used to suit
the congregation.*

6. SECOND EUCHARISTIC PRAYER OF CREATION (2008)

The Lord be . . . [[ELLC 6]] . . . **God thanks and praise.**
to] up unto

We thank and praise you, almighty Father.
In wisdom you guide the course of the
    world
and cherish us with tender care.

We thank you
that we can come together around this
    table
in the name of Jesus your Son,
the first born of creation.
In him all things, visible and invisible,
were created and hold together.

We thank you that you have sent your
    Holy Spirit
to make us a new community of faith
to serve you within your creation.

Specific Proper Preface to be inserted here

And so with the wonders of creation
 and the songs of praise of all your
    creatures
both in heaven and on earth
we join in one great act of awe and
    adoration:
Holy, holy . . . [[ELLC 7]] . . . **in the highest.**
Blessed is . . . [[ELLC 8]] . . . **in the highest.**

God of all creation, send your Spirit upon
    the goodness of the earth,
and upon these gifts of bread and wine,
that in them we may recognize and receive
the fullness of the Risen Christ:
bread broken and wine poured,
Body given and Blood shed.

On the night before he offered himself,
Jesus recalled with his disciples
the wonder of your creation
and the covenant you made with your
    chosen people.

Then he took bread, gave you thanks,
blessed it and broke it, saying:
'Take this all of you and eat it.
This is my Body, which will be given up
    for you.'

In the same way he took the cup
and giving you thanks and praise,
he gave the cup to his disciples and said:
'Take this all of you and drink from it,
this is the cup of my Blood,
the Blood of the new and everlasting
    covenant.
It will be shed for you and for all
so that sins may be forgiven.
Do this in memory of me.'

So we proclaim the mystery . . . [[CF 6(a)]]
    . . . **will come again.**

As we remember the death and
    resurrection of our Lord Jesus Christ,
we celebrate the goodness of the earth,
our companionship in this world
and the sharing of all skills and arts
that enrich our lives.
We share the cup of our humanity
matured over the unnumbered centuries
of the struggle that has gone into making
    this world;
our living and dying, fears and hopes,
    futility and fidelity.

Together with those who have drawn
    sustenance from this soil,
those with whom we share it,
and those to whom we pass it on,
we share this bread and raise this cup
in fulfilment of the Lord's command:
through him, with him, in him,
in the unity of the Holy Spirit,
all glory and honour is yours,
Almighty Father, forever and ever.
Amen.

*The Sanctus and Benedictus can be said or sung in any of the languages normally used to suit
the congregation.*

19. The Provinces of the Middle East and the Rest of Africa

The other Anglican provinces of the Middle East and Africa present a somewhat scattered picture, but without known new provincial eucharistic rites.

In Jerusalem and the Middle East, apart from some distant days in Iran, dioceses have tended to use English and American rites. The present Bishop in Egypt hopes to stimulate some diocesan liturgical creativity.

In West Africa, the 1980 rite, **WAfr**, published in **LAL**, continues in use in forms adapted to the different, somewhat disparate, dioceses.

In Sudan, though there is a concern for liturgical renewal, the political crises have not allowed this to have any priority. Forms derived from 1662 continue.

In Uganda, 1662 still provides the main forms.

In Rwanda and Burundi, the position is probably similar to Uganda.

In Central Africa, there is no provincial rite, but in different dioceses there continues considerable currency for the various Southern Africa Books.

In the Indian Ocean, there are different uses in different dioceses (and there has been a Madagascar rite since 1945, published as **Mad** in **MAL**).

F. Asia

20. The Church of Pakistan

The united Church of Pakistan was formed by a union of different denominations in 1970. Its constitution provided for the continuance of the inherited forms and patterns of worship of those denominations. However, the Church established a Liturgical Commission at an early point after its formation and the Commission immediately produced in Urdu (the common language of Pakistan) a set of experimental services, which were approved for occasional use at the Synod of the Church in 1971. The services were then published in English in pocket-book form in *Experimental Services* (1974). The language still addressed God as 'thou'. The Lord's Supper was almost entirely drawn from **CSI**, and acknowledged as such.

In 1985 a specifically Pakistan Book of official Urdu services (*Dua-e-Aam*) was produced and the eucharistic rite in it was a slightly revised and simplified form of the 1971 rite. It is presented here as **Pak**.

THE ORDER FOR THE HOLY COMMUNION FROM THE CHURCH OF PAKISTAN *BOOK OF COMMON PRAYER* 1985 (Pak)

[The translation is taken from a duplicated text checked and corrected against the original by Awais, Zabir and Dominic Moghal. The numbering and lining are editorial.]

THE PREPARATION

 1. [*Salutation]

 2. *Still standing, all join in saying aloud this prayer:*
    Almighty God, to whom . . . [CF 1] . . . Christ our Lord. Amen.

 3. [*The Summary of the Law, and/or The New Commandment]
    The Kyries [ELLC 2 in English and Greek]

 4. [Call to confession in preparation for communion]

 5. [Corporate confession]

 6. *Then shall the Priest proclaim the words of Scripture as follows:*
    Hear the gracious word of God to all who truly turn to him through Jesus Christ:
    [Texts of Matt. 11.28; John 3.16; 1 Tim. 1.15; 1 John 2.1]

 7. [Absolution, in part close to CF2]

 8. *The Gloria: all stand to sing or say together:*
    Glory to God . . . [ELLC 3] . . . God the Father. Amen.
    God's people] his people

THE MINISTRY OF THE WORD OF GOD

 9. [*Salutation]

10. [Announcement of the day in the Calendar, and reading of Collect]

11. [Epistle and other Lesson; *proclamation and response following]

12. [Gospel; announcement, *proclamation and response following]

13. *A sermon may be preached.*

14. *The Nicene Creed shall be said by all:*
    We believe in one God . . . ⟦ELLC 5 following 1974 ICET⟧ . . . world to come. Amen.
    [and the Son]] OMIT BRACKETS

THE PRAYERS

15–18. ⟦A set form with provision for other uses, and for the people to add their prayers⟧

THE BREAKING OF THE BREAD

19. *All stand and the Priest says:* ⟦Ps. 133.1 and 1 Cor. 10.17⟧ *All continue:*
    We will offer in his dwelling an oblation with great gladness,
    we will sing and speak praises to the Lord. *(Ps. 27.6)*

20. *The peace may be given here, first from the Celebrant to the people and then from one to another among the people by clasping the hands of his neighbour and saying:*
    The peace of the Lord be always with you.

    And he who receives the peace may reply:
    And also with you.

21. *A hymn may be sung. The bread and wine for the communion and the offering of the people shall be brought to be presented at the Altar Table. While those bearing them stand before the Table all shall join the following prayer:*
    Holy Father, who consecrated for us a new and living way
    through the blood of your dear Son,
    receive us unworthy as we are.
    Receive these offerings and use them
    for your glory and the extension of your kingdom.
    All things come from you
    and of your own do we give you.

    The bearers of the offertory shall then return to their places.

22. *All kneel and the Priest shall say:*
    Be present, be present, O Jesus, great high priest, as you were with your disciples,
    and make yourself known to us in the breaking of the bread.
    By your Holy Spirit sanctify this bread and wine
    that they may become for us your body and blood.
    For through you we all have access to the Father in the one Spirit.

23. *The Priest shall stand to lead the people in the Eucharist:*

The Lord be . . . ⟦ELLC 6⟧ . . . give thanks and praise.

It is both right and our duty,
at all times and in all places
to give you thanks, O Lord,
Holy Father, Almighty God through our
   Lord.

Here a proper preface may be read according to season.

Therefore with angels and archangels
and with all the company of heaven
we proclaim your glorious name,
forever praising you and saying:

Holy, holy . . . ⟦ELLC 7⟧ . . . Glory be to you, O Lord, most high.
Blessed is . . . ⟦ELLC 8⟧ . . . in the highest.

Holy and blessed heavenly Father,
who of your tender love for mankind
gave your only Son Jesus Christ
to take our nature on him
and to suffer death upon the cross for our
   redemption:

Who made there by his one oblation once
   offered
a full, perfect and sufficient sacrifice,
   oblation and satisfaction

for the sins of the whole world:
We recall before you his suffering and death,
remembering his sacrifice.
Have mercy on us and all your church;

Who in the same night that he was betrayed
took bread and after giving you thanks
he broke it and gave it to his disciples,
saying, Take, eat, this is my body
which is given for you:
do this in remembrance of me.

Again after supper he took the cup,
gave you thanks and gave it to them,

saying: Drink this all of you,
for this is my blood of the new covenant,
which is shed for you and for many
for the forgiveness of sins.
Do this as often as you drink it,
in remembrance of me.

All shall respond heartily in saying together:
**Amen O Lord, we commemorate your
    death,
we confess your resurrection
and we wait for your return.
Glory be to you, O Christ.**

24. As our Saviour Christ commanded and taught us we are bold to say:
    Our Father in heaven . . . ⟦ELLC 1⟧ . . . for ever. Amen.
    Save us from the time of trial and] Do not bring us to the time of trial but

25. *After a short silence all may say:*
    We do not presume . . . ⟦CF 3⟧ . . . he in us. Amen.
    that our sinful . . . precious blood and] OMIT

26. *The Priest shall stand and break the bread saying:*
    The bread which we break is a communion in the body of Christ. *(1 Cor. 10.16)*

27. *After receiving himself the Priest shall lead the people in the following devotion:*
    O Lamb of God . . . ⟦ELLC 9(b) with 'O Lamb' three times⟧ . . . grant us your peace.

28. *When all have received the Sacrament of the body and blood of Christ, Let us give thanks:*

29. Almighty God, our heavenly Father,
    who have accepted us as your children in your Son our Lord Jesus Christ
    and fed us with the spiritual food of his most precious Body and Blood
    and have promised us forgiveness of sins and life everlasting,
    we give thanks to you and glorify you for your indescribable gifts,
    and offer ourselves, our souls and bodies, in your presence
    to be a reasonable, holy and living sacrifice, as a spiritual act of worship.
    Grant us grace not to conform any longer to the pattern of this world,
    but to be transformed by the renewing of our minds
    and to know your good and perfect and pleasing will;
    and so to obey you in this world,
    that in the end we may rejoice with all your saints in your heavenly kingdom
    through Jesus Christ our Lord,
    who with you and the Holy Spirit lives and reigns for ever and ever.
    **Amen! Praise and glory and wisdom and thanks
    and honour and power and strength be to our God for ever and ever. Amen.**
    or
    Almighty and everliving . . . ⟦1662 prayers of thanksgiving and oblation combined as
    in CSI⟧ . . . for ever.
    Amen! Praise and glory . . . ⟦as above⟧ . . . for ever and ever. Amen.

30. *A hymn of praise and thanksgiving, or of dedication to service, may be sung.*

31. *The Priest pronounces this or a seasonal blessing:*
    The peace of God . . . ⟦CF 12(a)⟧ . . . remain with you always. **Amen.**

32. *The Priest may then dismiss the people saying:*
    Go in peace and serve the Lord.

21. The Church of North India

The Church of North India was formed from a union of different denominations in 1970, and first produced its own forms of the eucharist in 1973. This text was slightly revised in 1974 and was then published in **FAL** as **CNI**. Three further editions of the booklet came in the years to 1983, all following **Eng3** at many points. The 1983 edition was shown by a table of changes to **CNI** in **LAL**, and was coded as **CNIR**. In 1990 the Church became a full member of the Anglican Communion.

The booklet form of the eucharistic rite was clearly provisional, and was treated as experimental. The aim developed of providing a complete volume of all the normal liturgical provision to mark the Silver Jubilee of the Church, and this was authorized by the Synod Executive Committee in March 1995, and then published as *The Book of Worship*.[77] Its authorization does not inhibit the continued use of inherited forms (or lack of forms) of the uniting denominations.

Because of the varied languages in use in North India, the Book was compiled in English, and specifically in inclusive language. The Preface states a policy of drawing upon the different traditions represented within the united Church, and the Introductory Notes encourage expression in people's own culture.

The Book contains two eucharistic rites, and a separate 'Service of the Lord's Supper with Feet-Washing and Love-Feast'. The first two are presented here, coded as **CNI1** and **CNI2**; and the separate third service does not present different eucharistic material. All the rites include the optional provision, inherited from non-Anglican denominations, that the narrative of institution can be read as a preliminary 'warrant' text, and then be omitted from the actual eucharistic prayer. **CNI1** otherwise retains the **Eng3** tradition so visibly continued in the earlier booklets, but **CNI2** draws upon different sources. In addition the Church is involved in a concordat with the Church of South India and the Mar Thoma Syrian Orthodox Church, and a joint eucharistic rite to give expression to the concordat is contained within the Church of South India *Book of Common Worship*, and its text, coded as **ILC**, is shown at the end of the South India chapter below.

'THE LORD'S SUPPER' FROM THE CHURCH OF NORTH INDIA'S 1995 *BOOK OF WORSHIP* (CNI1)

[Both the numbering and the lining are original to the rite]

AN ORDER FOR THE LORD'S SUPPER OR THE HOLY EUCHARIST

General Notes
[Five notes concern the setting and conduct of worship]

---

77 Published by the ISPCK, Post Box 1585, Kashmere Gate, Delhi-110006.

Explanatory Notes on the Service
[[Over three pages of detailed direction]]

The Structure of the Lord's Supper
[[A list of nine sub-headings under the two cross-headings shown in the rite]]

The Lord's Supper

THE PROCLAMATION OF THE WORD AND THE PRAYERS

THE PREPARATION

1. *At the beginning of the Service the minister may give a Call to Worship (see Section 47).*

2. *Before or after this a hymn, a canticle or a psalm may be said or sung.*

3. *The minister greets the people, saying*
   The grace of our Lord Jesus Christ and the love of God and the fellowship of the Holy Spirit be with you all. (2 Cor. 13.14)
   And also with you.

4. *The minister and people say together*
   Almighty God, to whom . . . [[CF 1]] . . . Christ our Lord. Amen.
       hidden] hid

5. *All sing or say*
   Glory to God . . . [[ELLC 3]] . . . God the Father. Amen.
       God's people] his people

   Or, the Kyries
   Lord, have mercy . . . [[ELLC 2, six-line responsive in English]] . . . **Lord, have mercy.**

   Or, the Trisagion, thrice repeated
   Holy, God,
   Holy and mighty, holy and immortal, have mercy on us.

6. *The minister prays in his/her own words.*

7. *The minister may then pray in the words of the Collect of the Day.*

THE MINISTRY OF THE WORD

8. [[*The Old Testament, with *proclamation and response, and *silence]]

9. *A psalm may be said.*

10. *The Epistle* [[with *proclamation and response, and *silence]]

11. *A Canticle, a hymn or a psalm may be sung or said.*

12. *The Gospel* [[with *response to announcement, *proclamation and response at conclusion, and *silence]]

13. *The Sermon, beginning with a short invocation.*

14. *The Nicene Creed is said or sung, at least on Sundays and greater Festivals.*
    We believe in one God . . . [[ELLC 5]] . . . world to come. Amen.
        of one Being] one in Being
        was incarnate . . . truly human] by the power of the Holy Spirit he was born of the Virgin Mary and
            became man
        in accordance with] in fulfilment of
        [and the Son]] OMIT BRACKETS
    Or, in place of the Nicene Creed, the Apostles' Creed may be said or sung.
    I believe in God . . . [[ELLC 4]] . . . life everlasting. Amen.
    Or, a suitable canticle, hymn, or lyric, affirming the faith of the Church, may be sung.

15. *Brief announcements may be given now or at any other convenient time.*

THE INTERCESSION

16. [Two responsive forms of intercession, with reference to an Explanatory Note permitting other ways]

THE CONFESSION OF SIN

17. *The minister may read the Summary of the Law*
    [Standard text]

18. God so loved the world . . . [largely as in **EngA**] . . . love and peace with all people.

19. *After a short silence the presbyter and people say* [corporate confession as in **Eng3**]

20. Almighty God, who forgives all who forgive one another and truly repent . . . [CF 2]
    . . . Christ our Lord. **Amen. Thanks be to God.**
    [permission to use 'us' and 'our' for 'you' and 'your']

THE MINISTRY OF THE SACRAMENT

21. *If the Scripture Warrant is to be used, it is read now, or after Section 27.*
    Beloved in the Lord, let us attend to the words of institution of this Holy Sacrament, as they are given by Saint Paul in the first Epistle to the Corinthians:
    I received from the Lord what I also delivered to you, that the Lord Jesus on the night when he was betrayed took bread, and when he had given thanks, he broke it, and said, 'This is my body which is for you. Do this in remembrance of me.' In the same way also the cup, after supper, saying, 'This cup is the new covenant in my blood. Do this as often as you drink it, in remembrance of me.' For as often as you eat this bread and drink the cup, you proclaim the Lord's death until he comes. *1 Cor. 11.23–26*

THE PEACE

22. We are the body of Christ. In the one Spirit we were all baptized into one body. Let us pursue all that makes for peace and builds up our common life. *1 Cor. 12.27, 13; Rom. 14.19*

    The peace of the Lord be always with you.
    And also with you.

23. *The peace may be given here. The manner of giving the peace is according to custom. The people also may greet one another.*

THE PREPARATION OF THE BREAD AND WINE

24. *A lyric or hymn may be sung, and the offerings of the people may be collected and presented.*

25. *The bread and wine are brought forward and placed on the Table, or, where it is the custom, unveiled.*

26. Let us present these offerings, and with them ourselves, for the service of the Divine Majesty.

27. **All things come from you,**
    and of your own do we give you.
    Almighty God, creator of the world.
    We ask you to accept these *(offerings and)
    gifts of bread and wine
    for the glory of your name
    and the good of your people;
    through Jesus Christ our Lord. Amen.

    * *Omit these words if there is no offering other than bread and wine.*

28. The Lord is here . . . ⟦CF 5⟧ . . . **him thanks and praise.**

29. It is not only right,
it is our duty and our joy,
holy Father, heavenly King,
almighty and eternal God,
always and everywhere to offer you
thanks and praise through Jesus Christ,
your only Son, our Lord;

For he is your true and living Word;
through him you have created all things
    from the beginning,
and formed us in your own image;

Through him you enlighten every one
who comes into the world,
and from age to age have raised up
prophets and wise men and women
to point the way to you;

Through him you have freed us
from the slavery of sin,
giving him to be born as man,
to die upon the cross,
and to rise again for us;

Through him you give your holy and life-
    giving Spirit,
to make us your children
and the first-fruits of your new creation.

30. *When an additional special thanksgiving is
provided for the season of the Christian Year or
for some other special occasion, it follows here (see
Section 47, page . . .).*

31. **Therefore we join our praises to the
    never-ending song**
of saints and angels before your throne,
**we proclaim the glory of your name, and
say:**
Holy, holy . . . ⟦ELLC 7⟧ . . . **in the highest.**

Accept our praises, heavenly Father,
through your Son, our Saviour Jesus
    Christ,
and as we follow his example
and obey his command,
grant that by the power of your Spirit
these gifts of bread and wine

may be to us the body and blood
of him who died for us and rose again.

32.* For in the same night that he was
    betrayed,
he took bread;
and after giving you thanks, he broke it,
and gave it his disciples, and said:
'Take, eat; this is my body
which is given for you.
Do this in remembrance of me.'
In the same way, after supper he took the
    cup;
and having given you thanks,
he gave it to them, and said:
'Drink this, all of you;
for this is my blood of the new Covenant,
which is shed for you and for many,
for the forgiveness of sins.
Do this, as often as you drink it,
in remembrance of me.'

33. Therefore, heavenly Father,
in remembrance of him
we set apart this bread and this cup;
we celebrate and proclaim his perfect
    sacrifice made once for all upon the
    cross,
his resurrection from the dead,
and his ascension into heaven;
and we look for his coming in glory.
Christ . . . ⟦CF 6(a)⟧ . . . shall come again.

Accept through him, our great high priest,
this our sacrifice of thanks and praise;
and as we eat and drink these holy gifts
in the presence of your divine majesty,
renew us by your Spirit,
inspire us with your love,
and unite us in the body of your Son, Jesus
    Christ our Lord.

With him, and in him, and through him,
by the power of the Holy Spirit,
with all who stand before you in earth and
    heaven,
we worship you, Father almighty,
in songs of everlasting praise:
Blessing . . . ⟦CF 7⟧ . . . and ever. Amen.

---

* *When the Scripture Warrant (Section 21) has already been read, Section 32 may be omitted.*

THE COMMUNION

THE BREAKING OF THE BREAD AND THE SHARING OF THE BREAD AND WINE

34. *The presbyter breaks the consecrated bread, saying*
    We break this bread that we may share in the body of Christ.
    We are one body, for we all share in the one bread.

35. *The presbyter may take the cup into his/her hands in the sight of the people and say*
    The cup which we bless is a sharing of the blood of Christ.
    His life is in us and we live in him.

36. As our Saviour Christ has taught us, so we pray:
    Our Father in heaven . . . ⟦ELLC 1⟧ . . . for ever. Amen.
    Save us from the time of trial and] Do not bring us to the time of trial but

    Silence

37. *The Prayer of Humble Access may be said.*
    We do not presume . . . ⟦CF 3(a)⟧ . . . he in us. Amen.
    sinful bodies . . . most precious blood] sinful bodies and souls may be made clean
                                        by his most precious body and blood

    One or both of the following may be said or sung:
    Blessed is he . . . ⟦ELLC 8⟧ . . . in the highest.
    Jesus, Lamb of God . . . ⟦ELLC 9(a)⟧ . . . world, give us your peace.

38. **Draw near in faith . . . ⟦CF 9(a)⟧ . . . with thanksgiving.**
    Eat and drink in remembrance] Remember

39. *The presbyters and people receive the consecrated bread and wine.*

40. *The following words of administration may be used**
    The body of our Lord Jesus Christ, which was given for you.
    The blood of our Lord Jesus Christ, which was shed for you.

    The communicant may reply each time: **Amen.**

41. *Any consecrated bread or wine which is not required for purposes of communion is con-*
    sumed at the end of the administration or after the Blessing.

AFTER COMMUNION

42. *A Sentence (Section 47) may be said by the presbyter.*

    Silence may be kept.

43. Having now with faith received this holy sacrament, let us give thanks to God.

44. *The presbyter may pray in his/her own words.*

    One of the following is then said by all:
    Almighty God, we thank you . . . ⟦CF 11(a)⟧ . . . praise and glory. Amen.
    souls and bodies] ourselves

---

* *Alternative words of administration which may be used*
⟦Three sets of alternatives: (1) based on CF 10(a) and (b); (2) 'The body of Christ, the bread of life' and 'The blood of Christ, the true vine'; (3) drawn from the institution narrative⟧

Or

Heavenly Father,
you have fed us with the spiritual food
of the most precious body and blood
of your Son, our Saviour Jesus Christ.
You have assured us,
in these holy Mysteries,
of your favour and goodness towards us,
and that we are living members of the body of your Son,
and heirs of your eternal kingdom.
For these great benefits we thank you
and in union with your Son
we offer you ourselves
as a living sacrifice.
And now, Father, send us out
to do the work you have given us to do,
to love and serve you
as faithful witnesses of Christ our Lord.
To him, to you, Father, and to the Holy Spirit,
be honour and glory, now and for ever.
Amen.

45. *The presbyter gives this or the appropriate blessing (Section 47).*
The peace of God . . . ⟦CF 12(a)⟧ . . . with you always. **Amen.**

Go in peace . . . ⟦CF 12(b)⟧ . . . **of Christ. Amen.**

The ministers and people leave and greet each other.

47.[78] *SENTENCES, THANKSGIVINGS AND BLESSINGS FOR THE SEASONS OF THE CHRISTIAN YEAR OR SOME OTHER SPECIAL OCCASIONS* ⟦Four texts (including a proper preface) for 19 seasons or occasions in the year, followed by General sentences for 'Call to Worship' and 'After Communion'. Finally comes this rubric⟧

Where the people receive the Consecrated Bread and Wine by 'Tables', each 'Table' being dismissed by a brief word of encouragement, exhortation or blessing, some of the sentences above may be used at the dismissal of each 'Table' ⟦Then there is reference to the opening notes which provide for receiving by 'Tables'⟧

48. *CONSECRATION OF ADDITIONAL BREAD OR WINE*
If either or both of the consecrated elements are likely to prove insufficient, the presbyter returns to the holy Table, and adds more with these words
Having given thanks to you, Father, over the bread and the cup, according to the institution of your Son Jesus Christ, who said 'Take, eat, this is my body', we pray that this bread also may be to us his body, and be received in remembrance of him.

Having given thanks to you, Father, over the bread and the cup, according to the institution of your Son Jesus Christ, who said: 'Drink this, this is my blood', we pray that this wine also may be to us his blood, and be received in remembrance of him.

(The basic principle is that of bringing additional bread or wine into the sacramental action by associating them with the already consecrated bread and wine before the supply of the latter has been completely exhausted. For this there is good historical precedent.)

---

78 ⟦There is no Section 46⟧

183

'AN ALTERNATIVE ORDER FOR CELEBRATING THE LORD'S SUPPER' FROM THE CHURCH OF NORTH INDIA'S 1995 *BOOK OF WORSHIP* (CNI2)

A Recommended Outline for a celebration of the Lord's Supper in which a set text is not used

⟦The numbering is original to the rite⟧

ABOUT THIS OUTLINE

⟦Four notes referring to the provisions of the *CNI Constitution*, the Introductory Notes from CNI1, the freedom to continue any forms in use at the time of union, the desirability of 'a truly indigenous setting', and the roles of presbyters, deacons and laypeople⟧

The Alternative Order

1. *THE PROCLAMATION OF THE WORD*

1. When the people have assembled, **the Minister calls them to worship** in words of Holy Scripture, or other appropriate words.

   A **Psalm, Hymn** or **Lyric** may be sung, setting forth the glory of God, or invoking the presence of the Holy Spirit.

2. The Minister briefly offers **prayer in his/her own words** – a prayer of Adoration, Confession and Supplication; or appropriate traditional prayers may be said together.

3. (a) **Passages of Holy Scripture** from the Old and New Testaments – especially from the Gospels – are read; and a **Sermon** is preached, setting forth God's glory and love, and encouraging those present to Christian faith and discipleship.

   (b) **The Congregation responds to the Word of God in appropriate hymns or lyrics, and by declaring their faith** in the words of the Apostles' or the Nicene Creed, or in some other traditional or contemporary affirmation of faith.

4. **Intercession** is offered for the world and for the Church, remembering particular needs. The presbyter, or others invited by him/her, may pray in their own words. Or the prayers of intercession in the CNI Order of the Lord's Supper may be used in any of the alternative forms there suggested. (See that Order, Section 16, and the relevant Note on page . . .).

5. We do not approach this Sacrament trusting in our own righteousness or merit, but pleading the all-sufficient merit of Christ's Sacrifice 'once for all offered'. This may be expressed in a '**Prayer of Humble Access**' in traditional or contemporary words, or in a suitable **Hymn** or **Lyric**.

6. The **Offerings of the People** may be received; and where it is the custom, **Bread and Wine** may also be placed on the Table now. **The presbyter and those who are assisting him/her** (e.g., elders or lay deacons) **take their places at the Table.**

Note: Part 1 and 2 of the service form a unity of Word and Sacrament. Presbyters should therefore plan the service as a whole, avoiding over-lengthy prayers, readings or sermon, and taking care that there are no 'vain repetitions' either in Part 1 or Part 2.

2. *THE COMMUNION*

1. **The Presbyter greets the people.** He/she may read the **Scripture Warrant** for the Celebration of the Lord's Supper (1 Cor. 11.23–26). (See also para 2(b) below.) He/she may also read **words of Comfort and Encouragement** from the Holy Scripture. **Or he/she may give a brief exhortation**, reminding the people of the meaning of the Sacrament, warning against carelessness or self-righteousness, and encouraging them to true repentance and living faith.

2. The presbyter and people follow the Lord's example in word and action:

(a) **The presbyter takes Bread and Wine** in the sight of the people and sets them apart 'to this sacred use and mystery'.

(b) He/she offers **a Prayer of Thanksgiving and Invocation** in traditional or modern language. The prayer should include joyful commemoration of all God's mighty acts, in creation, in the incarnation, death and resurrection of Christ, and in the gift of the Spirit, and a prayer that the Holy Spirit may bless us and our gifts of Bread and Wine so that they may be for us the Body and the Blood of Christ, who died for us and rose again.

If the Scripture Warrant (para 1, above) has not already been read, the Lord's words instituting the Sacrament should also be included in this prayer.

(c) **The presbyter breaks the Bread and gives it to the people. In the same way he/she gives the Cup.**

The method of administering the Bread and Wine will be according to local custom. It may be administered by the presbyter and those assisting him/her to the people coming forward and standing or kneeling near the Table; or it may be by distributing the Bread and Wine to the people in their places, by elders and lay deacons; or it may be by passing the Bread and Wine from person to person. On Diocesan and Synodical occasions, the method of administration will be decided in advance and announced to the people by the Presiding Minister.

3. **During the administration of the Bread and Wine Hymns or Lyrics** may be sung, or appropriate verses from Scripture may be spoken, where this is the custom. But time shall also be allowed for **silence and meditation** as the worshippers wait in the presence of the Lord.

4. When all have partaken, **any remaining consecrated Bread and Wine shall be replaced on the Table,** and consumed now or after dismissal of the people.

5. The Celebration of the Lord's Supper concludes with a '**Post-Communion Prayer**' of thanksgiving and self-dedication in traditional or modern language, followed by a **Hymn or Psalm of Thanksgiving** (such as Psalm 103) and by the **Benediction** pronounced by the presbyter.

22. The Church of Bangladesh

The Church of Bangladesh was formed originally from the union of Churches in Pakistan in 1970 just prior to the severance of Bangladesh from Pakistan early in 1971. While the Church was immediately separated from the Church of Pakistan, its autonomy was fully recognized in 1974. According to its constitution the worship traditions of the uniting churches were continued and sustained. The existence of the common language with the neighbouring parts of North India meant that there developed a regular use of the Bengali (Bangla) version of **CNI**. However, from the early 1980s a Liturgical Committee was developing drafts which were distinctively Bangladeshi in character. In 1989 a semi-definitive eucharistic rite gave rise to an English-language translation. At this stage the rite included four eucharistic prayers and in this and elsewhere went far beyond being simply a translation of **CNI**.

In 1990 the Church of Bangladesh became a full member of the Anglican Communion. In 1997 the Church provided a full Bengali Prayer Book, into which the 1989 eucharistic rite was incorporated with certain enrichments. Most notably a new eucharistic prayer was added, and the rite edited below includes this in translation as the first prayer in the new order. In the one English-speaking congregation in Bangladesh, the use of the 1989 rite has run on with some local further developments, but it is the Bengali text which the edition here is intended to demonstrate.

THE LORD'S SUPPER of THE CHURCH OF BANGLADESH, 1997 (Bangla)

[The official translation of 1989 was by John Webber, which he has here supplemented for the 1997 rite. The numbering is that of the 1997 rite, with the points of change from 1989 editorially indicated by 1989 numbers in brackets, or a cross ('x') where the section was not in 1989. Nos 28–32 are editorial. The lining is editorial.]

THE MINISTRY OF THE WORD

PREPARATION

1. *The minister gives a call to worship.*

2. *The minister greets the people, saying:*
   The grace of our Lord Jesus Christ, the love of God and the fellowship of the Holy Spirit be always with you.
   And also with you.

3[x]. *A hymn may be sung.*

4[3]. *An opening prayer is said (pages . . .)* [i.e. Appendix A]

5[4]. *The minister invites the people to confess their sins (pages . . .)* [[i.e. Appendix B]]. *(The confession may also be made following the intercession.)*
He then says
Let us call to mind our sins, and confess them with penitence and faith.

[5] [[Two forms of corporate confession]]

The bishop or presbyter says

[6] Almighty God, have mercy . . . [[CF 2]] . . . Christ our Lord. **Amen. Thanks be to God.**

6[7]. *All sing or say*
Glory to God in the highest . . . [[ELLC 3]] . . . God the Father. Amen.
God's people] his people

7[8]. Let us pray
[[Trisagion or Kyries (ELLC 2) in English]]

8[9]. *Taking up the theme of the day, the minister may pray in his own words. He may then say the collect of the day.*

THE READINGS

9[10]. *Taking the Bible, the minister may stand before the congregation and all may say*
O Lord, give us the grace to know and understand your heavenly Word.
Fill us with the truth of your Holy Gospel.
Make us gladly to obey your commands, and may we perfectly fulfil your will.
Make us worthy to receive your blessing and mercy, now and at all times;
through Christ our Lord. Amen.

10[11]. *Lessons from the Old Testament and the Epistles may be read* [[with proclamation and response after each]]

[12] *Silence may be kept, and a hymn or psalm sung.*

[13] *The Gospel is read. All stand* [[Announcement and response before and proclamation and response after.]]

[14] *A sermon is preached.*

11[15]. *The Nicene or Apostles' Creed may be said, or a suitable hymn affirming the faith of the Church may be sung.*

Nicene	*Apostles'*
We believe . . . [[ELLC 5]] . . . world to come. Amen.	**I believe in God . . .**
is, seen and] is seen and	**[[ELLC 4]] . . . life**
of one Being] one in Being	**everlasting. Amen.**
was incarnate . . . human] by the power of the Holy Spirit	
he was born of the Virgin Mary	
and became man	
in accordance with] in fulfilment of	

12[16]. *Announcements may now be given.*

13[17]. *THE INTERCESSION*
Prayers are offered
[[Topics for prayer are listed, and permission given for the minister's own words or the use of those on pages . . . (i.e. Appendix C)]]

14[18]. *If the confession has not already been said, it is said now.*[79]

---

79 [[1989 provided [19] *'A prayer of preparation for the celebration of the Supper may now be said'.*]]

THE COMMUNION

THE PEACE

15[20].   *The presbyter says these or other appropriate words*

We are the body of Christ.	*Or*
By the one Spirit we were baptized	Our Lord Jesus Christ said,
into one body.	Peace I leave with you
Let us then pursue all that builds up	my peace I give to you.
our common life.	

The peace of the Lord be always with you
And also with you.
The people may greet each other with a sign of peace.

[21]   *Where it is the custom, the Scripture Warrant may be read from 1 Corinthians 11.23–26*

THE TAKING OF THE BREAD AND WINE

16[22].   Let us present our offerings, and with them ourselves, for the service of God.

A hymn may be sung, and the offerings of the people collected. The bread and wine are brought to the Holy Table.

[23]   **All things come from you and of your own do we give you,**
Almighty God, creator of the world.
We ask you to accept these offerings, and gifts of bread and wine,
and, with them, the offering of ourselves
for the glory of your name and the good of your people.
Amen.

THE GREAT THANKSGIVING

17[x].   Be present, be present, O Jesus, our good High Priest,
as you were with your disciples,
and make yourself known to us in the breaking of the bread. **Amen.**[80]

[24]   *The presbyter begins the Great Thanksgiving, saying* [This form from the dialogue to the sanctus is common to all five prayers]

The Lord be with . . . [ELLC 6] . . . **him thanks and praise.**
It is good and right, our duty and our joy,
holy Father, heavenly king, almighty and eternal God,
always and everywhere to offer you thanks and praise
through Jesus Christ your only Son, our Lord.

[25]   *Here a proper preface is said, at least on Sundays and Feast days.*

[26]   **Therefore we join our praises**
to the never-ending songs of saints and angels before your throne;
we proclaim the glory of your name and say:
Holy, holy, holy . . . [ELLC 7] . . . in the highest.
Blessed is he who comes . . . [ELLC 8] . . . in the highest.

---

80 [1989 had this prayer in Appendix D, as the first of the 'Prayers of Preparation']

First Eucharistic Prayer[81]

Heavenly Father,
through your Son, our Saviour and Lord,
     Jesus Christ
accept our praise and offering.
As we follow his example and obey his
     command,
grant that, through the power of your
     Spirit,
this bread and wine may be changed into
     the body and blood
of him who died and was raised for us.

On the night he was delivered into hostile
     hands,
he took the bread in his hands, and giving
     thanks to you, broke it up,
and giving it to his disciples, said:
Take, eat, this is my body delivered up for
     you,
do this in my memory.

In the same way, after supper,
he took the cup in his hands,
and giving thanks to you gave it to them,
and said: All of you, drink from this cup,
because this is my blood, poured out to
     establish a new covenant
and for the wiping away of your sin and
     that of many.
As often as you drink it, do it in my
     memory.

Therefore, heavenly Father,
we offer up this bread and cup
set apart in his memory,
we remember and proclaim the act of
     effective atonement
offered for everybody once upon the cross,
his resurrection from the dead and
     ascension into heaven,
and we await his glorious coming again.
Therefore, with joy, together we sing with
     adoration:
Christ has . . . ⟦CF 6(a)⟧ . . . come again.

Through the mediation of our High Priest,
     Christ,
receive this offering of thanksgiving and
     praise.
Almighty King, when we receive this holy
     food before you,
make us new by your Spirit,
awaken the heart with your love
and join us to the body of your Son,
our Lord, Jesus Christ.

Almighty Father, joined to him,
through him and in the strength of the
     Holy Spirit,
with all who worship you in heaven and
     on earth,
we praise you with an unending hymn:
**Blessing and . . . ⟦CF 7⟧ . . . and ever.
     Amen.**

---

81 ⟦The First Prayer here was new in 1997; the next four came in 1989 in the order 3, 2, 4, 5⟧

[27] *Second Eucharistic Prayer*

Blessed are you, O Lord our God,
the Father of our saviour, Jesus Christ.
We will not cease to give you thanks,
for through him we are chosen in love
  to be your children
and destined to live for the praise of your
  glory.
He came and proclaimed good news,
peace to those who were afar off
and those who were near,
so that all might come to you, our Father,
you who are so rich in mercy.
Even when we were dead in sin
we were made alive with him,
and saved by his grace.
We are now no longer aliens in a foreign
  land,
but fellow citizens with the saints,
and members of your own household.

When the hour had come
for him to be glorified by you, his heavenly
  Father,
having loved his own who were in the
  world,
he loved them to the end.
At supper with them, on the night he was
  handed over to suffering and death,
he took bread, and after giving you thanks,
he broke it, gave it to his disciples and
  said,
'Take, eat, this is my body, which is given
  for you.
Do this in remembrance of me.'

Again after supper, he took the cup,
and having given you thanks,
he gave it to them and said,
'Drink this all of you,
for this is my blood of the new covenant,
which is shed for you and for many
for the forgiveness of sins.
Do this, as often as you drink it,
in remembrance of me.'
Amen, to Christ be the glory.

He is our great high priest, holy and
  blameless,
your beloved Son,
who, through the sacrifice of himself,
put away sin and won for us an eternal
  inheritance,

and now ever lives to make intercession
  for us.
Through him, we have confidence
to draw near to the throne of grace,
and with this bread and cup
to recall that sacrifice,
and show forth his death until his coming
  again,
rejoicing and saying,
Christ has . . . ⟦CF 6(a)⟧ . . . come again.

We come to him,
that living stone, rejected by men,
but in your sight chosen and precious,
and on him are built into a living temple,
a holy priesthood, to offer spiritual
  sacrifices
and to declare the wonderful deeds
of him who called us out of darkness
into his marvellous light.
In him, alone, we ask you to accept these
  praises,
and, with your Holy Spirit,
to bless these gifts of bread and wine,
that they may be to us his body and his
  blood.

Bless us, as here we offer ourselves
as a holy and living sacrifice,
restore, establish and strengthen us,
and grant that we, and all who share in
  this bread and this cup,
may receive all the benefits of his passion.

Be mindful of your church,
deliver it from evil,
make it perfect in your love,
and, as grain once scattered on the
  hillsides
was in this bread made one,
we pray that you will gather all your
  children from every place
into the Kingdom of Christ Jesus, your
  Son, our Lord.

With him and in him and through him,
in the power of the Holy Spirit,
with all who stand before you in earth and
  heaven,
we worship you, Father Almighty,
in songs of everlasting praise,
Blessing . . . ⟦CF 7⟧ . . . and ever. Amen.

You are indeed holy and blessed,
O gracious Father, endless is your mercy.
Accept our praises and thanksgiving
for all your mighty works.
And as we follow the example of your
   Son,
our Saviour, Jesus Christ,
and obey his commands,
grant that, by the power of your Spirit,
these gifts of bread and wine may be to us
the body and blood of him
who died for us and rose again.

For in the same night that he was
   betrayed,
he took bread, and, after giving you
   thanks,
he broke it, gave it to his disciples and
   said:
'Take, eat, this is my body,
which is given for you.
Do this in remembrance of me.'
Again, after supper, he took the cup,
and having given you thanks,
he gave it to them and said,
'Drink this all of you,
for this is my blood of the new covenant,
which is shed for you and for many
for the forgiveness of sins.
Do this, as often as you drink it,
in remembrance of me.'
Amen, to Christ be the glory.

Therefore, heavenly Father, in
   remembrance of him,
we set apart this bread and this cup;
we celebrate and proclaim his birth and
   life among us,
his perfect sacrifice made once for all upon
   the cross,
his resurrection from the dead
and his ascension into heaven,
rejoicing and saying,
Christ has . . . ⟦CF 6(a)⟧ . . . come again.

And we pray you to accept,
through him, our great High Priest,
this our sacrifice of thanks and praise.

Send your blessing upon us, O Lord,
that as we eat these gifts in the presence of
   your divine majesty,
we may be renewed by your Spirit,
strengthened in your love,
and united in the body of your Son.

Be mindful of your church and all your
   people,
and gather us with your saints
into the Kingdom of Christ our Lord.

With him, and in him, and through him,
by the power of the Holy Spirit,
with all who stand before you in earth and
   heaven,
we worship you, Father Almighty,
in songs of everlasting praise:
Blessing and . . . ⟦CF 7⟧ . . . ever. Amen.

Fourth Eucharistic Prayer

Father, we give you thanks, through your
beloved Son, Jesus Christ.
He is your Word and by him we are
saved.
He came down from heaven,
and won for you a holy people.
He bore suffering, so that we might be
freed from suffering.
He freely accepted death, so that he might
destroy death,
crush Satan underfoot, and make known
the resurrection.

For on the same night that he was
betrayed,
he took bread;
after giving you thanks, he broke it,
gave it to his disciples and said,
'Take, eat, this is my body, which is given
for you.
Do this in remembrance of me.'

Again, after supper, he took the cup,
and, having given you thanks,
he gave it to them and said,
'Drink this, all of you,
for this is my blood of the new covenant,
which is shed for you and for many
for the forgiveness of sins.
Do this, as often as you drink it, in
remembrance of me.'
Amen, to Christ be the glory.

Remembering, then, his death and
resurrection,
we present this bread and cup before you,
giving you thanks that you have made us
worthy
to stand before you and serve you as your
priestly people,
rejoicing and saying,
Christ has . . . ⟦CF 6(a)⟧ . . . come again.

And we pray you, send your Spirit upon
these,
the gifts of your Church,
that they may be to us his body and his
blood.

Gather into one all who share this bread
and wine.
Fill us with your Holy Spirit,
that we may be established firmly in your
faith and truth,
and may praise you through your Son,
Jesus Christ.

With him, and in him, and through him,
by the power of the Holy Spirit,
with all who stand before you in earth and
heaven,
we worship you, Father Almighty,
in songs of everlasting praise:
**Blessing and honour . . . ⟦CF 7⟧ . . . and
ever. Amen.**

Fifth Eucharistic Prayer

O God, Lord of the universe,
you are holy and your glory is beyond
    measure.
Upon your eucharist send the life-giving
    Spirit,
who spoke by Moses and the prophets,
who overshadowed the Virgin Mary with
    grace,
who descended upon Jesus in the river Jordan,
and upon the apostles on the day of
    Pentecost.
May the outpouring of this Spirit of fire
transfigure this thanksgiving meal,
that this bread and wine may become for us
the body and blood of Christ.

May this Creator Spirit accomplish the
    words of your beloved Son,
who, in the night in which he was betrayed,
took bread, and when he had given thanks
    to you,
broke it, and gave it to his disciples, saying,
'Take, eat, this is my body which is given for
    you.
Do this in remembrance of me.'
After supper he took the cup,
and, when he had given thanks,
he gave it to them and said,
'Drink this, all of you,
for this is my blood of the new covenant,
which is shed for you and for many
for the forgiveness of sins.
Do this in remembrance of me.'
Amen, to Christ be the glory.

Wherefore, Lord, we celebrate today the
    memorial of our redemption;
we recall the birth and life of your Son
    amongst us,
his baptism by John,
his last meal with the apostles,
his death and descent to the abode of the
    dead;
we proclaim Christ's resurrection and
    ascension in glory,
where as our High Priest he ever intercedes
    for all people,
and we look for his coming at the last,
rejoicing and saying,
Christ has . . . ⟦CF 6(a)⟧ . . . come again.

United in Christ's priesthood,
we present to you this memorial.
Remember the sacrifice of your Son,

and grant to people everywhere
the benefits of Christ's redemptive work.
Behold, Lord, this eucharist,
which you yourself gave to the Church,
and graciously receive it,
as you accept the offering of your Son,
whereby we are reinstated in the
    Covenant.
As we partake of Christ's body and
    blood,
fill us with your Holy Spirit
that we may be one body, one spirit in
    Christ,
a living sacrifice to the praise of your
    glory.

Remember, Lord, your one holy, catholic
    and apostolic Church,
redeemed by the blood of your Christ.
Reveal its unity, guard its faith,
and preserve it in peace.
Remember, Lord, all the servants of your
    Church,
bishops, presbyters, and deacons,
and all to whom you have given special
    gifts of ministry.
Remember _____
Remember also our sisters and brothers
who have died in the peace of Christ,
and those whose faith is known to you
    alone;
guide them to that joyful feast,
prepared for all peoples in your presence,
with the blessed Virgin Mary,
with the patriarchs and prophets,
the apostles and martyrs,
with _____ and all the saints,
for whom your friendship was life.
With all these we sing your praise
and await the happiness of your
    Kingdom,
where with the whole creation,
finally delivered from sin and death,
we shall be enabled to glorify you,
through Christ our Lord.

With him and in him and through him,
in the power of the Holy Spirit,
with all who stand before you in earth
    and heaven,
we worship you, Father Almighty,
in songs of everlasting praise,
Blessing . . . ⟦CF 7⟧ . . . and ever. Amen.

18[28]. *The presbyter breaks the bread, saying*
We break this bread that we may share in the body of Christ.
We are one body, because we all share in the one bread.
The presbyter then takes the cup into his hands and says
The cup which we bless is a sharing of the blood of Christ.
His life is in us and we live in him.

19[29]. As our Saviour Christ has taught us, we now pray
Our Father, who art . . . ⟦modified traditional text⟧ . . . **and ever. Amen.**
Silence may be kept.

20[x]. **We do not presume** . . . ⟦CF 3(a)⟧ . . . **he in us.**[82]
     that our sinful . . . precious blood and] OMIT

     There may be said or sung:
21[30]. **Lamb of God** . . . ⟦ELLC 9(b)⟧ . . . **grant us peace.**

22[31]. **Draw near in faith** . . . ⟦CF 9(a)⟧ . . . **with thanksgiving.**
     Eat and drink in remembrance] Remember
   or
   Behold, our Lord Jesus Christ, the living Bread, the source of eternal life.
   Blessed are we who are called to his supper.
   The ministers and people receive the Bread and Wine.

[32] *The following words of administration may be used.*
   The Body of Christ, given for you   *or*   The Body of Christ, the living bread
   The Blood of Christ, shed for you   *or*   The Blood of Christ, the true vine
   The communicant may reply **Amen.**

AFTER COMMUNION

23[33]. *A sentence from the Bible may be read.*

24[34]. *The minister will then give thanks, praying in his own words, or using one of the
   forms given (pages . . . ⟦i.e. appendix E⟧). All may then say*
[35] **Almighty God, we thank you** . . . ⟦CF 11(a)⟧ . . . **praise and glory. Amen.**
     you our souls and bodies] ourselves

   The Bishop or Presbyter gives this or another appropriate blessing.
25[36]. **The peace of God** . . . ⟦CF 12(a)⟧ . . . **with you, now and for ever. Amen.**
     be among] rest upon

26[37]. **Go in peace** . . . ⟦CF 12(b)⟧ . . . **name of Christ. Amen.**

27[38]. *If either or both or both of the consecrated elements are likely to prove insufficient, the
   presbyter returns to the Holy Table, and adds more with these words:*
   Having given thanks to you, Father, over the bread and the cup, according to the
   institution of your Son Jesus Christ, who said 'Take, eat, this is my body', [*and/or*
   'Drink this; this is my blood'] we pray that this bread/wine also may be to us his
   body/blood, and be received in remembrance of him.

28. *APPENDIX A – OPENING PRAYERS*[83]

29. *APPENDIX B – INVITATIONS TO CONFESSION* ⟦three forms⟧

30. *APPENDIX C – INTERCESSIONS* ⟦six forms⟧

31. *APPENDIX D – PRAYERS OF PREPARATION* ⟦including CF 3(c), and, in 1989, CF 3(a)
   also⟧

32. *APPENDIX E – AFTER COMMUNION* ⟦four forms⟧

---

82 ⟦1989 had this prayer in Appendix D, as the second of the *'Prayers of Preparation'*⟧
83 ⟦This includes the Collect for Purity, CF 1⟧

23. The Church of South India

The Church of South India (CSI), formed in 1947 from a union of Anglican, Methodist and Reformed (Presbyterian and Congregationalist) Churches, has had a greatly respected position as a pioneer Church in the revising of eucharistic liturgy in a unitive and creative way. This reputation began with the first liturgical proposal from its Liturgy Committee in January 1950, and that liturgy, marginally revised in 1954, was published in **LiE** and was labelled **CSI**, and was included in the full *Book of Common Worship* (*BCW*) in 1963, with a large range of proper material added to it. A modernizing of the English of **CSI** came in 1972, and this new text was published in **FAL** and labelled **CSIR**. An experimental rite was authorized in 1985 in order to relate the eucharist more appropriately to Indian cultural ways. In 1994 the Synod directed the Liturgy Committee to revise the *BCW*, and this led to a new text for the eucharist being completed in 2001, and a 'Short Order' being agreed in 2003. Both these rites were duly included in the new *Book of Common Worship*, which was accepted by the Synod in 2004 and published as a hardback book in 2006. While they exhibit many new features, one of the most surprising is the moving of the Peace to follow, as reconciliation, after the confession of sin in the 'Preparation' part of the service. Eucharistic prayers B and C are innovatory, B in particular providing a kind of epiclesis in its last line, though one without mention of the Spirit. The two rites are presented here as **CSI1** and **CSI2** respectively.

However, there is a third rite in the 2006 *BCW*. There is a longstanding Concordat between CSI, CNI and the Mar Thoma Syrian Church of Malabar, and the three Churches, being fully in communion with each other, have sought, through their Commission on Worship and Mission of the Communion of Churches in India, to develop a common eucharistic liturgy. The agreed service is published after the CSI's own services in the 2006 *BCW*, and is edited and presented here as **ICL** (India Concordat Liturgy). The Mar Thoma Church, though reformed, retains (with some adaptation) its inherited Liturgy of St James, and is the only Church with Eastern rites with which the Anglican Churches worldwide are in communion.[84] The Introduction to it in the *BCW* says it has drawn upon the liturgies of the three Churches, but also upon the Lima liturgy and other resources.

---

84 The rite in use in the Mar Thoma Church is presented in English in Phillip Tovey (ed.), *The Liturgy of St James as Presently Used* (Alcuin/GROW Joint Liturgical Study 40, Grove Books, Cambridge, 1998).

THE ORDER FOR THE LORD'S SUPPER FROM THE CHURCH OF SOUTH INDIA *BOOK OF COMMON WORSHIP* (2006)(CSI1)

[The numbering and lining are editorial]

ORDER FOR THE LORD'S SUPPER

THE PREPARATION

1. *A hymn or psalm or bhajan may be sung or said.*

2. *As the ministers come to the Lord's Table, the congregation stands. The presbyter, or one of those with the presbyter, carries in both hands the Bible from which the lessons are to be read, and places it on the Table or on a lectern. The presbyter may stand behind the Table, facing the congregation.*

3. *The presbyter says while the congregation is still standing:*
   Let us pray: Almighty God, to whom . . . [CF 1] . . . Christ our Lord. **Amen.**
      hidden] hid
   or [three alternative opening prayers]

4. *All may be seated.*

LIGHTING OF THE LAMP

5. [Prayer for the flame of God's presence]

6. *Then, as the lamp is lit by some members suitably selected from the congregation, a bhajan such as **Asatoma sadgamaya, Tamasoma jyothirgamaya, Mrithyoma amrithamgamaya, Shanthi, shanthi, shanthi*** or some other suitable psalm is chanted.*

7. *Then all sing or say:*
   Glory to God in the highest . . . [ELLC 3] . . . **God the Father. Amen.**

   Or [Trisagion repeated thrice]

   Or This litany may be said, with the deacon leading the refrain:
   This is the feast of victory for our God. Alleluia, Alleluia, Alleluia.
   [Five lines of praise from the Book of Revelation with the refrain following each]

8. *If there has been no special service of preparation before the celebration of the Lord's Supper, the following may be read.*

OUR LORD'S SUMMARY OF THE LAW AND THE PROPHETS
   [Text from Mark 12 and Matt. 22, with congregational response]
   On festive occasions, the full form of the Ten Commandments (see page . . . [i.e. §38]) may be read, instead of the summary of the Law and the Prophets.

CONFESSION

9. [Call to kneel and to self-examination, then call to confession, based on 1662 Short Exhortation]

10. [Three alternative forms of congregational confession of sin, with a litany of penitence as fourth alternative]

11. *Then the presbyter stands and reads (a selection from the following):*
    Hear the gracious Word of God to all who truly turn to him through Jesus Christ:
    [Isa. 1.18; Jer. 31.33–34; Isa. 40.31; Matt. 11.28; John 3.16; 1 Tim. 1.15; 1 John 2.1–2]

12. [Two alternative absolutions, the first close to CF 2, the second fuller and original]

---

* *Asatoma sadgamaya*: From falsehood to truth.
Tamasoma jyothirgamaya: From darkness to light.
Mrithyoma amrithamgamaya: From death to eternal life.
Shanthi: Peace.

THE PEACE (all stand)

13. Having been forgiven and made whole through our Peacemaker, let us live together in peace. God's peace challenges us and guides us towards the acts of justice, peace and integration of the whole creation. Let us say 'Shalom' to one another and give each other a sign of reconciliation and peace.
    The peace of the Lord be with you:
    And also with you.
    (The peace is shared; either passed on by touch of hand, or by the gesture of namaskara or a handclasp.)

14. *The congregation kneels.*

THE COLLECT OF THE DAY

THE MINISTRY OF THE WORD OF GOD

15. *THE PRAYER FOR ILLUMINATION*
    [A short litany or a versicle and response from Ps. 119 followed by a prayer for guidance]
    (Then the Bible is given to the first reader who takes it to the lectern.)

16. [Readings from Old Testament and Epistles with congregational affirmation and *thanksgiving; *psalm, bhajan or canticle between]

17. *The congregation stands for the Gospel reading and joins in singing Gloria:*
    [Gloria chant with Hallelujahs, then the reading of the Gospel, and acclamation and Hallelujahs following]

18. *THE SERMON*

19. *AFFIRMATION OF FAITH*
    The Nicene Creed
    We believe in one God . . . [ELLC 5] . . . world to come. Amen.
    was incarnate . . . Virgin Mary] by the power of the Holy Spirit he became incarnate from the Virgin Mary
    [and the Son]] OMIT BRACKETS
    or The Apostles' Creed
    I believe in God . . . [ELLC 4] . . . life everlasting. Amen.
    [An asterisk leads to a footnote noting an earlier version of 'he descended to the dead']

    or [a cued Trinitarian affirmation by three paragraphs of the role the persons of the Trinity have in our lives]

    or [a paragraphed affirmation of how our discipleship follows from God's self-revelation]
    The congregation may be seated.

20. *The announcements may be made here. A hymn or lyric may also be sung, and the offering may be collected.*
    [Rubric referring to (monetary) offerings and to birthdays etc., and two prayers for these respective purposes]

21. *INTERCESSION*
    [Four alternative litanies, followed by one of three concluding prayers]

22. *The presbyter then gives the First Benediction:*
    The grace of our Lord Jesus Christ, and the love of God, and the fellowship of the Holy Spirit be with you all. **Amen.**

23. *Those who wish to leave may do so now.*

THE BREAKING OF THE BREAD

24. *All stand, and the presbyter says* ⟦Ps. 133.1 and 1 Cor. 10.17, with congregational response Ps. 27.6⟧

25. *A hymn or lyric is sung while the congregation's offering, and an offering of a tray of flowers with other signs of God's goodness in creation, are brought forward with the offerings of bread and wine for the Eucharist, and placed on the altar.*

26. Glory to God, source of all bounty and beauty
whose fullness and fragrance can transform us within and without:
Creator God, we lift our hearts to you in thanks.
Glory to God, who has made a covenant with all living creatures,
and has promised never to forsake the creation he loves:
Creator God, we lift our hearts to you in thanks.
Glory to God, who made us all in his image,
and entrusted the earth and her life to our care.
Creator God, we lift our hearts to you in thanks.
O God, Redeemer of all things,
with grateful thanks we offer these gifts and this bread and wine,
fruits of your earth and of our labour,
and signs of your redemptive purpose for our lives and for all creation.
By sharing in this bread and wine, you assure us, in Christ,
of a share in your being, your bliss, your purpose:
Glory to God, our Redeemer, who saves us by his grace.

Or Holy God, who through your dear Son has consecrated for us
a new and living way to your throne of grace,
we come to you through him, unworthy as we are,
and we humbly ask you to accept and use us and these our gifts for your glory.
All that is in heaven and earth is yours, and of your own we give to you. **Amen.**

Or O God, you have given us a new and living way to offer ourselves to you.
Though unworthy we come to you, as we are,
by that way, your Son, Jesus of Nazareth;
and in his name we ask you to accept and use us and these gifts
however it best pleases you.
All that is created is yours and everything that we can offer already belongs to you.
Amen.

The bearers of the offertory return to their places.

27. *The presbyter and congregation kneel and say together:*
Be present, be present, O Jesus you good High Priest,
as you were in the midst of your disciples,
and make yourself known to us in the breaking of the bread,
who lives and reigns with the Father and the Holy Spirit,
one God, world without end. Amen.

The presbyter stands.

THE GREAT THANKSGIVING

28. *The presbyter may use A or B or C for the Great Thanksgiving.*

A.

The Lord be with you.
And with your spirit.
Lift up . . . ⟦ELLC 6⟧ . . . **thanks and praise.**
It is indeed right, our duty and our highest
  joy,
that we should at all times, and in all places,
give thanks to you, O Lord,
holy, almighty and everlasting God;*
through Jesus Christ your Son our Lord,
through whom you created the heavens
  and the earth and all that is in them,
and made humankind in your own image,
and when it had fallen into sin you
  redeemed it
to be the first fruits of a new creation.
Therefore, with angels and archangels
and with all the company of heaven,
we laud and magnify your glorious name,
evermore praising you and saying:
Holy, holy, holy Lord God of hosts,
heaven and earth are full of your glory.
Glory be to you, O Lord most high.
Blessed is he that has come and is to come
in the name of the Lord.
Hosanna in the highest.

Truly holy, truly blessed are you,
O God our Saviour,
who of your tender love towards
  humankind
gave your only Son Jesus Christ
to take our nature upon him
and to suffer death upon the cross for our
  redemption;
who made there, by his one oblation of
  himself once offered,
a full, perfect, and sufficient sacrifice,
  oblation and satisfaction,
for the sins of the whole world;
and instituted and in his holy Gospel
  commanded us to continue
a perpetual memory of his precious death,
until he comes again;
who, in the same night when he was
  betrayed,
took bread, and after having given thanks,
broke it, and gave it to his disciples,
saying: Take, eat:
this is my body which is given for you,

do this in remembrance of me.
Likewise, after supper he took the cup,
and after he had given thanks
he gave it to them, saying,
Drink this, all of you:
this is my blood of the new covenant,
which is shed for you and for many
for the remission of sins,
do this, as often as you drink it, in
  remembrance of me.
Amen. Your death O Lord we
  commemorate,
your resurrection we confess,
and your coming we await.
Glory be to you, O Christ.

Therefore, O Lord our God,
remembering the precious death and
  passion
and glorious resurrection and ascension,
of your Son our Lord,
we your servants do this in remembrance
  of him as he commanded,
until his coming again,
giving thanks to you for the perfect
  redemption
which you have brought about for us in
  him.
We give thanks to you,
we praise you,
we glorify you, O Lord our God.

And we most humbly ask of you, O
  merciful God,
to sanctify with your Holy Spirit
us and these your own gifts of bread and
  wine,
that the bread which we break
may be the communion of the body of
  Christ,
and the cup which we bless
the communion of the blood of Christ.
Grant that, being joined together in him,
we may all attain to the unity of the faith,
and may grow up in all things, unto him
who is the Head, even Christ, our Lord,
by whom and with whom, in the unity of
  the Holy Spirit,
all honour and glory be yours,
O God almighty, world without end.
Amen.

* ⟦A footnote provides for proper prefaces in place of the following text as far as 'new creation'.⟧

B.
Our Creator God is with us to bless us;
*Saranam, saranam, saranam.**
The risen Lord is with us to bless us;
Saranam, saranam, saranam.
The transforming Spirit is with us to bless
us;
Saranam, saranam, saranam.

O God, Redeemer of fallen creation,
at the last meal that your Son, Jesus
Christ,
shared with his disciples before his death,
he took bread in his hands of compassion,
gave you praise and thanks,
and broke bread.
Then he said, Take, eat: this is my body,
which is given for you.
Do this in remembrance of me.
**We celebrate through this bread,
the self-offering of our Saviour Christ.**

Then after the meal he took the cup,
offered praise and thanks to you,
gave the cup to his disciples and said:
Drink this, all of you;
this is my blood of the new covenant,
which is shed for you and for many
for the forgiveness of sins.
Do this, whenever you drink it,
in remembrance of me.
**We celebrate through this cup
the new covenant of our Saviour Christ.**

As this bread is broken and this wine
poured out,

O Seeker and Saviour of the lost,
we remember again the poor and
oppressed of the earth.
We recall that your body was broken
that the hungry might be nourished,
the oppressed set free,
replenished with the bread of new hope
and new life.
Christ has . . . ⟦CF 6(a)⟧ . . . come in glory.

As this bread was once scattered seed,
O Bread of life sown in the earth to die
and rise to new life:
so gather all peoples together
in one humanity of your coming reign.
Restore the broken life of your creation;
heal the disfigured body of your world;
draw all creatures unto yourself
through the cross and in the power of your
risen life.
And grant to all the faithful departed a
share in your bliss,
that with them we too at the end
may be welcomed into your eternal
Kingdom
through your inexhaustible grace,
and through the guidance of your
indwelling Spirit.
**Sanctify us,
sanctify this bread,
sanctify this wine,
so that together
we may be the body of Christ. Amen.**

C.
The Lord be with you . . . ⟦ELLC 6⟧ . . .
 give God thanks and praise.

Truly it is right and good
to glorify you at all times and in all places,
by offering you our thanksgiving
O Lord, holy Father/Parent.
You spoke and the light shattered
 darkness,
order arose from confusion.
You breathed into the dust of the earth
and we were formed in your image.
Through your Son, our Lord Jesus,
you came to us while we wandered.
He met us as a refugee, a threatened child.
He called us by name
to leave what is comfortable
to be his disciples, friends and partners.
With his outstretched arms on the cross,
and through his death he bore our sins
and through his resurrection we are saved.
And through your Holy Spirit
you brood over the chaos we create,
mothering us and shaping a new creation.
You enlighten everyone coming into the
 world.
You inspired the prophets and apostles
to find the right word at the right time.
You liberate, equip and commission your
 people
for the continuance of your mission
to make everything new.
Therefore, with angels and archangels
and with all the company of heaven
we proclaim and sing your glory:
**Holy, holy . . . ⟦ELLC 7⟧ . . . in the highest.
Blessed is he . . . ⟦ELLC 8⟧ . . . the highest.**

Our Lord Jesus Christ, on the night in
 which he was betrayed,
took the bread and when he had given

thanks to you,
broke it and gave it to his disciples,
saying: Take, eat: this is my body,
which is given for you.
Do this in remembrance of me.

In the same way after supper, he took the
 cup
and when he had given thanks,
he gave it to them saying:
Drink this, all of you:
this is my blood of the new covenant,
which is shed for you and for many
for the forgiveness of sins.
Do this, whenever you drink it,
in remembrance of me.
**Lord we commemorate your death on the
 cross,
we celebrate your resurrection,
and we await your coming.**

Eternal God,
let your Holy Spirit move in power
over us and over these earthly gifts of
 bread and wine,
that they may be the communion of the
 body and blood of Christ,
and that we may become one in him.
May his coming in glory find us
ever watchful in prayer, strong in truth
 and love,
and faithful in the breaking of the bread.
Then, at last, all peoples will be free, all
 divisions healed,
and with your whole creation,
we will sing your praise,
through your Son, Jesus Christ.
Through Christ, with Christ, in Christ,
in the unity of the Holy Spirit,
all glory and honour are yours,
almighty God, for ever and ever. **Amen.**

29. *The presbyter may kneel.*
    As our Saviour has taught us, so we pray:
    Our Father . . . ⟦ELLC 1⟧ . . . for yours is the kingdom,
    the power and the glory, for ever and ever. Amen.
       hallowed] holy
       as in heaven] as it is in heaven
       today] this day
       Save us . . . trial and] and lead us not into temptation but
    A moment's silence is kept, all kneeling.

30. *The prayer of humble access may be said:*
    We do not presume . . . ⟦CF 3(a)⟧ . . . and he in us. Amen.
       that our sinful . . . precious blood] that our sinful bodies and souls may be made clean
                               by his most precious body and blood

THE SHARING

31. *As the bread is lifted up and broken, prior to the congregation's coming forward to share together in it, the following sentences may be said:*
    When we break the bread, do we not share in the body of Christ?
    We seek to share your life, gracious God.

    As the cup is lifted up:
    When we lift the cup, do we not share in the life-blood of Christ?
    We seek to share your life, gracious God.

32. *During this time these words may be said or sung:*
    O Lamb of God . . . ⟦ELLC 9(b)⟧ . . . grant us your peace.
       Lamb] O Lamb THRICE

33. *The ministers and congregation receive the bread and the wine. The following words of administration may be used:*
    The Body of our Lord Jesus Christ, the Bread of life.
    The Blood of our Lord Jesus Christ, the true vine.

34. *[If the bread and wine set apart be insufficient, the presbyter taking more, may say:*
    Obeying the command of our Lord Jesus Christ, we take this bread (wine) to be set apart for this holy use, in the name of the Father and of the Son and of the Holy Spirit. **Amen.**]

THANKSGIVING

35. *When all have partaken, the minister says:*
    Having now by faith received the sacrament of the Body and Blood of Christ, let us give thanks.

    O gracious God, you have fed us
    with the spiritual food of the most precious body and blood
    of your Son, our Saviour Jesus Christ.
    You have assured us, in these holy mysteries, of your favour and goodness towards us,
    and that we are living members of the body of your Son,
    and heirs of your eternal kingdom.
    For these great benefits we thank you,
    and in union with your Son we offer you ourselves as a living sacrifice.
    And now, Lord, send us out to do the work you have given us to do,
    to love and serve you as faithful witnesses of Christ our Lord. **Amen.**
    Blessing, and glory, and wisdom, and thanksgiving,
    and honour, and power, and might, be unto our God, forever and ever. Amen.

Or

Merciful God of all creation, holy Father/Parent of all people,
who through our Lord Jesus Christ united all things in his fullness,
we join your whole creation in exultant praise of your bountiful goodness.
You have touched us with new life and filled us with new hope
that your reign will come,
that the hungry will be fed,
that the oppressed will be set free from evil,
that your reconciling work will be done,
that love and faithfulness will meet together,
that justice and peace will kiss each other
and the whole creation will be filled with your glory. **Amen.**
Blessing, and glory, and wisdom, and thanksgiving,
and honour, and power, and might, be unto our God, forever and ever. Amen.

Or

Glorious God, you have made us one with all your people in heaven and on earth.
You have fed us with the bread of life, and renewed us for your service.
Help us who have shared Christ's body and received his cup, to be his faithful
      disciples
so that our daily living may be part of the life of your Kingdom,
and our love be your love reaching out into the life of the world. **Amen.**
Blessing, and glory, and wisdom, and thanksgiving,
and honour, and power, and might, be unto our God, forever and ever. Amen.

36. *The presbyter gives the Second Benediction:*
    Go out into the world in peace; have courage; hold onto what is good; return no one
    evil for evil; strengthen the faint-hearted; support the weak, and help the suffering;
    honour all people; love and serve the Lord, rejoicing in the power of the Holy Spirit,
    and may the blessing . . . [[CF 12(a)]] . . . always. **Amen.**
    Or
    The peace of God, which surpasses all . . . [[CF 12(a)]] . . . always. **Amen.**

37. *PROPER PREFACES (to be used with the Great Thanksgiving A)* [[14 Proper Prefaces]]

38. *THE TEN COMMANDMENTS* [[Old Testament Text with congregational responses after
    each commandment]]

SHORT ORDER FOR THE LORD'S SUPPER FROM THE CHURCH OF SOUTH INDIA *BOOK OF COMMON WORSHIP* (2006)(CSI2)

⟦The 'Short Order' consists entirely of liturgical text from CSI1, but with a simple route through some of the options, as shown below. The Introduction to it in the *BCW* says that it may be further reduced in length by specified optional omissions (the 'Gracious Word', the first lesson, the sermon, the creed, the prayer of humble access, and 'hymns, lyrics, songs, except at the offertory') – and anything else from the full Order (CSI1) may be added⟧

THE PREPARATION
1. ⟦As §1 in CSI1⟧
2. ⟦As §2 in CSI1⟧
3. ⟦The third prayer from §3 in CSI1⟧
4. *(Lighting of the lamp – invoking the presence of God)*
5. ⟦As §5 in CSI1⟧
6. ⟦As §6 in CSI1, including the footnote⟧

ADORATION
7. ⟦Trisagion only from §7 in CSI1⟧
8. ⟦No provision from §8 in CSI1⟧

CONFESSION
9. ⟦No provision for the Summary of the Law and the Ten Commandments, but otherwise as §9 in CSI1⟧
10. ⟦The second confession only from §10 in CSI1⟧
11. ⟦As §11 in CSI1⟧
12. ⟦The second absolution only from §12 in CSI1⟧

THE PEACE
13. ⟦As §13 in CSI1⟧

THE COLLECT OF THE DAY
14. ⟦As §14 in CSI1⟧

THE MINISTRY OF THE WORD OF GOD
15–18. ⟦As §§15–18 in CSI1⟧

AFFIRMATION OF FAITH
19. ⟦The Apostles' Creed only from §19 in CSI1⟧
20. ⟦As §20 in CSI1⟧

INTERCESSION
21. ⟦One litany only from §21 in CSI1⟧
22. ⟦As §22 in CSI1⟧
23. ⟦No provision corresponding to §23 in CSI1⟧

THE BREAKING OF THE BREAD
24. ⟦As §24 in CSI1⟧
25. ⟦As §25 in CSI1⟧
26. ⟦The third prayer only from §26 in CSI1⟧
27. ⟦As §27 in CSI1⟧
28. ⟦Prayer C only from §28 in CSI1⟧
29. ⟦As §29 in CSI1⟧
30. ⟦As §30 in CSI1⟧

THE SHARING
31. ⟦As §31 in CSI1⟧
32. ⟦As §32 in CSI1⟧

33. [As §33 in CSI1]
34. [As §34 in CSI1]

THANKSGIVING
35. [The second prayer only from §35 in CSI1]
36. [As §36 in CSI1]

[There are no appendices in CSI2 corresponding to §§37 and 38 in CSI1]

THE 'COMMON LITURGY OF THE EUCHARIST/HOLY COMMUNION FOR THE COMMUNION OF THE CHURCHES IN INDIA' (ICL)

[The numbering and lining are editorial]

THE PREPARATION
CALL TO WORSHIP
1. *One of these verses or any other verse from the Bible may be used by the leader or presiding minister.*
   [Ps. 95.6–7; Ps. 100.4–5; Ps. 105.1–3]

PRAYER
2. Let us pray: Holy and gracious God, you are the source of all life.
   Your eyes watch over us. You know the secrets of our hearts.
   Draw us into your presence, move us into obedience
   and summon us to your lotus feet
   that we may worship you with gratefulness and humility
   through Jesus Christ our Lord.
   Amen.
   Or
   [Five versicles and responses, followed by brief congregational prayer, all concerning mutual sharing]

GRACE/GREETING
3. Grace, mercy and peace from God, the Father, and the Son and the Holy Spirit be with us.
   Thanks be to God, Hallelujah.

LAMP, BIBLE AND INCENSE
4. *Here a lamp, or a candle may be lit, and a Bible be carried to the altar, and incense may be used to symbolize God's presence amongst us. An appropriate bhajan may be sung.*

ADORATION
5. *One of the following forms of adoration of the Trinity may be used by repeating thrice. Any other form of adoration of the Trinity may also be used.*
   Holy are you, O God;
   Holy are you, Almighty Lord;
   Holy are you, Immortal God;
   O Lord, the Messiah, who was crucified for us, have mercy on us.
   Or
   Holy God,
   Holy and mighty, holy and immortal, have mercy on us.

CONFESSION OF SINS

6. *Silence may be kept for a few minutes. Then the leader may give an exhortation for confession. One of the following forms or any other form of confession or litany or a penitential psalm may be used as a prayer of confession.*
   [A congregational confession or a lengthy responsive form concluding with a short corporate prayer]

ABSOLUTION

7. *One of the following or some other biblical verses in the form of absolution may be used by the presiding minister.* [Three short absolutions, each with differing grammatical form]

   A hymn, lyric or bhajan of praise or thanksgiving may be sung.

MINISTRY OF THE WORD OF GOD

8. *After each reading from the Bible, a chant or a hymn or a psalm may be sung.*

9. *Old Testament:*

10. *Psalm/Hymn:*

11. *Epistle:*

12. *Gospel:*

13. SERMON/HOMILY

14. CREED
    The Nicene Creed is said or sung, at least on Sundays and greater Festivals. Or, in place of the Nicene Creed, the Apostles' Creed may be said or sung.

THE NICENE CREED
   We believe in one God . . . [ELLC 5] **. . . world to come. Amen.**
       was incarnate . . . Virgin Mary] **by the power of the Holy Spirit he became incarnate from the Virgin Mary**
   [and the Son]] OMIT BRACKETS
   or THE APOSTLES' CREED
   I believe in God . . . [ELLC 4] **. . . life everlasting. Amen.**

ANNOUNCEMENTS

15. *Announcements, if any, may be made here, or at some other suitable place in the liturgy. Notices of marriages or special observances, as well as special biddings for intercessory prayers may also be given here.*

INTERCESSION

16. *The following or any other litany or an extempore intercessory prayer may be offered.*
    [A single litany of intercession]

RECONCILIATION AND PEACE

17. Hear the words of Jesus Christ calling us to care for one another: [John 15.12–13]
    or
    Jesus said: 'Before you offer your gift, go and be reconciled.' As brothers and sisters in God's family, we come together to ask God for forgiveness.
    or
    My brothers and sisters, as we prepare to celebrate the presence of Christ in word and sacrament, let us call to mind and confess our sins.

    A moment of silence is observed.

    [A litany of penitence, especially in relation to unity, or a congregational confession]

WORDS OF FORGIVENESS
18. *One of the following may be used:*
   ⟦Three short absolutions⟧

SHARING OF PEACE
19. Having been forgiven and made whole through Christ our Peace, let us live together
   in peace. Let us say *shalom* to each other as a sign of reconciliation and peace.
   The peace of the Lord be with you:
   And also be with you.

   or
   Let there be peace:
   Peace among nations,
   Peace among people,
   Peace among neighbours,
   Peace among friends,
   The peace of Christ above all.

   Here, peace may be exchanged by handclasp or according to the custom of the particular
   cultural tradition by saying: 'The peace of our Lord Jesus Christ be with you' / Shanthi /
   Shalom.

OFFERTORY
20. *A hymn or lyric may be sung during the collection of the offering.*

THANKOFFERING
21. *Here the celebrant may remember those who have celebrated special days in their lives or*
   thank for the special grace received by members of the congregation. Special thankoffering
   may be received in the sanctuary.

EUCHARISTIC ELEMENTS
22. *A man, a woman and a child may carry the eucharistic elements and the offerings to the altar.*
   The following prayer may be offered by all.

OFFERTORY PRAYER
23. **O God, you have given us through Jesus Christ our Lord**
   a new and living way to offer ourselves to you.
   We come to you with the fruits of the earth
   and the labour of our hands.
   Accept and use us, and these our gifts
   however best it pleases you.
   All that is created is yours.
   And everything that we can offer already belongs to you.
   Amen.
   Brothers and sisters, with reverence and purity of heart,
   with love and true faith and devotion,
   let us participate in this Holy Eucharist / Qurbana / Communion,
   which is now being offered.
   To God be the glory, honour and praise for ever and ever. **Amen.**

24. *THE GREAT THANKSGIVING*

Peace be with you . . . ⟦ELLC 6⟧ . . . **give thanks and praise.**
lift them to] lift them unto

It is truly right and good to glorify you
at all times and in all places,
by offering you our thanksgiving,
O Lord Holy Father.
You spoke, and light shattered darkness,
order arose from chaos.
You breathed into the dust of the earth,
and we were formed in your image.
Through your Son, our Lord Jesus,
you met us while we wandered.
He called us by name to leave aside what is
    comfortable
to be his disciples, friends and partners.
With his outstretched arms on the cross,
and through his death he bore our sins
and through his resurrection we are saved.
And through your Holy Spirit you brood
    over us,
mothering us and shaping a new creation.
You enlighten everyone coming into the
    world.
You inspired the prophets and the apostles.
You liberate, equip and commission your
    people
for the continuance of your mission.
Therefore, with angels and archangels
and with all the company of heaven
we proclaim and sing your glory:
Holy, holy . . . ⟦ELLC 7⟧ . . . in the highest.

Words of Institution

When the sinless One of his own will
chose to suffer death for us sinners,
he took bread in his holy hands.
Bless, O Lord.

He gave thanks (blessed + sanctified)* and
    broke it
and gave it to his disciples saying:
Take, eat, this is my body,
which is given for you.
Do this in remembrance of me. **Amen.**

In the same way he took the cup.
Bless, O Lord.

He gave thanks (blessed + sanctified)*
and gave it to his disciples saying:
Drink this all of you,
this is the blood of the new covenant
for you and for many (for the forgiveness
    of sins)**.
Do this in remembrance of me. **Amen.**

Anamnesis (Memorial of Christ's death and resurrection)

As often as we eat this bread and drink
    this cup,
we proclaim the Lord's presence with us,
we commemorate his death,
we celebrate his glorious resurrection,
we await his coming.
May God's blessing be upon us all.
**Christ . . . ⟦CF 6(a)⟧ . . . again –
Hallelujah**

Epiclesis (Invocation of the Holy Spirit)

Our heavenly Father, have mercy upon
    us.
Send your Holy Spirit to sanctify us,
and this offering of bread and wine.
Lord, have mercy *(thrice).*

May the Holy Spirit sanctify this bread
that it may be the Body of our Lord Jesus
    Christ. **Amen.**

May the Holy Spirit sanctify this wine in
    the chalice
that it may be the Blood of our Lord
    Jesus Christ. **Amen.**

**Accept this our offering of praise and
    thanksgiving;
make us one body Jesus Christ our Lord,
by whom and with whom
in the unity of the Holy Spirit
all honour and glory be to you,
almighty Father, world without end.
Amen.**

+ *Here the presbyter makes the sign of the cross*
* *Eastern liturgies include these words*
** *Some traditions include these words*

LORD'S PRAYER

25. **Our Father in heaven . . . ⟦ELLC 1⟧ . . . yours is the kingdom, the power and the glory, for ever and ever. Amen.**
    hallowed] holy
    as in heaven] as it is in heaven
    today] this day
    Save us . . . trial and] and lead us not into temptation but

THE SHARING (Communion)

26. *The celebrant breaks the consecrated bread, saying:*
    We break this bread that we may share in the Body of Christ
    We are one body, for we share in the one bread.

    The celebrant may take the cup into his/her hands in the sight of the congregation and say:
    The cup which we bless is sharing of the Blood of Christ
    His life is in us and we live in him.

27. *The celebrant invites the people to receive the holy sacrament by saying:*
    The things of God for the people of God. Come to the Lord's Table.
    Or
    Any other suitable words of invitation may be used.

28. *During the time of sharing, Agnus Dei 'Lamb of God' or any other suitable hymn may be sung.*
    O Lamb of God . . . ⟦ELLC 9(b)⟧ . . . grant us your peace.
    Lamb] O Lamb THRICE

29. *The ministers and the congregation receive the holy sacrament. The following words of administration may be used.*
    The Body of our Lord Jesus Christ, the Bread of life.
    The Blood of our Lord Jesus Christ, the true Vine.

THANKSGIVING

30. *One or both of the following prayers may be offered.*
    Let us rejoice and be thankful in what we have received.
    Merciful God, God of all creation, we join your whole creation
    in exultant praise of your bountiful goodness.
    You have now touched us with new life
    and filled us with new hope that your reign will come,
    that the hungry will be fed,
    that the oppressed will be set free from evil,
    that your reconciling work will be done,
    that love and faithfulness meet together,
    that justice and peace will kiss each other
    and the whole creation be filled with your glory. Amen.

    Blessing and glory, and wisdom, thanksgiving,
    and honour and power, and might, be unto our God, forever and ever. Amen.

Almighty God, we thank you . . . ⟦CF 11(a)⟧ . . . praise and glory. Amen.
offer you our souls and bodies] offer you ourselves, our souls and bodies

**Blessing and glory, and wisdom, thanksgiving,
and honour and power, and might, be unto our God, forever and ever. Amen.**

BENEDICTION

31. Go into the world, do whatever is true, whatever is honourable, whatever is just,
    whatever is pure, whatever is pleasing, whatever is commendable,
    if there is any excellence and if there is anything worthy of praise,
    and the God of peace will be with you.
    The blessing of the Father, the Son and the Holy Spirit be amongst you
    and remain with you always. **Amen.**
    or
    Unto God's gracious mercy and protection we commit you.
    The Lord bless you and keep you,
    the Lord make his face shine upon you, and be gracious to you;
    the Lord lift up his countenance upon you, and give you peace. **Amen.**
    or
    The peace of God . . . ⟦CF 12(a)⟧ . . . remain with you always. **Amen.**

24. The Church of Ceylon (Sri Lanka)

The two dioceses of the Anglican Church of Ceylon (Sri Lanka) have continued in an extra-provincial role since the previous Church of India, Pakistan, Burma and Ceylon gave way to united Churches and to the Province of Myanmar (Burma) in 1970. The distinctive diocesan use, **Cey**, from 1938 retained its standing alongside the rites in the CIPBC 1960 Book of Common Prayer (**Ind, IndR** and **IndS**). The dioceses have since made informal joint arrangements for common liturgical usage, beginning with a Joint Liturgical Commission appointed in 1976. This Commission was responsible for a minor adaptation of **Cey** in an English-language use for a specific occasion on the visit of the Archbishop of Canterbury in 1982, mentioned briefly in **LAL**.

In the 1980s the Commission revised **Cey**, and provided it in contemporary English, as well as in Sinhala and Tamil. The resultant rite, labelled here **Cey1**, was in 1988 authorized by the bishops of the two dioceses, with the concurrence of the Archbishop of Canterbury, the Metropolitan, as formally 'for experimental use' alongside the existing rites; however, the bishops' preface urged 'we strongly commend its use as the Chief Sunday Service of every Anglican congregation'. There was a minor revision of its text in 1997, and this was favoured in Colombo diocese, but not used at all in Kurunagala diocese. In 2007 a constitution bound the two dioceses together, and a fully official Church of Ceylon Liturgical Committee was appointed. It revised the rite, and the resultant text, labelled here **Cey2**, was first approved by the two bishops separately, then approved by the two jointly as an episcopal synod and finally authorized by the General Assembly in 2009, initially for experimental use. It is intended to replace other existing rites, and the two bishops state in their 'Authorization' preface to the rite that permission to use **Cey1** will be withdrawn after three years, and the standing of earlier rites will also be decided then. **Cey2** is authorized in English, Sinhalese and Tamil, the three versions having equal standing and being printed side by side. At some points Sinhalese and Tamil texts are found within the English version, with English translations provided also.

A LITURGY OF SRI LANKA, THE LORD'S SUPPER OR THE HOLY EUCHARIST OF THE ANGLICAN CHURCH OF CEYLON 2009 (Cey2)

[The numbering here is original to Cey2. The text of Cey1 (1988), where it varies significantly, is shown by *apparatus*, though the numbering of Cey1 does not wholly coincide with the numbering here. In the eucharistic prayer variants in 1997 are also shown. The lining is editorial.]

NOTES
[13 Notes (lettered (a) to (m)) explain the format of the rite and make suggestions re posture, singing, and cultural adaptation, and give directions for the Presider and permission for parts of the service to be led by a deacon or trained layperson.]

AUTHORIZATION
[The two bishops provide a substantial preface to the rite, the salient points of which are reported in the introductory paragraphs above. Cey1 has a preface appropriate to 1988]

THE GATHERING

1. *Entrance Psalm or Hymn*

2. *All stand* [rubric concerning clergy and people exchanging greetings]

3. [Introductory sentence from scripture, silence and *versicle and response of praise]
   Silence
   The lighting of the lamp
      Cey1 OMITS LAST RUBRIC

4. *PRAYER OF PREPARATION or some other suitable chant or prayer of INVOCATION may be said by all.*
   Almighty God, . . . [CF 1] . . . Christ our Lord. Amen.
   or
   [12–line Sinhala chant of worship, with English translation]
   or
   [One of two 12–line Tamil invocations, with English translation]
   Silence

5. *THE CONFESSION OF SINS*
   (The confession may be done here or after or before 14)
   The People are invited to make confession of their sins on their knees by saying the Ten Commandments or the Summary of the Law or by using the following or a seasonal invitation or the comfortable words from Appendix 3
   [Texts of (5.1.1) Ten Commandments (with New Testament parallels), of (5.1.2) the Lord's Summary of the Law, and of (5.1.3) the invitation to confession]

   All kneel in penitence and a short silence is kept after which all say together
      Cey1: IN PLACE OF ALL THE ABOVE *Deacon:* Let us make humble confession of our sins to God

5.2 *CORPORATE CONFESSION*
   [Congregational confession]

   Or
5.2.2 *THE KYRIES*
   Lord, have mercy . . . [ELLC 2, ninefold in English] . . . Lord, have mercy.
   Or [Kyries ninefold in Tamil]
   Or [Kyries ninefold in Sinhalese]
   Or [Kyries ninefold in Greek]
      Cey1 OMITS THE LAST THREE OPTIONS

Or

5.2.3 THE TRISAGION *repeated three times (Traditionally used at Eastertide standing and pre-Lent)*

⟦Text of Trisagion⟧
Presider:
Almighty God, who forgives all who forgive one another and truly repent of their sins, have mercy on you, pardon . . . ⟦CF 2⟧ . . . through Jesus Christ our Lord. **Amen.**
Cey1: May the Almighty and Merciful Lord grant unto you pardon and remission of all your sins, time for amendment of life, and the grace and comfort of the Holy Spirit.

6. *As a form of preparation for worship and to receive the Word of God all may sing or say the* GLORIA *except in Lent and Advent.*
Glory to God . . . ⟦ELLC 3⟧ . . . God the Father. Amen.
king] sovereign

Or ⟦Traditional text of Gloria in Excelsis as in 1662 – not in **Cey1**⟧

Or A CANTICLE
Cey1: ADDS *may be sung such as the Gloria, Magnificat, Benedictus, or Te Deum* AND IT REPLACES THE FIRST RUBRIC

7. *Silence for personal prayers of the people*

The Collect for the day
Cey1: ADDS *(or the collect may be said at the end of the Prayers of the People at Section 14)*

THE MINISTRY OF THE WORD

All sit (Either two or three readings from the Scriptures follow, the last of which is always the Gospel.)

8. *THE FIRST READING: The Old Testament (or during Eastertide from the Acts of the Apostles)*
Silence ⟦proclamation and response at conclusion⟧

9. *RESPONSORIAL PSALM OR CANTICLE*

10. *THE SECOND READING: New Testament*
Silence ⟦proclamation and response at conclusion⟧

A Gradual Hymn may be sung and a Gospel Procession or lesser entrance may take place.
Cey1: OMITS RUBRIC

11. *THE GOSPEL*
All remain standing (Preceded by an Hallelu Yah acclamation except during Lent)
⟦announcement and acclamation before reading⟧

Silence

⟦proclamation and response at conclusion⟧

12. *THE SERMON – All sit*

13. THE AFFIRMATION OF FAITH
    *The **Nicene Creed** or an **Affirmation of Faith** may be said or sung by all standing*
    We believe in one God . . . [ELLC 5] . . . the world to come. Amen.
        was incarnate . . . truly human] **by the power of the Holy Spirit he became incarnate of the Virgin**
                        Mary, and was made man

    [and the Son]] OMIT

    *If the confession has not been said earlier it may be said after or before the Prayers of the
    People.*
        Ce**y1** OMITS RUBRICS BEFORE AND AFTER, BUT PERMITS THE APOSTLES' CREED
        (ELLC 4) WHEN THERE IS NO COMMUNION. IT HAS SEPARATE SECTION
        '*Notices*' (§29 below) FOLLOWING HERE

14. THE PRAYERS OF THE PEOPLE *takes place here in the following or other suitable form.*
    [A form of prayer, with versicle and response at intervals]

    (Other collects may be added here)
        Ce**y1** [not in 1997]: **OF THE PEOPLE** *takes place . . . form*] **OF THE PEOPLE OR BIDDINGS**
                        (Alternately, this may be said after the Offertory, all may stand)
        Ce**y1** HAS CROSS-HEADING '*THE MINISTRY OF THE SACRAMENT*' FOLLOWING

15. THE PEACE
    The Peace may be preceded by a sentence from scripture or a seasonal invitation
    The Lord is / be with you (*Bishop*: Peace be with you)
    And also with you.
    Beloved, let us love one another for love is of God. (*1 John* 4.7)
    All exchange a sign of peace with one another according to the appropriate customs.
        Ce**y1** HAS 'GREETING OF PEACE', NO INITIAL RUBRIC, AND FINAL RUBRIC *All may
        exchange a sign of Peace.*

THE MINISTRY OF THE SACRAMENT

16. **THE TAKING**
    An appropriate offertory sentence may be said or as given in the appendix.

    *Hymn (During the Hymn the elements of Bread and Wine and the alms and other gifts
    may be taken through an Offertory Procession or great entrance.)*
        Ce**y1** HAS TITLE 'Offertory Sentence' AND TITLE 'Presentation of offerings of the people'

17. *The following or other prayers may be said at the preparation of the table.*
    Blessed are you, Lord God of the universe,
    you are the giver of this bread,
    fruit of the earth and of human labour,
    let it become the bread of life.
    Blessed be God, now and forever!

    Blessed are you, Lord God of the universe,
    you are the giver of this wine,
    fruit of the earth and of human leisure,
    let it become the wine of the eternal kingdom.
    Blessed be God, now and forever!

    As the grain once scattered in the fields and the grapes once dispersed on the hillside
    are now reunited on this table in the bread and wine,
    so, Lord, may your church soon be gathered together
    from the corners of the earth into your kingdom.
    Maranatha! Come Lord Jesus!

        Ce**y1** OMITS

18. *The Offertory prayer or song to be said by all*
    All things come from you, and of your own do we give you,
    O creator and Lord of the universe,
    who is forever adored by the holy angels.
    Out of what you have given we again give you these gifts,
    which we present at your holy table,
    and with them our very lives and service,
    to be taken for the service of you our servant Lord;
    through Jesus Christ our Saviour.
    Amen.
        Cey1 HAS 1 Chron. 29.11, 14b

Or [[Sinhala]]
Nithi saga duthun gena puda labana
    devidune
(God who is forever by angels adored)
Obamaya mavum karu mulu lowehi
    Samidune
(You are Creator and Lord of the whole
    world)
Oba gena nikuth wei siyalu deya sondine
(All good things created come to us from
    you)
Pudamuva obe deya obtama bathi sithine
(Now out of what you gave we give again
    to you)
Puja sanaya matha apa thabana deemana
(Lord upon the altar this offering)
Sawdiv mahima athi samiduni pidum
    mena
(We gift to you Lord all sovereign)
E ha apadha obtama piduna vun mena
(In this our very selves offer we in love)
Jesu himi namina piliganu daya ve na
(Father accept our gift through Jesus our
    Lord)

Or [[Tamil with similar meanings]]
Kaanikai padaithom iraiva – Ullam
Kaninthey padaitom nin peedam
Tharuvana ellam unnathuvey – Nitham
Tharuvathu ellam nin karame

Thanthom emaye kaanikkaiyai – Nin
Seveiku uriya thiraviamaai
Ertpaai umathu kodaithanaye – Nin
Paathathil vaiththa malarenavey

Cey1 OMITS BOTH COLUMNS, ALLOWS OTHER SONGS, AND PROVIDES LEFT COLUMN AS PASTE-IN

19. THE EUCHARISTIC PRAYER

The Presider then uses the following or one of the EUCHARISTIC PRAYERS in the Appendix after which the Service will continue from Section 20 (Proper and extended prefaces are in the Appendices).

Ce¥1: *THE EUCHARISTIC PRAYER . . . Appendices*)] THE GREAT THANKSGIVING

The Lord is/be with you
And also with you
Or
The Lord is here
God's Spirit is with us
Lift up your hearts . . . ⟦ELLC 6⟧ . . . **God
thanks and praise.**
> to] up to

It is right and a good and joyful thing,
always and everywhere to give thanks to
 you,
almighty Father, creator of heaven and
 earth.
A Proper preface shall follow

Therefore we praise you,
joining our voice with angels and
 archangels
and with all the company of heaven,
who for ever sing this hymn
to proclaim the glory of your name.
**Holy, holy . . . ⟦ELLC 7⟧ . . . your glory.
(Hosanna in the highest.)**

People may sit, kneel or remain standing
Holy indeed are you, almighty Father,
 eternal Sovereign
who in all your gifts and works,
manifests your holiness to all humanity.
Holy is your Only Begotten Son, Jesus
 Christ
through whom you did order the universe.
And Holy is your ever-blessed Spirit
who reveals all things,
even the deep things of you, O God.

Just as you yourself are holy,
so also you created us in your own image
that we might live in holy fellowship.
And when we disobeyed your
 commandments,
you did not abandon us
but you guided us as a merciful Father,
you revealed yourself to us

through the sages, the Law and the
 Prophets,
and through your redeeming acts in
 history,
and when the time was ripe,
you came to us through your Son Jesus,
whom you sent into the world
to share our human nature
in order that he might revive your own
 image in us.
**Father, Jesus loved us
and sacrificed himself for us
and heralded the new age
in breaking bread with friends**
(The congregation may raise a hand)

On the very night that he was betrayed
to suffer death upon the cross for us,
the Lord Jesus took bread
and when he had given thanks to you,
 almighty Father,
he broke it and gave it to his disciples
saying: Take, eat, this is my body that is
 given for you.
Do this in remembrance of me.
In the same manner after supper,
he took the cup also, and after giving
 thanks,
he gave it to them saying:
Drink, all of you from this,
for this is my blood of the new covenant
which is poured out for many for the
 forgiveness of sins.
Do this, as often as you drink it,
in remembrance of me.
**We proclaim the Lord's death,
we live by his resurrection,
we look for his coming again.**

And so Father, we present this bread and
 cup
in communion with your whole church,
in fellowship with (Blessed Mary, and
 _____ and) all the saints,
and in union with all creation
we celebrate your Son's death and victory;

and preparing us for what lies ahead
and giving thanks for all that Christ has
  done for us.

The congregation may raise a hand

And we entreat you, most merciful Father,
that your All-Holy Spirit may + bless and
  hallow us and these your gifts
by his life-giving power
that they may be for us the body and
  blood
of your most dearly loved Son,
and unite us with your new creation
that all who share in this Holy
  Communion
may obtain remission of our sins
and be worthy of integration into Christ
and in all humanity
and all other benefits of Christ's life,
suffering, resurrection and session in glory
and eagerly await Christ's coming again.

Or

And we entreat you, most merciful Father,
that your Holy Spirit may hallow the
  whole earth
and us, as we partake in the body and
  blood
of your dearly loved Son,
and unite us with your new creation
that we may obtain remission of our sins
and all other benefits of Christ's life,
suffering, resurrection and session in glory
and eagerly await Christ's coming again.

**Accept this our sacrifice of praise and
  thanksgiving;
make us one body in Jesus Christ our
  Lord,**

by whom and with whom and in whom
in the unity of the Holy Spirit
all honour and glory be to you,
almighty Father, world without end.
Amen.

NB: In this *apparatus* the 1997 text continued
Cey1 at each point marked with an asterisk (*),
but anticipated Cey2 where no other specific 1997
text is recorded.

Cey1: **God thanks and praise**] him thanks and
  praise
  (Hosanna . . . highest)] Glory be to you, O Lord
    most high*
  revealed yourself] spoke
  sages] great sages*
  redeeming acts] acts*
  came to us] spoke to us* [[1997 ADDS specially]]
  bread with friends] bread with his friends*
  when he had given] after he gave [[1997 after
    giving]]
  disciples saying] disciples to share saying*
  cup also . . . gave it] cup of wine. After he gave
    thanks to you, he gave it [[1997: after giving]]
  poured out for many] shed for you and all
    mankind [[1997: for you and for many]]
  Do this . . . drink it] Whenever you drink it, do
    this*
  the Lord's death] his death*
  and preparing . . . all that Christ] giving thanks
    for all that he*
  FIRST OPTION ON LEFT:
  and these your gifts . . . loved Son] IN BRACKETS
  and unite us . . . Christ's coming again] OMIT
  1997 OMITS WHOLE OPTION
  SECOND OPTION ON LEFT:
  Cey1 OMITS
  1997 OMITS that we . . . coming again

20. **BREAKING OF THE BREAD**[85]
The bread which we break is it not a sharing of the body of Christ?
We being many are one bread, one body for we all partake of one bread.

21. **THE COMMUNION**
As our Saviour Christ has taught us, we now pray:
Our Father in heaven, holy be . . . ⟦ELLC 1⟧ . . . for ever. Amen.
    Save us from the time of trial and] Do not bring us to the test and
or
Our Father, who art . . . ⟦modified traditional text⟧ . . . and ever. Amen.
    Cey1 OMIT TRADITIONAL OPTION

22. *A piece of bread may be placed in the chalice to symbolize the resurrection followed by the Easter Greeting.*
The peace of the Lord be always with you
And also with you.
    Cey1: ADDS (*or* **God's Spirit is with us**)

23. The gifts of God for the people of God
Hosanna in the highest. Blessed is he . . . ⟦ELLC 8⟧ . . . in the highest.

All kneel or prostrate

Deep silence

24. **PRAYERS OF APPROACH**
One of the following or other appropriate prayers of approach may be used.
Most merciful Lord,
your love compels us to come in.
Our hands were unclean,
our hearts were unprepared;
we were not fit
even to eat the crumbs from under your table.
But you, Lord, are the God of our salvation,
who share your bread with sinners.
So cleanse and nourish us
and come to us through the precious body and blood of your Son,
that he may live in us and we in him;
so that we, with the whole community of Christ,
may one day soon sit and eat together with you in your kingdom. Amen.
    Cey1: who shares] and share
        cleanse and nourish . . . through the most precious] cleanse and feed us with the most
                                                                                precious
        community . . . eat together in] company of Christ may sit and eat in
Or
We do not come . . . ⟦CF 3(a)⟧ . . . he in us. Amen.
    our sinful . . . precious blood and that] OMIT
    Cey1 ⟦not 1997⟧: do not come] do not dare to come
Or
Lamb of God . . . ⟦ELLC 9(b)⟧ . . . grant us peace.

---

85 ⟦At 20, 21, 25 and 28 the first line is appointed to be said by a deacon.⟧

25. *THE INVITATION*
Draw near with faith and take this Holy Sacrament to your comfort.
Or
Jesus is the Lamb of God . . . ⟦CF 9(b)⟧ . . . **I shall be healed.**
  Blessed . . . his supper] Happy . . . the supper of the Lord
Or any other suitable invitation may be used
  Cey1 OMITS THE ALTERNATIVE

26. *THE DISTRIBUTION*
The following or other suitable words may be used at the distribution
The Body of Christ (The Bread of Life).
The Blood of Christ (the Chalice of Life).
  Cey1 ADDS +Amen TO EACH

27. *ADDITIONAL CONSECRATION*
In the event the consecrated elements are not enough a presbyter may use the following prayer for an additional consecration.
We entreat you, Father, having given thanks over the bread and the cup according to the institution of your Son Jesus Christ, that your all-Holy Spirit may hallow this bread (wine) also, that it too may be for us the Body (Blood) of your Son Jesus, who took bread (the cup) gave thanks and gave it to the disciples saying, 'This is my Body (Blood).' **Amen.**
  Cey1 OMITS RUBRIC
    having given . . . Son Jesus Christ] OMIT
    be for us] become for us

A period of silence is kept after communion

All may stand

28. Give thanks to the Lord for God is gracious
God's mercy endures for ever.

An after communion sentence from scripture may be said (see appendix)
Almighty God . . . ⟦CF 11(a)⟧ . . . praise and glory. Amen.
  Cey1: through him . . . our souls and bodies] through whom we offer you ourselves

Or Father of all . . . ⟦CF 11(b)⟧ . . . through Jesus Christ our Lord. Amen.
  May we who share . . . light to the world] SAID BY ALL

Or The Thisaranaya (Triple refuge)

Oba piya devikara saranaya ganimi	(I take refuge in you Parent God)
Oba kithu himikara saranaya ganimi	(I take refuge in you Christ Lord)
Oba sudha tindukara saranaya ganimi	(I take refuge in you blest Spirit)
Oba eka devikara saranaya ganimi	(I take my refuge in you three as one God)
Obe sura sasunehi saranaya pathami	(I look for refuge in your holy church)
Obe ana vinayehi saranaya pathami	(I look for refuge in your own precepts laws)
Obe subha dahamehi saranaya pathami	(I look for refuge in your noble word)
Obe mema sasunehi saranaya pathemi	(I look for refuge in this your community)

  Cey1 REVERSES THE ORDER OF THE FIRST TWO OPTIONS

29. *THE NOTICES*

Brief announcements, notices may be given now or at any other suitable point in the service.
Banns of Marriage may be published.
   Cey1 PROVIDES NOTICES AFTER THE CREED (§13)

30. *THE DISMISSAL*

The Bishop or Presider may pronounce a suitable blessing such as the following.
(Other examples before the blessing or dismissal are given in the appendix)
The peace of God . . . ⟦CF 12(a)⟧ . . . remain with you always. **Amen.**

Or ⟦said by deacon⟧
Brothers and sisters, to the mercies of the glorious Trinity we commit you, go now
in the food of your pilgrimage in peace and gladness. Serve the Lord and help to free
others.
Thanks be to God.
   Cey1: glorious] holy and glorious
         in the food] with the food

Or ⟦said by deacon⟧
Go in peace and serve the Lord.
In the name of Christ. Amen.
   Cey1 OMITS BRACKETED MENTION OF APPENDIX

APPENDICES (only in the Presider's Edition)

         Cey1 OMITS APPENDICES

APPENDIX 1 (Children's Liturgy / Liturgy in the absence of an ordained presbyter)
⟦Provision for extended communion, and guidelines for children's liturgy⟧

APPENDIX 2: Alternative Eucharistic Prayers and exhortation
Prayer A: From the Ecumenical Lima Liturgy (2 Jan 1982)
⟦The Lima Text is in Appendix A on page 315 below⟧

Prayer B: From the 1960 Provincial Liturgy
⟦Text of **IndR** recast in modernized English⟧

Prayer C: From the Ceylon Liturgy (1938)
⟦Text of **Cey** recast in modernized English⟧

Prayer D: From 1552/1662 Liturgy
⟦Text of 1662, recast in modernized English, beginning '*Comfortable Words from the appendix*
may be said here', and continuing from 'Lift up your hearts'. Cf. **EngCW2A**⟧

APPENDIX 3: Proper Prefaces

APPENDIX 4: Seasonal Material

APPENDIX 5: Comfortable Words

APPENDIX 6: Canticles

25. The Church of the Province of Myanmar (Burma)

The Church of the Province of Myanmar (Burma) was formed when the other components of the Church of India, Pakistan, Burma and Ceylon went separate ways in 1970. At that stage, the existing CIPBC 1960 BCP, containing **Ind** and **IndR,** continued in use, in Burmese and also tribal languages. The Book was republished without change of content in 1984 as *The Book of Common Prayer of Christ's Church of Burma.* The Province, however, took steps to provide a rite reflecting some of the developments of the decades since 1960, and the Provincial Council authorized a new rite, published in booklet form bilingually in Burmese and English, in 1999. A large part of the eucharistic prayer is, unusually, addressed to the Son of God.

THE HOLY COMMUNION OF THE CHURCH OF THE PROVINCE OF MYANMAR (BURMA) 1999 (Burm)

[[The numbering and lining are editorial]]

THE HOLY COMMUNION

1. *(The congregation stands and sings a hymn when the priest enters the church. At the end of the hymn the congregation kneels while the priest remains standing.)*

2. In the name of the Father, and of the Son, and of the Holy Spirit. **Amen.**

3. *TAKING REFUGE*
[[Four versicles and responses of taking refuge in the three persons of the Trinity, and blessing the Trinity]]

4. *GREETING*
The grace of our Lord Jesus Christ, and the love of God, and the fellowship of the Holy Spirit be with you.
And also with you.

5. *PRAYER* [[three prayers for three seasons of the year. Trinity season has the Collect for Purity CF 1]]

6. *THE RECEIVING OF THE TEN COMMANDMENTS (OR) THE BEATITUDES OR THE THREE VIRTUES*
[[Texts of the Commandments, the Beatitudes, and of 'Faith, Hope and Love', each with a response, the latter two allocated to seasons]]

7. *THE COLLECT* [[rubric directing]]

THE MINISTRY OF THE WORD

8. *OLD TESTAMENT READING* [[announcement, *proclamation and response at the end, *anthem following]]

9. *NEW TESTAMENT READING (EPISTLE)* ⟦announcement, *proclamation and response at the end, *hymn following⟧

10. *THE GOSPEL* ⟦salutation, announcement and response, and proclamation and response at the end⟧

11. *THE SERMON*

12. *THE CONFIRMATION OF OUR FAITH*
As we have one Lord, one faith, one Baptism, and only one Father who is holier than others, let us stand and say together the Nicene Creed that is confirmed by our forefathers and all Christians in the world.
(Then shall be sung or said the Creed, the people still standing as before; except that at the discretion of the Minister it may be omitted on any day, not being a Sunday or a greater Festival.)

13. *THE NICENE CREED*
We believe in one God . . . ⟦ELLC 5⟧ . . . world to come. Amen.
⟦A footnote permits genuflection at 'he came down'⟧
for us] **for us men**
was incarnate . . . truly human] **by the power of the Holy Spirit he became incarnate of the Virgin Mary and was made man**
[and the Son]] OMIT BRACKETS

14. *THE INTERCESSION* ⟦A single prayer, with threefold Kyrie responses at three points⟧

PRAYERS OF PENITENCE

15. *EXHORTATION*
(The priest or deacon stands, turns to the congregation, says the following exhortation.)
You that do truly . . . ⟦as in 1662⟧ . . . upon your knees.

16. *GENERAL CONFESSION* ⟦text of **EngA**⟧

17. *ABSOLUTION*
(The priest or bishop stands up, and turning himself to the people, pronounces this absolution.)
Almighty God, who forgives . . . ⟦CF 2⟧ . . . Christ our Lord. **Amen.**

18. *THE COMFORTABLE WORDS*
(The priest or deacon may say.) ⟦Matt. 11.28, John 3.16, 1 Tim. 1.15, 1 John 2.1⟧

THE OFFERTORY

19. *THE ANNOUNCEMENTS (Only those which are permitted)*
Let us present our offerings to the Lord with reverence and godly fear.

20. *THE OFFERTORY SENTENCES* ⟦eight sentences, primarily about giving money, and nine thematic seasonal ones, and permission to use others for festival days⟧

THE MINISTRY OF THE SACRAMENT

21. *(While a hymn is being sung, the priest may take of the Bread and Wine prepared for the Sacrament as much as he thinks is sufficient. Then the priest may present the Bread and Wine, and the alms and other offerings of the people.)*
Let us pray.
**All things come of you, and of your own do we give you,
O Creator of the world, who are ever adored by the holy angels.
We humbly beseech you to accept at our hands these (*alms and*) oblations,
which we present at your holy Table,
and with them the offering of ourselves to the service of your divine Majesty;
through Jesus Christ our Lord. Amen.**

22. THE CONSECRATION [The symbols in the narrative appear to indicate manual acts]

The Lord be with you . . . [ELLC 6] . . .
him thanks and praise.

It is indeed our duty to give you thanks
and praise.
Almighty Father, remove all the
hindrances from us
with your Word which was with you in
creation.
You chose the Church as your partner
and your own by your incarnation.

*Here shall follow the Proper Preface, according to
the time. If there is no specially appointed preface
the priest can say the following.*

Therefore with Cherubin and Seraphin
we proclaim bravely and hopefully, saying:
Holy, holy . . . [ELLC 7] . . . of your glory.
Glory be to you, O Lord most high. Amen.
Blessed is he who now . . . [ELLC 8] . . . in
the highest.

[Nine Proper Prefaces are printed here]

THE EUCHARISTIC PRAYER

Holy in truth are you, and blessed in truth,
O merciful and Almighty God.
You gave us the care and encouragement
at the beginning,
and the Law and sacrifice for fallen human
beings.
When the time was fulfilled,
you also gave us the redeemer, Lord,
to nullify human's sins.

Lord, by your incarnation through the
Holy Virgin Mary,
you are true man and true God.
By your temptation, you lived as human
being without sin.
As you walked willingly towards the Cross
for us,
our redemption was made

by your one oblation of yourself once
offered,
a full, perfect, and sufficient sacrifice.

Holy and Almighty, the Eternal,
the Pureness and Creator, by your hand,
took bread* and gave thanks;
you broke it and gave it to your disciples,
saying, Take, eat;**
this is my body which is given for you;
do this in remembrance of me.

In the same way, after supper,
you took the cup* and gave thanks;
you took the cup yourself
and gave it your holy and chosen disciples
at the table,
saying, Drink this, all of you;
** this is my blood of the new covenant,
which is shed for you and for many
for the forgiveness of sins.
Do this, as often as you drink it,
in remembrance of me. **Amen.**

Father, we celebrate this sacrifice
by the remembrance of the death of Jesus
Christ,
the proclamation of his resurrection,
and looking for his coming again with
power and great glory.
And we humbly pray to you, Lord,
to send down the Holy Spirit to us and to
these gifts;
and that all who are partakers of this Holy
Communion
may be one with Jesus Christ and become
living sacrifices.

Through him, with him, and in him,
by the power of the Holy Spirit
all honour and glory be yours,
Almighty Father, for ever and ever.
Amen.

---

* [There is no explanation, but the position suggests a manual act of 'taking']
** [There is no explanation, but the position suggests a manual act of laying a hand on the particular element]

23. The peace of the Lord be always with you
    And also with you.

24. *THE PRAYER OF HUMBLE ACCESS*
    (*This prayer may be said by the priest and congregation, together while kneeling*)
    We do not presume . . . ⟦CF 3(a)⟧ . . . and he in us. Amen.
       our sinful . . . and that] OMIT

25. **Lamb of God . . . ⟦ELLC 9(b)⟧ . . . grant us peace.**
       sin] sins THREE TIMES

26. *(The priest who celebrates the Communion, may say to the congregation by lifting up the*
    Bread and Wine while standing and turning to them.)
    Draw near and receive the Body and Blood of our Lord Jesus Christ,
    which were given for you,
    and feed on him in your hearts by faith with thanksgiving.

27. *(When the priest delivers the Bread, he may say)*
    The body of Christ keep your body and soul to eternal life.
    (When the priest delivers the Cup, he may say)
    The blood of Christ keep your body and soul to eternal life.

THE THANKSGIVING

28. The Lord be with you.
    And also with you.
    Let us boldly say together with thanksgiving the Lord's Prayer, which was
    commanded and taught by Christ himself.
    Our Father in heaven . . . ⟦ELLC 1⟧ . . . for ever. Amen.
       Save us . . . trial and] **Lead us not into temptation but**

29. Let us pray
    Almighty and everliving God . . . ⟦prayer of thanksgiving as in 1662⟧ . . . Christ our
    Lord. **Amen.**

30. ⟦Rubric re saying or singing, and using or omitting, Gloria in Excelsis⟧

    GLORIA IN EXCELSIS
    Glory to God in the highest . . . ⟦ELLC 3⟧ . . . God the Father. Amen.
       God's people] his people

31. *THE BLESSING*
    The peace of God . . . ⟦CF 12(a)⟧ . . . with you always. **Amen.**

26. The Provinces of South East Asia and Hong Kong

The Province of South East Asia, formed in 1995 from the joining together of four separate extra-provincial diocese, inherited separate diocesan rites in Kuching and Sabah. The Sabah rite of 1984 was not shown in **LAL**, but is similar to **Kuch** of 1973, and to **Pak** in this volume, in having a 1662-based eucharistic prayer (without Humble Access in it), but ending with the narrative followed solely by the acclamation '**Christ has died** . . .' (CF 6(a)). The province does not appear to have created any provincial rite.

Hong Kong and Macau became a separated extra-provincial diocese when the Anglican Church in China was suppressed, and the diocese produced its own somewhat conservative eucharistic rites in 1957 and 1965, and these were presented in **MAL** as **HK1** and **HK2**. **HK1** came within the main Chinese Prayer Book of the diocese, and remained in normal use for three decades, while **HK2**, an experimental rite, did not have the same lasting role. With the lapse of time the 'traditional' English of these rites gave them a dated feel in English, but a more modern rite was needed in Chinese also. So the coming of semi-definitive modern English texts elsewhere led the diocesan Liturgical Committee to draw upon the text of **Amer2-2** and, to a lesser extent, upon **EngA**, and make that the basis of a new Chinese-language rite in 1985. This was authorized by the diocesan synod as 'Rite 2', as it was seen as the successor to **HK1**, the rite in authoritative use. After the transference of the colony in 1997 to Chinese rule as the Special Administrative Region, the diocese was divided into three and became the province of Hong Kong in 1998. The province ordered the publication of 'Rite 2' in a bilingual form, which occurred in 2000, and the rite is shown below as **HK3**. Its dependence upon **Amer2-2** is very obvious, and there is a move within the Province to create their own rites for the future.

'THE HOLY EUCHARIST RITE TWO' AUTHORIZED IN THE PROVINCE OF HONG KONG, 2000 (HK3)

⟦The numbering is original, the lining partly editorial⟧

THE HOLY EUCHARIST RITE TWO

THE PREPARATION

1. *A hymn, psalm, or anthem may be sung.*

2. *A appropriate sentence may be used (see the Lectionary).*

3. ⟦Opening greeting and response as in **Amer2-2**, with seasonal variants, the people standing⟧

4. *All remain standing.*
   Almighty God, to whom . . . ⟦CF 1⟧ . . . **Christ our Lord. Amen.**
   hidden] hid

5. ⟦Gloria in Excelsis, called 'Glory to God', (ELLC 3) in Christmas and Easter, Kyries (ELLC 2) or Trisagion in Advent and Lent⟧

6. *THE COLLECT OF THE DAY* ⟦Greeting, the collect, all standing⟧

THE PROCLAMATION OF THE WORD

THE LESSONS

7. ⟦First lesson, the people standing, proclamation and response⟧

8. ⟦*Silence, psalm⟧

9. ⟦On Sundays etc. second lesson, proclamation and response⟧

10. ⟦*Silence, *canticle, hymn or anthem⟧

11. ⟦All standing, Gospel, announcement and response before, proclamation and response after⟧

12. *THE SERMON*

13. *THE NICENE CREED* ⟦Rubric re Sunday use etc.⟧
    Let us confess our faith, as we say:
    We believe in one God . . . ⟦ELLC 5⟧ . . . world to come. Amen.
    was incarnate . . . truly human] by the power of the Holy Spirit,
    he became incarnate from the Virgin Mary
    and was made man
    [and the Son]] OMIT BRACKETS

14. *THE PRAYERS OF THE PEOPLE* ⟦rubric re topics and reference to forms in Appendix 1⟧

CONFESSION OF SIN

15. *The people may stand or kneel. The Celebrant may read one of the following sentences.* ⟦texts of Matt. 22.37–40; 1 John 1.8–9; Heb. 4.14, 16⟧

16. Let us confess our sins against God and our neighbour.

17. *Silence may be kept.*

18. ⟦congregational confession, largely based on **Amer2-2**⟧

19. ⟦absolution as in **Amer2-2**⟧

20. ⟦rubric providing for the bishop to absolve⟧

21. *THE PEACE All stand.*
    The peace of the Lord be always with you.
    And also with you.

22. *Then the Celebrant and People may greet one another in the name of the Lord*

23. *Announcements*

THE CELEBRATION OF THE EUCHARIST

THE OFFERTORY

24. *All stand. The Celebrant may begin the OFFERTORY with one of the following sentences.* ⟦texts of Ps. 50.14; 96.8; Eph. 5.2; Rom. 12.1; Heb. 13.15, 16⟧

25. *During the OFFERTORY, a hymn, psalm, or anthem may be sung.*

26. *Representatives of the congregation bring the People's offerings of bread and wine, and money and other gifts, to the Deacon or Celebrant. The People stand while the offerings are presented. One of the following may be said or sung.*
    All things come from you, O Lord,
    and of your own do we give you.
    Or

Yours, Lord, is the greatness, the power, the glory, the splendour, and the majesty;
for everything in heaven and on earth is yours.
All things come from you,
and of your own do we give you.

THE GREAT THANKSGIVING

27. *The Celebrant uses one of the four* EUCHARISTIC PRAYERS *which follow.*

28. *EUCHARISTIC PRAYER (A) The people remain standing*

The Lord . . . [ELLC 6] . . . **him thanks**
  and praise.

It is right, and a good and joyful thing,
always and everywhere to give thanks to
  you,
Father Almighty, Creator of heaven and
  earth.
[Proper Preface on stated occasions]

Therefore we praise you,
joining our voices with Angels and
  Archangels
and with all the company of heaven,
who for ever sing this hymn
to proclaim the glory of your Name:
Holy, holy . . . [ELLC 7] . . . in the highest.
Blessed is . . . [ELLC 8] . . . in the highest.

Holy and gracious Father:
In your infinite love you made us for
  yourself;
and, when we had fallen into sin
and become subject to evil and death,
you, in your mercy, sent Jesus Christ,
your only and eternal Son,
to share our human nature,
to live and die as one of us,
to reconcile us to you,
the God and Father of all.

He stretched out his arms in the cross,
and offered himself, in obedience to your
  will,
a perfect sacrifice for the whole world.

[rubric re manual acts in footnote 67 on p. 95 above]
On the night he was handed over to
  suffering and death,
our Lord Jesus Christ took bread;
and when he had given thanks to you,
he broke it, and gave it to his disciples,
and said, 'Take, eat:

This is my Body, which is given for you.
Do this for the remembrance of me.'

After supper he took the cup of wine;
and when he had given thanks,
he gave it to them, and said,
'Drink this, all of you:
This is my Blood of the new Covenant,
which is shed for you and for many
for the forgiveness of sins.
Whenever you drink it,
do this for the remembrance of me.'

Therefore we proclaim the mystery . . .
  [CF 6(a)] . . . **come again.**

We celebrate the memorial of our
  redemption,
O Father, in this sacrifice of praise and
  thanksgiving.
Recalling his death, resurrection and
  ascension,
we offer you these gifts.

Sanctify them by your Holy Spirit
to be for your people
the Body and Blood of your Son,
the holy food and drink of new and
  unending life in him.
Sanctify us also
that we may faithfully receive this holy
  Sacrament,
and serve you in unity, constancy and peace;
and at the last day bring us with all your
  saints
into the joy of your eternal kingdom.

All this we ask through your Son Jesus
  Christ.
By him, and with him, and in him,
in the unity of the Holy Spirit
all honour and glory is yours,
Almighty Father, now and for ever.
Amen.

The service continues with the Lord's Prayer (§ 32 . . .)

29. EUCHARISTIC PRAYER (B) *The people remain standing*

The Lord be . . . [ELLC 6] . . . **him thanks and praise.**

It is right, and a good and joyful thing,
always and everywhere to give thanks to
  you,
Father Almighty, Creator of heaven and
  earth.

[Proper Preface on stated occasions]

Therefore we praise you,
joining our voices with Angels and
  Archangels
and with all the company of heaven,
who for ever sing this hymn
to proclaim the glory of your Name:
Holy, holy . . . [ELLC 7] . . . in the highest.
Blessed is . . . [ELLC 8] . . . in the highest.

We give thanks to you, O God,
for the goodness and love which you have
  made known to us in creation;
in the calling of Israel to be your people;
in your Word spoken through the
  prophets;
and above all in the Word made flesh,
Jesus, your Son.
For in these last days you sent him
to be incarnate from the Virgin Mary,
to be the Saviour and Redeemer of the
  world.
In him, you have delivered us from evil,
and made us worthy to stand before you.
In him, you have brought us out of error
  into truth,
out of sin into righteousness,
out of death into life.

[rubric re manual acts in footnote 67 on p. 95 above]

On the night before he died for us,
our Lord Jesus Christ took bread;
and when he had given thanks to you,
he broke it, and gave it to his disciples,
and said, 'Take, eat: this is my Body,
which is given for you.
Do this for the remembrance of me.'

After supper he took the cup of wine;
and when he had given thanks,
he gave it to them, and said,
'Drink this, all of you;
this is my Blood of the new Covenant,
which is shed for you and for many
for the forgiveness of sins.
Whenever you drink it,
do this for the remembrance of me.'

Therefore, according to his command, O
  Father,
We remember his death.
We proclaim his resurrection.
We await his coming in glory.

And we offer our sacrifice of praise and
  thanksgiving
to you, O Lord of all;
presenting to you, from your creation,
this bread and this wine.

We pray you, gracious God,
to send your Holy Spirit upon these gifts
that they may be the Sacrament
of the Body of Christ and his Blood of the
  new Covenant.
Unite us to your Son in his sacrifice,
that we may be acceptable through him,
being sanctified by the Holy Spirit.
In the fullness of time,
put all things in subjection under your
  Christ,
and bring us to that heavenly country,
where with [_____ and] all your saints,
we may enter the everlasting heritage of
  your sons and daughters;
through Jesus Christ our Lord,
the firstborn of all creation,
the head of the Church,
and the author of our salvation.

By him, and with him, and in him,
in the unity of the Holy Spirit
all honour and glory is yours,
Almighty Father, now and for ever.
Amen.

The service continues with the Lord's Prayer (§ 32 . . .)

The Lord be . . . ⟦ELLC 6⟧ . . . **him thanks and praise.**

God of all power, Ruler of the Universe,
you are worthy of glory and praise.
Glory to you for ever and ever.

At your command all things came to be:
the vast expanse of interstellar space,
galaxies, suns, the planets in their courses,
and this fragile earth, our island home.
**By your will they were created and have
their being.**

From the primal elements you brought
forth the human race,
and blessed us with memory, reason, and
skill.
You made us the rulers of creation.
But we turned against you, and betrayed
your trust;
and we turned against one another.
**Have mercy, Lord, for we are sinners in
your sight.**

Again and again, you called us to return.
Through prophets and sages you revealed
your righteous Law.
And in the fullness of time you sent your
only Son,
born of a woman, to fulfil your Law,
to open for us the way of freedom and peace.
By his blood, he reconciled us.
By his wounds, we are healed.

And therefore we praise you,
joining with the heavenly chorus,
with prophets, apostles, and martyrs,
and with all those in every generation
who have looked to you in hope,
to proclaim with them your glory,
in their unending hymn:
Holy, holy . . . ⟦ELLC 7⟧ . . . in the highest.
Blessed is . . . ⟦ELLC 8⟧ . . . in the highest.

And so, Father, we who have been
redeemed by him,
and made a new people by water and the
Spirit,
now bring before you these gifts.
Sanctify them by your Holy Spirit,

that we who eat and drink at this holy table
may share the divine life of Christ our
Lord.

⟦rubric re manual acts in footnote 67 on p. 95 above⟧
On the night he was betrayed he took
bread,
said the blessing, broke the bread,
and gave it to his friends, and said,
'Take, eat: This is my Body, which is given
for you.
Do this for the remembrance of me.'

After supper, he took the cup of wine,
gave thanks, and said,
'Drink this, all of you:
This is my Blood of the new Covenant,
which is shed for you and for many
for the forgiveness of sins.
Whenever you drink it,
do this for the remembrance of me.'

Remembering now his work of redemption,
and offering to you this sacrifice of
thanksgiving,
**We celebrate his death and resurrection,
as we await the day of his coming.**

Lord God of our Fathers;
God of Abraham, Isaac, and Jacob;
God and Father of our Lord Jesus Christ:
Open our eyes to see your hand at work in
the world about us.
Deliver us from the presumption
of coming to this Table for solace only,
and not for strength;
for pardon, and not for renewal.
Let the grace of this Holy Communion
make us one body, one spirit in Christ,
that we may worthily serve the world in
his name.
**Risen Lord, be known to us
in the breaking of the Bread.**

Accept these prayers and praises, Father,
through Jesus Christ our great High Priest,
to whom, with you and the Holy Spirit,
your Church gives honour, glory and
worship,
from generation to generation.
Amen.

The service continues with the Lord's Prayer (§ 32 . . .)

The Lord be . . . ⟦ELLC 6⟧ . . . **him thanks and praise.**

It is truly right to glorify you, Father,
and to give you thanks;
for you alone are God, living and true,
dwelling in light inaccessible
from before time and for ever.

Fountain of life and source of all goodness,
you made all things
and fill them with your blessing;
you created them to rejoice
in the splendour of your radiance.

Countless throngs of angels stand before
  you
to serve you night and day;
and, beholding the glory of your presence,
they offer you unceasing praise.
Joining with them,
and giving voice to every creature under
  heaven,
we acclaim you, and glorify your Name,
as we sing (say),
Holy, holy . . . ⟦ELLC 7⟧ . . . in the highest.
Blessed is . . . ⟦ELLC 8⟧ . . . in the highest.

We acclaim you, holy Lord, glorious in
  power.
Your mighty works reveal your wisdom
  and love.
You formed us in your own image,
giving the whole world into our care,
so that, in obedience to you, our Creator,
we might rule and serve all your creatures.
When our disobedience took us far from
  you,
you did not abandon us to the power of
  death.
In your mercy you came to our help,
so that in seeking you we might find you.
Again and again you called us into
  covenant with you,
and through the prophets you taught us to
  hope for salvation.

Father, you loved the world so much
that in the fullness of time
you sent your only Son to be our Saviour.
Incarnate by the Holy Spirit,
born of the Virgin Mary,
he lived as one of us, yet without sin.
To the poor he proclaimed the good news
  of salvation;
to the prisoners, freedom;

to the sorrowful, joy.
To fulfil your purpose he gave himself up
  to death;
and, rising from the grave,
destroyed death, and made the whole
  creation new.

And, that we might no longer live for
  ourselves,
but for him who died and rose for us,
he sent the Holy Spirit,
his own first gift for those who believe,
to complete his work in the world,
and to bring to fulfilment the sanctification
  of all.

⟦rubric re manual acts in footnote 67 on p. 95 above⟧

When the hour had come
for him to be glorified by you, his heavenly
  Father,
having loved his own who were in the
  world,
he loved them to the end;
at supper with them he took bread,
and when he had given thanks to you,
he broke it, and gave it to his disciples,
and said, 'Take, eat:
this is my Body, which is given for you.
Do this in remembrance of me.'

After supper he took the cup of wine;
and when he had given thanks,
he gave it to them, and said,
'Drink this, all of you:
This is my Blood of the new Covenant,
which is shed for you and for many
for the forgiveness of sins.
Whenever you drink it,
do this for the remembrance of me.'

Father, we now celebrate this memorial of
  our redemption.
Recalling Christ's death and his descent
  among the dead,
proclaiming his resurrection and ascension
  to your right hand,
awaiting his coming in glory;
and offering to you,
from the gifts you have given us,
this bread and this cup,
we praise you and bless you.
We praise you, we bless you,
we give thanks to you,
and we pray to you, Lord our God.

Lord, we pray that in your goodness and
  mercy
your Holy Spirit may descend upon us,
and upon these gifts, sanctifying them
and showing them to be holy gifts for your
  holy people,
the bread of life and the cup of salvation,
the Body and Blood of your Son Jesus
  Christ.

Grant that all who share this bread and
  cup
may become one body and one spirit,
a living sacrifice in Christ,
to the praise of your Name.

Remember, Lord, your one holy catholic
  and apostolic Church,
redeemed by the blood of your Christ.
Reveal its unity, guard its faith,
and preserve it in peace.

The petitions in [ ] may be omitted.

[Remember (our Bishop _____ and) all
  who minister in your Church.]
[Remember all your people, and those who
  seek your truth.]

[Remember _____.]
[Remember all who have died in the peace
  of Christ,
and those whose faith is known to you
  alone;
bring them into the place of eternal joy
  and light.]

And grant that we may find our
  inheritance
with [the Blessed Virgin Mary,
with prophets, apostles, martyrs,
(with _____) and] all the saints
who have found favour with you in ages
  past.
We praise you in union with them
and give you glory through your Son Jesus
  Christ our Lord.

Through Christ, and with Christ, and in
  Christ,
all honour and glory are yours,
Almighty God and Father,
in the unity of the Holy Spirit,
for ever and ever.
Amen.

THE COMMUNION

32. *THE LORD'S PRAYER The People kneel*
    As our Saviour Christ has taught us, we now pray
    Our Father in heaven . . . ⟦ELLC 1⟧ . . . for ever. Amen.
    Save us from the time of trial and] Lead us not into temptation but

33. *THE BREAKING OF THE BREAD*
    The Celebrant breaks the consecrated bread.
    We break this bread . . . ⟦CF 8(a)⟧ . . . **in one bread.**

34. **Lamb of God . . . ⟦CF 9(b)⟧ . . . grant us peace.**
    . sin] sins THREE TIMES

35. *The following prayer may be said.*
    We do not presume . . . ⟦CF 3(a)⟧ . . . he in us.
    that our sinful . . . precious blood and] OMIT

36. *Facing the People, the Celebrant says the following invitation.*
    The Gifts of God for the People of God. Take them in remembrance that Christ died
    for you and feed on him in your hearts by faith, with thanksgiving.

37. *The ministers receive the Sacrament in both kinds, and then immediately deliver it to the*
    People.
    At the distribution of the Bread,
    The Body of Christ keep you in eternal life. *or* The Body of Christ, the bread of heaven.
    At the distribution of the Cup,
    The Blood of Christ keep you in eternal life. *or* The Blood of Christ, the cup of
    salvation.

38. *During the ministration of Communion, hymns, psalms, or anthems may be sung.*

39. *If the consecrated Bread or Wine does not suffice for the number of communicants, the celebrant is to return to the Holy Table, and consecrate more of either or both, by saying:*
Hear us, O heavenly Father, and with your Word and Holy Spirit bless and sanctify this bread (wine) that it, also, may be the Sacrament of the precious Body (Blood) of your Son Jesus Christ our Lord, who took bread (the cup) and said, 'This is my Body (Blood).' **Amen.**

40. *Any consecrated Bread and Wine which is not required for purposes of communion is consumed at the end of the distribution. The vessels are also cleansed.*

AFTER COMMUNION

41. *The People kneel.* Let us pray
Eternal God, heavenly Father,
you have graciously accepted us as living members
of your Son our Saviour Jesus Christ,
and you have fed us with spiritual food
in the Sacrament of his Body and Blood.
Send us now into the world in peace,
and grant us strength and courage
to love and serve you
with gladness and singleness of heart;
through Christ our Lord. Amen.

or
Almighty and everliving God,
we thank you for feeding us with the spiritual food
of the most precious Body and Blood
of your Son our Saviour Jesus Christ;
and for assuring us in these holy mysteries
that we are living members of the Body of your Son,
and heirs of your eternal kingdom.
And now, Father, send us out
to do the work you have given us to do,
to love and serve you
as faithful witnesses of Christ our Lord.
To him, to you, and to the Holy Spirit,
be honour and glory, now and for ever.
Amen.

42. *The Bishop, when present, or the Priest, may bless the People. The following or an alternative blessing (Appendix 3 on pp . . .) may be used.*
The peace of God . . . ⟦CF 12(a)⟧ . . . with you always. **Amen.**

43. *All stand. The Deacon, or the Celebrant, dismisses the People with these words.* ⟦'Alleluia' may be added in Eastertide⟧
Let us go forth in the name of Christ. **Thanks be to God.**
Go in peace to love and serve the Lord. **Thanks be to God.**
Let us go forth into the world, rejoicing in the power of the Spirit. **Thanks be to God.**
Let us bless the Lord. **Thanks be to God.**

44. *A hymn may be sung as the ministers depart.*

27. The Episcopal Church in the Philippines

The Episcopal Church in the Philippines became an independent Province of the Anglican Communion in 1990. It inherited the rites of the 1979 BCP of the Episcopal Church in the USA, of which it had until then been a constituent part. These were **Amer1-1**, **Amer2-2**, and **Amer3-3**, translated into various vernacular languages. However, a National Commission on Liturgics and Church Architecture had already been formed in the Philippines, and its tasks had included preparing draft liturgies specifically for the Philippines. In 1987 this Commission had put out a draft *Liturgy of the Holy Mass* in pamphlet form for trial use. This was to hand when the granting of autonomy to the Province in 1990 included the agreement that a new provincial BCP would be sought by the new Province. The Commission was asked by the Executive Council of the Church to work on with the existing eucharistic draft with a view to revising and enriching it to take its place in the projected BCP. This finally came to pass in 1999. The Commission worked in English, and it was an English-language BCP which was authorized, though the expectation was that it would be both translated and culturally adapted to the various different cultures in which the Episcopal Church lives in the Philippines.

The eucharistic rite was developed primarily from **Amer2-2**, though Tomas Maddela writes of the Commission drawing generally upon Roman Catholic sources, the Lima liturgy and Anglican rites in England, Australia and the Church of South India.[86] With the eucharistic prayers he identifies an Hippolytan ancestry for Prayer B, an Eastern Orthodox point of reference in Prayer C, an overtly Roman family likeness in Prayer D and large elements of **Amer2-2** in Prayers A and E. He reports a concurrent need to retain a visibly Anglican style, partly in order to distinguish the Episcopal Church from the Philippines Independent Church, which, being a breakaway from Rome and in full communion the Anglican Communion, has a more Roman Catholic flavour to its rites.

---

86 Tomas Maddela, 'The Episcopal Church in the Philippines' in *The Oxford Guide*, pp. 388–90.

THE EUCHARIST FROM THE EPISCOPAL CHURCH IN THE PHILIPPINES
BOOK OF COMMON PRAYER, 1999 (Philp)

[The numbering is editorial. The lining is original]

1. ### DIRECTIONS CONCERNING THE SERVICE
   [Functions of ministers and lay people; provision for services without communion; directions for communion from reserved sacramental elements]

2. ### THE ASPERGES
   [Elaborate provision for blessing water and sprinkling the congregation to begin the rite, as an alternative to the Penitential Order, but the rite may begin at §8 without either preliminary]

THE PENITENTIAL ORDER
[For optional use on Fridays and Sundays outside of Christmas and Easter]

3. ### THE ENTRANCE
   All stand. A hymn, psalm, or anthem may be sung.
   The Celebrant makes the sign of the cross over the people and says:
   Blessed be God: Father, Son, and Holy Spirit.
   And blessed be his kingdom, now and forever. Amen.
   [Other greetings for Easter and Lent and penitential occasions. *Ten Commandments with responses]

   Then, one of the following sentences is read:
   [Mark 12.29–31; 1 John 1.8–9; John 3.16; 1 John 2.1b–2]

4. ### THE EXHORTATION
   On the first Sunday in Advent, the first Sunday in Lent, and Trinity Sunday, the Exhortation is used in place of the above sentences from Scripture. The Exhortation may be used also on other occasions.
   The Exhortation may be used in whole or in part. The people sit.
   [Text closely modelled on the Long Exhortation in 1662]

5. ### INVITATION TO CONFESSION
   The Deacon or Celebrant may say one of the following:
   All you who truly and earnestly repent of your sins, seek reconciliation with your neighbours, and intend to lead a new life, following the Commandments of God and walking in his holy ways; draw near with faith, and make your humble confession to Almighty God.
   or
   Since we have a great high priest who passed through the heavens, Jesus, the Son of God, let us with confidence draw near to the throne of grace, that we may receive mercy and find grace to help in time of need.
   or
   Let us humbly confess our sins against God and our neighbour.
   All kneel. Silence is kept for a time.

6. ### THE GENERAL CONFESSION
   Most merciful God . . . [congregational confession as §59 in **Amer2-2**] . . . **your Name. Amen.**

7. THE ABSOLUTION

The Bishop, when present, or the Priest, stands and turning to the people, says:
Almighty God, have mercy . . . [similar to CF 2] . . . in eternal life. **Amen.**

A deacon or layperson using the preceding form substitutes 'us' for 'you' and 'our' for 'your'.

All stand. The Liturgy continues with the Gloria in Excelsis, the Trisagion, the Te Deum, or another song of praise.

THE LITURGY OF THE WORD

8. THE ENTRANCE

All stand. A hymn, psalm or anthem may be sung.
[Greetings as at §3 above]

The Celebrant says the following Collect. The people may join him.
Almighty God, to you . . . [CF 1] . . . through Jesus Christ our Lord. Amen.
  whom] you
  hidden] hid
  Cleanse our hearts] Purify our hearts

On Sundays and feast days, except in Lent and Advent, the following hymn is used, all standing:
Gloria in Excelsis Deo
Glory to God . . . [ELLC 3] . . . the glory of God the Father. Amen.
  God's people] his people
or
Te Deum Laudamus
[Standard text as far as 'glory everlasting', not reproduced in this volume]

On other occasions, the following is used.
Kyrie Eleison [ELLC 2, single] or **Trisagion**
or, some other appropriate anthem may be used.

9. THE COLLECT OF THE DAY
The Lord be with you.
And also with you.
Let us pray. *The Collect*

10. THE LESSONS
[One or two readings, *preceded by responsive acclamation, and then by announcement, *gradual psalm between, *Alleluia Verse or Sequence Hymn following, Gospel reading with announcement and closing proclamation and response]

11. SERMON

All stand after Sermon for the Nicene Creed.
12. THE NICENE CREED
We believe . . . [ELLC 5] . . . world to come. Amen.
  was incarnate . . . truly human] by the power of the Holy Spirit
                                he became incarnate from the Virgin Mary
                                and was made man

  [and the Son]] OMIT

13. *THE PRAYERS OF THE PEOPLE*
    One of the following forms of Intercession shall be used.
    ⟦Five forms of intercession, the fifth being extemporary prayer by Celebrant and people, then a choice of concluding collects⟧

14. *THE PEACE*
    Beloved in the Lord, we are the Body of Christ.
    In one Spirit we were all baptized into one Body.
    Let us strive to keep the unity of the Spirit in the bond of peace.
    The peace of the Lord be always with you.
    And also with you.
    The people greet each other in peace.

THE GREAT THANKSGIVING

15. *THE OFFERTORY*
    The Celebrant begins the offertory with one of the following sentences or any other appropriate sentence. At Eastertide, Alleluia may be added to the offertory sentence.
    ⟦Ps. 50.14; 96.8; 27.6; Deut. 16.16b–17; Lev. 27.30; Matt. 5.23–24; Acts 20.35; Rom. 12.1; Heb. 13.15–16; 1 Chron. 29.11⟧

    The following sentence may be used, or added.
    Let us with gladness present the offerings of our life and work to the Lord.

    The Minister and People sit. The deacon, or another Minister, prepares the Holy Table. The People's gifts are collected.

    During the above preparations, a hymn or anthem may be sung, or instrumental music played. When everything is ready, the Celebrant stands behind the Altar, facing the people.

    The people stand. Representatives of the Congregation bring the offerings to the Altar. A Doxology may be sung while the gifts are being brought to the Altar.

    As the offerings are placed on the altar, the following prayers may be said by the Celebrant and People:

    MONEY AND OTHER GIFTS:
    Everlasting God,
    you have given us all we have;
    your bounty supplies all our needs.
    We offer you this token of our gratitude
    for all your mercies. Amen.

    THE BREAD
    Eternal God,
    you have caused the grain to grow,
    and from it this bread has been made.
    We offer it to you.
    May it become for us the Bread of Life. Amen.

THE WINE
God Almighty,
from your gifts this wine has been made.
We offer it to you.
May it become for us the Drink of Salvation. Amen.

In place of the above, the following prayer may be used.
Holy Father,
through the blood of your dear Son
you have consecrated for us
a new and living way to your throne of grace.
We come to you through him, unworthy as we are,
humbly asking you to accept us
and these our gifts for your glory.
All that is in heaven and earth is yours,
and of your own do we give you.

Incense may be offered. The offerings, Altar, Ministers and People may be censed. Or, incense
may be burned near the Altar. The following prayer may be used at the kindling of incense:
Incense and a pure offering, O Lord Almighty,
your holy Church presents to your Name;
and when the cloud ascends to the heavenly altar,
look upon your people and declare mercy.

A hymn may be sung during the time of censing.

16. *All stand throughout the Eucharistic Prayer. The following introductory verses may be*
    used.
    The merciful goodness of the Lord
    endures forever and ever upon those who fear him,
    and his righteousness from generation to generation.
    Even on those who keep his covenant,
    and remember his commandments and do them.
    The Lord has set his throne in heaven;
    and his kingdom has dominion over all.
    Praise the Lord you angels of his,
    you mighty ones who do his bidding,
    and listen to the voice of his word.
    Praise the Lord, all you works of his;
    you ministers of his who do his will.
    Praise the Lord, all you works of his;
    in all places of his dominion, praise the Lord!

17. *One of the Eucharistic Prayers following shall be used.*
    ⟦After each prayer a rubric directs that the Lord's Prayer follows⟧

The Lord be with . . . [[ELLC 6]] . . . **him thanks and praise.**

It is right, and a good and joyful thing,
always and everywhere to give thanks to you,
Father Almighty, Creator of heaven and earth.
[[Proper Prefaces, 25 in all including three for Sundays]]

Therefore with angels and archangels
and with all the company of heaven,
we joyfully proclaim your glory,
evermore praising you and saying:
Holy, holy . . . [[ELLC 7]] . . . in the highest.
Blessed is . . . [[ELLC 8]] . . . in the highest.

Holy and gracious Father:
in your infinite love you made us for yourself;
and, when we had fallen into sin
and become subject to evil and death,
you, in your mercy, sent Jesus Christ,
your only and eternal Son, to share our human nature,
to live and die as one of us,
to reconcile us to you, the God and Father of all.

He stretched out his arms upon the cross,
and offered himself in obedience to your will,
a perfect sacrifice for the whole world.

[[rubric re manual acts in footnote 67 on p. 95 above]]

On the night he was handed over to suffering and death,
our Lord Jesus Christ took bread;
and when he had given thanks to you, he broke it,
and gave it to his disciples, and said,
'Take, eat: This is my Body, which is given for you.

Do this for the remembrance of me.'

After supper he took the cup of wine;
and when he had given thanks, he gave it to them, and said,
'Drink this, all of you: This is my Blood of the new Covenant,
which is shed for you and for many for the forgiveness of sins.
Whenever you drink it, do this for the remembrance of me.'

Therefore we proclaim the mystery of faith:
Christ has . . . [[CF 6(a)]] . . . come again.

We celebrate the memorial of our redemption, O Father,
in this sacrifice of praise and thanksgiving.
Recalling his death, resurrection, and ascension,
we offer you these gifts.

Sanctify them by your Holy Spirit
to be for your people the Body and Blood of your Son,
the holy food and drink of new and unending life in him.

Sanctify us also
that we may faithfully receive this holy Sacrament,
and serve you in unity, constancy, and peace;
and at the last day bring us with all your saints
into the joy of your eternal kingdom.

All this we ask through your Son Jesus Christ.
By him, and with him, and in him,
in the unity of the Holy Spirit all honour and glory is yours,
Almighty Father, now and for ever.
Amen.

EUCHARISTIC PRAYER B

The Lord be with you . . . [ELLC 6] . . .
him thanks and praise.

It is right, and a good and joyful thing,
always and everywhere to give thanks to
you,
Father Almighty, Creator of heaven and
earth.

[Proper Preface of Sundays and other occasions]

Therefore with angels and archangels
and with all the company of heaven,
we joyfully proclaim your glory,
evermore praising you and saying:
Holy, holy . . . [ELLC 7] . . . in the highest.
Blessed is . . . [ELLC 8] . . . in the highest.

All glory to you, Almighty God, heavenly
Father,
for of your love and mercy,
you gave your Son Jesus Christ
to take our nature upon him,
and to suffer death upon the cross for our
redemption.
He made there, by the one offering of
himself,
a full and perfect sacrifice for the sins of
the whole world.

On the night in which he was betrayed,
he instituted and commanded us to
continue
a memorial of his precious sacrifice until
his coming again.

[rubric re manual acts in footnote 67 on p. 95 above]

At supper with his disciples,
our Lord Jesus Christ took bread,
and when he had given thanks to you,
he broke it, and gave it to them, and said,
'Take, eat: This is my Body, which is given
for you.
Do this for the remembrance of me.'

After supper, he took the cup of wine,
and when he had given thanks,
he gave it to them, and said,
'Drink this, all of you: this is my Blood of
the New Covenant,

which is shed for you and for many for the
forgiveness of sins.
Whenever you drink it, do this for the
remembrance of me.'

Therefore, we proclaim the mystery of
faith.
Christ has . . . [CF 6(a)] . . . come again.

Wherefore, O Lord and heavenly Father,
we your people celebrate and make the
memorial which your Son commanded.
Having in remembrance his blessed
passion and precious death,
his mighty resurrection and glorious
ascension
and awaiting his coming in glory,
we offer you this Bread of Life and this
Cup of salvation.
And with these gifts we offer ourselves,
asking you to accept upon your heavenly
altar,
this our sacrifice of praise and
thanksgiving.

Gracious Father, by the power of your
Holy Spirit,
sanctify bread and wine, that they may be
to us
the most precious Body and Blood of your
Son Jesus Christ.
May all who receive this holy Sacrament
be filled with your grace and heavenly
blessing,
and be made one body with him,
that he may dwell in us, and we in him.

And, although we are not worthy to offer
you any sacrifice,
yet we ask you to accept this our duty and
service,
through Jesus Christ our Lord,
by him, and with him, and in him
in the unity of the Holy Spirit,
all honour and glory is yours, O Father
Almighty,
now and forever. **Amen.**

EUCHARISTIC PRAYER C

The Lord be with you . . . [ELLC 6] . . .
  him thanks and praise.

It is truly right and good to glorify you,
always and everywhere, to give thanks to
  you,
Father Almighty and Everlasting God.

Through Jesus Christ our Lord;
you made all things good
and made us in your image
to share your life and reflect your glory.
In your appointed time you gave Jesus
  Christ to us as the life of the world.
He accepted baptism and consecration as
  your servant to announce the good news
  to the poor.
He gave us the eucharist,
the memorial of his cross and resurrection,
and his presence among us as the Bread of
  Life.

Therefore, Lord, with the angels and all
  the saints,
we proclaim and sing your glory.
Holy, holy . . . [ELLC 7] . . . **in the highest.**
Blessed is . . . [ELLC 8] . . . **in the highest.**

O holy and gracious God, Lord of the
  universe,
as your life-giving Spirit spoke of old by
  Moses and the prophets,
filled the Blessed Virgin Mary with grace,
descended upon Jesus in the river Jordan,
and upon the apostles on the day of
  Pentecost;
so pour your life-giving Spirit upon this
  eucharist,
transfiguring this thanksgiving meal,
that this bread and wine may become for
  us the Body and Blood of Christ.
**Come, Holy Spirit, and fill us with the gift
  of grace.**

[rubric re manual acts in footnote 67 on p. 95 above]

May this Creator Spirit accomplish the
  words of your beloved Son,
who, in the night in which he was betrayed,
took bread, and when he had given thanks
  to you,
broke it and gave it to his disciples, saying:

'Take, eat: This is my body, which is given
  for you.
Do this for the remembrance of me.'

After supper, he took the cup,
and when he had given thanks,
he gave it to them and said:
'Drink this, all of you:
This is my blood of the new covenant,
which is shed for you and for many for the
  forgiveness of sins.
Do this for the remembrance of me.'

Great is the mystery of faith!
Your death, Lord Jesus, we proclaim!
Your resurrection we celebrate!
Your coming in glory we await!

Wherefore, Lord, we make memorial of
  our redemption;
the birth and life of your Son among us,
his baptism by John, his meal with the
  apostles,
his death and descent to the abode of the
  dead,
his resurrection and ascension in glory,
where he, our Great High Priest,
  intercedes for all people.

United in Christ's priesthood,
we present to you this memorial, the
  sacrifice of your Son.
Grant to all people everywhere the benefits
  of Christ's redemptive work.
Come, Lord Jesus!

O Lord, as you accept the offering of your
  Son,
receive this eucharistic offering,
whereby you call us back to your
  covenant.
Fill us with the Holy Spirit
that as we partake of the body and blood
  of Christ,
we may be united in one single body and
  spirit in him,
a living sacrifice to the praise of your glory.
Come, Holy Spirit,
and fill us with the gift of your grace!

Guide us to the joyful feast
prepared for all people in your presence,
with all your saints, (with blessed *N*.)

[the blessed Virgin Mary, patriarchs and
    prophets,
the apostles and martyrs . . .]
for whom your friendship was life.
With these we sing your praise
and await the happiness of your kingdom
where with the whole creation,
finally delivered from sin and death,

EUCHARISTIC PRAYER D

The Lord be with you . . . ⟦ELLC 6⟧ . . .
    him thanks and praise.

It is right and a good and joyful thing,
always and everywhere to give thanks to
    you,
Father Almighty, creator of heaven and
    earth,
through Jesus Christ our Lord,
who by the power of the Holy Spirit,
took flesh as your Son, and was born of
    the Virgin Mary.
By his death and resurrection, you freed us
    from sins and death;
and through him you sent your holy and
    life-giving Spirit
to make us your people.

Therefore, with angels and archangels,
and with all the company of heaven,
we proclaim your glory evermore
praising you and saying:
Holy, holy . . . ⟦ELLC 7⟧ . . . in the highest.
Blessed is . . . ⟦ELLC 8⟧ . . . in the highest.

⟦rubric re manual acts in footnote 67 on p. 95 above⟧

Accept our praise, heavenly Father,
as we, made a new people by baptism,
bring you these gifts of bread and wine.
Sanctify them by your Holy Spirit
to be for us the Body and Blood
of your Son Jesus Christ our Lord,
who, on the night that he was betrayed,
    took bread;
and when he had given thanks to you,
    broke it,
and gave it to this disciples, saying:
'Take, eat: This is my Body, which is given
    for you.
Do this for the remembrance of me.'
In the same way after supper he took the
    cup,

we shall be enabled to glorify you,
through Jesus Christ our Lord
Come, Lord Jesus! Come soon!

Through Christ, with Christ, in Christ,
all honour and glory is yours,
Almighty God and Father,
in the unity of the Holy Spirit,
now and forever. **Amen.**

and when he had given thanks;
he gave it to them saying,
'Drink this, all of you: This is my Blood of
    the new covenant
which is shed for you and for many for the
    forgiveness of sins.
Do this as often as you drink it, in
    remembrance of me.'

Let us proclaim . . . ⟦CF 6(a)⟧ . . . **come
again.**

Therefore, heavenly Father,
in remembrance of his perfect sacrifice
    upon the cross,
and rejoicing in his resurrection and
    glorious ascension,
and looking for his coming in glory,
we offer you this memorial of our
    redemption.
Receive, O Lord, this our sacrifice of
    praise and thanksgiving,
that as we partake of the Body and Blood
    of Jesus Christ,
we may be filled with your heavenly grace
    and blessing, and grow into his likeness.

Remember, Lord, all who have died
    marked with the sign of faith,
(especially those for whom we now pray,
    N. and N.).
Bring them into your light and peace.
Grant that with them and all your saints,
    (especially blessed N.),
united with one heart and one voice,
we may praise and glorify your Name;
through Jesus Christ our Lord,
by whom, and with whom, and in whom,
in the unity of the Holy Spirit,
all honour and glory is yours, Almighty
    Father,
now and forever. **Amen.**

EUCHARISTIC PRAYER E

The Lord be with you . . . [ELLC 6] . . .
him thanks and praise.

It is truly right, Almighty Father,
to give thanks and praise.
You alone are God, source of light and life.
You have created all things for your
honour and glory.
Countless throngs of angels stand before
you to do you service night and day.
United with them, we acclaim you and
glorify your Name, as we *sing* (say),
Holy, holy . . . [ELLC 7] . . . in the highest.
Blessed is . . . [ELLC 8] . . . in the highest.

Father Almighty, Lord of heaven and earth,
your mighty works reveal your wisdom
and love.
You created us in your image.
You gave us the whole world to care for
so that in obedience to you, our Creator,
we might rule and serve all your creatures.
In your mercy, when we disobeyed and
turned from you,
you did not abandon us to the power of
death.
You provided a means of salvation for us.
Again and again, through the prophets,
the law, the saints, and angels,
you taught us to hope for salvation.

In the fullness of time,
you sent your only Son to be our Saviour.
Incarnate of Mary, the Virgin,
he became one of us yet without sin.
He proclaimed the good news of salvation,
and taught us how to know you, the true
God.
In fulfilment of your will,
he gave himself up to death on the cross;
and, rising from the grave, he destroyed
death and restored life, and made the
whole creation new.
He ascended into heaven,
and sent the Holy Spirit from you, Father,
as his first gift to those who believe,
to complete his work on earth,
and bring us the fullness of grace.

[rubric re manual acts in footnote 67 on p. 95 above]

When the time had come for him
to be glorified by you, his heavenly Father,

having loved those who were his own in
the world,
he showed them the depth of his love.
While they were at supper, he took bread,
and when he had given thanks to you,
he broke it and gave it to his disciples, and
said,
'Take, eat: This is my Body, which is given
for you.
Do this for the remembrance of me.'

After supper, he took the cup of wine,
and when he had given thanks to you,
he gave it to them and said,
'Drink this, all of you: This is my Blood of
the new covenant,
which is shed for you and for many for the
forgiveness of sins.
Whenever you drink it, do this for the
remembrance of me.'

Let us proclaim . . . [CF 6(a)] . . . **come**
again.

Father, we now celebrate the memorial of
our redemption;
recalling Christ's death, his descent among
the dead,
his resurrection and ascension to heaven,
where he sits at your right hand;
and, looking forward to his coming in
glory,
we offer you this bread and wine.
For all your blessings,
we praise you, we bless you,
we pray to you, Lord our God.

Father, we pray that your Holy Spirit
may descend upon us and upon these gifts
that they may become the Bread of Life
and the Cup of Salvation,
the Body and Blood of your Son Jesus
Christ.

May all who share this bread and cup
be united with one another
in the fellowship of the one Holy Spirit,
to the praise of your glorious Name.

We pray for your one, holy, catholic,
and apostolic Church, redeemed by the
blood of Christ.
Reveal its unity, guard its faith, and
preserve it in peace.
[Remember N. N. and all who minister in
your Church.]

[Remember all your people, and all who seek your truth.]
[Remember _____.]
[Remember all who have died in the peace of Christ, especially N.;
bring them into the place of eternal joy and light.]

In your mercy, may we find our
  inheritance with all your saints
(with blessed _____) who have found
  favour with you in ages past.
Grant that, in union with them,
we may praise and glorify your Name;
Through Christ, and with Christ, and in
  Christ,
all honour and glory are yours, Almighty
  God and Father,
in the unity of the Holy Spirit, forever and
  ever. **Amen.**

18. *The Lord's Prayer*
    As our Saviour Christ has taught us, we now pray,
    Our Father in heaven . . . ⟦ELLC 1⟧ . . . for ever. Amen.

THE BREAKING OF BREAD

19. *The Celebrant may say:*
    Lord, we ask you to deliver us from evil,
    and to grant peace in our time.
    In your mercy, keep us free from sin
    and safe from anxiety
    as we await in joyful hope
    the coming of our Lord and Saviour Jesus Christ. **Amen.**

    The Celebrant breaks the consecrated Bread, saying:
    Broken is the Lamb of God, broken but not divided;
    ever eaten yet never consumed,
    sanctifying all who partake of it. **Amen.**

20. *Then one of the following anthems is sung:*
    1. (Alleluia) Christ our Passover is sacrificed for us:
       Therefore let us keep the feast. (Alleluia)
    2. Lamb of God . . . ⟦ELLC 9(b)⟧ . . . **Grant us your peace.**
    3. ⟦Anthem based on John 6.55⟧
    4. ⟦Anthem based on John 6.51 and 1 Cor. 10.17⟧
    5. ⟦Anthem based on Luke 24.35 and 1 Cor. 10.16–17⟧

21. *There is a period of silence. The people and celebrant may say the following:*
    We do not presume to come to your table . . . ⟦CF 3(a) slightly altered⟧ . . . drink his blood,
    that being renewed and strengthened by his risen life,
    we may evermore dwell in him, and he in us. Amen.

THE HOLY COMMUNION

22. The gifts of God for the people of God.
    The following may be added:
    Take them in remembrance that Christ died for you,
    and feed on him in your hearts by faith with thanksgiving.

23. *The Celebrant receives communion in both kinds, and then delivers them to the people with these words:*
    The Body of Christ, the bread of heaven. **Amen.**
    The Blood of Christ, the cup of salvation. **Amen.**
    or
    The Body (Blood) of our Lord Jesus Christ keep you in eternal life. **Amen.**

24. *If the consecrated elements do not suffice for the communicants, the Celebrant consecrates more of either or both by saying again the words of the eucharistic prayer and ending with the invocation, or may use the following form:*

Hear us, O heavenly Father, and with your Word and Holy Spirit bless and sanctify this bread (wine) that it, also, may be the Sacrament of the precious Body (Blood) of your Son Jesus Christ our Lord, who took bread (the cup) and said: 'This is my Body (Blood).'

THE CONCLUDING RITE

25. *After the Communion, all stand and the Celebrant says:*

Let us pray.
Eternal God, heavenly Father,
we thank you because you have accepted us
as living members of the Body of your Son Jesus Christ,
and have nourished us with the Sacrament of his victorious life.
May we be bread broken and given for the world,
may your love in us heal the wounds we have made,
may your words on our lips speak peace to all people.
Send us with vision and courage
to love and serve your Son Jesus Christ in his brethren.
So will your Name be praised and glorified, now and in time to come,
until all be fulfilled in your kingdom. Amen.

or

Almighty and eternal God,
now that we have partaken of the banquet
you have prepared for us in the world to come,
may we all one day share in the life of your heavenly city,
through Jesus Christ your Son, our Lord,
who lives and reigns with you,
in the unity of the Holy Spirit,
one God, world without end. Amen.

26. *Celebrant may bless the people, using an appropriate form provided from page . . . and following.*

27. THE DISMISSAL [led by the deacon]
Go in peace to love and serve the Lord.
Thanks be to God.
or
Go forth in the Name of Christ.
Thanks be to God.
or
Go out and bear witness to Christ rejoicing in the power of the Spirit.
Thanks be to God.
or
Go in the strength of the food and drink of your pilgrimage in joy and gladness.
Thanks be to God.

From the Easter Vigil through the Day of Pentecost, 'Alleluia, alleluia' is added to the Dismissal and to the response of the people.

28. OCCASIONAL POST-COMMUNION PRAYERS
[Prayers for use at marriage, ministration to the sick, burial and ordination]

29. BLESSINGS [Proper blessings for ten seasons and occasions with three for 'ordinary time', including CF 12(a)]

28. The Anglican Church of Korea

The Anglican Church of Korea became a province of the Anglican Communion in 1993, but it already had a long history of a liturgical independence and the provision of its own eucharistic rites. The diocese authorized its own Korean-language rite in 1939, and this was published in **LiE**, coded as **Kor**.[87] The text was included in a complete Korean BCP in 1965. A revised eucharistic text in 1973 was printed in **FAL**, coded as **Kor1**, and some adjustments to that in 1982 were printed in **LAL**, coded as **Kor1A**.[88] With the coming of the province a project developed for a new Prayer Book in a contemporary style. The Book was adopted in 2004, and replaced existing rites.

The eucharistic rites were compiled in Korean, and have not previously been available in English. The first, coded here as **Kor2**, gives a range of choices at most stages; the second, coded as **Kor3**, provides a single shorter route through the liturgical provision; but much of the material is interchangeable between the two rites. The eucharistic prayers do not appear to exhibit much relationship to the threefold prayer in **Kor1**, and most are determinedly western in their epiclesis, though Form 3 (like one of the three strands in **Kor1**) is interestingly eastern.

THE EUCHARIST 'RITE 1' FROM THE ANGLICAN CHURCH OF KOREA PRAYER BOOK, 2004 (Kor2)

⟦The translation is that of Br Christopher John SSF and Nak-Hyon Joo, with reference to the English-language text used by Paul Mooney, ministering in English in Seoul. The translation has been done for this collection, with a view to faithfulness to the original rather than liturgical smoothness. The numbering is original to the translation. The lining is largely editorial.⟧

---

87 The first known translation of **Kor** was that provided to Bernard Wigan for **LiE**, but the text used in the first edition of **LiE** (1962) was then declared defective, and an improved translation was included in the second edition in 1964.

88 Nak-Hyon Joo, in his excellent chapter about Korea in *The Oxford Guide*, allocates **Kor1** to 1982. As, however, the rite he describes seems to be the text of 1973 which was published in **FAL** in 1975 (and he makes no reference to a rite of 1973), the **FAL** dating should stand, and it is **Kor1A** (as in **LAL**) which is allocated to 1982.

INTRODUCTORY NOTES

⟦13 introductory notes provide for the relevant roles of presbyters, deacons and laity in the service, and give guidance re vesture, posture and ceremonial. Two are printed here in full.⟧

11. *If there is insufficient consecrated bread, extra may be consecrated by repeating the consecratory words marked with a ✠ in the eucharistic prayer. But this way of consecration cannot be used outside the eucharist.*

12. *If there is any consecrated bread remaining after holy communion, it is consumed either during or after the eucharist. But the consecrated bread may be kept in a tabernacle in preparation for church members unable to participate in the eucharist because of sickness, or for places without a priest.*

Liturgy of the Eucharist – Rite 1

OPENING

1. *Entrance: An opening hymn may be sung as the presider and the procession enter. If there is no entrance procession a suitable hymn may be sung.*

2. *Opening Prayer*
Let us pray: Almighty God . . . ⟦CF 1⟧ . . . Christ our Lord. **Amen.**

3. *Confession of sin*
The presider uses the following sentence or some other suitable to the season. The Ten Commandments may be used, or may be omitted, according to circumstances.
My brothers and sisters, as we prepare to celebrate this holy communion in a fitting manner, let us be at peace with one another and humbly confess our sins.

⟦Pause for reflection, congregational confession, and presidential absolution (akin to CF 2)⟧

4. *Invocational Anthem*
The presider may use one of the following Invocational Anthems according to the intention of the worship. ⟦Directions concerning which anthem at which season⟧
1) *Kyrie Eleison* ⟦text of ELLC 2 sixfold in vernacular or Greek⟧
2) *Trisagion* ⟦text of Trisagion said responsively⟧
3) *Come to Us* ⟦text of short responsive anthem⟧
4) *Gloria in Excelsis*
Glory to God . . . ⟦ELLC 3, set out responsively for first half, then congregationally⟧
. . . **God the Father. Amen.**
God's people] his people

THE LITURGY OF THE WORD

5. *The Collect of the Day*
The Lord be with you
And also with you.

After the response there may be some appropriate greeting or explanation of the intention of the worship.
Let us pray: *The collect of the day*

6. *The First Reading* ⟦Announcement at beginning, proclamation and response at end⟧

    A psalm or hymn may follow the reading.

7. *The Second Reading*   *If there is a second reading the format follows that of the first reading.* ⟦then as §6⟧

    A psalm or hymn may follow the reading.

8. *The Gospel Acclamation*   *Before the gospel reading there may be an acclamation.* ⟦'Alleluias' are set out with provision for seasonal variants⟧

9. *The Gospel Reading* ⟦Salutation, announcement and response at beginning, proclamation and response at end⟧

    All sit for a short time of reflection on the gospel reading.

10. *The Sermon*

11. *The Confession of Faith*
    One of either the Nicene Creed or Apostles' Creed may be chosen. On Sundays and greater feast days the Nicene Creed is recommended. The Nicene Creed may be read antiphonally between the presider and the congregation.
    1) *The Nicene Creed*
        We believe in one God . . . ⟦ELLC 5, set out responsively⟧ . . . **world to come. Amen.**
            [and the Son]] OMIT BRACKETS
    2) *The Apostles' Creed*
        I believe **in God** . . . ⟦ELLC 4⟧ . . . **life everlasting. Amen.**

    The presider may announce pastoral notices here

12. *Prayers for the Church and the World*
    ⟦Three forms of intercessory prayer interspersed with versicles and responses⟧

THE LITURGY OF HOLY COMMUNION

13. *The Greeting of Peace*
    The presider may select either the following sentence, or some other suitable for the season.
    You together are the body of Christ and each is one of its members. Christ sacrificed himself that there may be peace. Let us be united in God.
    The peace of the Lord be always with you.
    And also with you.
    Let us share with one another the blessing of peace.

14. *The Offertory*
    During the offertory a hymn may be sung. After the offering is prepared either the following or some other sentence suitable for the season is said.
    Everything comes from God,
    and we offer to God what we have already received from God.
    Lord, may these gifts be used to proclaim your gospel throughout the world. **Amen.**

    When the things for holy communion are prepared, the presider offers the eucharistic prayer.

15. The Eucharistic Prayer

Eucharistic Prayer – Form 1

The Lord . . . ⟦ELLC 6⟧ . . . **and praise.**

Almighty God, it is right and our joy
at all times and in all places
to give you thanks and praise
through Jesus Christ, our Lord.

The seasonal preface follows here.

Therefore with all the angels and saints in
   heaven,
we lift our voices
to praise your holy and glorious name,
Holy, Holy . . . ⟦ELLC 7⟧ . . . in the highest!
Blessed is . . . ⟦ELLC 8) . . . in the highest!

All glory to you, almighty God;
who in your tender mercy
sent your only Son Jesus Christ to this
   world
to hang on the cross for our redemption;
making in his body one perfect sacrificial
   offering
to take away the sins of the world,
and who instituted and commanded us to
   follow
the offering of this holy communion
that we might remember his precious
   death
until he comes again.

Hear our prayer, merciful God,
and sanctify for us by the ✠ Holy Spirit
this bread and wine
that the mystery of salvation
which our Lord Jesus commanded
may be fulfilled.

Christ, on the evening before he suffered,
took bread and after offering a prayer of
   thanksgiving;
broke it and gave it to his disciples saying,
'Take, eat: this is my body which is given
   for you;

do this in remembrance of me.'

He also took the cup,
and after offering a prayer of thanksgiving,
gave it to the disciples saying,
'Drink this,
this is my blood of the new covenant,
which is shed for you and for many
for the forgiveness of sins.
Whenever you drink it,
do this in remembrance of me.'

We proclaim the mystery of faith:
Christ has . . . ⟦CF 6(a)⟧ . . . come again.

Therefore, recalling the passion, death,
resurrection and ascension of Jesus Christ,
and until his coming again,
we offer you this bread and wine
as our sacrifice of praise and thanksgiving.

We earnestly beseech you, Lord God,
to accept this our wholehearted offering of
   thanksgiving,
and to make your whole church obtain the
   grace of salvation
by the merits of the passion and death
of our Lord Jesus Christ.
Send your Holy Spirit
to all those who receive this bread of life
   and cup of salvation
to share the heavenly blessings,
and to make our bodies and souls
an acceptable living sacrifice unto God
and also to make all of us
become one body with Jesus Christ.

Through Christ, with whom, and in
   whom,
in the unity of the Holy Spirit,
all honour and glory are yours,
almighty God, for ever and ever. **Amen.**

Eucharistic Prayer – Form 2

The Lord . . . [ELLC 6] . . . **and praise.**

Almighty God, it is right and our joy
at all times and in all places
to give you thanks and praise
through Jesus Christ, our Lord.

The seasonal preface follows here

And so with all the angels and saints in
    heaven,
we lift our voices
to praise your holy and glorious name:
Holy, Holy . . . [ELLC 7] . . . **in the highest!**
Blessed is . . . [ELLC 8) . . . **in the highest!**

God of love, by your word you created
    this world
and from your love for all your creatures
you sent your only Son Jesus Christ to this
    earth;
by his death on the cross and his
    resurrection
you opened up for us the way of salvation.

As we follow the word of the Lord
and offer this sacrifice of thanks and
    praise,
send your Holy Spirit upon this bread and
    wine,
and grant that it may become
the sacrament of the new covenant
of the body and blood of ✠ Jesus Christ.

On the night that he was arrested,
Christ took bread and after offering a
    prayer of thanksgiving,
broke it and gave it to the disciples
saying, 'Take, eat: this is my body
which is given for you;
do this in remembrance of me.'

He also took the cup,
and after offering a prayer of thanksgiving,
gave it to the disciples saying,
'Drink this, this is my blood of the new
    covenant,
which is shed for you and for many
for the forgiveness of sins.
Whenever you drink it,
do this in remembrance of me.'

Therefore, Lord, we offer before you
this bread of life and cup of salvation;
we remember Jesus Christ's offering of
    himself
made once for all upon the cross;
and until he comes again in glory
we proclaim the death and resurrection of
    Christ.
By the death of Christ, death is no more;
**By the resurrection of Christ, new life is
    won;**
Lord Jesus, come again in glory!

Lord of life, assist us we beseech you,
to gather the strength
to practise justice and mercy in this world
until the coming of the kingdom of God.
Look again with grace upon your people
and gather us in the bosom of your love
so that we can come together
with all your saints (especially N.)
at the eternal heavenly feast.

Through Christ,
with whom, and in whom,
in the unity of the Holy Spirit,
all honour and glory are yours,
Almighty God, for ever and ever.
Amen.

Eucharistic Prayer – Form 3

The Lord . . . [ELLC 6] . . . **and praise.**

Almighty God, it is right and our joy
at all times and in all places
to give you thanks and praise
through Jesus Christ, our Lord.

The seasonal preface follows here

And so with all the angels and saints in
heaven,
we lift our voices
to praise your holy and glorious name:
Holy, Holy . . . [ELLC 7] . . . **in the highest!**
Blessed is . . . [ELLC 8) . . . **in the highest!**

You are holy, almighty creator God.
You are holy, our saviour, Jesus Christ.
You are holy, life-giving Holy Spirit.

You made humankind in your image
so that they could be holy,
but they fell to sin.
In your great love, your only Son Jesus
Christ
was born of the Virgin Mary,
so that whoever believes in him
would not perish but receive eternal life
and live in the hope of resurrection.

On the night that he was arrested,
Christ took bread and after offering a
prayer of thanksgiving,
he blessed the bread, broke it
and gave it to the disciples saying,
'Take, eat: this is my body which is given
for you;
do this in remembrance of me.'
He also took the cup,
and after offering a prayer of thanksgiving,
gave it to the disciples saying,
'Drink this, this is my blood of the new
covenant,
which is shed for you and for many
for the forgiveness of sins.

Whenever you drink it,
do this in remembrance of me.'

Therefore, we remember God the Son,
Jesus Christ,
who died for us, was buried,
rose after three days, ascended to heaven,
is seated at the right hand of God the
Father,
and who will come again in glory,
and we offer this thanksgiving offering,
praying that you receive it with joy.

Lord, accept this bloodless offering
as a suitable sacrifice
and send your ✠ Holy Spirit on us and this
offering,
that this bread and wine may be for us
Christ's precious body and blood.
Forgive the sins of those who receive this
sacrament,
that they may come before you with a pure
heart.

We humbly beseech you,
remember all the bishops, priests and
deacons of your holy church,
that they may properly preserve and teach
your word.
Grant that all the faithful who serve you
may receive your mercy, and praise you
with one heart.
Remember those who rest
in the hope of eternal life and salvation
(especially *N.*),
that they may come to the joy of eternal
rest in your light.

Through Christ, with whom, and in
whom,
in the unity of the Holy Spirit,
all honour and glory are yours,
Almighty God, for ever and ever.
Amen.

Eucharistic prayer – Form 4

The Lord . . . [ELLC 6] . . . and praise.

God the Father, our one true God,
it is right and proper and our joy,
always and everywhere,
to offer you thanks and praise.

From the beginning of the world
you dwelt eternally in unapproachable
   light
as the spring of life and the source of all
   goodness.
You cared for all things
and filled them with your blessing,
so that they delighted
to live in your marvellous light.

Therefore, the countless angels of heaven
serve you day and night,
and, in that light seeing your face,
they praise you without ceasing.
We with them and all things under heaven
lift our voices
to praise your holy and glorious name:
Holy, Holy . . . [ELLC 7] . . . in the highest!
Blessed is . . . [ELLC 8) . . . in the highest!

Holy God of mighty, glorious power,
you created all things in your wisdom and
   love,
and made us in your image.
You asked us to live in obedience to you
and to take care of all things.
In our disobedience we went far from you
but you did not abandon us to death,
and in your great love gave us Jesus Christ
born of the Virgin Mary by your Holy
   Spirit.

Jesus Christ came to this world,
giving good news of redemption to the
   poor,
freedom to the imprisoned and joy to the
   sad.
In obedience to you he gave himself up to
   death,
vanquished death by rising from the tomb
and renewed all things in this world.

While Jesus Christ was with the disciples
   at the last supper,
you, God the Father, glorified him.
He took bread, and after offering you a
   prayer of thanksgiving,
gave it to them, saying:

'Take, eat: this is my body
which is given for you;
do this in remembrance of me.'

He took the cup,
and after offering a prayer of thanksgiving,
gave it to them, saying:
'Take, drink: this is my blood of the new
   covenant,
shed for you and for many
for the forgiveness of sins.
Whenever you drink it,
do this in remembrance of me.'

Therefore, in doing this we remember
   Christ's death,
and proclaim his resurrection and
   ascension
to the right hand of God the Father.
We await his coming again in glory,
and offer you this bread and wine
in memory of our salvation.

Lord, by your goodness and mercy,
send your Holy Spirit upon us and this
   offering
to make it ✠ holy; Jesus Christ's body and
   blood for your people,
and the bread of life and cup of salvation.
May all who share these holy gifts
be of one heart and one body in Christ,
and be one holy living offering.

We earnestly beseech you,
remember your one, holy and apostolic
   church,
saved by the blood of Christ;
keep our faith, make us show the unity of
   the church
and preserve it in peace.
Remember all those who belong to your
   body the church,
and grant that with the Blessed Virgin
   Mary and all the saints,
they may receive your heavenly
   inheritance,
and, united with them
in the name of our Lord Jesus Christ,
may forever praise your name.

Through Christ, with whom, and in whom,
in the unity of the Holy Spirit,
all honour and glory are yours,
Almighty God, for ever and ever.
Amen.

16. *The Lord's Prayer*
As our Saviour Christ has taught us, we pray:
Our Father in heaven . . . ⟦ELLC 1⟧ . . . now and for ever. Amen.

17. *The Breaking of the Consecrated Bread*
We break this bread to share in the body of Christ.
We differ from one another,
but sharing in the one bread,
we become one body.

Silence may be kept while the bread is broken.

Agnus Dei
Lamb of God . . . ⟦ELLC 9(b)⟧ . . . grant us peace.

18. *Communion*
After breaking the bread the presider says the following invitation
Behold the Lamb of God who takes . . . ⟦CF 9(b)⟧ . . . **and I shall be healed.**

The presider receives the consecrated bread, saying 'May the sacred body and precious blood
of Christ keep me in eternal life.'
While sharing the consecrated bread and wine the following is said:
The sacred body of Christ. **Amen.**
The precious blood of Christ. **Amen.**

19. *Post Communion Prayer*
The presider selects the following or some other post communion prayer chosen for the
season:
Let us pray.
Almighty God, we thank you
that by feeding us with the spiritual food
of Christ's sacred body and precious blood
you have made us one with the body of Christ.
We earnestly beseech you, by your Holy Spirit,
help us in your love to be in communion with each other,
and serve you as you have commanded.
We pray this in the name of our Lord Jesus Christ.
Amen.

SENDING OUT

20. *The Blessing*
The Lord be with you.
And also with you.
The presider may choose a different blessing prayer, depending on the season.
May the eternal peace of God be with you,
may you remain in the love of Christ
and may the blessing . . . ⟦CF 12(a)⟧ . . . be with you. **Amen.**

21. *The Dismissal*
The presider chooses one of the following dismissals:
  1) Let us go out and proclaim the gospel of the Lord.
  2) Let us go out and make the peace of the Lord.
  3) Let us go out and share the love of the Lord.
     In the name of Christ. Amen.
⟦Provision to use 'proclaim the Lord's resurrection' and add Alleluias in Easter⟧

A dismissal hymn may be sung.

THE EUCHARIST 'RITE 2' FROM THE ANGLICAN CHURCH OF KOREA PRAYER BOOK, 2004 (Kor3)

⟦The translation is that of Br Christopher John SSF and Nak-Hyon Joo.
The numbering is original to the translation. The lining is largely editorial.⟧

Liturgy of the Eucharist – Rite 2

Opening

1. *Entrance*
   An opening hymn may be sung as the presider and the procession enter the church. If there is no entrance procession a suitable hymn may be sung.

2. *Confession of Sin*
   Brothers and sisters, as we prepare to celebrate this eucharist in a fitting manner, let us confess our sins.
   ⟦Pause for reflection, one-line biddings to confess, Kyrie responses and a brief absolution⟧

The Liturgy of the Word

3. *The Collect of the Day*
   The Lord be with you.
   And also with you.
   After the response there may be some appropriate greeting or explanation of the intention of the worship.
   Let us pray.
   The collect of the day

4. *The Reading(s)*
   One of either an Old Testament or New Testament reading, or both.
   ⟦Announcement at beginning, proclamation and response after⟧
   A psalm or hymn may follow the reading.

5. *The Gospel Reading*
   The Lord be with you.
   And also with you.
   ⟦Announcement and response at beginning, proclamation and response after⟧

6. *The Sermon*

7. *Prayers for the Church and the World*
   ⟦One responsive prayer, 'Form 4', suggesting interchangeability with the three in **Kor2**⟧

The Liturgy of Holy Communion

8. *The Greeting of Peace*
   The presider may select either the following sentence, or some other.
   Christ is our peace; through the cross he made us one.
   We gather in the Lord's name to share his peace.
   The peace of the Lord be always with you.
   And also with you.
   Let us share with one another the blessing of peace.

9. *The Offertory*
   During the offertory a hymn may be sung. After the offering is prepared the following sentence is said.
   We give thanks for all the Lord has given us in this land
   and ask God to receive our offering with joy.
   We pray this in the name of our Lord Jesus Christ.
   Amen.

10. *The Eucharistic Prayer*
     [As this is 'Form 5', it would appear to be interchangeable with the four prayers in **Kor2**]

Eucharistic Prayer – Form 5

The Lord . . . [ELLC 6] . . . **and praise.**

Almighty God, we thank you
that you made this world with your great
  love
and sent your only Son Jesus Christ
as a perfect sacrifice to save humanity
who had fallen into sin.

May the Holy Spirit ✠ sanctify this bread
  and wine
we offer with thanksgiving
that it may be for us the body and blood
  of Christ.

The Lord, on the evening before he suffered,
took bread and after offering a prayer of
  thanksgiving,
broke it and gave it to the disciples
saying, 'Take, eat:
this is my body which is given for you;
do this in remembrance of me.'

He also took the cup,
and after offering a prayer of thanksgiving,
gave it to the disciples saying,

'Drink this, this is my blood of the new
  covenant,
which is shed for you and for many
for the forgiveness of sins.
Whenever you drink it,
do this in remembrance of me.'

Therefore, remembering Christ's passion
  and resurrection
we offer you this bread and wine
until the Lord comes again.

We earnestly beseech you
to send your Holy Spirit on us
who receive this bread of life and cup of
  salvation,
that we may be one body with our Lord
  Jesus Christ
and a living sacrifice of praise and
  thanksgiving.

Through Christ, with whom, and in whom,
in the unity of the Holy Spirit,
all honour and glory are yours,
Almighty God, for ever and ever.
Amen.

11. *The Lord's Prayer*
     As our Saviour Christ has taught us, we pray:
     Our Father . . . [ELLC 1] . . . now and for ever. Amen.

12. *The Breaking of the Consecrated Bread and the Holy Communion*
     We break this bread to share in the body of Christ.
     We differ one from another, but sharing in the one bread, we become one body.
     After breaking the bread the presider says the following invitation.
     Come with a believing heart,
     and receive with thanks the sacred body and precious blood of Jesus Christ. **Amen.**
     The presider receives the consecrated bread first, then it is shared in the ordinary way.

13. *Post Communion Prayer*
     Almighty God . . . [as **Kor2**, §19] . . . as you have commanded. **Amen.**

Sending Out

14. *The Blessing*
     The Lord be with you.
     And also with you.
     May the eternal peace . . . [as **Kor2**, §20] . . . be with you. **Amen.**

15. *The Dismissal*
     Let us go out and proclaim the gospel of the Lord.
     In the name of Christ, Amen.
     A dismissal hymn may be sung.

     [Appendices of Ten Commandments and Propers]

29. The Holy Catholic Church of Japan (Nippon Sei Ko Kai)

Nippon Sei Ko Kai has had its own vernacular Prayer Book, drawn by translation from English and American sources, since 1895. Its first truly Japanese Book, compiled in Japan by its own liturgical scholars, was authorized in 1959, and its eucharistic rite appears in **LiE** as **Jap**. A long essay in **MAL** indicated the problems the Book was already setting the Church in that the Japanese language used was in 'classic literary style'. In 1971 the General Synod called for a wholesale revision of the Book, and this was finally brought to pass in 1990. Its key feature is that it employs 'modern colloquial Japanese'.[89] The eucharistic rite follows the general pattern of Anglican rites, and has two eucharistic prayers, one adopted almost verbatim from the First Eucharistic Prayer in **EngA**, the other drawn from Hippolytus, though with reference to latterday embellishments of it. The rite is presented here as **Jap1**.

The Holy Eucharist
According to the Use of the Nippon Sei Ko Kai 1990 (Jap1)

[The translation here is unofficial, but is supplied by Shintaro Ichihara, a member of the NSKK Liturgical Commission. The numbering here is editorial; the lining is original.]

THE ENTRANCE

1. *All stand. Here a hymn may be sung as the priest and choir enter.*

2. Come, Lord Jesus Christ.
   Show yourself to us as once you revealed
   your risen self to the disciples,
   among whom you stood after your resurrection.

3. *Prayer of Preparation*
   Let us pray.
   Almighty God, to whom . . . [CF 1] . . . through Jesus Christ our Lord. **Amen.**

4. *Use one of the following three.*
   [i] Glory to the Father and to the Son, and to the Holy Spirit:
   as it was beginning is now and shall be for ever. Amen.
   [ii] *The following is then said or sung three times:*
   Lord, have mercy . . . [ELLC 2, in vernacular or Greek] . . . Kyrie eleison.
   [iii] Praise God the Father almighty,
   Praise the Son Lord Jesus Christ,
   Praise the Holy Spirit who dwells among us,
   as it is now and shall be for ever. Amen.

---

89 The phrases 'classic literary style' and 'modern colloquial Japanese' are direct quotes from the chapter by John M. Yoshido in Hefling and Shattuck (eds), *The Oxford Guide to the Book of Common Prayer*.

5. *Gloria in Excelsis*
   On Sundays and Principal Holy Days the Gloria in Excelsis is used, except on days in Advent and Lent.
   Glory to God in the highest . . . ⟦ELLC 3⟧ . . . **glory of God the Father. Amen.**
   God's people] his people

6. *The Collect for the Day*
   The Lord be with you.
   And also with you.
   Let us pray.   *The Priest says the Collect for the Day, and people respond*   **Amen.**

THE LITURGY OF THE WORD

7. Let us hear the Word of the Scripture.   *All sit*

   THE OLD TESTAMENT ⟦with announcement before and proclamation and response after⟧

8. THE PSALM   *Here a psalm is sung or read.*

9. THE EPISTLE ⟦with announcement before and proclamation and response after⟧

10. *All stand*   *Here a Gradual or a hymn may be sung.*

11. THE GOSPEL   *All face the Gospeller* ⟦with salutation, announcement and response before and *proclamation and response after⟧

12. *All sit*   THE SERMON

13. *Here the Priest gives notices of forthcoming services, teachings of the Bishop, banns of marriage, and other information.*

14. *All stand*   THE NICENE CREED   *On Sundays and Principal Holy Days the Nicene Creed is used.*
    We believe in one God, . . . ⟦ELLC 5⟧ . . . **the life of the world to come. Amen.**
    incarnate of] **incarnate from**
    became truly human] was made man
    [and the Son]] OMIT BRACKETS

15. *PRAYERS OF INTERCESSION*   *All stand*   ⟦A single form with regular versicle and response⟧

16. *PRAYER OF PENITENCE* ⟦Call to penitence, then kneel, with the priest confessing in the presence of the people and being absolved by them, and the people confessing in the presence of the priest and being absolved by the priest⟧

THE LITURGY OF THE SACRAMENT

17. THE PEACE   *All stand*
    The Peace of the Lord be always with you.
    And also with you.
    Let us greet one another in Peace.
    All may exchange a sign of peace, and saying; The peace of the Lord. (Shu no Heiwa)

18. *THE OFFERTORY*
    Let us offer our gifts to the Lord, rendering him the glory which is proper to his name.
    An offertory hymn is sung and the collection taken. Representatives of the people bring bread, wine and offerings to the Priest. After the collection is offered, the priest may say . . .
    Heavenly Father, accept these gifts that they may be used for your holy work.
    All things come from you, O Lord,
    and we offer to you only what we have received from you. Amen.

19. *THE THANKSGIVING AND CONSECRATION*
    Priest uses one of the two Eucharistic Prayers which follow. Kneel

20. *First Eucharistic Prayer*

The Lord be . . . ⟦ELLC 6⟧ . . . **him thanks and praise.**

It is indeed right,
it is our duty and our joy,
at all times and in all places
to give you thanks and praise,
holy Father, almighty and eternal God,
through Jesus Christ your only Son our
  Lord.

For he is your living Word;
through him you have created all things
  from the beginning,
and formed us in your own image.

Through him you have freed us from the
  slavery of sin,
giving him to be born as man and to die
  upon the cross;
you raised him from the dead
and exalted him to your right hand on
  high.

Through him you have sent upon us
your holy and life-giving Spirit,
and made us a royal priesthood
called to serve you for ever.

Here the Proper Preface may be said or sung

Therefore with angels and archangels,
and with all the company of heaven,
we proclaim your great and glorious name,
for ever praising you and saying:
Holy, holy . . . ⟦ELLC 7⟧ . . . in the highest.
This Anthem may also be used.
Blessed is . . . ⟦ELLC 8⟧ . . . in the highest.

Accept our praises, heavenly Father,
through your Son our Saviour Jesus Christ;
and as we follow his example and obey his
  command,
grant that by the power of your Holy
  Spirit
these gifts of bread and wine
may be to us his body and blood;

Who in the same night that he was
  betrayed,

took bread and gave you thanks;
he broke it and gave it to his disciples,
  saying,
Take, eat; this is my body which is given
  for you;
do this in remembrance of me.
In the same way, after supper
he took the cup and gave you thanks;
he gave it to them, saying,
Drink this, all of you;
this is my blood of the new covenant,
which is shed for you and for many for the
  forgiveness of sins.
Do this as often as you drink it,
in remembrance of me.
Christ has . . . ⟦CF 6(a)⟧ . . . come again.

Therefore, heavenly Father,
we remember his offering of himself
made once for all upon the cross,
and proclaim his mighty resurrection
  and glorious ascension.
As we look for his coming in glory,
we celebrate with this bread and this cup
his one perfect sacrifice.
Accept through him, our great high priest,
this our sacrifice of thanks and praise;
and as we eat and drink these holy gifts
in the presence of your divine majesty,
renew us by your Spirit,
inspire us with your love,
and unite us in the church which is the
  body of your Son, Jesus Christ our Lord.

Together with the whole company of
  heaven,
may we for ever praise your holy name.
**To him who by the power at work within
  us
is able to do far more abundantly
than all that we ask or think,
to him be glory in the church and Christ
  Jesus
to all generations, for ever and ever.
Amen.**

21. Second Eucharistic Prayer

The Lord be . . . [ELLC 6] . . . **him thanks
and praise.**

We give you thanks, Father most holy,
through your beloved Son, Jesus Christ,
your Word through whom you made all
   things,
whom you sent as our Saviour and
   Redeemer,
incarnate by the Holy Spirit and born of
   the Virgin.
Fulfilling your will and gaining for you a
   holy people,
he stretched out his hands as he endured
   his Passion,
so as to break the bonds of death and
   manifest the resurrection.

Therefore with angels and archangels,
and with all the company of heaven,
we proclaim your great and glorious name,
for ever praising you and saying:
Holy, holy . . . [ELLC 7] . . . **in the highest.**
This anthem may also be used.
Blessed is . . . [ELLC 8] . . . **in the highest.**

We give thanks to you, God,
through your beloved Son Jesus Christ,
whom you sent to us in former times
as Saviour, Redeemer, and Messenger of
   your Will,
who is your inseparable Word,
through whom you made all,
and in whom you were well-pleased,
whom you sent from heaven into the
   womb of a virgin,
who, being conceived within her, was
   made flesh,
and appeared as your Son,
born of the Holy Spirit and the virgin.
It is he who, fulfilling your will
and acquiring for you a holy people,
extended his hands in suffering,
in order to liberate from sufferings
those who believe in you.
Who, when he was delivered to voluntary
   suffering,

in order to dissolve death,
and break the chains of the devil,
and tread down hell,
and bring the just to the light,
and set the limit,
and manifest the resurrection,
at the time he was betrayed
and entered willingly into his Passion,
took bread and gave you thanks;
he broke it and gave it to his disciples,
   saying,
Take, eat; this is my body which is given
   for you;
do this in remembrance of me.
In the same way, after supper
he took the cup and gave you thanks;
he gave it to them, saying,
Drink this, all of you;
this is my blood of the new covenant,
which is shed for you and for many for the
   forgiveness of sins.
Do this as often as you drink it,
in remembrance of me.
Christ has . . . [CF 6(a)] . . . **come again.**

Therefore, remembering his death,
   resurrection and ascension,
we offer to you the bread and the cup,
giving thanks to you, who has made us
   worthy
to stand before you and to serve as your
   priests.
In their gathering together,
give to all those who partake of your holy
   mysteries the fullness of the Holy Spirit,
toward the strengthening of the faith in
   truth,
that we may praise you and glorify you,
through your Son Jesus Christ,
**through whom to you be glory and
   honour,
Father and Son,
with the Holy Spirit,
in your Holy Church,
now and throughout the ages of the ages.
Amen.**

The Communion

23. As our Saviour Christ has taught us, we are confident to say,
    Our Father in heaven . . . ⟦ELLC 1⟧ . . . and for ever. Amen.
    Save us from the time of trial and] Lead us not into temptation but

24. *The priest breaks the bread and says:*
    When we break the bread,
    We partake of the Body of Christ.
    We who are many are one body in Christ,
    for we all share in the one bread.

25. *All may use the following prayer*
    We do not presume . . . ⟦CF 3(a)⟧ . . . in Christ and he in us. Amen.
    our sinful . . . most precious blood] our sinful bodies and souls may be made clean
    by Christ's precious Body and Blood,

26. *The following hymn may be said or sung.*
    Lamb of God . . . ⟦ELLC 9(b)⟧ . . . grant us your peace.

27. *Then the priest and the communicants receive the Sacrament. The following words are said
    to each at the distribution and each responds, saying 'Amen'.*
    The Body of our Lord Jesus Christ, which is given for you. **Amen.**
    The Blood of our Lord Jesus Christ, which is shed for you. **Amen.**

28. *During the Communion, an anthem may be sung, followed by a post-Communion hymn.*

Post-Communion

29. *Kneel*
    Let us pray.
    Almighty and everliving God, we thank you for feeding us
    with the precious body and blood of your Son, our Saviour, Jesus Christ.
    We thank you for this assurance of your goodness and love,
    and that we are living members of his body
    and heirs of his eternal kingdom.
    Accept this our sacrifice of praise and thanksgiving,
    and help us to grow in love and obedience,
    that with all your saints we may worship you for ever.
    Father, we offer ourselves to you as a living sacrifice
    through Jesus Christ our Lord.
    Send us out, in the power of your Spirit,
    to live and work to your praise and glory.
    Amen.

30. *THE DISMISSAL*
    The blessing of God almighty . . . ⟦CF 12(a)⟧ . . . remain with you always. **Amen.**
    All stand
    Alleluia! Let us go in peace . . . ⟦CF 12(b)⟧ . . . **Name of Christ. Alleluia!**

31. *A recessional hymn may be sung*

G. Australasia

30. The Anglican Church of Australia

The Anglican Church of Australia went through various stages of revising its eucharistic liturgies over the 30 years from the first experimental rite, 'A Modern Liturgy', in 1966, coded as **Aus2** in **MAL**. This rite had pioneered addressing God as 'you'. It was followed by two further experimental liturgies in 1969 (**Aus3** in **FAL**) and in 1973 (**Aus4** in **FAL**), and these led to the more definitive alternatives in the hardback *An Australian Prayer Book* (*AAPB*) in 1978. One of these was the modernized 1662, coded as **Aus1B**, but the rite in succession to Aus4, after various stages of drafting and re-touching in 1976–77, took its place as **Aus5** and was printed in **LAL** with an *apparatus* showing these latter changes.

   The coming of inclusive language put pressure upon all the services in *AAPB*, and the hardback book provided sufficient years in use for other changes to become desired. In the early 1990s the Commission started to work towards a new Book, and provided a draft new eucharistic rite for comment and experimental use in 1993. It included six eucharistic prayers. The Commission completed its work in 1994, retouching the eucharistic prayers, and changing their order; and the new Book, *A Prayer Book for Australia* (*APBA*), was brought in draft to General Synod in July 1995. There were now three 'Orders' of holy communion, the first the next stage in retouching the modern 1662, coded here as **Aus1C**, the second the mainstream order with the fullest provision, coded here as **Aus6**, and the third a brisker, shorter, simpler rite which was less doctrinally and didactically ambitious, and also conserved some traditionalist features.[90] It is coded here as **Aus7**. The fifth and sixth eucharistic prayers of 1993 were now interchanged and allocated to the 'Third Order', though still available for use in the 'Second Order'. However, General Synod relocated what was now the sixth one, bringing it back into the main 'Second Order' as the fifth prayer there, and leaving what had been the fifth prayer (itself largely a simplification of the first prayer) as the sole 'Great Thanksgiving' in that rite, i.e. the final sixth one in the two rites taken together. Synod, however, found itself embroiled in other, rather tenser, drafting. 'Thanksgiving 3', a prayer drawn from Hippolytus (though with considerable adjustment), was deleted; and a new prayer was created at the instigation of David Silk, Bishop of Ballarat, and with long experience on the Church of England's Liturgical Commission behind him. A small group, meeting

---

90 It did, however, have its own surprising features – not the least of which is a congregational responsive intervention of '**Come, Lord Jesus**' (Marana Tha?) when the anamnesis mentions the parousia.

behind the scenes and presenting David Silk with clear Australian desiderata, produced with him this new Thanksgiving 3, and got it accepted on the third day of the debate.

All the eucharistic prayers had dropped the rubric about manual acts which was in **Aus5**, but the 'Great Thanksgiving' in the Third Order restored the possibility of the fraction during the narrative of institution. All six are distinctively western in their structure and receptionist in their wording of that preliminary consecratory epiclesis. Nevertheless, despite the overwhelming vote in favour in General Synod, Archbishops of Sydney have precluded the use of some parts of *APBA* in that diocese, and there was a hint of unspoken controversy in the insistence at Synod that the services should be, as the Book's subtitle now says, for 'use together with' 1662 and *AAPB*, and should be labelled on the title page as 'Liturgical Resources authorized by General Synod' – which suggests no pre-eminence.

THE HOLY COMMUNION FIRST ORDER FROM *A PRAYER BOOK FOR AUSTRALIA*, 1995 (Aus1C)

⟦The 'First Order' reproduces the modernized 1662 of **Aus1B** in *AAPB* almost exactly, though sufficiently to change the numbering of the sections. The chief changes (using the **Aus1B** numbering) are as follows.

§4 Rubric re use of litanies omitted.
§6 Text of Ten Commandments stripped down to a single line for most commandments.
§§8–10 Provision for first two readings conflated.
§13 Text of Nicene Creed from ELLC 5 rather than ICET 3.
§18 Provision for when there is no communion omitted.
§20 The long exhortation has an alternative printed before the **Aus1B** one.
§21 In the confession 'judge of all men' becomes 'judge of all people'.
§29 Provision for alternative words for distributing the elements and for hymns during communion is omitted.
§31 Implicit permission to consume the remains at this point and explicit reference to a sentence of scripture are omitted.
§32 In the Lord's Prayer 'Save us from the time of trial and' replaces 'Lead us not into temptation but'.
The 'Alternative Order for §§20–27' is omitted.⟧

THE HOLY COMMUNION SECOND ORDER FROM *A PRAYER BOOK FOR AUSTRALIA*, 1995 (Aus6)

⟦The numbering and lining are original. The original has its rubrics in red.⟧

GATHERING IN GOD'S NAME

1. *A psalm, hymn or anthem may be sung when the ministers enter or after the greeting. A seasonal sentence may be used here or after §3.*

2. *An Invocation, or an Acclamation such as follows, may be said before or after the greeting.*
Blessed be God: Father, Son and Holy Spirit.
Blessed be God's kingdom, now and for ever.

⟦Other texts for Lent and penitential seasons⟧

3. *The Greeting. The priest greets the people in these or other suitable words.*
The grace of our Lord Jesus Christ, and the love of God and the fellowship of the Holy Spirit, be with you all.
And also with you.
or
The Lord be with you.
And also with you. [*or in Easter* Christ is risen [Alleluia.]. **He is risen indeed [Alleluia.]**]

4. *The Prayer of Preparation may be said.*
[Let us pray.]
Almighty God, to whom . . . [CF 1] **. . . Christ our Lord. Amen.**

    §§5 to 10 may be used according to local and seasonal custom, in any appropriate form and sequence.[91]

5. *The Two Great Commandments, the Ten Commandments (see page . . .), or other suitable passages are said when the confession follows.*
[Text of Two Great Commandments (our Lord's Summary of the Law)]

6. *A deacon or other minister may introduce the Confession with a seasonal introduction (see pages . . .) or other suitable words. Silence may be kept.*
[Congregational confession]

7. *The Absolution. Standing, the priest says*
[Absolution, akin to CF 2]

8. *'Lord, have mercy' (Kyrie eleison)*
[Kyries, ELLC 2, threefold in English and Greek]

9. *The Hymn of Praise, Gloria in excelsis. It may be omitted during Advent and Lent (see note 4* [note 4 suggests Trisagion as in §10 below]).
Glory to God . . . [ELLC 3] **. . . God the Father. Amen.**

10. *Especially during Advent and Lent, the following (Trisagion) may be said.*
Holy God, holy and mighty, holy and immortal, have mercy on us.

11. *The Collect of the Day. The priest says*
Let us pray.   *The community may pray silently. The priest says or sings the collect.*

THE MINISTRY OF THE WORD

12. *All sit for the Reading from the Old Testament or as appointed.*
After each reading the reader may say
Hear the word of the Lord,
thanks be to God.   *Silence may follow each reading.*

13. *A Psalm, hymn or anthem may be sung.*

14. *The Reading from the New Testament (other than from the gospels).*

15. *A hymn or anthem may be sung.*

16. *All stand for the Gospel Reading.*
[*greeting; announcement and response before; proclamation and response after]

17. *The Sermon.   Silence may follow.*

---

91 [A grey vertical line down beside §§5–8 suggests that they may be omitted, presumably for the particular reason that confession and absolution come again at §§22 and 23]

18. *On Sundays the Nicene Creed or the Apostles' Creed (see page . . .) is said or sung, all standing.*
    [The minister may say these or similar words.
    Let us together affirm the faith of the Church:]
    We believe in one God . . . ⟦ELLC 5⟧ . . . world to come. Amen.
        [and the Son]] OMIT BRACKETS

THE PRAYERS OF THE PEOPLE

19. ⟦*Provision for prayers to take any form, with reference to forms later in the Book, with possible responses and conclusion, to which the Lord's Prayer is an alternative as follows, if it is not being used later [see §27]*⟧
    Accept our prayers through Jesus Christ our Lord, who taught us to pray,
    Our Father in heaven . . . ⟦ELLC 1⟧ . . . for ever. Amen.

[PREPARATION][92]

20. *A selection from the following or other suitable sentences of scripture may be used.*
    ⟦*Texts of Matt. 11.28, John 6.35, John 13.34, Mark 11.25, John 3.16*⟧

    and/or
21. *This Prayer of Approach may be used.*
    [Let us pray.] **We do not presume to come to your . . . ⟦CF 3(a)⟧ . . . he in us. Amen.**
        our sinful . . . precious blood and] OMIT

CONFESSION AND ABSOLUTION

22. *At least on Sundays and other Holy Days a general Confession is made here if it has not been said at §6.*
    ⟦*Rubric describing ways of introducing the confession; *silence; congregational confession as at §6*⟧

23. ⟦*Absolution as at §7*⟧

THE GREETING OF PEACE

24. *All stand. The Greeting of Peace is introduced with these or other suitable words:*
    We are the body of Christ
    His Spirit is with us.
    or
    Christ has reconciled us to God in one body by the cross.
    We meet in his name and share his peace.

    The peace of the Lord be always with you.
    And also with you.
    All may exchange a sign of peace.

    A hymn may be sung.

25. *The gifts of the people are brought to the Lord's Table. They may be presented in silence or a suitable prayer, such as follows, may be used.*
    Blessed are you, Lord, God of all creation.
    Through your goodness we have these gifts to share.
    Accept and use our offerings to your glory
    and for the service of your kingdom.
    Blessed be God for ever.

---

92 ⟦*The use of square brackets for the cross-heading and a grey vertical line down the side of the page suggest that §§20 and 21 are for occasional use only.*⟧

THE GREAT THANKSGIVING

26. *The priest takes the bread and wine for the communion, places them on the Lord's Table, and says the following (Thanksgiving 1) or another authorized Prayer of Thanksgiving and Consecration.*

   [[Rubric listing where Thanksgivings 2–5 and 'The Great Thanksgiving (Third Order)' are to be found]]

Thanksgiving 1

[The Lord be with you.
And also with you.]
Lift up . . . [[ELLC 6]] . . . **thanks and praise.**

A Seasonal Preface (see pages . . .) may be substituted for 'All glory and honour . . . saying:'
All glory and honour be yours always and
   everywhere,
mighty Creator, everliving God.

We give you thanks and praise for our
   Saviour Jesus Christ,
who by the power of your Spirit was born
   of Mary
and lived as one of us.

By his death on the cross
and rising to new life,
he offered the one true sacrifice for sin
and obtained an eternal deliverance for his
   people.

Therefore with angels and archangels,
and with all the company of heaven,
we proclaim your great and glorious name,
for ever praising you and saying:
Holy, holy . . . [[ELLC 7]] . . . **in the highest.**
[**Blessed is** . . . [[ELLC 8]] . . . **in the highest.**]

Merciful God, we thank you
for these gifts of your creation,
this bread and wine,
and we pray that by your Word and Holy
   Spirit,
we who eat and drink them
may be partakers of Christ's body and
   blood.

On the night he was betrayed Jesus took
   bread;
and when he had given you thanks

he broke it, and gave it to his disciples,
   saying,
'Take, eat. This is my body given for you.
Do this in remembrance of me.'

After supper, he took the cup,
and again giving you thanks
he gave it to his disciples, saying,
'Drink from this, all of you.
This is my blood of the new covenant
shed for you and for many
for the forgiveness of sins.
Do this, as often as you drink it, in
   remembrance of me.'

The memorial acclamation is used here or below.

Christ has . . . [[CF 6(a)]] . . . **come again.**

Therefore we do as our Saviour Christ has
   commanded:
proclaiming his offering of himself
made once for all upon the cross,
his mighty resurrection and glorious
   ascension,
and looking for his coming again,
we celebrate, with this bread and this cup,
his one perfect and sufficient sacrifice
for the sins of the whole world.

The memorial acclamation may be used here.

Renew us by your Holy Spirit,
unite us in the body of your Son,
and bring us with all your people
into the joy of your eternal kingdom;
through Jesus Christ our Lord,
with whom, and in whom,
in the fellowship of the Holy Spirit,
we worship you, Father,
in songs of never-ending praise:
Blessing . . . [[CF 9]] . . . **and ever. Amen.**
   be] are

Thanksgiving 2

[The Lord be with you.
And also with you.]
Lift up . . . ⟦ELLC 6⟧ . . . **thanks and praise.**

It is right to praise you, faithful God,
always and everywhere,
for with your only begotten Son
and life-giving Spirit,
you are the one true God from everlasting
to everlasting.

At the dawn of time you wrought from
nothing
a universe of beauty and splendour,
bringing light from darkness
and order from chaos.

You formed us, male and female, in your
image,
and endowed us with creative power.

We turned away from you but you did not
abandon us.
You called us by name and searched us
out,
making a covenant of mercy,
giving the law, and teaching justice by the
prophets.

And so we praise you,
joining with your faithful people of every
time and place,
singing the eternal song:
Holy, holy . . . ⟦ELLC 7⟧ . . . **in the highest.**
[**Blessed is** . . . ⟦ELLC 8⟧ . . . **in the highest.**]

When the fullness of time was come,
you sent your Son to be born of Mary.

Bright image of your glory,
he learnt obedience to you in all things,
even to death on a cross,
breaking the power of evil,
freeing us from sin, and putting death to
flight.

You raised him from death,
exalting him to glory,
and the new day dawned.

On the night he was betrayed
Your Son Jesus Christ shared food with his
friends,
his companions on the way.

While at table he took bread,
blessed, and broke it,
and giving it to them, said:
'Take, eat; this is my body.'

He took a cup of wine,
and, giving thanks, he gave it to them, and
said,
'This is my blood of the covenant,
which is poured out for many.
Do this in remembrance of me.'

The memorial acclamation is used here or below.

Christ has . . . ⟦CF 6(a)⟧ . . . **come again.**

Therefore, living God, as we obey his
command,
we remember his life of obedience to you,
his suffering and death,
his resurrection and exaltation,
and his promise to be with us for ever.
With this bread and this cup
we celebrate his saving death until he
comes.

The memorial acclamation may be used here.

Accept, we pray, our sacrifice of praise and
thanksgiving,
and send your Holy Spirit upon us and our
celebration
that all who eat and drink at this table
may be strengthened by Christ's body and
blood
to serve you in the world.

As one body and one holy people,
may we proclaim the everlasting gospel
of Jesus Christ our Lord,
through whom, with whom, and in whom,
in the unity of the Holy Spirit,
all glory is yours, eternal God, now and
for ever. **Amen.**
or **Blessing** . . . ⟦CF 7⟧ . . . **and ever. Amen.**
be] are

Thanksgiving 3

[The Lord be with you.
And also with you.]
Lift up . . . [ELLC 6] . . . **and praise.**

*The following Preface is omitted if a Seasonal or
other Proper Preface is used.*
It is indeed right,
it is out duty, our joy and our salvation,
that we should at all times and in all places
give thanks to you, almighty and
    everlasting God,
through Jesus Christ your only Son our
    Lord.

For he is the true high priest,
who has freed us from our sins
and made us a royal priesthood
to serve you, our God and Father.

Therefore with angels and archangels,
and with all the company of heaven,
we proclaim your great and glorious name,
for ever praising you and saying:
Holy, holy . . . [ELLC 7] . . . **in the highest.**
[**Blessed is** . . . [ELLC 8] . . . **in the highest.**]

Holy and gracious God,
all creation rightly gives you praise.
All life, all holiness, comes from you
through your Son, Jesus Christ our Lord,
whom you sent to share our human nature,
to live and die as one of us,
to reconcile us to you,
the God and Father of all.

Hear us, merciful Lord;
through Christ accept our sacrifice of
    praise;
and, by the power of your Word and Holy
    Spirit,
sanctify this bread and wine,
that we who share in this holy sacrament
may be partakers of Christ's body and
    blood.

Who, when his hour had come,
on the night before he went up to the cross
to make full atonement for the sins of the
    whole world,
offering once for all his one sacrifice of
    himself,
took bread and gave you thanks;
he broke it and gave it to his disciples,
    saying,

'Take, eat:
this is my body which is given for you;
do this in remembrance of me.'

In the same way, after supper
he took the cup and gave you thanks;
he gave it to them, saying,
'Drink this, all of you;
this is my blood of the new covenant
which is shed for you and for many
for the forgiveness of sins.
Do this, as often as you drink it,
in remembrance of me.'

[Let us proclaim the mystery of faith:]
Christ has . . . [CF 6(a)] . . . **come again.**

Therefore, in obedience to his command,
we commemorate and celebrate
his saving passion and death,
his mighty resurrection and ascension into
    heaven
and we eagerly await his coming again in
    glory.

We thank you that by your grace alone
you have accepted us in Christ;
and here we offer you a spiritual sacrifice,
holy and acceptable in your sight.
Through Christ, receive this our duty and
    service,
and grant that we who eat and drink these
    holy gifts
may, by your Holy Spirit,
be one body in Christ,
and serve you in unity and peace.

In your grace and mercy,
bring us to the joy of your eternal
    kingdom
with all the company of the redeemed.
May we praise you in union with them,
and give you glory through your Son, Jesus
    Christ.

Through him, with him, in him,
in the unity of the Holy Spirit,
either all glory and honour is yours,
    gracious Father,
    for ever and ever. **Amen.**
or we worship you, Father eternal,
    in songs of never-ending praise:
Blessing . . . [CF 7] . . . **and ever. Amen.**

Thanksgiving 4

[The Lord be with you.
And also with you.]
Lift up . . . ⟦ELLC 6⟧ . . . **thanks and praise.**

All thanks and praise, glory and honour,
be yours at all times, in every place,
holy and loving Father, true and living
God.

We praise you that through your eternal
Word
you brought the universe into being
and made us in your own image.

You have given us this earth to care for
and delight in,
and with its bounty you preserve our life.

We thank you that you bound yourself to
the human race
with the promises of a gracious covenant
and called us to serve you in love and
peace.

Above all, we give you thanks for your
Son,
our Saviour Jesus Christ:
born as one of us, he lived our common
life
and offered his life to you in perfect
obedience and trust.

By his death he delivered us from sin,
brought us new life,
and reconciled us to you and to one
another.

Therefore with angels and archangels,
with apostles, and prophets,
with holy men and women of every age,
we proclaim your great and glorious name:
Holy, holy . . . ⟦ELLC 7⟧ . . . in the highest.
[**Blessed is . . . ⟦ELLC 8⟧ . . . in the highest.**]

Holy God, we thank you
for these gifts of your creation, this bread
and wine,
and we pray that we who eat and drink
them
in obedience to our Saviour Christ,
by the power of the Holy Spirit,
may be partakers of his body and blood.

and be made one with him and with each
other
in peace and love.

On the night he was betrayed Jesus took
bread;
and when he had given you thanks
he broke it, and gave it to his disciples,
saying,
'Take, eat. This is my body given for you.
Do this in remembrance of me.'

After supper, he took the cup,
and again giving you thanks
he gave it to his disciples, saying,
'Drink from this, all of you.
This is my blood of the new covenant
shed for you and for many
for the forgiveness of sins.
Do this, as often as you drink it, in
remembrance of me.'

The memorial acclamation is used here or below.

Christ has . . . ⟦CF 6(a)⟧ . . . come again.

Therefore we do as our Saviour has
commanded:
proclaiming his offering of himself
made once for all upon the cross,
his mighty resurrection and glorious
ascension,
and looking for his coming again,
we celebrate, with this bread and this cup,
his one perfect and sufficient sacrifice
for the sins of the whole world.

The memorial acclamation may be used here.

As we eat and drink this holy sacrament,
renew us by your Spirit
that we may be united in the body of your
Son
and serve you as a royal priesthood
in the joy of your eternal kingdom.

Receive our praises, Father,
through Jesus Christ our Lord,
with whom and in whom,
by the power of the Holy Spirit,
we worship you in songs of never-ending
praise:
Blessing . . . ⟦CF 7⟧ . . . and ever. Amen.
be] are

Thanksgiving 5

[The Lord be with you.
And also with you.]
Lift up . . . ⟦ELLC 6⟧ . . . **and praise.**

*Special thanksgivings appropriate for the season or
the occasion may be inserted at appropriate places
in this prayer.*

Loving God,
we thank you for this world of wonder
    and delight.
You have given it to us to care for,
so that all your creatures may enjoy its
    bounty.
Lord our God,
we give you thanks and praise.

We thank you that when we turned away
    from you,
you sent Jesus to live and work as one of
    us,
and bring us back to you.
He showed us how to love you
and set us free to love and serve one
    another.
Lord our God,
we give you thanks and praise.

We thank you that on the cross
Jesus took away our sin,
all that keeps us from each other and from
    you.
He frees us from hate and fear,
from all that destroys love and trust.
Lord our God,
we give you thanks and praise.

And so with everyone who believes in you,
with all the saints and angels,
we rejoice and praise you, saying:
Holy, holy . . . ⟦ELLC 7⟧ **. . . in the highest.**

And now we thank you
for these gifts of bread and wine;
may we who receive them,
as Jesus said,
share his body and his blood.

On the night he was betrayed, he took
    bread
and gave you thanks.
He broke the bread and gave it to his
    friends, and said,
'Take and eat. This is my body given for
    you.
Do this in remembrance of me.'

After supper he took the cup
and gave you thanks.
He shared the cup with them and said,
'This is my blood poured out
so that sins may be forgiven.
Do this in remembrance of me.'

The memorial acclamation is used here or below.

Christ has . . . ⟦CF 6(a)⟧ **. . . come again.**
You have gathered us together
    to feed on Christ
and to remember all he has done for us:

The memorial acclamation may be used here.

Fill us with your Spirit
that we may follow Jesus
in all we do and say,
working for justice and bringing your
    peace
to this world that you have made.

Accept our prayers through Jesus Christ
    our Lord.
Blessing . . . ⟦CF 7⟧ **. . . and ever. Amen.**
    be] are

27. *If the Lord's Prayer has not already been said, it is said here or after the communion.*
As our Saviour has taught us, we are confident to pray,
Our Father in heaven . . . ⟦ELLC 1⟧ . . . for ever. Amen.

THE BREAKING OF THE BREAD AND THE COMMUNION

28. *The priest breaks the bread. One of the following may be said.*
[We break this bread to share in the body of Christ.]
We who are many are one body,
for we all share in the one bread.
or
As this broken bread was once many grains,
which have been gathered together and made one bread:
**so may your Church be gathered
from the ends of the earth into your kingdom.**

29. *The priest and other communicants receive the Holy Communion.*
The sacrament is given with the following words.
The body of our Lord . . . ⟦CF 10(a)⟧ . . . with thanksgiving.
and
The blood of our Lord . . . ⟦CF 10(b)⟧ . . . be thankful.
or the priest says
[The gifts of God for the people of God.]
Come let us take this holy sacrament of the body and blood of Christ
in remembrance that he died for us,
and feed on him in our hearts by faith with thanksgiving.
The sacrament is given with the following words, after which the communicant responds
Amen.
The body of Christ [the bread of heaven] keep you in eternal life. **Amen.**
The blood of Christ [the cup of salvation] keep you in eternal life. **Amen.**

*During the communion, psalms, hymns or anthems such as those on pages . . . may be sung
or said.*

THE SENDING OUT OF GOD'S PEOPLE

30. *The priest says one of the following or another suitable prayer (see the Seasonal
Variations, pages . . .)*

(a) Gracious God,
we thank you that in this sacrament
you assure us of your goodness and love.
Accept our sacrifice of praise and thanksgiving
and help us to grow in love and obedience
that we may serve you in the world
and finally be brought to that table
where all your saints feast with you for ever.

or

(b) Bountiful God,
   at this table you graciously feed us
   with the bread of life and the cup of eternal salvation.
   May we who have stretched out our hands to receive this sacrament
   be strengthened in your service;
   we who have sung your praises
   tell of your glory and truth in our lives;
   we who have seen the greatness of your love
   see you face to face in your kingdom
   and come to worship you with all your saints for ever.

or

(c) Living God,
   in this holy meal you fill us with new hope.
   May the power of your love,
   which we have known in word and sacrament,
   continue your saving work among us,
   give us courage for our pilgrimage,
   and bring us to the joys you promise.

or

(d) Father of all . . . ⟦CF 11(b)⟧ . . . light to the world.
   Keep us in this hope that we have grasped;
   so we and all your children shall be free
   and the whole earth live to praise your name.
   If this prayer is said, §31 may be omitted.

31. *either*
   Father,
   we offer ourselves to you
   as a living sacrifice . . . .⟦CF 11(a)⟧ . . . **praise and glory.**

   or
   Most loving God,
   you send us into the world you love,
   Give us grace to go thankfully and with courage
   in the power of your Spirit.

32. *A hymn may be sung.*

33. *The priest says this or an appropriate seasonal Blessing.*
   The peace of God . . . ⟦CF 12(a)⟧ . . . with you always. **Amen.**

34. *The deacon may say*
   Go in peace . . . ⟦CF 12(b)⟧ . . . **name of Christ. Amen.**
   or
   Go in the peace of Christ
   Thanks be to God. ⟦Alleluias may be added in Easter⟧

⟦There follow 'Additional Prayers and Anthems' and 'Seasonal Variations'⟧

THE HOLY COMMUNION THIRD ORDER FROM
A PRAYER BOOK FOR AUSTRALIA, 1995 (Aus7)

[The numbering and lining are original. The original has its rubrics in red.]

GATHERING IN GOD'S NAME

1. *The priest greets the people. The service may begin with songs or hymns of praise and thanksgiving.*

2. *The minister says this or another suitable Sentence of Scripture.*
   [Our Lord's Summary of the Law, Matt. 22.37–40; Mark 12.30–31]
   Let us pray. **Almighty God . . . [CF 1] . . . Christ our Lord. Amen.**

3. *'Glory to God in the Highest' (page . . .) or some other hymn of praise may be sung.*

4. *The Collect of the Day*

THE MINISTRY OF THE WORD

5. *The Bible readings follow, one from the Old Testament and one or two from the New Testament. A reading from the Gospels is always included.* [*Proclamation and response after each]

6. *A psalm or portion of a psalm may be sung or said and a suitable hymn or song may follow any of the readings.*

7. *All stand for the Gospel reading.* [*Announcement and response before; proclamation and response after]

8. *The Sermon is preached here or after the creed.*

9. *On Sundays the Nicene Creed or the Apostles' Creed is said or sung, all standing.*
   We believe in one God . . . [ELLC 5] . . . world to come. Amen.
     [and the Son]] OMIT BRACKETS
   or
   I believe in God . . . [ELLC 4] . . . life everlasting. Amen.

10. *The Sermon is preached here if it has not been preached earlier.*

11. *A hymn or song may follow.*

THE PRAYERS OF THE PEOPLE

12. [One or more persons lead prayers, with a text here and reference to suitable alternatives. The prayers conclude with a set congregational doxology or with a link to the Lord's Prayer as follows.]
    or Accept our prayers through Jesus Christ our Lord, who taught us to pray
    Our Father in heaven . . . [ELLC 1] . . . for ever. Amen.

PREPARATION FOR THE LORD'S SUPPER

13. *An exhortation may be read (see page . . .). One of the following or a suitable alternative may be read.*
    [1 Cor. 11.26–28; Isa. 55.6–8; 1 John 3.2–3]

14. *A time of silence may follow.* [Call to confession, short congregational confession]

15. [Declaration of forgiveness by printed or other authorized text; *further assurance by John 3.16; Ps. 103.12; 1 Pet. 2.24]

THE GREETING OF PEACE

16. *All stand. The Greeting of Peace is introduced with these or other suitable words.*
    We are the body of Christ.
    His Spirit is with us.
    The peace of the Lord be always with you.
    And also with you.

    All may exchange a sign of peace.

17. *The gifts of the people are brought to the Lord's Table. A hymn or song may be sung.*

THE GREAT THANKSGIVING

18. *Bread and wine for the communion are placed on the Lord's Table. The priest says the following or another authorized Prayer of Thanksgiving and Consecration.*

[The Lord be with you.
And also with you.]
Lift up ... [[ELLC 6]] ... **thanks and praise.**

You are worthy, our Lord and God,
to receive all glory and honour and power,
for you created all things,
making us in your own image.

We praise for your Son,
our Saviour Jesus Christ,
who by his death on the cross
and rising to new life
offered the one true sacrifice for sin
and obtained an eternal deliverance for his
  people.

Therefore, we lift our voices to praise you,
  saying:
Holy, holy ... [[ELLC 7]] ... in the highest.

And now, gracious God, we thank you
for these gifts of bread and wine,
and we pray that we who receive them,
in the fellowship of the Holy Spirit,
according to our Saviour's word,
in remembrance of his suffering and death,
may share his body and blood.

On the night before he died Jesus took
  bread;
and when he had given you thanks
he broke it, and gave it to his disciples,
  saying,
'Take and eat. This is my body which is
  given for you.

Do this in remembrance of me.'

[*If the bread is broken here, the priest may say*

We who are many are one body in Christ
for we all share in the one bread.]

After supper, he took the cup,
and again giving you thanks
he gave it to his disciples, saying,
'Drink from this, all of you.
This is my blood of the new covenant
which is shed for you and for many
for the forgiveness of sins.
Do this, as often as you drink it, in
  remembrance of me.'

We eat this bread and drink this cup
to proclaim the death of the Lord.
We do this until he returns.
Come. Lord Jesus!

Father, as we recall his saving death and
  glorious resurrection
may we who share these gifts
be renewed by your Holy Spirit
and united in the body of your Son.

Bring us with all your people
into the joy of your eternal kingdom;
there to feast at your table and
join in your eternal praise:
Worthy is the Lamb, who was slain,
to receive praise and honour
and glory and power
for ever and ever. Amen.

THE BREAKING OF THE BREAD AND THE COMMUNION

19. *If the bread has not already been broken, the priest does so here. This may be done in silence, or the following may be said.*
[We break this bread to share in the body of Christ.]
We who are many are one body,
for we all share in the one bread.

20. *Those who distribute the bread and deliver the cup may say*
The body . . . [CF 10(a)] . . . with thanksgiving.
The blood . . . [CF 10(b)] . . . be thankful.

    or the priest may say
Draw near with faith, to feed on Christ in your hearts with thanksgiving.

    Those who distribute the bread and deliver the cup may say
The body of Christ keep you in eternal life. **Amen.**
The blood of Christ keep you in eternal life. **Amen.**

THE SENDING OUT OF GOD'S PEOPLE

21. *If the Lord's Prayer has not been said earlier (at §12), it is said here.*
This or another thanksgiving is then said.
Gracious God, thank you for feeding us
with the spiritual food of the body and blood
of our Saviour Jesus Christ.
Thank you for assuring us of your goodness and love,
and that we are living members of Christ's body.

22. *All say together*
Father,
We offer ourselves to you
as a living sacrifice
through Jesus Christ our Lord.
Send us out . . . [CF 11(a)] . . . praise and glory.

23. *This hymn of praise or a suitable alternative may be said or sung.*
Glory to God . . . [ELLC 3] . . . God the Father. Amen.

24. *The priest say this or an appropriate seasonal blessing*
The peace of God . . . [CF 12(a)] . . . with you always. **Amen.**

25. *The deacon may say*
Go in peace . . . [CF 12(b)] . . . name of Christ. **Amen.**

31. The Anglican Church of Papua New Guinea

The Province of Papua New Guinea was formed in 1978, and its initial provincial eucharistic rite was an updated version of the former diocesan rite (**NG**). A detailed revision followed, and the resultant rite, authorized in 1983, was labelled **PNG** and published in **LAL**, largely by showing the revised details in *apparatus* style. The Province (now the Anglican Church of Papua New Guinea) published a full new *Anglican Prayer Book* in 1991, in part to celebrate the centenary of the first establishing of the Anglican Church in Papua New Guinea. The 'Acknowledgements' at the front of the Book states 'Most of the material included . . . has been used first elsewhere. England has provided us with the main Eucharistic rite . . .' The wording and structure are indeed heavily dependent upon **Eng3** of 1973, but the rite is far from being a straight reprint from the Church of England's uses. There are signs of continuity from **PNG** in the use of Roman 'offertory prayers' and in the oblation of the bread and the cup in the anamnesis, and in many places the language appears to have originated in English, before being first rendered into a local language and then rendered back into English.

The 'Acknowledgements' go on to state 'the second Eucharistic rite is the one in use by our neighbours in the Province of Melanesia'. This is **MelR** of 1984, and is not reproduced here.

'THE EUCHARIST: THE FIRST ORDER – THE RITE OF PAPUA NEW GUINEA' IN THE ANGLICAN CHURCH OF PAPUA NEW GUINEA'S *ANGLICAN PRAYER BOOK*, 1991 (PNGR)

[The numbering and lining are editorial; the † apparently indicates the use of the sign of the cross]

THE PREPARATION . . . The people make themselves ready

1. *A psalm, or part of a psalm, or a hymn may be sung.*
    The Lord be with you.
    And with you.
    Kneel
    Almighty God, to whom . . . [[CF 1]] . . . through Jesus Christ our Lord. Amen.
    desires] wants
    cleanse] clean
    magnify] praise

2. Lord have mercy . . . [[ELLC 2]] . . . Lord have mercy.
    We have a great High Priest who has passed into the heavens, Jesus the Son of God; so let us draw near with a true heart and a sure faith, and make our confession to our heavenly Father.

    Short silence. Priest and people will then make this confession
    [[Congregational confession and presidential absolution]]

3. **Glory to God . . . [[ELLC 3]] . . . God the Father. Amen.**
    God's people] his people

4. The Lord be with you.
   And with you.
   Let us pray
   COLLECT OF THE DAY

THE READINGS AND THE PREACHING . . . THE MINISTRY OF THE WORD

5. *Sit* ⟦One reading from the Bible – on Sundays two with canticle or psalm between them – and *proclamation and response after each; *then psalm, hymn or canticle⟧

   Stand ⟦Salutation, Gospel reading, † and acclamation preceding and *proclamation and response following⟧

6. *Sit   On Sundays and special days the SERMON follows.*

7. *On Sundays and other Holy Days the Nicene Creed shall be sung or said.*
   Stand
   We believe in one God . . . ⟦ELLC 5⟧ . . . dead, † and the life of the world to come.
   Amen.
   of one Being] one in Being
   for us and] for us men and
   was incarnate . . . truly human] by the power of the Holy Spirit he was born of the Virgin Mary, and
   became man
   accordance with] fulfilment of

THE PRAYERS OF THE CHURCH . . . THE INTERCESSION

8. *The Priest and one or more of the people shall offer the Prayers of the Church.*
   Kneel ⟦Litany-type intercession with versicle and response at intervals⟧
9. *Stand*
   The peace of the Lord be always with you.
   And with you.
   We are the body of Christ.
   By one Spirit we were all baptized into one body.
   Keep the unity of the Spirit and hold together in the way of peace.

THE OFFERING . . . THE PREPARATION OF THE BREAD AND WINE

10. *The bread and wine shall then be placed on the altar and the gifts of the people may be given at the same time.*

11. *These Offering Prayers may be said aloud*

At the offering of the bread	Blessed are you . . . ⟦CF 4(a)⟧ . . . **Blessed be God for ever.**
At the preparation of the chalice	By the mystery of this water and wine may we come to share in the divinity of Christ, who humbled himself to share our humanity.
At the offering of the chalice	Blessed are you . . . ⟦CF 4(b)⟧ . . . become our spiritual drink. **Blessed be God for ever.**

12. *Then shall always be said:*
    Lord, to you belong the greatness, and the power,
    and the glory, and the victory, and the majesty.
    All that is in the heavens and on the earth is yours,
    and of your own we give back to you.

    Then may be said:
    Lord God, we ask you to receive us
    and be pleased with the sacrifice we offer you,
    with humble and contrite hearts.

13. AT THE LAVABO

Lord wash away my evil and make me clean from my sin.
A hymn may be sung at this time

THE THANKSGIVING

14. *Stand*

The Lord be with you.
And with you.
Lift up . . . [[ELLC 6]] . . . **good and right to**
to so.
lift them to] lift them up to

It is good and right
that we should at all times and in all places
give thanks to you, Lord, holy Father,
   almighty, everlasting God,
through Jesus Christ your only Son, our
   Lord:
Because through him you made all things
   from the beginning
and made us in your own likeness:
Through him you saved us from being
   slaves to sin,
giving him to be born as man,
to die on the cross and to rise again for us:
Through him you made us a people for
   yourself,
lifting him to your right hand on high,
and sending out through him your holy
   and life-giving Spirit.

SPECIAL THANKSGIVINGS

And now we give you thanks,
[[ten proper thanksgivings, as in **Eng3**]]

So, with angels and archangels
and all the company of heaven,
we praise you with joy and say:
Holy, holy . . . [[ELLC 7]] . . . in the highest.
† Blessed is . . . [[ELLC 8]] . . . in the
   highest.
Kneel
Hear us, Father, through Christ your Son,
   our Lord.
Through him receive our sacrifice of praise
   and thanksgiving,
and by the power of the Holy Spirit
make these gifts of bread and wine
to be to us his Body and Blood;

In the same night that he was betrayed,
he took bread;
and, when he had given thanks to you,
he broke it,
and gave it to his disciples, saying,
'Take, eat, this is my Body which is given
   for you.
Do this in remembrance of me.'
Then after supper he took the cup;
and, when he had given thanks to you,
he gave it to them saying,
'Drink this, all of you;
for this is my Blood of the new covenant
which is shed for you and for many
for the forgiveness of sins;
do this, whenever you drink it,
in remembrance of me.'

And so, Father, we make the memorial
   of his saving passion,
his resurrection from the dead,
and his glorious ascension into heaven
and looking for his coming again in glory,
we offer you this Bread of eternal life
and this cup of everlasting salvation.
We ask you to receive this duty and service
   of ours,
and to let us eat and drink these Holy
   Gifts
so that we may be filled
with your grace and heavenly blessing.

Through the same Jesus Christ our Lord,
by whom and with whom and in whom
honour and glory be given to you,
Father Almighty,
from the whole company of heaven and
   earth,
throughout all ages, world without end.
Amen.
Christ has died † . . . [[CF 6(a)]] . . . come
   again.

15. As our Saviour Christ has commanded and taught us, we pray,
    Our Father in heaven . . . ⟦ELLC 1⟧ . . . for ever. Amen.
    Save us . . . trial and] Lead us not into temptation but

THE BREAKING OF THE BREAD

16. *Then the Priest shall break the Consecrated Bread*
    The Cup which we bless
    is a sharing in the Blood of Christ.
    The Bread which we break
    is a sharing in the Body of Christ.
    Because there is one Bread, we who are many are one body
    for we all share in the one Bread.

17. **Lamb of God . . . ⟦ELLC 9(b)⟧ . . . give us your peace.**

THE SHARING OF THE SACRAMENT

18. *The Priest invites the people to share the Holy Sacrament, saying: EITHER:*
    Come with faith; take the Body of our Lord Jesus Christ which was given for you
    and his Blood which was shed for you, and feed on him in your heart by faith with thanks-
    giving.
    OR: This is the Lamb of God . . . ⟦CF 9(b)⟧ . . . **I shall be healed.**
    Blessed] Happy

19. *Then the Priest and other Ministers receive the Blessed Sacrament, and then shall give It to
    the people, saying to each one who receives:*
    † THE BODY OF CHRIST *and* † THE BLOOD OF CHRIST

    Hymns may be sung while people receive the Sacrament.

THE ENDING . . . THE THANKSGIVING

20. *Kneel*
    The Lord be with you.
    And with you.
    Let us pray.
    Almighty and everliving God, we thank you for feeding us in this Holy Sacrament
    with the Body and Blood of your Son our Saviour Jesus Christ.
    We thank you for keeping us in the Mystical Body of your Son,
    which is the blessed company of all believing people.
    We pray that we may continue to be living members of that holy fellowship,
    and do all those good works you have made ready for us.
    And here we offer you ourselves, our souls and bodies,
    to be a living sacrifice through Jesus Christ our Lord.
    Send us out into the world in the power of your Spirit,
    to live and work to your praise and glory. Amen.

21. Go in peace; love and serve the Lord; be full of joy in the power of the Holy Spirit;
    and the blessing of God almighty, the Father, the Son, and the Holy Spirit,
    be with you and stay with for ever. **Amen.**

22. *Consecrated Bread and Wine which are not used for Communion shall be eaten and drunk
    by the Priest immediately after the Communion of the People, or by one of the other Minis-
    ters while the Priest continues the service, or it shall be left on the altar until the end of the
    service and then it will be eaten and drunk or reserved in the Tabernacle.*

32. The Anglican Church in Aotearoa, New Zealand and Polynesia

The General Synod of the Province of New Zealand in 1984 authorized three new rites, 'Liturgies of the Eucharist'. These were published as a booklet, and were reproduced in **LAL**, there labelled as **NZ1**, **NZ2** and (the outline structure) **NZ3**. In 1986 the General Synod asked the Prayer Book Commission to bring a 'proposed New Zealand Prayer Book' to a special session in May 1987, and the Commission retouched the eucharistic rites for inclusion in the Book. Services were provided within the one Book in English and in Maori, with some texts also in Fijian and Tongan. The diocesan synods considered the Book and returned it to General Synod for final approval in 1988. The Book, *A New Zealand Prayer Book: He Karakia Mihinare o Aotearoa*, was published in hardback and officially launched in November 1989. There were now five eucharistic rites, four of them in self-evident continuity from the three in 1984, the fifth a new 'Service of Holy Communion' designed for 'special pastoral needs', predominantly the sick and frail. The first four are presented here as **NZ1A**, **NZ2A**, **NZ2B** and **NZ3A**, and in each case shown as departures from **NZ1**, **NZ2** and **NZ3**, as there is a high degree of continuity in the texts from the 1984 rites. The new service is coded **NZ4**. In this the eucharistic prayer is a reduced form of 'The People of God' in **NZ1A**. Each of the English-language versions has Maori texts interspersed with the English, particularly in congregational texts. These are mostly not shown here.

In 1992 the Province adopted a new constitution which distinguished three separate 'tikanga' (cultural/ethnic strands) in church life – Maori, Pakeha (European) and Polynesian. The name became Aotearoa, New Zealand and Polynesia. The title of the Church became 'The Anglican Church in Aotearoa, New Zealand and Polynesia'

In 2004 the General Synod approved a framework for planning and arranging liturgy using the 1989 Book, and this was entitled the 'template'. It related to all liturgical services, and not specifically eucharistic ones. A succinct summary of the template, given at its start, is as follows:

> ### 'The Template
> The template directs us to three sections into which we assemble elements of our worship. Each of these sections
> 1. *Gathering* – to name and establish
> 2. *Story* – to form and nurture
> 3. *Going out* – to launch and empower
> is integral to the structure of the new community expressing itself in worship.'

In 2006 Synod added a rider to remind those conducting worship that the template was there to help them 'to make better use of existing prayer book services', but was not intended to relieve them of the need to follow rubrics and other directions within the services. The template is relevant in that it supplied extra cross-headings in another provision of the 2006 Synod, 'An Alternative Form for Ordering the Eucharist'. This is set out below as **NZ5**. While its apparent character is simply to provide an outline structure for the eucharist, its footnoted exposition of 'authorized' eucharistic prayers legitimizes the use of any eucharistic prayer from any province of the Communion.

In 2010 General Synod approved eight further eucharistic prayers, as alternatives to be used within the existing rites, and specified the eucharistic prayers to which they are the natural alternatives. These are presented here as **NZ6**. Prayers A–F, while close in language to their predecessors, are characterized by new congregational acclamations and doxology. The last two prayers are for use with children and are wholly innovatory.

A table may help demonstrate the relationships between the eucharistic prayers, with the lettering of each used in 2010 traced back to its point of origin.

1984 *The Liturgies of the Eucharist*	1989 *A New Zealand Prayer Book: He Karakia Mihinare o Aotearoa*	2010 *Alternative Eucharistic Prayers*
NZ1: Main text – no specified theme (Prayer A) Appendix: 'Celebrating the Grace of God' (Prayer B)	NZ1A: 'Thanksgiving of the People of God' (Prayer A) Appendix: 'Celebrating the Grace of God' (Prayer B)	NZ6: Prayer A: 'The People of God' Prayer B: 'Celebrating the Grace of God'
NZ2: 'Thanksgiving and Praise' (Prayer D)	NZ2A: 'Creation and Redemption' (Prayer C)	Prayer C: 'Creation and Redemption'
'Creation and Redemption' (Prayer C)	NZ2B: 'Thanksgiving and Praise' (Prayer D)	Prayer D: 'Thanksgiving and Praise'
NZ3: 'For Special Occasions' (Prayer E)	NZ3A: (in 'A Form for Ordering the Eucharist') (Prayer E)	Prayer E: 'A Form for Ordering the Eucharist'
	NZ4: 'A Service of Holy Communion' (Prayer F)	Prayer F: 'Service of Holy Communion'
		Prayer (G): 'For use with children A'
		Prayer (H): 'For use with children B'

'THANKSGIVING OF THE PEOPLE OF GOD' FROM
A NEW ZEALAND PRAYER BOOK, 1989 (NZ1A)

[The numbering here follows the editorial numbering of NZ1 in LAL, the structure and numbering of which is shown in the right-hand column. The lining is original.]

THANKSGIVING OF THE PEOPLE OF GOD (NZ1A)

THE MINISTRY OF THE WORD AND PRAYER
THE GATHERING OF THE COMMUNITY
  1. [Greeting – rubric only]
  2. [Introduction – rubric only]
  3. [Text of responsive greetings]
  4. [*The sentence of the day – see §14]
  5. [*Collect for Purity (CF1) with small variants]
  6. [*Gloria in Excelsis (ELLC 3) – or at §12]
  7. [*The Summary of the Law, or The New Commandment, or The Ten Commandments (in an appendix), each with response **Spirit of God, search our hearts** or *with Kyries (ELLC 2)]
  8. [*Sentences calling to repentance]
  9. [Promise of God's forgiveness, with silence]
  10. [Congregational confession]
  11. [Precatory absolution]
  12. [*Gloria in Excelsis if not at §6]

  13. [*Versicle/response of Col. 3.15–16, introductory to readings]
  14. [*Sentence of the day]
  15. [Collect of the day (or before or after the Sermon)]
THE PROCLAMATION
THE READINGS
  16. [One or two lessons with *proclamation/response]
  17. [Rubric *psalm, hymn or anthem to follow each]
  18. [Gospel, announcement, proclamation/response]
THE SERMON
  19. [The Sermon here or after §20]
  20. [*The Apostles' Creed (ELLC 4) (page . . .), A Liturgical Affirmation (page . . . i.e. §11 in NZ2B), or The Nicene Creed (ELLC 5) with text here]
      [and the Son]] OMIT BRACKETS
      who with the Father] who in unity with the Father

THE LITURGY OF THE EUCHARIST (NZ1)

THE MINISTRY OF THE WORD AND PRAYER

THE PREPARATION
  1. [Greeting – rubric only]
  2. [Introduction – rubric only]
  3. [Text of responsive greetings]
  4. [*The sentence of the day – see §14]
  5. [*Collect for Purity (CF1) with small variants]
  6. [*Gloria in Excelsis (ELLC 3) – or at §12]
  7. [*The Ten Commandments, or The Summary of the Law, or a New Commandment, with *Kyries (ELLC 2)]

  8. [*Sentences calling to repentance]
  9. [Promise of God's forgiveness, with silence]
  10. [Congregational confession]
  11. [Declaratory absolution]
  12. [*Gloria in Excelsis if not at §6]
THE READINGS
  13. [*Introductory versicle/response of Col. 3.15–16]
  14. [*Sentence of the day]
  15. [Collect of the day (or before or after the Sermon)]

  16. [One or two lessons with *proclamation/response]
  17. [Rubric *psalm, hymn or anthem to follow each]
  18. [Gospel, announcement, proclamation/response]
THE PROCLAMATION
  19. [*The Sermon]
  20. [*Nicene Creed]

THANKSGIVING OF THE PEOPLE OF GOD (NZ1A)

THE PRAYERS OF THE PEOPLE

21. ⟦Various ways of interceding, including three forms in appendix; *Lord's Prayer⟧

THE MINISTRY OF THE SACRAMENT

THE PEACE

22. ⟦Versicle and response of Peace⟧
23. ⟦Rubric re sharing the Peace⟧
24. ⟦Two versicles and responses re keeping Peace⟧

THE PREPARATION OF THE GIFTS

25. ⟦*Hymn or anthem⟧
26. ⟦Presentation of *elements, and of offerings⟧
27. ⟦*Versicle and response from 1 Chron. 29.11, 14a⟧
28. ⟦*Single prayer, variant on CF 5 re 'gifts to share'⟧

THE LITURGY OF THE EUCHARIST (NZ1)

THE PRAYERS OF THE PEOPLE

21. ⟦Various ways of interceding, including three forms in appendix; *Lord's Prayer⟧

THE MINISTRY OF THE SACRAMENT

THE PEACE

22. ⟦Versicle and response of Peace⟧
23. ⟦Rubric re sharing the Peace⟧
24. ⟦Two versicles and responses re keeping Peace⟧

THE PREPARATION OF THE GIFTS

25. ⟦*Hymn or anthem⟧
26. ⟦Presentation of *elements, and of offerings⟧
27. ⟦*Versicle and response from 1 Chron. 29.11, 14a⟧
28. ⟦*Single prayer, variant on CF 5 re offering 'gifts'⟧

29. ⟦Reference to an alternative Great Thanksgiving (§49) and to seasonal variants, i.e. proper prefaces⟧

THE GREAT THANKSGIVING ⟦text of **NZ1A** with **NZ1** shown by *apparatus*⟧

30. *It is recommended that the people stand or kneel throughout the following prayer.*

31. *The presiding priest says or sings*

The Lord is here
God's Spirit is with us.
Lift up your . . . ⟦ELLC 6⟧ . . . **offer thanks and praise.**

It is right indeed, it is our joy and salvation, holy Lord,
almighty Father, everlasting God, at all times and in all places
to give you thanks and praise through Christ your only Son.

You are the source of all life and goodness;
through your eternal Word
you have created all things from the beginning
and formed us in your own image;
male and female you created us.

Variations to the following section are found on pages . . .

When we sinned and turned away

you called us back to yourself
and gave your Son to share our human nature.
By his death on the cross,
he made the one perfect sacrifice for the sin of the world
and freed us from the bondage of sin.
You raised him to life triumphant over death;
you exalted him in glory.
In him you have made us a holy people
by sending upon us your holy and life-giving Spirit.

Additions from pages . . . may follow here.

Therefore with the faithful who rest in him,
with angels and archangels and all the company of heaven,
we proclaim your great and glorious name,

for ever praising you and saying:
Holy, holy . . . ⟦ELLC 7⟧ . . . in the highest.
And these words may be added
Blessed is . . . ⟦ELLC 8⟧ . . . in the highest.

All glory and thanksgiving to you, holy
    Father;
on the night before he died
your Son, Jesus Christ, took bread;
and when he had given you thanks,
he broke it, gave it to his disciples, and
    said:
Take, eat, this is my body
which is given for you;
do this to remember me.

After supper he took the cup;
when he had given you thanks,
he gave it to them and said:
Drink this, all of you,
for this is my blood of the new covenant
which is shed for you and for many
for the forgiveness of sins;
do this as often as you drink it,
to remember me.
Glory to you, Lord Christ;
Your death we show forth;
Your resurrection we proclaim;
Your coming we await;
Amen! Come Lord Jesus.

Therefore loving God,
recalling your great goodness to us in
    Christ,
his suffering and death,
his resurrection and ascension,
and looking for his coming in glory,
we celebrate our redemption with this
    bread of life
and this cup of salvation.
Accept our sacrifice of praise and
    thanksgiving
which we offer through Christ our great
    high priest.

Send your Holy Spirit
that these gifts of bread and wine which
    we receive
may be to us the body and blood of Christ,
and that we, filled with the Spirit's grace
    and power,
may be renewed for the service of your
    kingdom.

United in Christ with all who stand before
    you
in earth and heaven,
we worship you, O God,
in songs of everlasting praise.
Blessing, honour and glory be yours,
here and everywhere,
now and for ever. Amen.

NZ1: **offer thanks] give him thanks and praise**
    our joy and our salvation] the joy of our
      salvation
    we sinned and turned away] we turned away
      from you
    gave your Son] gave your only Son
    By his death . . . freed us] He made the one
                 perfect sacrifice for the
                 sin of the world
                 and by his death on the
                 cross he freed us
    you have made us] you have called us to be
    Send your Holy Spirit that these] Grant that
                 through your Holy Spirit these
    and that we . . . O God] Fill us with your Spirit,
                 by whose grace and power
                 you make us one in the body
                 of Christ.
                 With all who share these holy
                 things
                 we worship you

⟦The two rubrics have altered words without
change of sense⟧

THANKSGIVING OF THE PEOPLE OF GOD (NZ1A)	THE LITURGY OF THE EUCHARIST(NZ1)
THE COMMUNION	**THE COMMUNION**
32. [*The Lord's Prayer (ELLC 1)]	32. [*The Lord's Prayer (ELLC 1)]
33. [Fraction with variant on CF 8(a)]	33. [Fraction with CF 8(a)]
34. *Any of these additional prayers at Communion may be used before or during Communion or as private devotions.*	34. [*Prayer of Humble Access (CF 3(a)) with variants]
Most merciful . . . [CF 3(b)] . . . kingdom. **Amen.** *Or*	
We do not presume [CF 3(a) with variants] . . . he in us. **Amen.**	
Lamb of God . . . [ELLC 9(b)] . . . your peace.	
Or	
Jesus, Lamb of God . . . [ELLC 9(a)] . . . your peace.	
35. [Invitation with variant on CF 9(a)]	35. [Invitation with variant on CF 9(a)]
36. [Communion, one-line words of administration]	36. [Communion, one-line words of administration]
37. [Supplementary consecration]	37. [Supplementary consecration]
AFTER COMMUNION	**AFTER COMMUNION**
38. [*Sentence of scripture, *silence]	38. [*Sentence of scripture, *silence]
39. [The Lord's Prayer if not used before]	39. [The Lord's Prayer if not used before]
40. [*Seasonal prayer, with or without §41 or §42]	40. [*Seasonal prayer, with or without §41 or §42]
41. [CF 11(b), second half said congregationally]	41. [CF 11(b), second half said congregationally]
42. [Thanksgiving, second half said congregationally]	42. [Thanksgiving, second half said congregationally]
43. [*Blessing]	43. [*Blessing]
44. [Dismissal]	44. [Dismissal]
APPENDICES	**APPENDICES**
45–47. [Forms of intercession and thanksgiving]	45–47. [Forms of intercession and thanksgiving]
48. ['Seasonal variants', i.e. proper prefaces]	48. ['Seasonal variants', i.e. proper prefaces]
AN ALTERNATIVE GREAT THANKSGIVING	**AN ALTERNATIVE GREAT THANKSGIVING**

AN ALTERNATIVE GREAT THANKSGIVING [text of **NZ1A** with **NZ1** shown here by *apparatus*]

49. CELEBRATING THE GRACE OF GOD

Seasonal additions as provided on pages . . . [i.e. §85] may be inserted where indicated.

It is recommended that the people stand or kneel throughout the following prayer.

The presiding priest says or sings

The Lord is here
God's Spirit is with us.
Lift up your . . . [ELLC 6] . . . **offer thanks
and praise.**

Honour and worship are indeed your due,
our Lord and our God, through Jesus
    Christ,
for you created all things;
by your will they were created,
and for your glory they have their being.
Trinity

In your loving purpose you chose us
before the foundation of the world
to be your people;
you gave your promises to Abraham and
    Sarah
and bestowed your favour on the Virgin
    Mary.
Saints

Above all we give you thanks and praise
for your grace in sending Jesus Christ,
not for any merit of our own
but when we had turned away from you.
Christmas, Epiphany

We were bound in sin,
but in your compassion you redeemed us,
reconciling us to yourself with the precious
    blood of Christ.
Passiontide

In your Son you suffered with us and for
    us,
offering us the healing riches of salvation
and calling us to freedom and holiness.
Advent, Lent, Easter, Ascension, Pentecost

Therefore with people of every nation,
    tribe and language,
with the whole Church on earth and in
    heaven,
joyfully we give you thanks and say:
Holy, holy . . . [ELLC 7] . . . in the highest.

All glory and honour to you, God of grace
for you gave your only Son Jesus Christ
once for all on the cross
to be the one perfect sacrifice for the sin of
    the world,
that all who believe in him might have
    eternal life.

The night before he died
he took bread,
and when he had given you thanks,
he broke it, gave it to his disciples, and
    said:
Take, eat, this is my body
which is given for you;
do this to remember me.

After supper he took the cup,
and when he had given you thanks,
he gave it to them and said:
Drink this, all of you,
for this is my blood of the new covenant
which is shed for you and for many
for the forgiveness of sins;
do this as often as you drink it,
to remember me.

Therefore, heavenly Father,
in this sacrament of the suffering and
    death of your Son,
we now celebrate the wonder of your
    grace
and proclaim the mystery of our faith.
Christ has . . . [CF 6(a)] . . . come in glory.

Redeemer God, rich in mercy, infinite in
    goodness,
we were far off until you brought us near
and our hands are empty until you fill
    them.
As we eat this bread and drink this wine,
through the power of your Holy Spirit
feed us with your heavenly food,
renew us in your service,
unite us in Christ,
and bring us to your everlasting kingdom.
O the depth and riches of your wisdom, O
    God;
how unsearchable are your judgements
and untraceable your ways.
**From you, and through you, and for you
    are all things.**
To you be glory for ever. Amen.

NZ1: OMITS REFERENCE IN RUBRIC AND
    CUES TO SEASONAL INSERTIONS
      purpose] purposes
      gave your . . . Sarah] called Abraham, Isaac
                  and Jacob
      renew us . . . service] OMIT
      glory for ever. Amen] the glory for ever.
                  Through Christ our Saviour. Amen

Silence may be kept.

'CREATION AND REDEMPTION', AN ALTERNATIVE EUCHARISTIC LITURGY FROM *A NEW ZEALAND PRAYER BOOK*, 1989 (NZ2A)

[As there is a change of order (including the provision of a distinct Ministry of the Word) from NZ2 as presented in **LAL**, the editorial numbering begins from §1 again. The lining is original.]

THE MINISTRY OF THE WORD AND PRAYER
THE GATHERING OF THE PEOPLE
1. [Greeting – rubric only]
2. [Introduction – rubric only]
3. In the name of God: Creator, Redeemer and Giver of Life. **Amen.**
4. [*The sentence of the day]
5. [Responsive affirmation of God's presence and thanksgiving for his reign; *sign of peace between spoken text]
6. [*Psalm, hymn, waiata, or Benedicite Aotearoa⁹³]
7. [Two forms of call to confession, penitence, and assurance of God's forgiveness, the second with Kyries as response (ELLC 2)]
8. [*Sentence of the day]
9. *A Collect of the Day shall be said here, or before or after the Sermon.*

THE PROCLAMATION
THE READINGS
10. [One or two readings with *proclamation/response]
11. [Rubric *psalm, hymn or anthem to follow each]
12. [Gospel, announcement, proclamation/response]

THE SERMON
13. [The Sermon here or after §14]

THE AFFIRMATION OF FAITH
14. *The Nicene Creed* [ELLC 5] *(page . . .), or A Liturgical Affirmation (page . . .)* [i.e. §11 on page 290 below], *or The Apostles' Creed as follows, or Te Whakapono a nga Apotoro (page . . .)* [Apostles' Creed in Maori] *may be said here.*
    I believe in God . . . [ELLC 4] **. . . life everlasting. Amen.**

THE PRAYERS OF THE PEOPLE
15. [Various ways of interceding, including three forms in appendix; *Lord's Prayer]

THE MINISTRY OF THE SACRAMENT
THE PEACE
16. [Versicle and response of Peace]
17. [Rubric re sharing the Peace]

THE PREPARATION OF THE GIFTS
18. *The offerings of the people are presented. Bread and wine for communion are placed on the table.*
19. God of all creation, you bring forth
    bread from the earth
    and fruit from the vine.
    By your Holy Spirit this bread and wine
    will be for us
    the body and blood of Christ.
    All you have made is good.
    Your love endures for ever.
20. *Variations as provided on pages . . . may be used in the Great Thanksgiving.*

---

93 [This is a nine-verse canticle derived from the Benedicite Omnia Opera, but with a wholly local reference, as, for example: 6. Dolphins and kahawai, sealion and crab, / coral, anemone, pipi and shrimp: / **Give to our God your thanks and praise.**]

THE GREAT THANKSGIVING [text of **NZ2A** with **NZ2** appendix §79 shown by *apparatus*]

21. *It is recommended that the people stand or kneel throughout the following prayer.*

The Spirit of God be with you.
And also with you.
Lift your hearts to heaven
where Christ in glory reigns.
Let us give thanks to God.
It is right to offer thanks and praise.

It is right indeed to give you thanks most
loving God,
through Jesus Christ, our Redeemer,
the first born from the dead,
the pioneer of our salvation,
who is with us always,
one of us, yet from the heart of God.
For with your whole created universe,
we praise you for your unfailing gift of life.
We thank you that you make us human
and stay with us
even when we turn from you to sin.
God's love is shown to us:
while we were yet sinners,
Christ died for us.

In that love, dear God,
righteous and strong to save,
you came among us in Jesus Christ,
our crucified and living Lord.
You make all things new.
In Christ's suffering and cross
you reveal your glory
and reconcile all peoples to yourself,
their true and living God.

A Variation may follow as on pages . . .

In your mercy you are now our God.
Through Christ you gather us,
new-born in your Spirit,
a people after your own heart.
We entrust ourselves to you,
for you alone do justice
to all people, living and departed.

Now is the acceptable time,
now is the day of salvation.

Therefore with saints and martyrs,
apostles and prophets,
with all the redeemed,
joyfully we praise you and say:
Holy, holy, holy:
God of mercy, giver of life;
earth and sea and sky
and all that lives,
declare your presence and your glory.

All glory to you, Giver of life,
sufficient and full for all creation.

Accept our praises,
living God, for Jesus Christ
the one perfect offering for the world,
who in the night that he was betrayed,
took bread,
and when he had given thanks,
broke it, gave it to his disciples, and said:
Take, eat, this is my body
which is given for you;
do this to remember me.

After supper he took the cup,
and when he had given thanks,
he gave it to them and said:
Drink this, all of you.
This is my blood of the new covenant
which is shed for you, and for many,
to forgive sin.
Do this as often as you drink it,
to remember me.

Therefore, God of all creation,
in the suffering and death
of Jesus our redeemer,
we meet you in your glory.
We lift up the cup of salvation
and call upon your name.
Here and now, with this bread and wine,
we celebrate your great acts of liberation,
ever present and living in Jesus Christ,
crucified and risen,
who was, and is, and is to come.
Amen! Come Lord Jesus.

May Christ ascended in majesty
be our new and living way,
our access to you, Father,
and source of all new life.
In Christ we offer ourselves
to do your will.

Empower our celebration with your Holy
Spirit,
feed us with your life,
fire us with your love,
confront us with your justice,
and make us one in the body of Christ
with all who share your gifts of love.
Through Christ,
in the power of the Holy Spirit,
with all who stand before you
in earth and heaven,
we worship you, Creator God. Amen.

Silence may be kept.

NZ2:

your hearts to heaven] up your hearts
**where Christ in glory reigns] we lift them up to
God**
even when we turn from] when we turn from

while] in that while
forgive sin] forgive your sin
now with this bread and wine, we] now, we
Creator God] all loving God

THE COMMUNION

22. *The Lord's Prayer (which is to be used at least once in the service) may be said here,
    introduced by these or similar words.*
    As Christ teaches us we pray
    Our Father . . . [ELLC 1] . . . and for ever. Amen.

23. *The priest breaks the bread in silence and then says*
    The bread we break
    is a sharing in the body of Christ.
    **We who are many are one body
    for we all share the one bread.**

24. *The priest may lift the cup. The priest says*
    The cup of blessing
    for which we give thanks
    is a sharing in the blood of Christ.

THE INVITATION

25. Bread and wine; the gifts of God
    for the people of God.
    **May we who share these gifts
    be found in Christ
    and Christ in us.**

26. *The presiding priest and people receive communion.
    The minister says the following words (or any of those provided in the other Eucharistic
    Liturgies) to each person.*
    The body of Christ, given for you [or Maori text].
    The blood of Christ, shed for you [or Maori text].
    The communicant may respond each time **Amen** [or Maori text]

27. [*Supplementary consecration]

AFTER COMMUNION

28. [*Sentence of day or other scripture]

29. *The Lord's Prayer (if it has not been used before) shall be said here.*

30. *A seasonal prayer of thanksgiving (pages . . .) may be used.*

31. Most loving God, creator and redeemer,
    we give you thanks
    for this foretaste of your glory.
    **Through Christ, and with all your saints,
    we offer ourselves
    and our lives to your service.
    Send us out in the power of your Spirit,
    to stand with you in the world.
    We ask this through Jesus Christ, the servant,
    our friend and brother. Amen.**

    Silence may be kept.

THE DISMISSAL OF THE COMMUNITY

32. *A blessing may be given.*

33. *The congregation is sent out with these words*
    Grace be with you.
    Thanks be to God.
    Go in peace.
    Amen. We go in the name of Christ.

'THANKSGIVING AND PRAISE', AN ALTERNATIVE EUCHARISTIC LITURGY FROM *A NEW ZEALAND PRAYER BOOK*, 1989 (NZ2B)

[The eucharistic prayer and following material in this rite carry forward §§69–74 in NZ2 in LAL, but relocate them in a new rite here labelled **NZ2B**. It is printed on right-hand pages facing a Maori text opposite. As it is a new rite it is editorially numbered as such. The lining is original.]

THE MINISTRY OF THE WORD AND PRAYER

THE GATHERING OF THE COMMUNITY

1. [Rubric re informal greeting and introduction to the theme]

2. *Then all standing, the presiding priest or minister continues*
   E te whanau a te Karaiti,
   welcome to this holy table;
   welcome to you,
   for we are Christ's body,
   Christ's work in the world.
   Welcome to you whose baptism makes you
   salt of the earth and light to the world.
   Rejoice and be glad.
   Praise God who gives us forgiveness and hope.
   Amen.
   Christ is our light,
   the joy of our salvation.

   Praise and glory to Christ,
   God's new beginning for humanity
   making ritual water gospel wine,
   cleansing all our worship.
   Love and loyalty to Christ,
   who gives us the gospel.
   Praise to Christ who calls us to holiness.

3. *SONG OF PRAISE*
   A psalm, canticle or hymn may be used or the following [responsive material of praise and self-giving]

4. *FORGIVENESS*
   [Call to repentance, congregational confession, absolution, and congregational acclamation of praise]

5. *The Sentence of the Day may be read.*

6. *A Collect of the Day shall be said here, or before or after the Sermon.*
   The congregation sits.

THE PROCLAMATION

THE READINGS
7–9 ⟦As §§16–18 in **NZ1A**⟧

10. ### THE SERMON
    The Sermon is preached here or after the Affirmation of Faith.

11. ### THE AFFIRMATION OF FAITH
    The Apostles' Creed ⟦ELLC 4⟧, *The Nicene Creed* ⟦ELLC 5⟧, *or A Liturgical Affirmation as follows may be said or sung, all standing.*
    You, O God, are supreme and holy.
    You create our world and give us life.
    Your purpose overarches everything we do.
    You have always been with us.
    You are God.

    You, O God, are infinitely generous,
    good beyond all measure.
    You came to us before we came to you.
    You have revealed and proved
    your love for us in Jesus Christ,
    who lived and died and rose again.
    You are with us now.
    You are God.

    You, O God, are the Holy Spirit.
    You empower us to be your gospel in the world.
    You reconcile and heal; you overcome death.
    You are our God. We worship you.

12. ⟦A bidding and the *PRAYERS OF THE PEOPLE*, *the Lord's Prayer (ELLC 1)⟧

THE MINISTRY OF THE SACRAMENT

THE PEACE
13. *All standing, the presiding priest says to the people*
    Blessed be Christ the Prince of Peace
    who breaks down the walls that divide.
    The peace of God be always with you.
    Praise to Christ who unites us in peace.
    The presiding priest may invite the people to exchange a sign of peace according to local custom.

THE PREPARATION OF THE GIFTS
14. *The offerings of the people are presented. Bread and wine for communion are placed on the table.*

15. *Variations as provided on pages . . . may be used in the Great Thanksgiving.*

16. *It is recommended that the people stand or kneel throughout the following prayer.*
    The presiding priest says or sings

17. Christ is risen!
He is risen indeed.
Lift your hearts to heaven
where Christ in glory reigns.
Let us give thanks to God.
It is right to offer thanks and praise.

It is the joy of our salvation,
God of the universe,
to give you thanks
through Jesus Christ.
You said, 'Let there be light';
there was light.
Your light shines on in our darkness.
For you the earth has brought forth life
in all its forms.

You have created us
to hear your Word,
to do your will
and to be fulfilled in your love.
It is right to thank you.

You sent your Son to be for us
the way we need to follow
and the truth we need to know.
The variation for Advent, Christmas, Epiphany or
Palm Sunday may follow here.

You sent your Son to give his life
to release us from sin.
His cross has taken our guilt away.
The variation for Passiontide, Easter,
Ascensiontide, Pentecost, Marriage or a Saint may
follow here.

You send your Holy Spirit
to strengthen and to guide,
to warn and revive your Church.
Therefore, with all your witnesses
who surround us on every side,
countless as heaven's stars,
we praise you for our creation
and our calling,
with loving and with joyful hearts:
Holy God, holy and merciful, holy and just.
Glory and goodness come from you.
Glory to you most high and gracious God.

Blessed are you, most holy, in your Son,
who washed his disciples' feet.
'I am among you,' he said, 'as one who
serves.'

On that night before he died
he took bread and gave you thanks.
He broke it, gave it to his disciples, and
said:
Take, eat, this is my body
which is given for you;
do this to remember me.

After supper, he took the cup,
and gave you thanks.
He gave it to them and said:
Drink this. It is my blood of the new
covenant,
shed for you, shed for all,
to forgive sin;
do this to remember me.

Therefore with this bread and wine
we recall your goodness to us.
God of the past and present,
we your people remember your Son.
We thank you for his cross and rising
again,
we take courage from his ascension;
we look for his coming in glory
and in him we give ourselves to you.

Send your Holy Spirit,
that we who receive Christ's body
may indeed be the body of Christ,
and we who share his cup
draw strength from the one true vine.
Called to follow Christ,
help us to reconcile and unite.
Called to suffer,
give us hope in our calling.

For you, the heavenly one, make all things
new;
you are the beginning and the end, the last
and the first.
Praise, glory and love be yours
this and every day,
from us and all people,
here and everywhere. Amen.

Silence may be kept.

NZ2:

your hearts to heaven] up your hearts
Where Christ . . . reigns] We lift them up to God
that night] the night
Therefore . . . past and present]
        Therefore God of the past and present,
        with this bread and wine,

send your Holy Spirit that we] Through your Holy
        Spirit may we
may indeed be] may we be indeed
and we who] may we who
For you . . . everywhere. Amen.] OMIT
  (POSSIBLY IN ERROR)

THE COMMUNION

18. *The Lord's Prayer* ⟦rubric as §32 in **NZ2A** above; text as ELLC 1⟧

19. *The priest breaks the bread in silence and then says*
Christ's body was broken for us on the cross.
Christ is the bread of life.

The priest may lift the cup.
His blood was shed for our forgiveness.
Christ is risen from the dead.

THE INVITATION

20. *Lifting the bread and cup, the priest invites the people saying*
Come God's people,
come to receive Christ's heavenly food.

21. *The presiding priest and people receive communion.*

*The minister says the following words (or any of those provided in the other Eucharistic
Liturgies) to each person.*
The body of Christ keep you in eternal life.
The blood of Christ keep you in eternal life.
Or
The bread of life, broken for you.
The cup of blessing poured out for you.
The communicant may respond each time **Amen.**

22. ⟦Supplementary consecration⟧

PRAYER AFTER COMMUNION

23. *Silence may be kept*

The Lord's Prayer (if it has not been used before) shall be said here.

The presiding priest may use an appropriate collect.

24. *The priest says*
Blessed be God who calls us together.
Praise to God who makes us one people.
Blessed be God who has forgiven our sin.
Praise to God who gives hope and freedom.
Blessed be God whose Word is proclaimed.
Praise to God who is revealed as love.
Blessed be God who alone has called us.
Therefore we offer all that we are
and all that we shall become.
Accept, O God, our sacrifice of praise.
Amen. Accept our thanks for all you have done.
Our hands were empty, and you filled them.

THE DISMISSAL OF THE COMMUNITY

25. *A general blessing or one appropriate to the theme may be given.*

   The presiding priest or the bishop may use one of the Gospel sayings of Jesus.

26. *The congregation is sent out with these words*
   (Go now to love and serve the Lord.) Go in peace.
   Amen. We go in the name of Christ.

'A FORM FOR ORDERING THE EUCHARIST' FROM *A NEW ZEALAND PRAYER BOOK*, 1989 (NZ3A)

[The numbering follows the numbering of **NZ3** in **LAL**. But the Great Thanksgiving which was appended after the rite in **NZ3** as §90 is here placed in its actual position in the rite, so that §§89 and 90 are reversed. §§91–93 in this rite did not appear (possibly in error) in **NZ3**. The lining is original.]

86. *This rite requires careful preparation by the presiding priest and participants.*

   It is intended for particular occasions and not for the regular Sunday Celebration of the Eucharist.

   THE PEOPLE AND PRESIDING PRIEST

87. *Gather in the Lord's name*

   Proclaim and respond to the Word of God
   The proclamation and response may include readings, music, dance and other art forms, comment, discussion and silence. A reading from the Gospels is always included.

88. *Pray for the world and the church*

   Exchange the Peace

   Prepare the table and set bread and wine on it

   Make Eucharist

   The presiding priest gives thanks in the name of the assembly.

   The presiding priest uses one of the Great Thanksgivings provided (pages . . . [i.e. those in **NZ1A** *(both prayers),* **NZ2A** *and* **NZ2B**]*), or the following*

89. THE GREAT THANKSGIVING [[Text of **NZ3A**: with **NZ3** shown by *apparatus*]]

The following Great Thanksgiving may be used either as a framework within which insertions may be made or as a continuous whole. The presiding priest says or sings

The Lord is here.
God's Spirit is with us.
Lift up your . . . [[ELLC 6]] . . . **offer thanks and praise.**

The presiding priest gives thanks to God for the work of creation and God's self-revelation. The particular occasion being celebrated may also be recalled. The following or any other suitable words are used.

It is indeed right, always and everywhere,
to give thanks to you, the true and living
   God,
through Jesus Christ.
You are the source of life for all creation
and you made us in your own image.

The presiding priest now gives thanks for the salvation of the world through Christ. The following or any other suitable words are used.

In your love for us
you sent your Son to be our Saviour,
in the fullness of time he became incarnate,
and suffered death on the cross.
You raised him in triumph,
and exalted him in glory.
Through him you send your Spirit
upon your church
and make us your people.

If the Sanctus is to be included, it is introduced with these or similar words.

And so, we proclaim your glory, as we say
Holy, holy . . . [[ELLC 7]] . . . in the highest.

To you indeed be glory, almighty God,
because on the night before he died,
your Son, Jesus Christ, took bread;
when he had given you thanks,
he broke it, gave it to his disciples, and
   said:
Take, eat, this is my body
which is given for you;
do this to remember me.

After supper he took the cup;
when he had given you thanks,
he gave it to them and said:
This cup is the new covenant in my blood
poured out for you;
do this as often as you drink it
to remember me.

The people may say this or some other acclamation.
Christ has . . . [[CF 6(a)]] . . . come in glory.

Therefore, loving God,
recalling now Christ's death and
   resurrection,
we ask you to accept
this our sacrifice of praise.
Send your Holy Spirit upon us
and our celebration,
that we may be fed with the body and
   blood of your Son
and be filled with your life and goodness.
Strengthen us to do your work,
and to be your body in the world.
Unite us in Christ
and give us your peace.

The presiding priest may add further prayer that all may receive the benefits of Christ's work and renewal in the Spirit.

The prayer ends with these or similar words.
All this we ask through your Son
Jesus Christ our Lord,
to whom with you and the Holy Spirit
be all honour and glory,
now and for ever.
Amen.

NZ3: RUBRICS ARE WORDED DIFFERENTLY
to offer thanks] **to give thanks**
This cup] Drink this, all of you.
            This is my blood of the new covenant
poured out for you] shed for you and for many
                  for the forgiveness of sins

90. *Break the bread*

91. *Share the gifts of God*
    The bread and wine of the Eucharist are shared reverently.

    When all have received, any of the sacrament remaining is then consumed.

92. *Give thanks*

93. *Depart in the name of the Lord*

'A SERVICE OF HOLY COMMUNION' FROM *A NEW ZEALAND PRAYER BOOK*, 1989 (NZ4)

⟦The numbering is editorial. The lining is original.⟧

A Service of Holy Communion

For use with individuals or small groups to meet special pastoral needs

⟦Opening notes indicate that it is for sick or frail persons that the rite is provided. Provision is made at various points for a distribution of elements previously consecrated, and that is omitted here.⟧

The Preparation and Readings

1. *The minister may say*
   Grace and peace to you from God.
   God fill you with truth and joy.

2. *The following may be used*
   Almighty God . . . ⟦CF 1⟧ . . . through our Saviour Jesus Christ. **Amen.**
   perfectly] truly
   magnify] praise

3. *A collect may follow*

4. *The Gospel for the day or other Scripture may be read here or after the Confession.*

5. ⟦Call to confession, silence, brief confession, minimal absolution, silence, word of comfort⟧

6. *The Gospel for the day or other Scripture may be read here.*

7. *The Prayers* ⟦brief guidance⟧

8. *The bread and wine for communion are prepared*

9. *In the Great Thanksgiving, the marked passages may be omitted*

The Great Thanksgiving

The Lord is here
God's Spirit is with us.
Lift up your . . . ⟦CF 6⟧ . . . **offer thanks
and praise.**

It is right indeed, everliving God,
to give you thanks and praise through
Christ your only Son.

You are the source of all life and goodness;
through your eternal Word
you have created all things from the
beginning.

When we sinned and turned away
you called us back to yourself
and gave your Son to share our human
nature.
He made the one perfect sacrifice for the
sin of the world.
Therefore we proclaim your great and
glorious name, saying
Holy, holy . . . ⟦ELLC 7⟧ . . . **the highest.**
On the night before he died, he took bread;
when he had given you thanks,
he broke it, gave it to his disciples, and said:
Take, eat, this is my body
which is given for you;
do this to remember me.

After supper he took the cup;
when he had given you thanks,

he gave it to them and said:
Drink this, all of you,
for this is my blood of the new covenant
which is shed for you and for many
for the forgiveness of sins;
do this as often as you drink it,
to remember me.

Therefore loving God,
recalling your great goodness to us in Christ,
we celebrate our redemption with this
bread of life
and this cup of salvation.

Send your Holy Spirit
that these gifts of bread and wine which we
receive
may be to us the body and blood of Christ,
and that we, filled with the Spirit's grace
and power,
may be renewed for the service of your
kingdom.

United in Christ with all who stand
before you
in earth and heaven,
we worship you, O God,
in songs of everlasting praise.
**Blessing, honour and glory be yours,
here and everywhere,
now and forever.**
Amen.

The Communion

10. *After The Great Thanksgiving the priest breaks the bread and says*
    We break this bread . . . ⟦CF 6(a) with variants⟧ . . . **the one bread.**

11. *One of the following may be said*
    Jesus, Lamb of God . . . ⟦ELLC 9(a)⟧ . . . give us your peace.
    Lamb of God . . . ⟦ELLC 9(b)⟧ . . . grant us your peace.

12. *The following may be used as a preparation to receive communion*
    We do not presume . . . ⟦CF 3(a), with variants⟧ . . . he in us. **Amen.**

13. *The Bread and the Cup are given to each person with the following or other authorized
    words.*
    The body of Christ given for you. The blood of Christ shed for you.
    Or The body and blood of Christ given for you.
    The communicant may respond each time **Amen.**

14. *The Lord's Prayer (which is to be said at least once in the service) may be said here,
    introduced by these or similar words*
    As Christ teaches us, we pray
    Our Father in heaven . . . ⟦ELLC 1⟧ . . . for ever. Amen.

The Blessing

15. ⟦Options re the blessing⟧

'AN ALTERNATIVE FORM FOR ORDERING THE EUCHARIST', 2006 (NZ5)

⟦The cross-headings 'GATHER', 'STORY' and 'GO' originate in the 'template'⟧

Forms used at the discretion of the minister conducting the service on any occasion shall be neither contrary to, nor indicative of any departure from the doctrine and authority of the Anglican Church in Aotearoa, New Zealand and Polynesia in any essential matter.

GATHER
The Gathering of God's People
    Greet
    Penitential Rite*
    Song/Act of Praise
    Opening Prayer (Collect)

STORY
Proclaiming & Receiving the Word
    First Reading
    Psalm
    Second Reading
    Gospel
    Sermon
    Creed
    Silence, Songs & Other Responses*
Prayers of the People
    Prayer
    The Lord's Prayer*
    Penitential Rite*
    Peace
Celebrating at the Lord's Table
    Preparing the Table
    Prayer over the gifts
    Eucharistic Prayer (any authorized Great Thanksgiving/Eucharistic Prayer may be used)
    The Lord's Prayer*
    Silence
    Breaking of the Bread
    Invitation
    Communion

GO
Going out as God's People
    Silence
    Hymns
    Prayer after Communion
    Blessing
    Dismissal

Indicates elements of the liturgy which may appear at one point or another in the rite.

*The five section headings and the related subsections are those agreed by the International Anglican Liturgical Consultation for Common Use throughout the Anglican Communion. See the Dublin Report 1995, **Renewing the Anglican Eucharist**.*

Authorized means approved by the General Synod/Te Hinota Whanui, or equivalent, of any member church of the Anglican Communion.

'ALTERNATIVE GREAT THANKSGIVINGS' APPROVED IN 2010 (NZ6)

1. *Alternative Great Thanksgiving A (alternative to Thanksgiving of the People of God)*

The Lord is here.
God's Spirit is with us.
Lift up . . . [ELLC 6] . . . **offer thanks and praise.**

It is right indeed, everliving God,
to give you thanks and praise through
    Christ your only Son.

You are the source of all life and goodness;
through your eternal Word
you have created all things from the
    beginning.

*Variations to the following section are found in
NZPB pages . . .*
When we sinned and turned away
you called us back to yourself
and gave your Son to share our human
    nature.
He made the one perfect sacrifice for the
    sin of the world.
In him you have made us a holy people
by sending upon us your holy and life-
    giving Spirit.

Additions from NZPB pages . . . may follow here.

Therefore with the faithful who rest in
    him,
with angels and archangels and all the
    company of heaven,
we proclaim your great and glorious name,
forever praising you and singing/saying:
Holy, holy . . . [ELLC 7] . . . in the highest.
Blessed is . . . [ELLC 8] . . . in the highest.

All glory and thanksgiving to you, holy
    Father;
on the night before he died
your Son, Jesus Christ, took bread;
when he had given you thanks,
he broke it, gave it to his disciples, and
    said:
Take, eat, this is my body
which is given for you; do this to
    remember me.

After supper he took the cup;
when he had given you thanks,
he gave it to them and said:

Drink this, all of you,
for this is my blood of the new covenant
which is shed for you and for many
for the forgiveness of sins;
do this as often as you drink it,
to remember me.

Therefore loving God,
recalling your great goodness to us in
    Christ,
his suffering and death,
his resurrection and ascension,
and looking for his coming in glory,
we celebrate our redemption with this
    bread of life
and this cup of salvation.

Either
With thanksgiving and hope we sing/say:
Glory to you, Lord Christ;
your death we show forth;
your resurrection we proclaim;
your coming we await;
Amen! Come Lord Jesus.
Or
And so we proclaim the mystery of our
    faith:
Christ has . . . [CF 6(a)] . . . come in glory.

Accept our sacrifice of praise and
    thanksgiving
which we offer through Christ our great
    high priest.

Send your Holy Spirit
that these gifts of bread and wine which
    we receive
may be to us the body and blood of Christ,
and that we, filled with the Spirit's grace
    and power,
may be renewed for the service of your
    kingdom.

United in Christ with all who stand before
    you
in earth and heaven,
we worship you, O God,
in songs of everlasting praise.
Blessing, honour and glory be yours,
here and everywhere,
now and forever. Amen.

2. *Alternative Great Thanksgiving B (alternative to Celebrating the Grace of God)*

Seasonal additions as provided in NZPB pages . . . may be inserted where indicated.

The Lord is here.
God's Spirit is with us.
Lift up . . . ⟦ELLC 6⟧ . . . **offer thanks and praise.**

Honour and worship are indeed your due,
our Lord and our God, through Jesus
    Christ,
for you created all things;
by your will they were created,
and for your glory they have their being.
Trinity

In your loving purpose you chose us
before the foundation of the world
to be your people;
Saints

Above all we give you thanks and praise
for your grace in sending Jesus Christ,
when we had turned away from you.
Christmas, Epiphany

In your Son you suffered with us and for
    us,
calling us to freedom and holiness.
*Advent, Lent, Passiontide, Easter, Ascension,
Pentecost*

Therefore with people of every nation,
    tribe and language,
with the whole Church on earth and in
    heaven,
joyfully we give you thanks and sing/say:
Holy, holy . . . ⟦ELLC 7⟧ . . . **in the highest.**
Blessed is . . . ⟦ELLC 8⟧ . . . **in the highest.**

All glory and honour to you, God of grace,
for you gave your only Son Jesus Christ
once for all on the cross
to be the one perfect sacrifice for the sin of
    the world,
that all who believe in him might have
    eternal life.
The night before he died,
he took bread,
and when he had given you thanks,
he broke it, gave it to his disciples, and
    said:

Take, eat, this is my body
which is given for you;
do this to remember me.

After supper he took the cup,
and when he had given you thanks,
he gave it to them and said:
Drink this, all of you,
for this is my blood of the new covenant
which is shed for you and for many
for the forgiveness of sins;
do this as often as you drink it,
to remember me.

Therefore heavenly Father,
in this sacrament of the suffering and
    death of your Son,
we now celebrate the wonder of your
    grace.
Either
And proclaim the mystery of our faith:
Christ has . . . ⟦CF 6(a)⟧ . . . **come in glory.**
Or
With thanksgiving and hope we say:
Glory to you, Lord Christ;
your death we show forth;
your resurrection we proclaim;
your coming we await;
Amen! Come Lord Jesus.

Redeemer God, rich in mercy, infinite in
    goodness,
we were far off until you brought us near
and our hands are empty until you fill
    them.
As we eat this bread and drink this wine,
through the power of your Holy Spirit
feed us with your heavenly food,
renew us in your service,
unite us in Christ,
as we offer you our songs of everlasting
    praise.
Blessing, honour and glory be yours,
here and everywhere,
now and forever. Amen.

3. Alternative Great Thanksgiving C (alternative to Thanksgiving for Creation and Redemption)

The Lord is here.
God's Spirit is with us.
Lift up . . . [ELLC 6] . . . **offer thanks and praise.**

It is right indeed to give you thanks most loving God,
through Jesus Christ, our Redeemer,
the pioneer of our salvation,
one of us, yet from the heart of God.

For with your whole created universe,
we praise you for your unfailing gift of life.
Your love is shown to us, for while we were yet sinners,
Christ died for us.

In that love, dear God,
righteous and strong to save,
you came among us in Jesus Christ,
our crucified and living Lord.

You make all things new.
In Christ's suffering and cross
you reveal your glory
and reconcile all peoples to yourself,
their true and living God.

A Variation may follow from NZPB pages . . .

Through Christ you gather us,
new-born in your Spirit,
a people after your own heart.
Therefore with saints and martyrs,
apostles and prophets,
with all the redeemed,
joyfully we praise you and sing/say:
Holy, holy . . . [ELLC 7] . . . in the highest.
Blessed is . . . [ELLC 8] . . . in the highest.

Accept our praises, living God, for Jesus Christ,
the one perfect offering for the world,
who in the night that he was betrayed,
took bread,
and when he had given thanks,
broke it, gave it to his disciples, and said:
Take, eat, this is my body
which is given for you; do this to remember me.

After supper he took the cup;
and when he had given thanks,

he gave it to them and said:
Drink this, all of you.
This is my blood
of the new covenant
which is shed for you, and for many, to forgive sin.
Do this as often as you drink it
to remember me.

Therefore, God of all creation,
in the suffering and death of Jesus our redeemer,
we meet you in your glory.
Here and now, with this bread and wine,
we celebrate your great acts of liberation,
ever present and living in Jesus Christ,
crucified and risen,
who was and is and is to come.

Either
With thanksgiving and hope we say:
Glory to you, Lord Christ;
your death we show forth;
your resurrection we proclaim;
your coming we await;
Amen! Come Lord Jesus.
Or
Let us proclaim the mystery of our faith:
Christ has . . . [CF 6(a)] . . . come in glory.

May Christ ascended in majesty
be our new and living way.
In him we offer ourselves to do your will.

Empower our celebration with your Holy Spirit,
feed us with your life,
fire us with your love,
confront us with your justice,
and make us one in the body of Christ
with all who share your gifts of love.

Through Christ,
in the power of the Holy Spirit,
with all who stand before you
in earth and heaven,
we worship you, Creator God,
in songs of everlasting praise.
Blessing, honour and glory be yours,
here and everywhere,
now and forever. Amen.

4. *Alternative Great Thanksgiving D (alternative to Thanksgiving and Praise)*

The Lord is here.
God's Spirit is with us.
Lift up . . . ⟦ELLC 6⟧ . . . **offer thanks and
praise.**

It is the joy of our salvation,
God of the universe,
to give you thanks through Jesus Christ.

You said, 'Let there be light';
there was light.
Your light shines on in our darkness.
For you the earth has brought forth life
in all its forms.

You have created us
to hear your Word,
to do your will
and to be fulfilled in your love.
You sent your Son to be for us
the way we need to follow
and the truth we need to know.
*A Variation from NZPB pages . . . may follow
here.*

You send your Holy Spirit
to strengthen and to guide,
to warn and to revive your Church.
Therefore, with all your witnesses
who surround us on every side,
countless as heaven's stars,
we praise you for our creation
and our calling,
with loving and with joyful hearts as we
sing/say:
**Holy, holy . . . ⟦ELLC 7⟧ . . . in the highest.
Blessed is . . . ⟦ELLC 8⟧ . . . in the highest.**

Blessed are you, most holy, in your Son;
On that night before he died
he took bread and gave you thanks.
He broke it, gave it to his disciples, and
said:
Take, eat, this is my body
which is given for you;
do this to remember me.

After supper, he took the cup,
and gave you thanks.

He gave it to them and said:
Drink this. It is my blood of the new
covenant,
shed for you, shed for all,
to forgive sin;
do this to remember me.

Therefore with this bread and wine
we recall your goodness to us.

God of the past and present,
we your people remember your Son.
We thank you for his cross and rising
again,
we take courage from his ascension;
we look for his coming in glory
and in him we give ourselves to you.

Either
With thanksgiving and hope we say:
**Glory to you, Lord Christ;
your death we show forth;
your resurrection we proclaim;
your coming we await;
Amen! Come Lord Jesus.**
Or
We celebrate and proclaim the mystery of
our faith:
Christ has . . . ⟦CF 6(a)⟧ . . . come in glory.

Send your Holy Spirit,
that we who receive Christ's body
may indeed be the body of Christ,
and we who share his cup
draw strength from the one true vine.

Called to follow Christ,
help us to reconcile and unite.
Called to suffer,
give us hope in our calling.

For you, the heavenly one, make all things
new;
you are the beginning and the end, the last
and the first,
to whom we bring our songs of everlasting
praise.
**Blessing, honour and glory be yours,
here and everywhere,
now and forever. Amen.**

5. Alternative Great Thanksgiving E (alternative to Form for Ordering the Eucharist)

The Lord is here.
God's Spirit is with us.
Lift up . . . ⟦ELLC 6⟧ . . . **offer thanks and praise.**

It is indeed right, always and everywhere,
to give thanks to you, the true and living
    God,
through Jesus Christ.
You are the source of life for all creation
and you made us in your own image.

In your love for us
you sent your Son to be our Saviour.
In the fullness of time he became incarnate,
and suffered death on the cross.
You raised him in triumph,
and exalted him in glory.
Through him you send your Holy Spirit
upon your church
and make us your people.

And so, we proclaim your glory, as we
    sing/say:
Holy, holy . . . ⟦ELLC 7⟧ . . . **in the highest.**
Blessed is . . . ⟦ELLC 8⟧ . . . **in the highest.**

To you indeed be glory, almighty God,
because on the night before he died,
your Son, Jesus Christ, took bread;
when he had given you thanks,
he broke it, gave it to his disciples, and
    said:
Take, eat, this is my body
which is given for you;
do this to remember me.

After supper he took the cup;
when he had given you thanks,

he gave it to them and said:
This cup is the new covenant in my blood
poured out for you;
do this as often as you drink it
to remember me.

Either
With thanksgiving and hope we say:
Glory to you, Lord Christ;
your death we show forth;
your resurrection we proclaim;
your coming we await;
Amen! Come Lord Jesus.
Or
And so we celebrate and proclaim the
    mystery of our faith:
Christ has . . . ⟦CF 6(a)⟧ . . . **come in glory.**

Therefore, loving God,
recalling now Christ's death and
    resurrection,
we ask you to accept
this our sacrifice of praise.
Send your Holy Spirit upon us
and our celebration,
that we may be fed with the body and
    blood of your Son
and be filled with your life and goodness.
Strengthen us to do your work,
and to be your body in the world.
United in Christ,
through the power of the Holy Spirit,
we raise to you, O God, our songs of
    everlasting praise.
Blessing, honour and glory be yours,
here and everywhere,
now and forever. Amen.

6. *Alternative Great Thanksgiving F (alternative to Service of Holy Communion)*

The Lord is here.
God's Spirit is with us.
Lift up . . . [[ELLC 6]] . . . **offer thanks and
   praise.**

It is right indeed, everliving God,
to give you thanks and praise through
   Christ your only Son.

You are the source of all life and goodness;
through your eternal Word
you have created all things from the
   beginning.
When we sinned and turned away
you called us back to yourself
and gave your Son to share our human
   nature.
He made the one perfect sacrifice for the
   sin of the world.

Therefore we proclaim your great and
   glorious name, singing / saying,
**Holy, holy . . . [[ELLC 7]] . . . in the highest.
Blessed is . . . [[ELLC 8]] . . . in the highest.**

On the night before he died, he took
   bread;
when he had given you thanks,
he broke it, gave it to his disciples, and
   said:
Take, eat, this is my body
which is given for you;
do this to remember me.

After supper he took the cup;
when he had given you thanks,
he gave it to them and said:
Drink this, all of you,
for this is my blood of the new covenant
which is shed for you and for many
for the forgiveness of sins;

do this as often as you drink it,
to remember me.

Therefore loving God,
recalling your great goodness to us in
   Christ,
his suffering and death,
his resurrection and ascension,
and looking for his coming in glory,
we celebrate our redemption with this
   bread of life
and this cup of salvation.

Either
With thanksgiving and hope we say:
**Glory to you, Lord Christ;
your death we show forth;
your resurrection we proclaim;
your coming we await;
Amen! Come Lord Jesus.**
Or
And so proclaim the mystery of our faith:
Christ has . . . [[CF 6(a)]] . . . come in glory.

Send your Holy Spirit
that these gifts of bread and wine which
   we receive
may be to us the body and blood of Christ,
and that we, filled with the Spirit's grace
   and power,
may be renewed for the service of your
   kingdom.

United in Christ with all who stand before
   you
in earth and heaven,
we worship you, O God,
in songs of everlasting praise.
**Blessing, honour and glory be yours,
here and everywhere
now and forever.
Amen.**

7. [G] *Alternative Great Thanksgiving For Use With Children A*

God is here.
We praise God together.
Let us say thank you to God
who has done so much for us.

God, you made us, and the world and
    everything in it.
All the good we see comes from you.
You have always loved us
but people have not always loved you.
You sent Jesus to show us how to live
and to bring us back to you again.
Amen. We are alive in Jesus.

He died for us on the cross
so that through your Spirit
we can all be your people.
And so with thanks we praise you.
Amen. We are alive in Jesus.

We are here because on the night before
    he died
Jesus shared a meal with his friends.
There he took some bread
and gave thanks to you, God.
He broke it into pieces, and gave it to
    them.
'This is my body', he said.
'Do this, and know that I am with you.'
Amen. We are alive in Jesus.

Later, he took a cup of wine and gave
    thanks to you.
He shared it with them, and said
'This is my blood, which brings new life.
Do this, and know that I am with you.'
Amen. We are alive in Jesus.

And so, remembering Jesus, who died,
was raised to new life by you,
and is alive forever,
we are glad to share that life and live in
    him.
Amen. We are alive in Jesus.

Send your Holy Spirit
so that this bread and wine
can be for us the body and blood of Jesus,
and through this food
give us strength to live as your people.
Amen. We are alive in Jesus.

Help us care for your world and for each
    other
in the way that
Jesus showed us.
Until he comes again,
with all your people
in every time and every land
we worship you and say:
We praise you.
We thank you.
We bless you.
Amen.

8. [H] *Alternative Great Thanksgiving For Use With Children B*

The Lord is here.
God's Spirit is with us.
Lift up . . . ⟦ELLC 6⟧ . . . **offer thanks and praise.**

God, you made us, and the world and everything in it.
All the good we see comes from you.
You have always loved us
but people have not always loved you.
You sent Jesus to show us how to live
and to bring us back to you again.

He died for us on the cross
so that through your Spirit
we can all be your people.
And so with thanks
we praise you singing/saying.
Holy, holy . . . ⟦ELLC 7⟧ . . . in the highest.
Blessed is . . . ⟦ELLC 8⟧ . . . in the highest.

We are here because on the night before he died
Jesus shared a meal with his friends.
There he took some bread
and gave thanks to you, God.
He broke it into pieces, and gave it to them.
'This is my body', he said,
'Do this, and know that I am with you.'

Later, he took a cup of wine and gave thanks to you.
He shared it with them, and said
'This is my blood, which brings new life.
Do this, and know that I am with you.'

And so, remembering Jesus, who died,
was raised to new life by you,
and is alive forever,
we are glad to share that life and live in him
and proclaim the mystery of our faith.
Christ has . . . ⟦CF 6(a)⟧ . . . come in glory.

Send your Holy Spirit
so that this bread and wine
can be for us the body and blood of Jesus,
and through this food
give us strength to live as your people.

Help us to care for your world and for each other
in the way that Jesus showed us.
Until he comes again,
with all your people
in every time and every land
we worship you in songs of everlasting praise.
Blessing, honour and glory be yours,
here and everywhere,
now and forever. Amen.

33. The Church of the Province of Melanesia

The Province of Melanesia was formed in 1975, and already possessed what became its provincial Book of Common Prayer, the *Melanesian English Prayer Book*, dating from 1973. The eucharistic rite in the Book was reprinted in **MAL**, coded as **Mel**. It has continued as the normative rite of the Province, and remains the text from which all vernacular translations are taken.[94]

The Provincial Commission on Liturgy and Worship began further revision in the 1980s, when there was a project for a new provincial Prayer Book. This led to a draft 'Second Order' issued in duplicated form in 1984, from which the eucharistic prayer was published in **LAL**, and was coded as **MelR**. The Prayer Book project was never realized, and 'Second Order' went through further drafts, in the process acquiring three new alternative eucharistic prayers (two of them thematic). In 2003 the Commission published in booklet form with a Preface what it called the 'proposed final version' of the rite with a view to its inclusion in a future Church of Melanesia Prayer Book. The Preface invited 'further suggestions for final revision' and to that extent advertised the rite as provisional (and one later change is reported in the footnote to the Peace at §5 below). For obvious reasons it is coded here as **Mel2**.[95] The Commission was in 2010 addressing the question of inclusive language.

THE 'SECOND ORDER' EUCHARISTIC RITE OF THE ANGLICAN CHURCH OF MELANESIA, 2003 TEXT (Mel2)

[The numbering is editorial, the lining partly editorial, the capitalization typically original.]

The Holy Eucharist
Second Order

INTRODUCTION
1. *At the entry of the Ministers, a Hymn, a Canticle, or a Psalm may be sung.*
   The Celebrant may announce the Special Intentions for the day and read the Introductory Sentence.

2. *THE GREETING*
   All stand
   In the Name of the Father, and of the Son, and of the Holy Spirit. **Amen.**

---

94 Terry Brown, in his chapter in *The Oxford Guide*, records that **Mel** included twice within the narrative of institution (imitating a use in the Canadian diocese of Qu'Appelle) an addition to 'in remembrance of me' reading 'and know that I am with you' (see **FAL**, pp. 119 (Qu'Appelle), 379 and 387). This addition was excised by the provincial Synod in 1989.

95 This rite clearly had to be labelled 'Mel2', but it should be noted there is no **Mel1**.

Or
The grace of our Lord Jesus Christ, and the love of God, and the fellowship of the
Holy Spirit be with you all.
And also with you.

Then one of the following or any other suitable greeting:
Suitable for daily use:
Arise, shine out, for your light has come.
The glory of the Lord is shining upon you.

Suitable for all Sundays in the year:
This is the day that the Lord has made.
Let us rejoice and be glad in it.
[Further greetings are for Lent and for Easter seasons]

3. *INVITATION TO CONFESSION*
   The Deacon or Celebrant may read the following: [The Summary of the Law]

   The Deacon or Celebrant then says:
   My brothers and sisters, to prepare ourselves to celebrate this Holy Eucharist,
   let us remember our sins,
   humbly confess them to our merciful Father,
   and ask for God's forgiveness.

   Silence

   Then is said together:
   [text of congregational confession]
   Then may be said or sung one of the following:
   [Kyrie Eleison (ELLC 2) responsively in English or Greek]

   Or may be said or sung the following:
   [Trisagion]

4. *FORGIVENESS OF SINS*
   Then the Bishop, when present, or Priest, stands and says:
   [An absolution similar to CF 2]
   [Rubric re deacon or lay person substituting 'us' for 'you']

5. *THE PEACE*[96]
   Brothers and sisters, we are reconciled with God and with one another. Let us express
   our unity in the Body of Christ.
   The Peace of the Lord be with you always.
   And also with you.
   Priest and people exchange the sign of peace.

6. *HYMN OF PRAISE*
   When appointed, the following hymn of praise (Gloria in excelsis) may be said or sung:
   Glory to God . . . [ELLC 3] . . . **God the Father. Amen.**
   God's people] his people

7. *THE COLLECT*
   Let us pray.
   The Collect for the day is then said or sung. **Amen.**

---

96 [The Preface to the rite says that this position for the Peace is an 'ancient practice'. However, the
position was not well received and the provincial Commission of Liturgy, Worship and Doctrine soon after
thought again, and now reports in the annual Lectionary that it 'agreed that the sharing of the Peace in the
Second Order should be returned to its position before the Offertory'.]

THE LITURGY OF THE WORD

8. THE READINGS ⟦one or two readings from Scripture with announcement before and proclamation and response after, *psalm or *hymn between⟧

9. *All Stand*
   THE GOSPEL *is then proclaimed.* ⟦announcement and response before, proclamation and response after⟧

10. THE SERMON
    On Sundays and Holy Days there shall be a Sermon. On other days there shall be a homily or short reflection, followed by silence.

    On Sundays and other major feasts there follows, all standing:

11. THE NICENE CREED
    We believe in one God . . . ⟦ELLC 5⟧ . . . world to come. Amen.
    was incarnate . . . Virgin] by the power of the Holy Spirit
    ⁣   **he became incarnate from the Virgin**

    truly] OMIT
    death] died
    [and the Son]] OMIT BRACKETS

12. THE PRAYERS OF THE PEOPLE
    ⟦Four differing forms of prayer are printed, with permission to vary them or to use other forms.⟧

THE LITURGY OF THE EUCHARIST

13. THE OFFERTORY
    Members of the congregation will bring the offering of bread and wine forward to be placed on the Altar, to be prepared by the Deacon or Celebrant.

    An offertory hymn may be sung.

    When all preparations and hymn are completed, the Celebrant says aloud the following offertory prayer:
    Blessed are you . . . ⟦CF 4(a)⟧ . . . bread of life. **Blessed be God forever.**
    Blessed are you . . . ⟦CF4(b)⟧ . . . become our spiritual drink. **Blessed be God forever.**

    Offerings of money and other gifts are brought, to be blessed.

    The Celebrant may wash his hands, saying:
    Lord, wash away my iniquity: cleanse me from my sins.

    The Celebrant may then say:
    Pray, brothers and sisters, that our sacrifice may be acceptable to God, the Almighty Father.
    May the Lord accept the sacrifice we offer
    for the praise and glory of his name,
    for our good, and the good of all his Church.
    Or
    Pray, brothers and sisters, that we may prepare our hearts to receive Christ.

The Lord is here.
God's Spirit is with us.
Lift up . . . ⟦CF 6⟧ . . . **give God thanks and praise.**

Father, all-powerful and everliving God,
it is right that we give you all glory and honour,
thanksgiving and praise,
through Jesus Christ your Son, our Lord.
This PREFACE is used when no proper preface is provided. See page . . . for special prefaces.

He is your eternal Word
through whom you created the whole world,
the Saviour you sent to redeem us.

By the power of the Holy Spirit
he was born of the Virgin Mary
and became human.

For our sake he died upon the cross
and rose again from the dead
in fulfilment of your will,
and so called us to be a holy people.

He is our great High Priest
seated at your right hand on high
where he always lives to intercede for us.

Through him you have sent upon us
your holy and life-giving Spirit
and made us a royal priesthood
called to serve you forever.

And so we join the angels and saints
in proclaiming your glory as we say (sing):
Holy, holy . . . ⟦ELLC 7⟧ . . . in the highest!
Blessed is . . . ⟦ELLC 8⟧ . . . in the highest.

The people stand or kneel.
Holy and gracious Father,
we bring you these gifts,
this bread and this wine.
We ask you to make them holy
by the power of your Holy Spirit,
that they may become for us
the body and blood of your Son, our Lord Jesus Christ,
at whose command we celebrate this Eucharist.

He takes the bread into his hands and says:
For on the night in which he was betrayed,
he took bread,
and when he had given you thanks he broke it,
and gave it to his disciples and said:
TAKE THIS ALL OF YOU AND EAT.
THIS IS MY BODY WHICH IS GIVEN FOR YOU.
DO THIS IN MEMORY OF ME.

He takes the cup in his hands and says:
After supper he took the cup,
and again giving you thanks
he gave it to his disciples, saying:
TAKE THIS, ALL OF YOU, AND DRINK
THIS IS THE CUP OF MY BLOOD,
THE BLOOD OF THE NEW AND EVERLASTING COVENANT,
WHICH IS SHED FOR MANY
FOR THE FORGIVENESS OF SINS.
DO THIS IN MEMORY OF ME.

Let us proclaim the mystery . . . ⟦CF 6(a)⟧ . . . **come again.**

Father,
we offer you this bread of life
and this cup of salvation,
as our Saviour commanded.

We celebrate and show forth his perfect sacrifice,
made once for all upon the cross,
his mighty resurrection and glorious ascension;
and we look for his coming again
to fulfil all things according to your will.

Renew us by your Holy Spirit,
unite us in the body of your Son,
and bring us with all the saints,
into the joy of your eternal kingdom,
through Jesus Christ our Lord;
by whom, with whom, and in whom,
in the unity of the Holy Spirit,
all glory and honour is yours, Almighty Father,
for ever and ever. **AMEN.**

Silence

15. *THE LORD'S PRAYER*

As our Saviour Christ has taught us, we
  now pray:
**Our Father in heaven . . . ⟦ELLC 1⟧ . . .
  now and forever. Amen.**

As our Lord has taught us we say:
**Our Father in heaven
holy be your Name,
your rule come,
your will be done,
in the world as it is in heaven.
Give us this day our food for today.
Forgive us what we do wrong
as we forgive those who do wrong to us.
Bring us not into trouble to try us,
but save us from evil.
For yours is the rule and the power
and the glory for ever and ever. Amen.**

16. *THE BREAKING OF THE BREAD*
    The Celebrant breaks the consecrated bread in silence.

    *Then the following may be said or sung, adding the word 'Alleluia' from Easter to
    Pentecost:*
    (Alleluia!) Christ our passover is sacrificed for us.
    Therefore let us keep the feast. (Alleluia!)

    Then may be said or sung either of the following, whichever is appropriate:
    Lamb of God . . . ⟦ELLC 9(b)⟧ . . . **Give us your peace.**
    ⟦The alternative is for a funeral or requiem⟧

17. *INVITATION TO COMMUNION*
    *Facing the people, the Celebrant or Deacon says one of the following, holding up the
    chalice and paten:*
    THE GIFTS OF GOD FOR THE PEOPLE OF GOD.
    Jesus Christ is holy. Jesus Christ is Lord.
    Or
    COME, GOD'S PEOPLE. COME TO RECEIVE CHRIST'S HEAVENLY FOOD.
    Thanks be to God.
    Or
    BEHOLD THE LAMB . . . ⟦CF 9(b)⟧ . . . **shall be healed.**
      Blessed] HAPPY

18. *The ministers receive the sacrament in both kinds and then give it to the people, saying:*
    The Body (Blood) of our Lord Jesus Christ. (**Amen**).
    Or
    The Body of Christ, the Bread of heaven. (**Amen**).
    The Blood of Christ, the Cup of Salvation. (**Amen**).

19. *After the ablutions, the Communion Sentence may be read. The Celebrant then continues:*
Let us pray. *All kneel.*

> Glory to God,
> **whose power, working in us,**
> **can do infinitely more**
> **than we can ask or imagine.**
> **Glory to God from generation to generation,**
> **in the Church and in Christ Jesus,**
> **for ever and ever. Amen.**

> *Or*
> Almighty and everliving God,
> **We thank you for feeding us with the spiritual food**
> **of the most precious Body and Blood**
> **of our Saviour Jesus Christ**
> **and for assuring us in these holy mysteries**
> **that we are heirs of your eternal kingdom;**
> **through Christ our Lord. Amen.**

> *Or*
> **Father of all . . . ⟦CF 11(b)⟧ . . . through Christ our Lord. Amen.**

20. *The Bishop when present, or the Celebrant, blesses the people using this or an appropriate seasonal Blessing. See page . . . for seasonal blessings.*
The Lord be with you.
And also with you.
The Blessing of Almighty God, the Father, the Son, and the Holy Spirit be upon you and remain with you forever. **AMEN.**

21. *Notices may be given here.*

22. *All stand. The Celebrant or Deacon dismisses the people with these words, adding the words 'Alleluia! Alleluia!' from Easter to Pentecost.*
Go in peace to love and serve the Lord.
Thanks be to God. (Alleluia! Alleluia!)
or
Let us go forth in the Name of Christ.
Thanks be to God. (Alleluia! Alleluia!)

---

23. *If there is not enough bread and wine for the number of communicants, the Celebrant has to return to the Altar and consecrate either or both, saying:*
Holy and gracious Father . . . ⟦as §14 above, adapted for either element⟧ . . .
MEMORY OF ME.

24. *DIRECTIONS*
⟦Six brief directions concern the details of conducting the rite⟧

⟦Without further labelling there follow three '*Alternative Great Thanksgivings*'⟧

25. An Alternative Great Thanksgiving (1) (Suitable for use at services where there are many Children)

Lift up your hearts . . . [[ELLC 6]] . . . is **good and right to do so.**

Father, it is good to celebrate your great love.
Our hearts are full of thanks
as we gather around Christ Jesus
to tell you of our joy.
You loved us so much
that you gave him to be born like one of us.
He came to heal the sick, forgive sinners,
and on the cross He gave himself to die
and reconcile us to you.

As our Saviour, Christ has taken away from us
the evil which stops us being friends,
and has enabled us to live as your free children.

In that great love, Jesus our friend,
has brought us together in this Eucharist
to celebrate your great act of redemption.
Therefore, loving God, with hearts full of praise
we lift our voices to sing your praises
as we join the children from all nations,
with angels and saints who worship you in heaven
and say (sing):
**Holy, holy . . . [[ELLC 7]] . . . in the highest!
Blessed is . . . [[ELLC 8]] . . . in the highest!**

The people kneel.
God of all mercies,
we ask you to send your Holy Spirit
to make this bread and this wine
become the body and blood of Jesus our Lord,
who told us to do what he did himself
the night before he suffered.

During the last meal Jesus shared with his disciples,
He took bread, gave thanks to God,
broke it and gave it to them, saying:
TAKE, EAT. THIS IS MY BODY
WHICH IS GIVEN FOR YOU.
DO THIS IN MEMORY OF ME.

He takes the cup into his hands and says:[97]
In the same way He did with the bread,
Jesus took the cup of wine, gave thanks to God,
passed it to his disciples, saying:
DRINK THIS, ALL OF YOU.
FOR THIS IS MY BLOOD OF THE NEW COVENANT,
WHICH IS SHED FOR YOU AND FOR ALL PEOPLE
FOR THE FORGIVENESS OF SIN.
DO THIS AS OFTEN AS YOU DRINK IT IN MEMORY OF ME.
**His death, Father, we show forth,
His resurrection we proclaim.
His coming we await.
Glory to you, O Lord most high.**

By this offering of Bread and Wine
we remember what Jesus did to save us.
Accept us your little ones in your Beloved Son
as we show forth His death and resurrection.
May Christ, our friend, who rose from the dead,
now fill the universe with His presence.
And now that he lives to be with us here
and children everywhere,
make us to be faithful to Him.
United with joy in the power of the Holy Spirit,
may this communion enable us to love like Jesus,
always for you and for others.
So that in the end with the angels and saints
and all the friends of Jesus,
we worship you in songs of unending praise.

Through him, with him, and in him,
in the unity of the Holy Spirit,
all glory and honour is yours, Almighty Father,
for ever and ever. **AMEN.**
Continue with the Lord's Prayer on page . . . [[i.e. at §15]]

---

97 [[It is unclear why the cup is taken, when no direction has been given concerning the bread. But see the lack of direction re both in §26, and one rubric only in §27.]]

Lift up your hearts . . . ⟦ELLC 6⟧ . . . **is
good and right to do so.**

Father, it is good and right
always and everywhere to give you thanks
through your beloved Son, Jesus Christ.
He is your eternal Word,
through whom you made the world.
He is the Saviour you sent to redeem us.
By the power of the Holy Spirit
he took flesh and was born of the Virgin
   Mary.

For our sake he opened his arms on the
   cross.
By his death he put an end to death
and by rising to life again
he opened your kingdom to us.
In this he fulfilled your will
and won for you a holy people.

And so we join the angels and saints
in proclaiming your glory as we say (sing):
Holy, holy . . . ⟦ELLC 7⟧ . . . **in the highest!**
Blessed is . . . ⟦ELLC 8⟧ . . . **in the highest!**

The people kneel.
Lord, you are truly holy
and all holiness comes from you.
Let your Holy Spirit come upon these gifts
to make them holy so that they become
   for us
the body and blood of our Lord Jesus
   Christ.

Before he freely gave himself up to death
he took bread and gave you thanks.
He broke the bread
and gave it to his disciples and said:
TAKE THIS ALL OF YOU AND EAT.
THIS IS MY BODY WHICH IS GIVEN
   FOR YOU.
DO THIS IN MEMORY OF ME.

When supper was ended, he took the cup.
Again he gave you thanks and praise,
gave the cup to his disciples, and said:
TAKE THIS, ALL OF YOU, AND DRINK
   FROM IT.
THIS IS THE CUP OF MY BLOOD,
THE CUP OF THE NEW AND
   EVERLASTING COVENANT.
IT WILL BE SHED FOR YOU AND FOR
   ALL PEOPLE,
SO THAT SINS MAY BE FORGIVEN.
DO THIS IN MEMORY OF ME.
In dying . . . ⟦CF 6(b)⟧ . . . **come in glory.**
Rising] In rising

And so, Father, we remember his death
   and resurrection,
and look forward to his coming in glory,
as we offer you this life-giving bread and
   cup.
We thank you for counting us worthy
to stand in your presence and serve you.
We ask that all of us who share in the
   body and blood of Christ,
may be brought together in unity by the
   Holy Spirit,
and be made worthy to share eternal life
with the Virgin Mary, the apostles and all
   your saints
who have done your will all down the
   ages.
May we praise you with them
and give you glory through Jesus Christ
   our Lord,
by whom, and with whom,
in the unity of the Holy Spirit,
all glory and honour is yours, Almighty
   Father,
for ever and ever.
AMEN.

Continue with the Lord's Prayer on page . . . ⟦i.e.
at §15⟧

The Lord . . . [ELLC 6] . . . **good and right
to give him thanks and praise.**

Father, it is good and right to give you
thanks and praise.
Through Jesus Christ your eternal Word,
you made these islands, beaches, reefs,
mountains and valleys;
the sky, sunrise, sunset, moon and stars at
night.
We praise you for the birds of the air,
for the fish of the sea,
and all the creatures of the land.
We thank you for the bush, palm trees,
lagoons and oceans,
the waves, rivers, and water falls,
for all these tell of your greatness,
your wonder, and your unending love for
us.

Through Him in the fullness of time,
you saved us when we had fallen into sin.
By the power of the Holy Spirit
He became man like us,
born of the Virgin Mary.
Out of love for us, He opened His arms on
the cross.
By His death He destroys our death,
and by His rising again
He opened the kingdom of heaven for us.
In this, He fulfilled your will
and won for you a holy people.
And we whom you have set to live on
these islands
now join the angels and saints
in proclaiming your glory as we say (sing):
Holy, holy . . . [ELLC 7] . . . in the highest!
of power and might] of hosts
**Glory to you, O Lord most high.
Blessed is . . . [ELLC 8] . . . in the highest!**

The people kneel.
On the night he was betrayed,
your Son Jesus Christ had a meal with his
friends
and while at table,

he took bread, blessed it and broke it,
and giving it to his friends he said:
TAKE, EAT. THIS IS MY BODY.

He takes the cup into his hands and says:
Then he took a cup of wine, and giving
thanks,
he gave it to them, and said:
THIS IS MY BLOOD OF THE
COVENANT,
WHICH IS POURED OUT FOR MANY.
DO THIS IN MEMORY OF ME.
Let us proclaim our faith:
**We remember his passion and death.
We celebrate his resurrection and
ascension.
And we look for the coming of his
kingdom.**

Therefore, Living God, as we obey his
command,
we remember his suffering and death,
his resurrection and ascension,
and his promise to be with us forever.
And with this bread and this cup,
we celebrate his saving death until he
comes.

Accept, we pray, our sacrifice of praise and
thanksgiving,
and send down your Holy Spirit upon us
and our celebration.
May we all who eat and drink at this
table,
be strengthened by Christ's body and
blood
to serve you in the world.

As one body and one holy people,
may we proclaim the everlasting gospel of
Jesus Christ our Lord,
through whom, with whom, and in whom,
in the unity of the Holy Spirit,
all glory is yours, eternal Father,
now and for ever. **AMEN.**

*Continue with the Lord's Prayer on page . . . [i.e.
at §15]*

Appendix A: The Lima Liturgy

The World Council of Churches' Faith and Order Commission, meeting at Lima, Peru, in January 1982, provided, in its 'Lima text', a theological consensus which it commended to the member Churches in its publication, *Baptism, Eucharist and Ministry* (WCC, Geneva, 1982). In this it included under a sub-section entitled 'The Celebration of the Eucharist' specific recommendations for eucharistic liturgy, including for the eucharistic prayer:

– thanksgiving to the Father for the marvels of creation, redemption and sanctification . . .;
– the words of Christ's institution of the sacrament . . .;
– the *anamnesis* or memorial of the great acts of redemption . . . which brought the Church into being;
– the invocation of the Holy Spirit (*epiclesis*) on the community, and the elements of bread and wine (either before the words of institution or after the memorial, or both; or some other reference to the Holy Spirit which adequately expresses the 'epikletic' character of the eucharist);
– consecration of the faithful to God;
– reference to the communion of saints;
– prayer for the return of the Lord . . .
– the Amen of the whole community.

Arising from the Lima text, there was composed at Lima by Max Thurian (from Taizé) an actual eucharistic liturgy which has become known as the 'Lima Liturgy'. While it was designed to comprehend all the ecumenical participants, it was also deliberately thematic, in that, rather than be for general use, it highlighted the actual three themes of the Lima text. It was used at Lima, and gained publicity through its use at the WCC Assembly in 1983. As a one-man composition it has never had the same status or authority as the Lima text, but it has become known round the world as an ecumenical model; and it is specifically cited as a source in the chapters above re the Church of South India and The Episcopal Church in the Philippines, and its eucharistic prayer, printed here, is included as an appended optional use in **Cey2**. **Cey2** varies it solely by omitting 'him' in line 6, providing an option of a proper preface, and by making the penultimate paragraph optional.

THE LIMA EUCHARISTIC PRAYER

⟦The text is taken from Max Thurian and Geoffrey Wainwright (eds), *Baptism and Eucharist: Ecumenical Convergence in Celebration* (WCC, Geneva, 1983), pages 252–4. The lining is editorial.⟧

The Lord be . . . ⟦ELLC 6⟧ . . . **him thanks and praise.**

Truly it is right and good to glorify you,
at all times and in all places,
to offer you our thanksgiving
O Lord, Holy Father, Almighty and
  Everlasting God.
Through your living Word you created all
  things,
and pronounced them good.
You made human beings in your own
  image,
to share your life and reflect your glory.
When the time had fully come,
you gave Christ to us as the Way, the
  Truth and the Life.
He accepted baptism and consecration as
  your Servant
to announce the good news to the poor.
At the last supper Christ bequeathed to us
  the eucharist,
that we should celebrate the memorial of
  the cross and resurrection,
and receive his presence as food.
To all the redeemed Christ gave the royal
  priesthood
and, in loving his brothers and sisters,
chooses those who share in the ministry,
that they may feed the Church with your
  Word
and enable it to live by your Sacraments.
Wherefore, Lord, with the angels and all
  the saints,
we proclaim and sing your glory:
Holy, Holy . . . ⟦ELLC 7⟧ . . . the highest.

O God, Lord of the universe,
you are holy and your glory is beyond
  measure.
Upon your eucharist send the life-giving
  Spirit,
who spoke by Moses and the Prophets,
who overshadowed the Virgin Mary with
  grace,
who descended upon Jesus in the river
  Jordan

and upon the Apostles on the day of
  Pentecost.
May the outpouring of this Spirit of Fire
transfigure this thanksgiving meal
that this bread and wine may become for
  us
the body and blood of Christ.
Veni Creator Spiritus!

May this Creator Spirit accomplish the
  words of your beloved Son,
who, in the night in which he was
  betrayed,
took bread, and when he had given thanks
  to you,
broke it and gave it to the disciples,
saying : Take, eat: this is my body,
which is given for you.
Do this for the remembrance of me.
After supper he took the cup
and when he had given thanks,
he gave it to them and said:
Drink this, all of you:
this is my blood of the new covenant,
which is shed for you and for many
for the forgiveness of sins.
Do this for the remembrance of me.
Great is the mystery of faith.
Your death, Lord Jesus, we proclaim!
Your resurrection we celebrate!
Your coming in glory we await!

Wherefore, Lord we celebrate today
the memorial of our redemption:
we recall the birth and life of your Son
  among us,
his baptism by John,
his last meal with the apostles,
his death and descent to the abode of the
  dead;
we proclaim Christ's resurrection and
  ascension in glory,
where as our Great High Priest
he ever intercedes for all people;
and we look for his coming at the last.
United in Christ's priesthood,
we present to you this memorial:

Remember the sacrifice of your Son
and grant to people everywhere
the benefits of Christ's redemptive work.
Maranatha, the Lord comes!

Behold, Lord, this eucharist
which you yourself gave to the Church
and graciously receive it,
as you accept the offering of your Son
whereby we are reinstated in your
  Covenant.
As we partake of Christ's body and blood,
fill us with the Holy Spirit
that we may be one single body
and one single spirit in Christ,
a living sacrifice to the praise of your
  glory.
Veni Creator Spiritus!

Remember, Lord, your one, holy catholic
  and apostolic Church,
redeemed by the blood of Christ.
Reveal its unity, guard its faith,
and preserve it in peace.
Remember, Lord, all the servants of your
  Church:
bishops, presbyters, deacons,
and all to whom you have given special
  gifts of ministry.

(Remember especially _____)

Remember also all our sisters and brothers
who have died in the peace of Christ,
and those whose faith is known to you
  alone:
guide them to the joyful feast
prepared for all peoples in your presence,
with the blessed Virgin Mary,
with the patriarchs and prophets,
the apostles and martyrs _____
and all the saints for whom your
  friendship was life.
With all these we sing your praise
and await the happiness of your Kingdom
where with the whole creation,
finally delivered from sin and death,
we shall be enabled to glorify you through
  Christ our Lord:
Maranatha, the Lord comes!

Through Christ, with Christ, in Christ,
all honour and glory is yours,
Almighty God and Father,
in the unity of the Holy Spirit,
now and for ever.
Amen.

Appendix B: Common Forms

As in **FAL** and **LAL**, the 'Common Forms' reproduced here are all English-language texts which address God as 'you', again divided into two, first the most recent ecumenical texts, and then others which, of whatever origin, have a commonality in the Anglican Communion.

The ecumenical texts are the recommendations of the English Language Liturgical Consultation (ELLC) published in *Praying Together* (Canterbury Press, 1990).

Where these texts are used within the rites around the world, cue words indicate the exact amount of the text which is being cited. Variants from the forms here are indicated within the cue words where appropriate and are otherwise shown by an indented *apparatus* below the citation. Whether texts are being said by one voice or by the congregation can be determined by inspection.

1 The English Language Liturgical Consultation (ELLC) Texts

ELLC 1 The Lord's Prayer

Our Father in heaven,
hallowed be your name,
your kingdom come,
your will be done,
on earth as in heaven.
Give us today our daily bread.
Forgive us our sins,
as we forgive those who sin against us.
Save us from the time of trial
and deliver us from evil.
For the kingdom, the power, and the glory are yours
now and for ever. Amen.

ELLC 2 Kyrie Eleison

Kyrie eleison.	Lord, have mercy.
Christe eleison.	Christ, have mercy.
Kyrie eleison.	Lord, have mercy.

ELLC 3 Gloria in Excelsis

Glory to God in the highest,
and peace to God's people on earth.
Lord God. heavenly King,
almighty God and Father,
we worship you, we give you thanks,
we praise you for your glory.
Lord Jesus Christ, only Son of the Father,
Lord God, Lamb of God,
you take away the sin of the world:
have mercy on us;
you are seated at the right hand of the Father:
receive our prayer.
For you alone are the Holy One,
you alone are the Lord,
you alone are the Most High,
Jesus Christ,
with the Holy Spirit,
in the glory of God the Father. Amen.

ELLC 4 Apostles' Creed

I believe in God, the Father almighty,
creator of heaven and earth.
I believe in Jesus Christ, God's only Son, our Lord,
who was conceived by the Holy Spirit,
born of the Virgin Mary,
suffered under Pontius Pilate,
was crucified, died, and was buried;
he descended to the dead.
On the third day he rose again;
he ascended into heaven,
he is seated at the right hand of the Father,
and he will come to judge the living and the dead.
I believe in the Holy Spirit,
the holy catholic Church,
the communion of saints,
the forgiveness of sins,
the resurrection of the body,
and the life everlasting. Amen.

ELLC 5 Nicene Creed

We believe in one God,
the Father, the Almighty,
maker of heaven and earth,
of all that is, seen and unseen.
We believe in one Lord, Jesus Christ,
the only Son of God,
eternally begotten of the Father,
God from God, Light from Light,
true God from true God,
begotten, not made,

of one Being with the Father;
through him all things were made.
For us and for our salvation
he came down from heaven,
was incarnate of the Holy Spirit and the Virgin Mary
and became truly human.
For our sake he was crucified under Pontius Pilate;
he suffered death and was buried.
On the third day he rose again
in accordance with the Scriptures;
he ascended into heaven
and is seated at the right hand of the Father.
He will come again in glory to judge the living and the dead,
and his kingdom will have no end.
We believe in the Holy Spirit, the Lord, the giver of life,
who proceeds from the Father [and the Son],
who with the Father and the Son is worshipped and glorified,
who has spoken through the prophets.
We believe in one holy catholic and apostolic Church.
We acknowledge one baptism for the forgiveness of sins.
We look for the resurrection of the dead,
and the life of the world to come. Amen.

ELLC 6 Eucharistic dialogue – Sursum Corda

The Lord be with you.
And also with you.

Lift up your hearts.
We lift them to the Lord.

Let us give thanks to the Lord our God.
It is right to give our thanks and praise.

ELLC 7 Sanctus

Holy, holy, holy Lord, God of power and might.
Heaven and earth are full of your glory.
Hosanna in the highest.

ELLC 8 Benedictus Qui Venit

Blessed is he who comes in the name of the Lord.
Hosanna in the highest.

ELLC 9 Agnus Dei

(a) Jesus, Lamb of God, have mercy on us.
   Jesus, bearer of our sins, have mercy on us.
   Jesus, redeemer of the world, grant us peace.

(b) Lamb of God, you take away the sin of the world, have mercy on us.
   Lamb of God, you take away the sin of the world, have mercy on us.
   Lamb of God, you take away the sin of the world, grant us peace.

2 Anglican Common Forms (CF)

Note: most of these forms are taken from **EngCW**. Other texts which could have been labelled common forms occur in some rites – such as ten commandments (with or without New Testament counterparts), our Lord's Summary of the Law, the beatitudes, the Trisagion etc. These generally occur within the first half of the rite, where their full text would not be printed anyway, and it is hoped that mere reference to them will suffice.

CF 1 Collect for Purity

Almighty God,
to whom all hearts are open,
all desires known,
and from whom no secrets are hidden:
cleanse the thoughts of our hearts
by the inspiration of your Holy Spirit,
that we may perfectly love you,
and worthily magnify your holy name;
through Christ our Lord.
Amen.

CF 2 Absolution

Almighty God, who forgives all who truly repent, have mercy upon you, pardon and deliver you from all your sins, confirm and strengthen you in all goodness, and keep you in life eternal: through Jesus Christ our Lord. Amen.

CF 3 Prayer of Humble Access

(a) We do not presume
    to come to this your table, merciful Lord,
    trusting in our own righteousness,
    but in your manifold and great mercies.
    We are not worthy
    so much as to gather up the crumbs under your table.
    But you are the same Lord,
    whose nature is always to have mercy.
    Grant us therefore, gracious Lord,
    so to eat the flesh of your dear Son Jesus Christ
    and to drink his blood,
    that our sinful bodies may be made clean by his body
    and our souls washed through his most precious blood,
    and that we may evermore dwell in him, and he in us.
    Amen.

(b) Most merciful Lord,
    your love compels us to come in.
    Our hands were unclean,
    our hearts were unprepared;
    we were not fit
    even to eat the crumbs from under your table.
    But you, Lord, are the God of our salvation,
    and share your bread with sinners.
    So cleanse and feed us
    with the precious body and blood of your Son,

that he may live in us and we in him;
and that we, with the whole company of Christ,
may sit and eat in your kingdom.
Amen.

CF 4 At the Preparation of the Table (ex Roman Catholic 'Offertory Prayers')

(a) Blessed are you, Lord God of all creation;
through your goodness we have this bread to offer,
which earth has given and human hands have made.
It will become for us the bread of life.
Blessed be God for ever.

(b) Blessed are you, Lord God of all creation;
through your goodness we have this wine to offer,
fruit of the vine and work of human hands.
It will become for us the cup of salvation.
Blessed be God for ever.

(c) (*Originally from* CSI)
Be present, be present,
Lord Jesus Christ,
our risen high priest;
make yourself known in the breaking of bread.

CF 5 Variant on opening of Eucharistic dialogue in ELLC 6

ELLC 6		CF 5
The Lord be with you.	*(or)*	The Lord is here.
And also with you.		**His Spirit is with us.**

CF 6 Acclamations

(a) Great is the mystery of faith:
Christ has died:
Christ is risen:
Christ will come again.

(b) Praise to you, Lord Jesus:
Dying you destroyed our death:
rising you restored our life:
Lord Jesus, come in glory.

(c) Christ is the bread of life:
When we eat this bread and drink this cup,
we proclaim your death, Lord Jesus,
until you come in glory.

(d) Jesus Christ is Lord:
Lord, by your cross and resurrection
you have set us free.
You are the Saviour of the world.

CF 7 Doxology

**Blessing and honour and glory and power
be yours for ever and ever. Amen.**

CF 8 Breaking the Bread

(a) We break this bread
to share in the body of Christ.
**Though we are many, we are one body,
because we all share in one bread.**

(b) Every time we eat this bread
and drink this cup,
**we proclaim the Lord's death
until he comes.**

CF 9 Invitation to communion

(a) Draw near with faith.
Receive the body of our Lord Jesus Christ
which he gave for you,
and his blood which he shed for you.
Eat and drink
in remembrance that he died for you,
and feed on him in your hearts
by faith with thanksgiving.

(b) Jesus is the Lamb of God
who takes away the sin of the world.
Blessed are those who are called to his supper.
**Lord, I am not worthy to receive you,
but only say the word, and I shall be healed.**

(c) God's holy gifts
for God's holy people.
**Jesus Christ is holy,
Jesus Christ is Lord,
to the glory of God the Father.**

CF 10 Words of Administration or Distribution

(a) [Bread] The body of our Lord Jesus Christ, which was given for you, preserve your body and soul to everlasting life. Take and eat this in remembrance that Christ died for you, and feed on him in your heart by faith with thanksgiving. **Amen.**

(b) [Cup] The blood of our Lord Jesus Christ, which was shed for you, preserve your body and soul to everlasting life. Drink this in remembrance that Christ's blood was shed for you, and be thankful. **Amen.**

CF 11 Post-communion prayers

(a) Almighty God,
      we thank you for feeding us
      with the body and blood of your Son Jesus Christ.
      Through him we offer you our souls and bodies
      to be a living sacrifice.
      Send us out
      in the power of your Spirit
      to live and work
      to your praise and glory.
      Amen.

(b) Father of all,
      we give you thanks and praise,
      that when we were still far off
      you met us in your Son and brought us home.
      Dying and living, he declared your love,
      gave us grace, and opened the gate of glory.
      May we who share Christ's body live his risen life;
      we who drink his cup bring life to others;
      we whom the Spirit lights give light to the world.
      Keep us firm in the hope you have set before us,
      so we and all your children shall be free,
      and the whole earth live to praise your name;
      through Christ our Lord.
      Amen.

CF 12 Blessing and Dismissal

(a) The peace of God,
      which passes all understanding,
      keep your hearts and minds
      in the knowledge and love of God,
      and of his Son Jesus Christ our Lord;
      and the blessing of God almighty,
      the Father, the Son, and the Holy Spirit,
      be among you and remain with you always.
      Amen.

(b) Go in peace to love and serve the Lord
      In the name of Christ. Amen.

(c) Go in the peace of Christ.
      Thanks be to God.